Microsoft® Active Platform™ Sourcebook

Donald R. Brewer

WILEY COMPUTER PUBLISHING

John Wiley & Sons, Inc.
New York • Chichester • Weinheim • Brisbane • Singapore • Toronto

Publisher: Robert Ipsen
Senior Editor: Cary Sullivan
Development Editor: Kathryn A. Malm
Managing Editor: Frank Grazioli
Text Design & Composition: Benchmark Productions, Inc., Boston, MA

Designations used by companies to distinguish their products are often claimed as trademarks. In all instances where John Wiley & Sons, Inc., is aware of a claim, the product names appear in initial capital or ALL CAPITAL LETTERS. Readers, however, should contract the appropriate companies for more complete information regarding trademarks and registration.

This text is printed on acid-free paper. ∞

Published by John Wiley & Sons, Inc.

Published simultaneously in Canada.

Library of Congress Cataloging-in-Publication Data:

ISBN 0 471-19068-3

Printed in the United States of America
10 9 8 7 6 5 4 3 2 1

Contents

Introduction

When the company that dominates the software application and operating systems market, with its products deployed on over 90 percent of existing personal computers, espouses a new technology platform, it pays to listen. Microsoft is currently proclaiming the Microsoft Active Platform as the technical solution for integrating the Internet into the personal computer desktop environment.

This book will give you an understanding of what the Microsoft Active Platform is, why you should create applications that utilize it, and how you can create these applications and deploy them on the Internet or your intranet. This book will explain the three elements of the Microsoft Active Platform—ActiveX, Active Client, and Active Server—and the role each element plays in your applications.

Microsoft Active Platform

The Microsoft Active Platform is an assortment of technologies and applications that run in a client/server network environment. The object of the Microsoft Active Platform is to provide the tools and applications that can allow for easy development, deployment, and use of applications in a distributed network like the Internet or an intranet. Successful development of applications based on the Microsoft Active Platform will usher in an entirely new computing environment. In this brave new world, applications that you run on your desktop system will be seamlessly integrated with components and information retrieved from anywhere on the Internet or a company's intranet. Applications that you encounter on the Internet can have sophisticated interfaces to powerful databases or legacy applications, rather than the clunky CGI front-ends that exist today.

In a Microsoft Active Platform world, users work with files, objects, and information available on the Internet or an intranet just as easily as they do with those located on their local systems. You can retrieve files or post files from such common applications as Word or Excel to remote servers anywhere in the world, just as easily as you save them to your local hard drive. When you load a particular Web page, it can contain actual applications in the form of ActiveX controls that are automatically downloaded, installed, and run on your system. You may no longer have to go to the local store and purchase the newest software upgrades; instead, you may visit a designated Web site and the upgrades will be installed. Of course, you may still have to pay for them, for it may be a brave new world, but it is most definitely a capitalist one.

New distributed network applications can be created that consist of objects located everywhere on the Internet. To run these applications, objects from around the world are simply downloaded and installed on your system —transparently to you. Developers can create applications using Distributed Component Object Model (DCOM), which lets objects on a server communicate across the Internet with objects installed on a user's system. These simple examples indicate the new computing environment created by the Microsoft Active Platform.

Of course, the key to the success of this new technology is cross-platform integration. When developers create applications to run on the Internet or an intranet environment, the performance and appearance of these applications, no matter what operating system the user has, must be identical. The technologies used to create usable network-based applications must be cross-platform ones.

The Microsoft Active Platform is designed to work smoothly with the Windows operating systems, such as Windows NT and Windows 95, which are used on nearly 90 percent of existing PCs, but what about operating systems such as Macintosh and Unix? Microsoft has worked to port the ActiveX technology and desktop applications, such as Internet Explorer and Office 97, to Macintosh and Unix, thereby making the Microsoft Active Platform viable for use in a distributed networking environment.

What Is It?

We have shown you a glimpse of what the Microsoft Active Platform can do, but before you can develop your own applications you must understand the Microsoft Active Platform. Here is how Microsoft defines the Active Platform:

> *The Microsoft Active Platform is an open, standards-based software architecture for delivering rich content and line-of-business applications over the Internet and intranets. It combines the power of PC and network computing to link people with information, anywhere, any time.*

If that statement gives you a clear picture of what the Microsoft Active Platform is, you're the only one. For the rest of us, this ambiguous, marketing-inspired fluff does not give a clear picture of what the Microsoft Active Platform is and why you should bother to use it.

The key to the Microsoft Active Platform is understanding its three main components and the role each component plays in the Active Platform applications you create. The three components are these:

ActiveX

Active Client

Active Server

A typical Microsoft Active Platform application works in the following simple example. A user running an Active Client application such as Internet Explorer 4.0 requests information from an Active Server, such as Internet Information Server. This information can consist of ActiveX objects that are downloaded to the user's system and run within the Active Client application. These objects can then communicate with other objects running on the Active Server application.

Of course, this example of how the Microsoft Active Platform works will appear simple to any Web developer. Other than the replacement of ActiveX objects for Web pages, you probably do not see much difference between this example and the current client/server system used on the Web and for other Internet protocols. That's the main point of the Microsoft Active Platform: It is based on the same basic client/server model as the Web. The difference is that you are no longer limited to Web servers delivering static Web pages to Web browsers. Now Active Clients can be any application that supports the ActiveX objects, HTML, and scripting. These clients can download objects from the Active Server that can be complete applications capable of communicating directly with objects running on the server. In essence, the Microsoft Active Platform makes the Internet part of a user's local system, rather than a remote network that you contact whenever you want to send and receive e-mail.

- Standard HTML
- Scripting such as JavaScript or Visual Basic Script
- Objects including ActiveX controls and Java applets

> **NOTE** In addition to the Active Client applications being able to communicate with Active Server applications, the objects loaded in an Active Client application can communicate directly with those other objects running on an Active Server, or even on several different Active Servers anywhere on the Internet.

ActiveX

ActiveX controls represent the underlying technology of the Microsoft Active Platform. The ActiveX technology consists of components that are interoperable across intranets or the Internet. The ActiveX model is built on COM (Common Object Model) and DCOM (Distributed Common Object Model), which allows components to communicate with each other across the network.

In the Microsoft Active Platform, Active Client applications can download and install these ActiveX controls on the local system. The ActiveX controls can then run within the Active Client application and do everything from displaying animated video files to allowing a user to travel through a 3D VRML world.

An ever-growing library of thousands of ActiveX controls are available for free, as shareware, or for purchase. Once you acquire any ActiveX control, you will spend as little as a few seconds to incorporate it into one of your applications. In some cases, you may even want to customize an existing ActiveX control or create your own ActiveX control. The Visual Basic Control Creation Editor is one of the you can use to create customized ActiveX controls for your applications.

Visual Basic Control Creation Editor The ability to create your own ActiveX controls has been built into Visual Basic 5.0 in the form of the Visual Basic Control Creation Editor, which also exists as a separate application. The Visual Basic Control Creation Editor allows you to generate an ActiveX control, digitally sign it, and then package the assortment of files needed to distribute the ActiveX control within your own Internet application. Figure I.1 illustrates the development environment of the Visual Basic Control Creation Editor.

Active Client

On the client side, the main interface to the desktop environment is the Internet Explorer Web browser. Internet Explorer 4.0 expands the role of the Web browser into an actual front-end interface to the Windows operating system. The Microsoft

Figure I.1 Use the Visual Basic Control Creation Editor to create your own ActiveX controls.

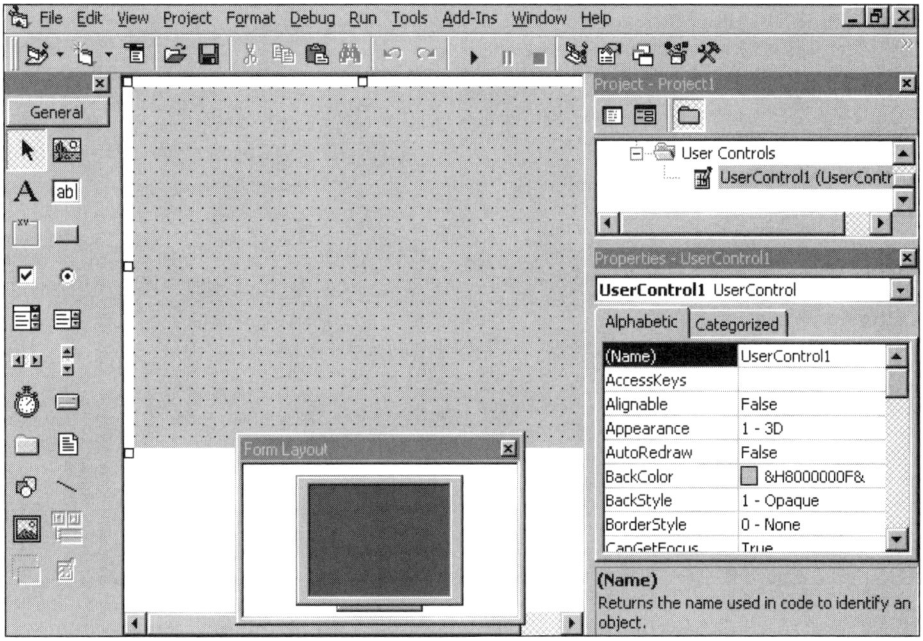

Active Platform allows for any application that supports the following technologies to be considered an Active Client:

- Component objects, including ActiveX controls and Java applets
- Standard HTML along with the new Dynamic HTML, as approved by the W3C consortium.
- Scripting within Internet applications using scripting languages such as Visual Basic Script and JavaScript.

Based on this description, Internet Explorer 4.0 is an ideal Active Client.

Internet Explorer 4.0 Software industry pundits often joke that it takes Microsoft three software releases to get an application right. The release of Internet Explorer 3.0 proved to be an equal competitor to the Netscape Navigator 3.0, but the recent release of Internet Explorer 4.0, illustrated in Figure I.2, showed that Microsoft was leaving its competition in the dust.

Figure I.2 Internet Explorer 4.0.

When Netscape boldly proposed that the browser could be the operating system it proved visionary, but it did seem to underestimate Microsoft. Internet Explorer 4.0 integrates the operating system with the Internet. Although it is only the first step, with other important features still needed, Internet Explorer brings the Internet to the desktop.

Dynamic HTML The Web is no longer static—it is dynamic. In Internet Explorer 4.0, Microsoft has included support for Dynamic HTML. Dynamic HTML allows you to use the design elements commonly available in conventional graphic design programs, including style sheets and 2D/3D layout capabilities, within your Web applications. Dynamic HTML allows you to develop Web applications that support several new capabilities:

- Dynamic styling and cascading style sheets
- Table manipulation
- Dynamic expansion

Once you go dynamic, you won't want to go back to the yesteryears of Web development. Those visiting your Web applications will be ever thankful.

Office97 Not only has the Internet become integrated into the operating system, it has also been integrated into one of the most popular business application suites, Microsoft Office. Office97 applications now allow you to retrieve and post information from the Internet; they even support ActiveX technology. These applications can include database connectivity and advanced multimedia such as PowerPoint presentations.

Most users will recognize the following business applications that constitute the Office97 product suite:

Word. The premier Word processing application, which now has excellent Web page development capabilities.

Excel. A spreadsheet program that has been recognized as one of the most widely used business applications.

PowerPoint. A presentations program that allows the generation and deployment of sophisticated slide presentations.

Access. The simple-to-use, ODBC-compliant database that can easily be integrated within the other Office97 applications.

Outlook. A sophisticated calendaring and e-mail application.

Not only are the Office97 applications compatible with the technologies of the Microsoft Active Platform, but they also allow someone who doesn't have any prior Web development experience to create sophisticated Internet applications.

Active Server

The Active Server component provides the basic infrastructure for the Microsoft Active Platform; the applications that it consists of respond to the services requested by the Active Client applications. Windows NT and the Internet Information Server are the two key applications that make up the backbone of the Active Server component. Here are some of the key services they provide:

Network services. Active Server supports DCOM, which allows for object-to-object communication using TCP/IP, HTTP, or other standardized protocols.

Data management services. Active Server allows you to store and access data anywhere on the network or to establish a connection with a database such as Microsoft SQL Server or any other ODBC-compatible database.

Directory and security services. The Active Server Directory provides a convenient way to control security access to objects and applications.

Visual InterDev Just as important to the services provided by the Active Server component are the tools you can use to create these high-performance, scalable Active Platform applications. Microsoft provides Visual InterDev as the premier Active Platform development tool (see Figure I.3).

Visual InterDev is a complete Internet application development environment that is used to create applications deployed on the Active Server. Some of the technologies of the Active Server include the following:

Active Server Pages. No longer do you have to create static Web pages; Active Server Pages allow the Active Server to dynamically generate the content delivered to the users.

Server Components. Because the Active Server uses the same ActiveX-based integration mechanisms built into all Microsoft BackOffice-based applications, Microsoft BackOffice-based applications can be integrated in Active Server Web sites like any other component, using the same consistent, component-based approach.

In addition to providing the numerous editors used to create applications and content, Visual InterDev also provides the FrontPage server extensions installed on the Web server you are currently running. These server extensions allow for the use of the FrontPage Web site management capabilities and for deploying nonstatic HTML content such as Active Server pages.

Distributed Common Object Model (DCOM) DCOM represents the next advance in COM-based technology. COM technology was originally designed for the communication of COM objects on the local system. DCOM takes it one step further, allowing for object communication across distributed networks, such as the Internet or even an intranet. Now objects can be downloaded to an Active Client on a user's system, and they can communicate with other objects residing on one or more Active Servers.

Internet Information Server A major component of the Active Server is Microsoft's Internet Information Server (IIS), which is integrated in Windows NT 4.0. IIS is a effective Web server application, one that you can use to deploy your

Figure I.3 Visual InterDev.

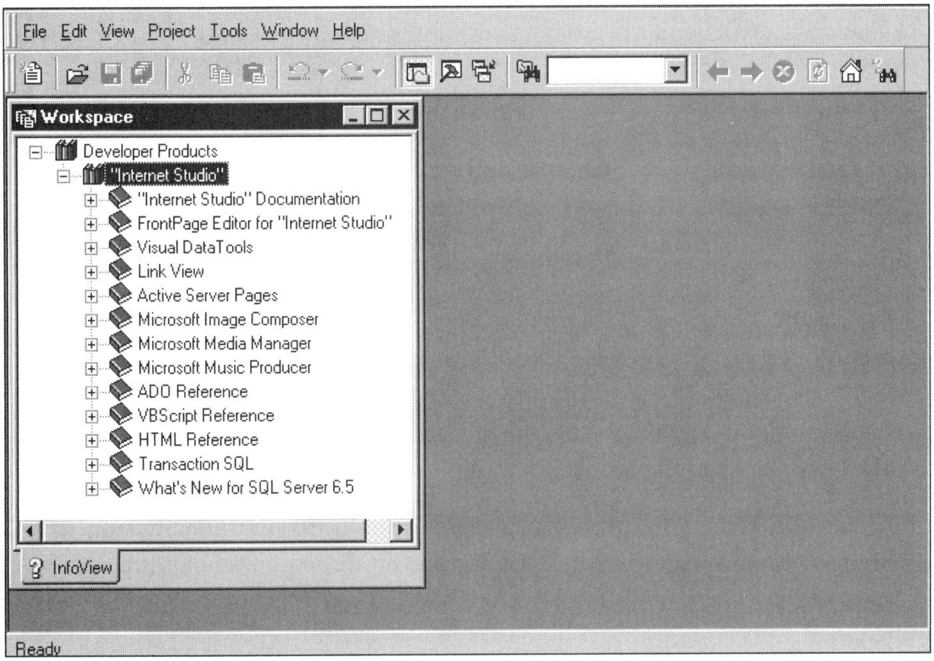

Microsoft Active Platform applications. IIS qualifies as an Active Server application with support for the following technologies:

- Scripting via Active Server Pages (ASPs), which provide a script-based programming model to let developers build "intelligent" Web sites
- Streaming media services for both audio and video with NetShow
- Searching and indexing of both Web pages and documents with Index Server
- Site and content management via FrontPage extensions

> **NOTE** This book is obviously geared to Web developers who are expected to already have the basic knowledge and experience with Web servers, such as the Internet Information Server. This book will therefore not contain detailed information about IIS, but if you are interested in getting more information check out the *Microsoft Internet Information Server 4.0 Sourcebook* by Michele Petrovsky, also published by Wiley.

Overview of This Book

The chapters in this book are grouped into three sections that cover the three main components of the Microsoft Active Platform. The first section introduces you to the ActiveX technology.

Part One—ActiveX Technology

Chapter 1, Internet Today—The Big Picture. This chapter provides a news update of the current and ongoing Internet trends. It introduces and describes Internet technologies, such as Java, plug-ins, and CORBA, that are competing against the ActiveX technology to establish themselves as "The Solution" for use in Internet applications. Of course, everyone has recognized that the interest from businesses has transformed the Internet from a curious ARPA project into the Information Highway. This chapter will point out some of the roadsigns along this highway, giving you some indication of where it is headed.

Chapter 2, ActiveX Controls. The chapter introduces you to the ActiveX technology and, more specifically, ActiveX controls. It describes how ActiveX controls operate and how you can deploy existing ActiveX controls in your Web pages.

Chapter 3, Creating ActiveX Controls. This chapter exposes the real strength of ActiveX controls, which is really their simplicity. In no time at all you should be designing, creating, and deploying customized ActiveX controls within your own applications by using the development tool Visual Basic Control Creation Editor.

Part Two—Active Client

Chapter 4, Internet Explorer. This chapter introduces you to Internet Explorer 4.0. With Internet Explorer 4.0 the Web browser has become the front-end to the Windows operating system, thereby integrating the Internet with your local system. This chapter will detail the features and capabilities of Internet Explorer 4.0, which allow you to maximize the performance of your Active Platform applications.

Chapter 5, Dynamic HTML. This chapter describes Dynamic HTML, which is supported by Internet Explorer 4.0. Using Dynamic HTML, you can create Web pages that feature dynamic styling, table manipulation, and even cascading style sheets. Web pages are no longer simply text and images, but now they can alter themselves in design and content based on information about the user or requested by the user.

Chapter 6, Office97. This chapter details the Internet-enabled features found in the Office97 applications. Create Word documents with ActiveX objects and hyperlinks to other content, or use Access to incorporate a database into your Web application. The Office97 applications, including Word, Excel, PowerPoint, Access, and Outlook, are excellent examples of what desktop applications can do when integrated into the Microsoft Active Platform.

Part Three—Active Server

Chapter 7, Visual InterDev. This chapter provides an introduction to the impressive Microsoft Active Platform development tool, Visual InterDev. Using Visual InterDev, you can create Web pages that contain ActiveX controls and script, Active Server pages that dynamically generate content, and Web applications with sophisticated database access capabilities. This chapter will also feature the various multimedia editors that you can use to create the content for your applications. Visual InterDev will become the development environment you use to create Microsoft Active Platform applications after you complete this chapter.

Chapter 8, Active Server Pages. This chapter instructs you on how to create Active Server pages. Using Active Server pages, you can integrate the database capabilities of Access 7.0 with your Web applications. After completing this chapter, you will be able to create Web applications in which users can make queries and even modify the data in the databases you make available.

Chapter 9, Active Server Components. This chapter details the capabilities of Active Server Components. One of the most difficult problems facing most developers today is the integration of legacy applications with Internet-based front-ends. Now you can treat a legacy application as a server component and integrate it into your existing applications.

Chapter 10, Distributed Component Object Model. This chapter will introduce you to creating Active Platform applications that use DCOM. These sample applications will illustrate how object-to-object communications operate for the applications you create.

Conclusion

The Microsoft Active Platform serves as the basis of the next generation of Internet applications. After completing this book you will have a solid understanding of the three elements of the Microsoft Active Platform and the technologies and tools that you can use to generate these type of applications.

You can remain up to date on the newest features added to the Microsoft Active Platform by checking out the following URL: www.microsoft.com/activeplatform.

Part One
ActiveX Technology

Chapter

1

Internet Today—The Big Picture

The Internet has often been referred to as the Information Superhighway. No one with a clue gets on a highway without first knowing where it goes. Any developer or company that plans to exploit the Internet should first have a very clear understanding of current trends and future opportunities. This understanding becomes even more important when choosing a particular technology solution, such as the Microsoft ActiveX Platform.

The Internet has proved to be a lasting communication system, rather than the CB radio of the 1990s. The many existing Internet startups must now prove that they can transform themselves from risky investments to established businesses. Although development on the Internet still can happen at break-neck speed, we now have a clearer picture of who the major players are, what the important technologies are, and which markets have the most potential.

In this chapter we will take a brief look at the more consumer-oriented aspects of the Internet. Most experts agree that the continual rise and importance of the Internet currently depend on two major forces, demographics and access.

Internet demographics are critical in determining the success of online business; this means there is a need for diversity among users. In turn, the number of individuals using the Internet for business and personal needs depends on the ease of access to the Internet. When nearly every Internet Service Provider (ISP) seems to have its modem banks overwhelmed and everyone is clamoring for higher bandwidth, the lack of quick and easy Internet access could become a stumbling block for business in the next several years.

Forces at Work

The Internet has truly permeated American culture. It seems that nearly every advertiser makes it a point to display its URL. This has helped draw the 37 million Americans, approximately 17 percent of the U.S. population, estimated to have access to the Internet as of November 1996. An estimated 150 million desktop computers are in use, with a significant portion already connected to the Internet. We can expect Internet usage to continue to increase, especially as other devices allow users to connect without using the conventional personal computer. These devices, include the following:

- WebTV
- Personal digital assistants
- Pagers
- Kiosks
- Cellular phones
- Network computers

Current estimates predict that there will be 200 million Internet users by the year 2000 and that about 50 percent of the American population will be cruising the Internet by then.

Two out of three Internet users are men, but the number of women on the Internet continues to increase. In the first quarter of 1994, women represented only 7 percent of all Internet users, but as of the first quarter of 1996 that number had increased to 33 percent. The average yearly salary of Internet users is $60,000, with 25 percent having annual incomes above $80,000. Internet users also represent the more educated portion of the population, with 64 percent having a college degree or higher. Obviously, as the Internet gains more and more users, the demographics will more closely reflect the population. Now many opportunities exist for businesses that market to individuals who are fairly well-to-do and educated.

Bandwidth

The current frenzy over the Internet appears similar to what occurred following Alexander Graham Bell's invention of the telephone in the 1870s. Everyone wanted a phone for both entertainment and business purposes. Within 30 years, the number of telephones in the United States grew from 1 to 11 million, more than the number of bathtubs in the United States at that time. In this rush to provide service to everyone, significant deficiencies in the quality of service occurred: many dropped calls; poor sound quality, which often required callers to scream into the phone just to be heard; and service often available only from 9:00 A.M. to 5:00 P.M. This account of the development of the telephone sounds much like the Internet of today, when major ISPs such as America Online experience frequent blackouts and many users can't even get online.

These are the growing pains experienced by any technological development that needs significant additional investment in capital to improve service and capabilities. Poor service and quality are significant factors in limiting the speed with which users adopt and come to depend on a particular technological innovation. One of the biggest issues for improving Internet access is to increase the bandwidth available to users for a reasonable price. Nearly everyone agrees on the numerous Internet opportunities that will exist with the development of inexpensive access to extensive bandwidth, including video conferencing and movies-on-demand. The jury is still out on which technology will deliver high bandwidth to the home. In the early 1990s many phone companies predicted fiber to the home within 10 to 15 years in the United States; their expectations, however, have diminished dramatically as they realized the capital expense required for such mass installation and the infrastructure that would be needed. Recently other technologies have emerged as potential options to provide reasonably high bandwidth to consumers at a feasible cost:

Cable modems

ADSL

Satellite

Power Lines

In the near future, we will see a variety of high-bandwidth candidates attempt to crush the competition and some that may emerge victorious. Companies such as @Home and Time Warner are pushing cable modems as "the solution," whereas the phone companies insist that ISDN (Integrated Services Digital Network) and the new ADSL (Asymmetric Digital Subscriber Line) technology are the answers.

The parallels that can be drawn between the emergence of the telephone and the Internet are interesting. When the telephone was first invented, it become instantly popular, much as the Internet is today. The telephone business environment in the late 1800s was created around AT&T (American Telephone & Telegraph), which owned the rights to Bell's invention. Soon many telephone companies were competing against AT&T by offering unlimited local calls for a basic monthly rate, much as ISPs do today. AT&T was significantly capitalized so that it could either purchase any of its competitors or drive them out of business by refusing to connect their competitors' customers' telephone lines with those of their own customers. In the end, AT&T monopolized the telephone system; then it was able to charge by the minute for local phone calls and prevent its customers from owning their own phones. This monopoly lasted nearly 100 years until the U.S. federal government forced the breakup of AT&T into the various Baby Bells of today. Consumers should remember that history often repeats itself and hope that more than one of these bandwidth solutions succeeds, thereby encouraging competition and, ideally, competitive pricing.

Cable Modems

With the recent deregulation of telecommunications, many cable companies have made it their mission to become significant competitors to the phone companies. Considering that a large number of American homes have cable wire already installed that is capable of transmitting real-time video information, the cable companies have sought to provide Internet access using this existing infrastructure.

The cable companies must overcome some problems in order to make cable modems a viable option for Internet access. The first is that the existing cable infrastructure is based on one-way information delivery, but little infrastructure is currently in place to allow significant two-way communication. The other problem is that all of the houses in a neighborhood, typically 500 to 2500, are connected to the same wire at a particular node, so when many users request information simultaneously, the bandwidth is effectively reduced proportionately to the number of the requesting users.

The cable companies already have several test markets currently under way to test and evaluate the performance of cable modems. The current systems promise the ability to transmit 10 Mbps download and 750 Kbps upload for approximately $50/month. Assuming that this sort of Internet access can be sustained, it looks quite promising, especially when we consider that a typical user currently pays $19.99/month for access to the Internet on a 28.8 Kbps dial-up connection.

Check out the following URLs for additional information about cable modems, manufacturers, and current providers of cable modem service. Who knows, you may even be able to order a cable modem in your area today and soon be cruising along at 10 Mbps for only $50/month.

www.cablemodems.com

rpcp.mit.edu/~gingold/cable/

ADSL (Asymmetric Digital Subscriber Lines)

The telephone companies are searching to find a competitive equal to cable modems. They do offer ISDN, which provides up to 110 Kbps transmission in both directions, several times faster than the typical 28.8 Kbps, but this technology has not been accepted by consumers to the degree anticipated. The problems stem from the telephone companies' poor service, along with higher costs in hardware and per-minute charges for online time. Consumers want a bandwidth solution that has more to offer, while the telephone companies have sought a solution that utilizes the twisted-pair wire that runs to nearly every home in the United States.

The telephone companies are currently promoting ADSL as a potential commercial solution. ADSL sends data over the copper wire at different frequencies than conventional voice calls. When the data reaches a local switch, the Internet portion is diverted to the Internet provider, while the voice data continues along the voice network system.

You can get additional technical and market information about ADSL at the following URL:

www.adsl.com

Power Lines

Nearly every company that has some sort of wire going to a large number of consumers, homes is seeking a way to transmit Internet information and cash in on the

Information Age. Cable companies and phone companies are slugging it out in mega-mergers on Wall Street, ongoing trials, and expensive PR campaigns, but people have paid little attention to the other type of company that has a wire in nearly every home in America: electric companies.

A small company called Adaptive Networks has been pursuing the use of power lines to provide high-bandwidth information transfer to consumers. It has already created power line products that operate at 100 Kbps that are being used in an assortment of products including vending machines and factory automation equipment. You can find out more about its technology and products on its Web site:

www.adaptivenetworks.com

Although the use of power lines as an Internet conduit has not generated the press that the telephone and cable technologies have, anything is possible in the world of telecommunications deregulation. Who knows, you may soon be unplugging the light in your hotel room, rather than the phone, to connect your computer to the Internet.

The Big Crash

We cannot ignore the pundits who claim that the Internet will fall victim to its very success. They expect that the ever-increasing number of Internet subscribers will simply crush the backbone of the Internet. Many Internet users may already be frustrated with the delays they encounter now when they try to download information from such popular Web sites as www.netscape.com or www.microsoft.com. The question is what will happen as the major cable and telecommunications companies continue to increase the bandwidth available to the average consumer using technologies such as cable modems and ADSL. Sure, the Internet Service Providers (ISPs) may be able to increase the bandwidth between the end user and the ISP, but a fast modem doesn't mean anything if the Internet backbone is crushed by too many users.

Almost every company, big and small, recognizes the current usage of and continuing potential for the Internet. The telecommunications companies also realize its potential; the only way to guarantee that they might be able to capitalize on this opportunity 5 to 10 years from now is to invest in infrastructure. The potential crash or slowdown of the Internet doesn't present a technical problem that must be solved; it merely requires enough capital to be invested. As long as significant capital continues to be invested the providers should be able to meet the ever-growing demand and prevent the collapse of the Internet.

Internet Opportunities

In the old days of ARPAnet, the precursor of the Internet, the vitality and growth of the network were based on how much the U.S. government was willing to invest. The Internet of today is driven solely by the amount of capital from commercial businesses and venture capital investors. In 1996 alone, the venture capitalists in Silicon Valley invested more than $800 million in Internet-related corporate ventures. Of course, this money is being invested with the expectation that significant Internet markets will soon be established.

In response to "Where's the money?", we think it's safe to say, "It's on the Internet."

Intranets

Netscape is fond of creating new terms, ranging from "intranets" to "extranets," to describe the Internet in the continual PR barrage of its founders, Marc Andreeson and Jim Barksdale. In the case of the intranet, Netscape once again proved insightful. An intranet is often described as an internal network of computers, typically associated with a company or similar organization, that runs applications based on TCP/IP (Transmission Control Protocol/Internet Protocol).

For years, companies such as Lotus Development Corp., with its Notes product, have pushed "groupware" solutions that allow everyone on a particular network to communicate using e-mail and a variety of collaboration tools. Of course, this all required proprietary Notes clients and Notes servers. With the emergence of the intranet, companies began to consider using TCP/IP applications that ran an assortment of different protocols to develop the same capabilities provided in existing groupware solutions.

E-mail clients (SMTP). Allows communication between employees on the intranet.

FTP clients. Used to provide file transfer capability.

Newsreader clients (NNTP). Allows for internal real-time question-and-answer forums.

Web browsers (HTTP). Allows for posting of an assortment of information; could also be used for internal collaboration and communication.

With Microsoft's dedicated efforts on Internet-related developments during 1996, many companies had to rethink their business strategy. Netscape realized its future might not be so rosy if its only source of income was Web browsers and Web servers, both of which could possibly be included for free as part of Microsoft's operating system. Netscape also realized that the real use of and customers for Internet-related products were not coming from the average consumer, but rather from businesses. Netscape's new business strategy was to offer a TCP/IP groupware solution for companies to use on its corporate intranets. This product line consisted of the Netscape Communicator product, which has the following components:

Navigator 4.0

Messenger

Conference

Composer

Collabra

Calendar

The client applications that constitute the Netscape Communicator product work in concert with the SuiteSpot servers product suite, which consists of the following servers:

Directory Server. A server that provides directory information about the users on the particular network.

Certificate Server. A server that allows for the issuance and management of certificates to control access for an intranet.

Enterprise Server. A Web server that allows for hosting of Web applications.

Mail Server. A server that allows for e-mail delivery to users.

News Server. A server that allows for hosting of NNTP newsgroups.

Collabra Server. A server that allows for real-time discussion capabilities that can work in concert with an open NNTP news server.

Calendar Server. A server that provides calendaring and scheduling capabilities for employees in an intranet environment.

Catalog Server. A server that can catalog an enormous amount of information for quick retrieval.

Proxy Server. A server that allows for replication and filtering of Web content to reduce network congestion.

Media Server. A server that can provide real-time streaming audio that can be synchronized with Web content.

Messaging Server. A server that provides messaging abilities.

This client-server product suite is spearheading Netscape's effort to compete against Lotus and Microsoft for market share of the intranet groupware market, which is expected to reach $5 billion by the year 2000. The war has begun in this winner-takes-all battle for ownership of intranet mind share, and as the computer industry has repeatedly shown, mind share equals market share.

Intranet Usage

As with any significant socio-economic paradigm shift resulting from a technology, such as the telephone a century ago or the personal computer almost 20 years ago, the main driving force is capital. In our society the group that has the most to gain from the development of the Internet, and that happens to retain a majority of the existing capital, is business. Although much of the hype and the press concerning the Internet have focused on personal use of the Internet, business has emerged as the real driving force at this time. One of the more telling elements involves business's use of intranets, thereby using the informational and communication capabilities of the Internet for a variety of different business applications.

As of mid-1996, nearly 50,000 businesses had their own Web pages on the Internet, and nearly 55 percent of all large and mid-sized businesses in the United States had some sort of intranet in use. Obviously, the use of an intranet by more and more employees is expected to lead to an increase in Internet use for personal reasons.

Electronic Commerce

One of the hottest Internet catch phrases is "electronic commerce." Electronic commerce can be broadly interpreted to be any online activity that contributes to commerce in any way, from actual direct online purchases to trading of stocks. Some believe that people will vacate the malls of America as they use their computers to purchase everything online, from their groceries to their clothes. Although this will probably never happen, electronic commerce has a promising future. Due in part to the existing limitations in bandwidth, certain industries will drive electronic commerce in the near term.

Banking and Finance

Banking and finance are simply service industries that provide spreadsheet types of information. Users are already using online banking services to handle their checking accounts, pay bills, and manage their portfolios (see Figure 1.1).

Research indicates that by the year 2000, banks representing at least 40 percent of the deposit base in the United States will be offering online banking services. These banks will serve the estimated 16 million U.S. households that will do their banking online by the year 2000. Of course, banks that provide online banking can do away with much of the paper and labor costs associated with that industry. Banking experts believe that banks will experience twice the profit from an online banking customer as from the average customer who banks in person. Increased demand for online banking may also require significant changes in marketing strategies. Today a person typically chooses the bank for convenience: How close is the nearest bank branch to where the customer lives or works? On the Internet, the actual location doesn't matter at all; in fact, a bank doesn't even have to have a

Figure 1.1 Banks such as Wells Fargo already allow users to do their banking online, requiring only a Web browser.

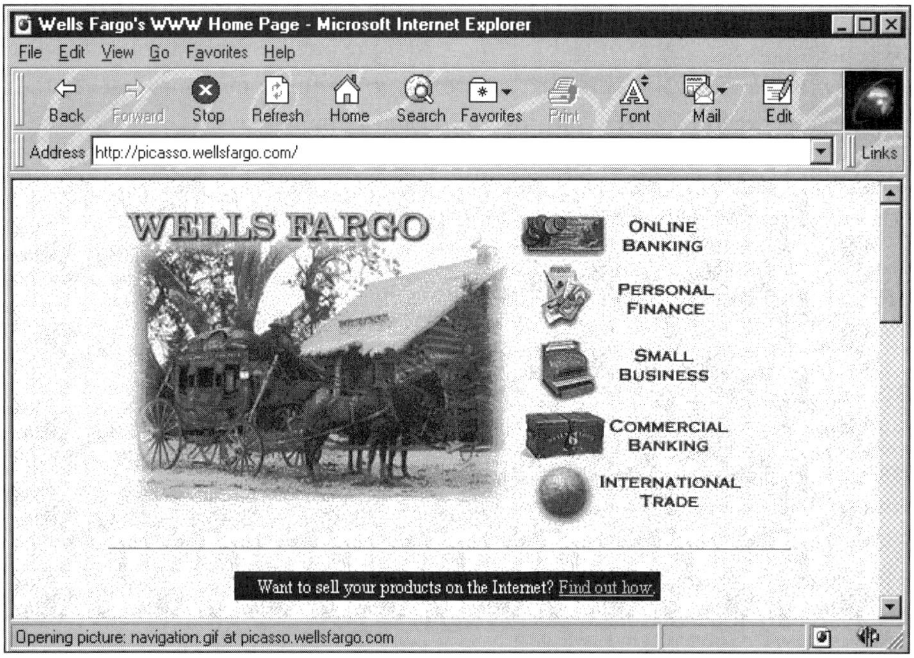

location. In this online banking marketplace, customers can select a bank based on a variety of other factors, including added services and better returns.

Banking and finance will become significant electronic commerce industries over the next several years, and the environment they create will most certainly echo throughout electronic commerce.

Online Shopping

An estimated 45 million people have access to the Internet. Nobody knows how many are active online purchasers as well, but the numbers are thought to be relatively few, in the tens of thousands. Online shoppers spent an estimated $350 million in 1995 on Internet purchases, which was less than 1 percent of the $63 billion spent on U.S. mail orders. Of course online purchases are expected to grow dramatically to $2.3 billion in 1997, half from travel-related purchases such as airline tickets, hotel reservations, and car rentals.

When you buy a shirt online you aren't exactly sure if it will fit or what it will look like once you put it on. Like the banking and finance industries' money products, travel can be described very accurately: You know what you are getting when you buy an airplane ticket from San Diego to New Orleans. In the travel industry, most purchases are made through travel agents who take 10 to 15 percent in commissions just to contact reservation servers with their computers and record the necessary information. Now online users can take a few minutes to find and reserve their desired travel arrangements, thereby cutting the travel agents out of the loop. Airline, cruise, and hotel companies can offer their products at 10 to 15 percent less without any loss in revenues, while the consumer can save significantly. Figure 1.2 illustrates a Web page for one of these travel-related companies.

Many retailers believe that conventional purchases will continue to predominate. It is important to recognize that 80 percent of Internet users are Americans, who live in a country where the nearest mall is typically 15 minutes away. With such a well-developed distribution system in the United States, the advantages offered by the Internet are minimized. It must be recognized that other parts of the world don't have the distribution system enjoyed in the United States. It is in these markets that online purchases of goods such as clothing are expected to see sizable growth. One can not ignore the fact that the combination of the Internet with worldwide delivery services such as FedEx and UPS will allow anyone, anywhere to purchase any items online and receive them within a couple of days.

Figure 1.2 There are already numerous online travel companies that users can contact to make airline, car rental, and hotel reservations.

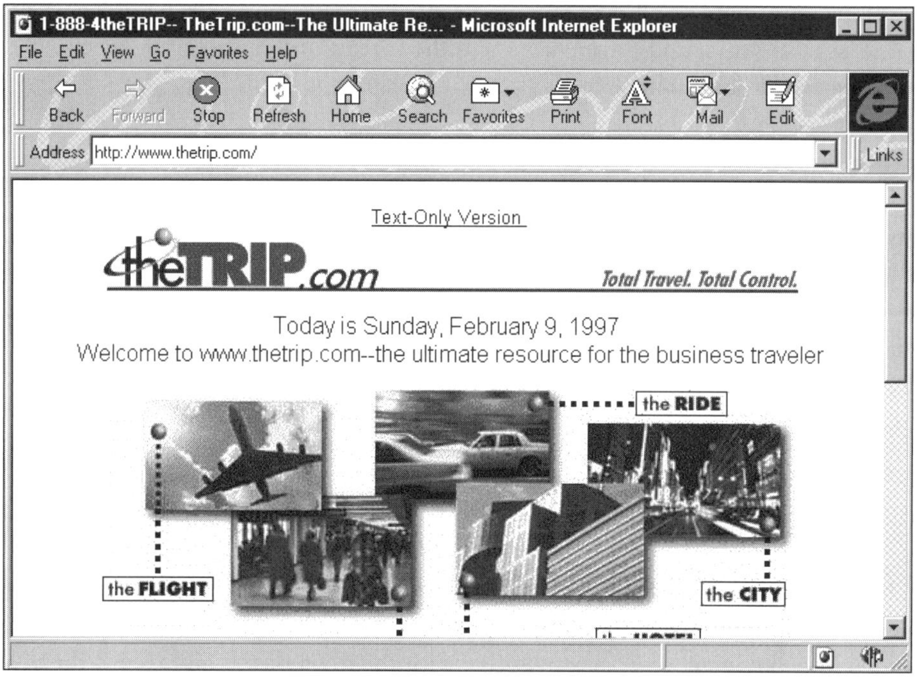

Figure 1.3 displays one of the more successful Internet retail companies, the Internet Shopping Network.

Microsoft and the Browser Wars

The actions of any company that commands 90 percent of the desktop operating system marketshare can post a significant road sign to the direction of the Internet. In late 1995, Bill Gates saw the potential of the Internet being seized by the recent upstart Netscape. Gates and company had believed that the market potential of the Internet would only be realized when bandwidth was significantly improved to allow such things as real-time video. The record Netscape IPO (Initial Public Offering) forced Microsoft to recognize opportunities even limited bandwidth provided.

The year 1996 was when Microsoft followed the model "embrace and extend." Adding Internet capabilities and features to nearly every software product became

Figure 1.3 Companies such as the Internet Shopping Network have geared their products to those most probably sought by current online shoppers.

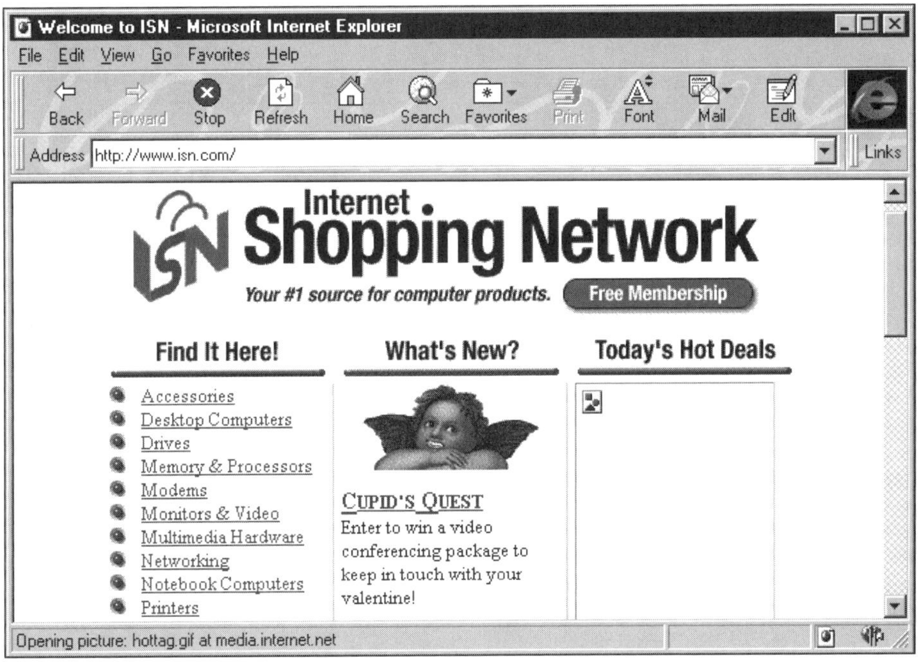

the priority. This has led to the release of numerous products in 1997 that feature Internet capabilities, such as Microsoft Office 97, Visual Basic 5.0, Visual J++, and a visual Internet development environment called Visual InterDev.

Microsoft's first task to establish itself in the new Internet marketplace was to compete directly with Netscape for the user interface to the Internet, namely the Web browser. The fact is that a Web browser in itself isn't all that complex a software application, as witnessed by the fact that the first Web browser, created by Marc Andreeson, was written in a couple of evenings in his college dorm room. Netscape Navigator did not have any proprietary technology, since the company completely embraced the philosophy of open standards. Open standards sound nice, but it is often hard to establish a business dependent on products and technologies that are based on open standards. Microsoft proved this by quickly producing an equal competitor to Netscape's Navigator Web browser, shown in Figure 1.4. Microsoft simply had to put a couple hundred programmers together and in a

Figure 1.4 Netcape's Navigator 4.0 Web browser is one component of the Netscape Communicator client product suite.

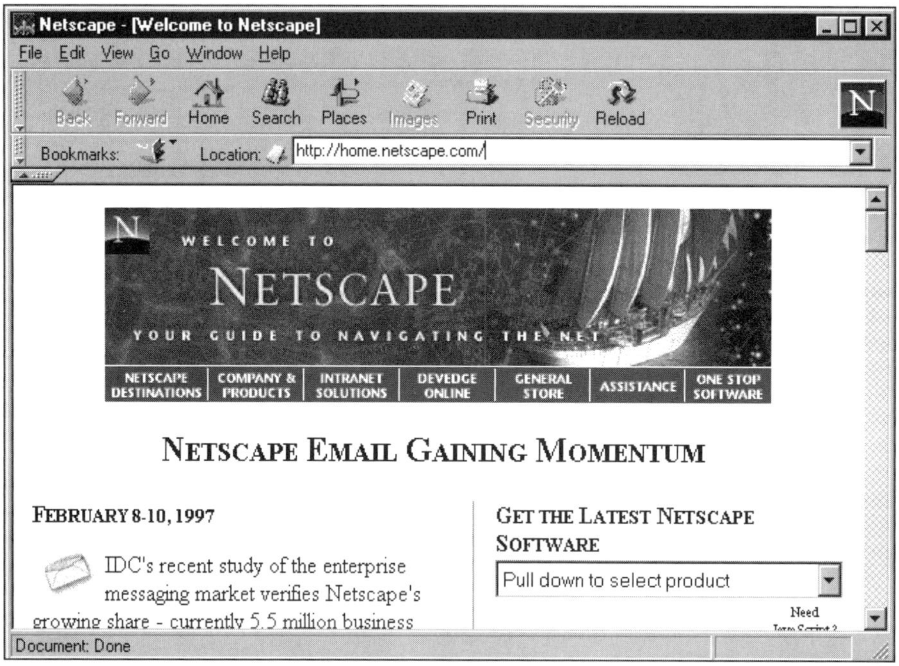

relatively short time produced Internet Explorer 3.0, which has since developed into Internet Explorer 4.0 (see Figure 1.5).

In the browser war, Microsoft's ace in the hole is that it still controls approximately 90 percent of the desktop operating system market. Netscape heralded the Web browser as the next operating system, and Microsoft has taken that advice to heart, incorporating Internet capabilities in its new operating system. Microsoft has made Internet Explorer 4.0 an integral part of the user's Active Desktop environment. Of course, that means a user who purchases Microsoft's operating system gets an impressive Web browser free as an integral component. This can be particularly disturbing for a company such as Netscape that obtains a sizable percentage of its revenues from sales of its Web browser.

In the client/server environment of the Internet the obvious complement to the client Web browser is the server. Microsoft's Windows NT operating system is gaining dramatically as the operating system of choice for business computing needs.

Figure 1.5 Microsoft's Internet Explorer 4.0 Web browser with Microsoft's home page loaded.

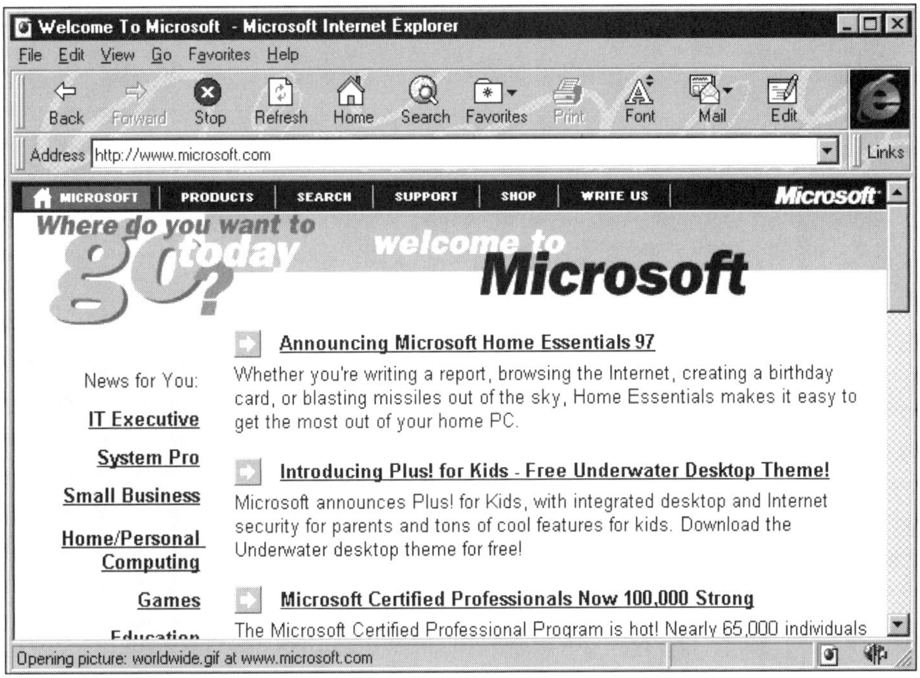

The Windows NT operating system comes with several different servers preloaded, one of which is Microsoft's Internet Information Web server. Anyone who purchases Windows NT gets for free several quality Internet servers including a Web server, an FTP server, and a Gopher server. This obviously makes it a little more difficult for a company such as Netscape to continue significant revenues due to server sales. It is awfully hard to sell something that most people already have for free.

More Than Just Pretty Pictures

The Internet frenzy that we all have observed over the last several years had its humble beginnings with the Mosaic Web browser that featured the ability to display images and text downloaded from the Internet. Images are great, but why stop there?

Several technology solutions have emerged to increase user interactivity and to deliver working applications that are capable of everything from displaying video or animation to providing database access. These technologies are proving that the

Internet is more than an interesting curiosity—it is a viable tool and resource. Here are just some of the technology solutions that are competing to provide value to Internet users:

- Scripting languages
- Java
- Plug-ins
- ActiveX

In many cases, these technologies have the same capabilities and features, making them direct competitors. A developer who wants to provide a customized application or multimedia presentation must choose which technology to use based on the various advantages and disadvantages of each solution.

Scripting Languages

The first Web browsers allowed users to view static text and images, but any sort of user interactivity or processing was handled through CGI (Common Gateway Interface) programs that were run on Web servers. Considering that the user's Web browser was running on a computer that had the same processing capability as existed on the Web server, why not allow much of the interactive programming to be done on the client side, rather than the server side? What was needed was a simple programming language.

In response, Netscape developed the JavaScript scripting language. JavaScript wasn't a full-fledged computer programming language because it was interpreted, rather than compiled. Although obviously named after the popular Java programming language, JavaScript has little else in common with Java. The main advantage of its being an interpreted language is that any JavaScript-compatible browser can download JavaScript code and run it regardless of the operating system platform that is running. This is a critical design feature for the Web where users running every kind of platform can interact in the same environment.

Netscape preached the philosophy of open standards but failed to make the intricacies of the JavaScript language readily available to companies attempting to build JavaScript support in their own browsers. Microsoft was forced to reverse-engineer its support of JavaScript in Internet Explorer and created its own implementation, often referred to as JScript. Microsoft also created its own competitive scripting language called Visual Basic Script, which was based on its own Visual Basic programming language.

Java

Java, developed by Sun Microsystems, is an object-oriented programming language that is similar to C++. Developers can create compiled Java applications that are platform-specific or Java applets. Java applets are applications written in Java and compiled into bytecode, which can then be interpreted by any machine or software application that has the Java Virtual Machine installed. Whenever a Java applet is encountered, the Java Virtual Machine interprets the bytecode and converts it into machine code specific to the platform it is currently running on and runs the application. The most popular Web browsers, including Netscape Navigator and Microsoft Internet Explorer, have a Java Virtual Machine that allows the Java applets encountered in Web pages to be downloaded to the user's computer and executed. You can find out everything you wanted to know about Java by checking out the following URL:

java.sun.com

Netscape Plug-ins

Before Microsoft took the Internet seriously Netscape felt that the Web browser could serve as the next development in operating systems. Netscape believed that users could download applications across the Internet and run them while in their Web browser or simply have existing applications on their system that would process information that was received from the Web. Plug-ins were compiled applications that represented the first step to this new future. A user would download the appropriate plug-in and install it on his or her computer; then, whenever content specific to that plug-in was encountered the content would be processed and displayed within the Web browser.

Plug-ins have shown the way to downloading applications or having applications process content encountered in Web pages, but they haven't proved simple in either creation or user implementation. They have shown the way to technologies such as ActiveX.

ActiveX

ActiveX controls represent Microsoft's competitive response to the need for application-specific components that can be downloaded from the Internet and executed on a user's computer system. ActiveX controls are actually based on software components called. OCXcontrols, which were derived from the old Visual Basic (.VBX) controls. The Microsoft developers recognized that .OCX controls carried too much baggage to allow them to be small, and easily down-loadable on the Internet. So they removed all of the required interfaces except IUNKNOWN and created ActiveX controls.

The obvious advantage of ActiveX controls over competitive solutions such as Java applets or plug-ins is that there are already hundreds, if not thousands, of already existent .OCX controls that could be quickly turned into ActiveX controls.

CORBA

"Objects" and "distributed objects" have been programming buzzwords for several years, and the success of the Internet over the last several years has only served to reignite the interest in object-based programming. Object-based programming solves a common problem. When a company like Microsoft develops a suite of products such as Microsoft Office, it handles the programming for each application separately. For example, one team creates Word, while another team creates Excel. Of course, both of these programs need similar features; they both need a spell checker, and they both need cut-and-paste features. In pre–object programming days each of these teams would create its own solutions for identical functionality in their respective applications. Obviously, this means a duplication of work and cost.

Object-oriented programming means that objects are created to perform specific tasks with known interfaces. A programmer can take a particular object and write code to provide and retrieve information from these known interfaces, thereby incorporating the functionality of that object in his/her program. With the proliferation of objects, the time and cost for programming decreases since all a programmer is doing is piecing together existing objects, or so goes the dream. The real strength of object-oriented programming isn't so much reducing the cost and complexity of the original code as easing updates: All you do is replace outdated objects with new objects.

The emergence of Internet and intranet networks has led to high expectations for distributed object computing. In a distributed object computing system, programs could consist of any number of objects found in various locations on the network. When a particular object is needed for a certain task, it would be requested across the network and downloaded onto the local machine.

The key to this model of distributed computing architecture is the ORBs (Object Request Brokers) that handle the various transaction requests. CORBA, Common Object Request Broker Architecture, is one potential solution to creating a distributed object computing on the Internet. Check out the following URL for more information about CORBA, and the organization that is spearheading its development: www.omg.com.

Where Do We Go from Here?

There are several stages in the development of a technology. The first stage is the actual invention of the technology, which is then followed by adoption. Technologies such as Java and ActiveX have been created, and we will now see how these technologies fare in the adoption stage. Quite possibly all of the technologies identified will manage to coexist, each with its own particular niche. Other developments such as network computers and WinFrame, are still in the early stages of development but may more closely suit your own needs.

Network Computers

Larry Ellison became the soothsayer and major cheerleader for the network computer. Like many of the other computer executives in Silicon Valley, he was tired of the stranglehold that Microsoft and Intel, often referred to as Wintel, had on the computer industry, and he saw the power of the Internet as the solution. Most businesspeople agree that computer support and maintenance costs exceed purchase price of the computer alone. Every time that a company needs to update the operating system or application software it must purchase a site license for every copy, have it installed, work out the inevitable bugs that occur, often have to add additional hardware such as memory, and finally retrain its employees. Not an enviable task, considering that many employees sample only a few applications on the computer, such as word processing, databases, and spreadsheets.

The network computer was to be a slimmed-down version of the PC, often not even having a resident hard drive. This would allow thc purchase price of a network computer to be in the $500 range, rather than the $1500-$2000 range for a typical PC. The network computer would access applications across the network from a server. These applications could even be Java-based, thereby requiring only that the network computer have the Java Virtual Machine to allow execution of the downloaded code. Users would not have their applications actually resident on their computers, software upgrades for a corporate system would be far easier: They would require an upgrade only on the servers on which the software was running.

If this sounds to you like the old days of terminals connected to mainframes, then you aren't alone. Has the computer industry gone full circle in 20 years, from terminals connected to mainframes to the desktop computer, and finally back to network computers connected to servers? Many advocates of network computers argue that the lessons were learned with the old terminals connected to mainframe model and that those apparent problems will not exist when new network computers are connected to multiple servers. Others argue that users aren't willing to give up the incredible functionality that the PC offers over the network computer.

Of course, cost is a significant driving factor. Companies should be wary of taking away high-end PCs from people who need high-end capabilities, but it is definitely worth considering replacing existing PCs with network computers for their part of the workforce that simply doesn't need all of the functionality and costs that are involved in supporting PCs. The network computer has promise, especially as bandwidth increases in the next few years on intranets and the Internet and as more and more applications are developed for this new computer model.

WinFrame

One very important network computer-related technology that you should check out is known as WinFrame, developed by a company called Citrix. Its URL is as follows:

www.citrix.com

WinFrame is a technology that allows a skinny client, such as Internet Explorer or Netscape Navigator, to run an assortment of applications across a network.

When you run WinFrame it may first appear like an ActiveX document (see Figure 1.6) but, in fact, the application you are running isn't even resident on your computer system. With the WinFrame technology the applications you choose to run are actually running on a Windows NT server, and the visual output is then downloaded to your browser. When you click on a particular button on the screen the information is transmitted to the Windows NT server running your application, the button is selected, and the resulting output display is then transmitted back to your client.

Figure 1.6 Here is a WinFrame application running in Internet Explorer.

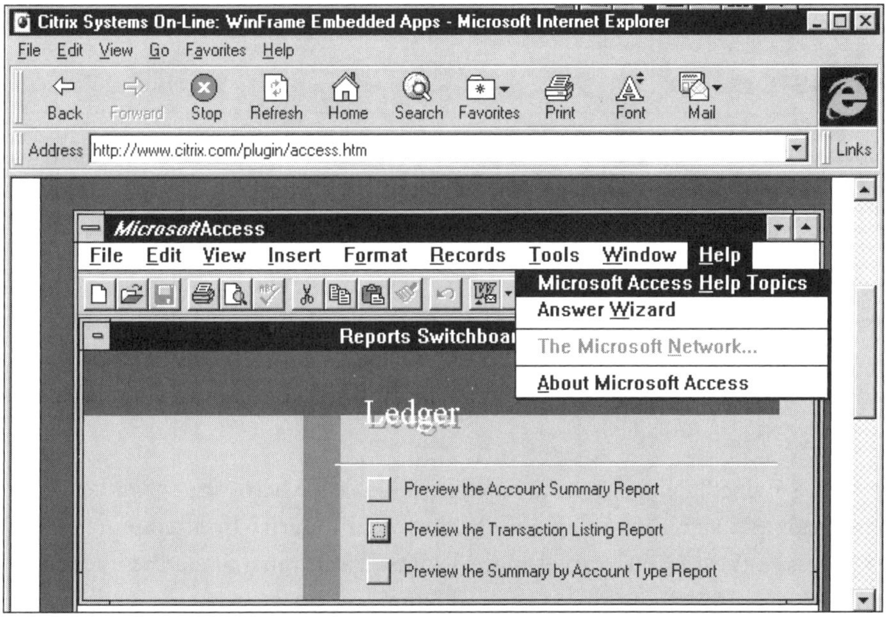

The advantages to this technology are instantly obvious. Now any PC, network computer, or palm-top computer that can run a skinny Web browser like Internet Explorer can then run any assortment of applications that you have loaded on your Windows NT server. All of the significant processing occurs on the server so the client's machine doesn't need the ever-increasing amount of RAM that today's applications require, nor does the client machine have to have any significant storage capability because all of the applications are stored on the server's hard disk space. Here are the basic requirements of the client's computer system needed to run WinFrame applications:

- Access to at least a 286 microprocessor and 640 KB RAM
- The ICA protocol, typically requiring only a bandwidth of 20 Kbps
- Works with any 16- or 32-bit Windows application

Of course, the WinFrame solution does place more significant hardware requirements on the server. For every user on a particular Windows NT server you should have at least 8 MB RAM. The flexibility of the WinFrame system and the prospect of decreasing both hardware cost and potentially software licensing cost have led many companies to consider implementing the WinFrame technology.

Conclusion

This chapter has served to recap the brief history of the explosive Internet growth of the last several years. Although the growth of the Internet will continue at still hyperactive rates, in terms of additional subscribers and companies, many of the big players have shown their hands.

Although the list of companies important to the development of the Internet would easily fill up this book, we feel that Netscape, Microsoft, and Sun Microsystems will play some of the most significant roles in Internet development over the next couple of years.

Netscape's immediate goal isn't to topple the Goliath Microsoft, but rather to establish itself as a significant player in the computer industry by attempting to obtain at least a third of the market in the groupware intranet arena spearheaded with its Netscape Communicator client and SuiteSpot server products. By doing so it will be able to justify its still high stock valuation, making many of those in the Netscape camp wealthy, and guarantee that Netscape will continue to be around.

Microsoft will make the terms "Internet access" and "operating system" one and the same. In addition, Microsoft is taking the Internet religion to heart by incorporating any Internet feature conceivable in all of its various products, most prominently in Office 97. Microsoft also appears to be leading the charge by providing some of the best development environments for programming languages such as Java, Visual Basic, C++, and the Internet with Visual InterDev, all of which encourage the adoption and use of the ActiveX technologies.

Sun Microsystems lives, breathes, and dreams Java; although Java still contributes a paltry sum compared to its other products, it effectively captures the soul of this organization. Java is a computer language that has been designed for the Internet, and it will most probably become the language of choice in the near future.

The next wave of technology, content, and products is waiting for needed increases in bandwidth to the consumer, which are two to three years away from being in the hands of enough consumers to have a significant impact.

Chapter

2

ActiveX Controls

ActiveX controls represent the next generation in the evolution of componentware and form the fundamental building blocks of the Microsoft Active Platform.

On the Web, ActiveX controls can be thought of as compact applications that can be downloaded from an Internet site, and run within an Active Client, such as Internet Explorer. The development of ActiveX controls indicates the end of static Web pages that contain only images and text and of form processing done with hard-to-use CGI programs. Here are just some of the different functions that you can now integrate into a Web page using ActiveX controls:

- Play video clips
- Play sound files of almost any type
- View and interact in a virtual reality environment
- Access and modify database information

In this chapter, we will introduce you to ActiveX controls and we will show you what led to their development and how best to deploy them within your own Microsoft Active Platform applications.

Once upon a Time ...

For many years software developers have sought the ideal of object-oriented programming. Forever frustrated with the need to build every new software program from scratch, developers hoped that one day they would construct their code using existing objects. These objects would have defined interfaces, properties, and methods that would allow them to be easily incorporated within an application. A programmer creating a payroll application, for example, could simply find several existing objects that applied the desired methods to payroll processing. One such method could calculate an employee's take-home pay after taxes. The programmer could simply define the proper interfaces to pass the needed information to the object. This information could include the employee's gross pay, marital status, number of dependents, and additional withholding desired; as well as the state and federal income tax withholding rates for the state in which the employee resides. The object would then return a value, the employee's net pay. Obviously, simply providing the necessary information to existing controls makes the work of program creation much easier.

The potential of object-oriented programming is also illustrated by Microsoft Office. Nearly every program in this suite, including Excel, Word, and PowerPoint, has a spell-checking feature. In the old days of computing programming, each development group working on an application would create its own code to provide spell-checking. This duplication of effort is obviously wasteful. The ideal solution would be to have a spell-checking object that could be inserted into whatever application is being created. In this case, one piece of code could be written and then reused. Another advantage of object-oriented programming involves the inevitable software updates. When Microsoft chooses to create Office 2000, not every function will need to be modified from the Office 97 version. In the conventional top-to-bottom programming style, the functions of different elements of an application often become integrated into each other: These functions' interdependencies make them more difficult to modify separately. The object-oriented programming approach avoids this problem.

The first development stage of Microsoft's componentware technology was Object Linking and Embedding 1 (OLE 1), which was a technology designed to allow users to work with compound documents. With this technology users could place Excel spreadsheets into Word documents, and they could make direct modifications to the spreadsheets while in Word. About the same time, Microsoft began the move to the "componentware" model of software programming by creating Visual Basic Extensions (.VBX), later called Visual Basic controls. Now, when a Visual Basic programmer needed a standard object such as a command button or a drop-down menu, he or she simply selected the appropriate VBX. There was no need to create the object from scratch, defining its design, appearance, methods, events, and properties. VBXs made programming simpler, but these controls were limited to only Visual Basic.

Microsoft then developed OLE 2, which represented the next generation of controls, superseding the old Visual Basic Extensions and OLE 1. OLE 2 supported compound documents and it was greatly expanded to include any objects that were based on the COM (Component Object Model). OLE controls used the COM to enable high-end characteristics, such as linking and embedding. Here are some of the basic capabilities all OLE controls were required to support:

- Display its own user interface
- Specify the properties of the OLE control that it hosted
- Send events to a control container

OLE controls required a large number of interfaces to support all of their capabilities and features. Here are all of the interfaces an OLE control needed to be considered an OLE control:

IOleinPlaceActiveObject

IOleControl

IOleinPlaceObject

IOleObject

IDataObject

IOleCache2

IViewObejct2

IRunnableObject

IPersistStorage

IPersistStreamInit

ISpecifyPropertyPages

IConnectionPointContainer

IConnectionPoint

IProvideClassInfo2

IDispatch

Obviously, the amount of overhead required to provide all of the numerous capabilities and features of OLE controls made them unsuitable for use on the Internet, where current bandwidth restrictions require slim components for reasonable download times. To understand OLE controls, you must first understand the Component Object Model.

Component Object Model

The Component Object Model (COM) serves as the foundation for OLE controls and now for ActiveX controls. COM provides the means for objects on a system to communicate with each other by setting the standard for object interfaces. The services of a particular object are accessed using the methods that are provided in the available interfaces. COM supports three main characteristics of object-oriented technology:

Polymorphism. Allows clients to treat different objects the same way. For example, a client could call the exact same method from two different objects that could each implement that method quite differently.

Inheritance. Allows a programmer to create a new object that automatically includes the properties or methods of another object.

Encapsulation. Means that objects can have their data accessed or modified using only the interfaces they provide, which protects the objects from incorrect changes by clients that access them.

One of the advantages of COM objects is that they can be written in any type of computer programming language because all that is required is that the object provides a binary interface. Chapter 10 will give you a complete understanding of COM.

Distributed Component Object Model

As useful as COM is, it is limited to allowing only those controls found on one computer system to communicate with each other. In response to the explosive growth of distributed networks, especially the publicly distributed network we commonly refer to as the Internet, Microsoft developed DCOM to allow the communication of COM objects across connected networks.

DCOM allows objects to provide their services to other objects residing on other machines, just as COM does locally. To do this, DCOM uses the Remote Procedure Call (RPC). A client makes a call for a particular object as if the object resided on the same machine, but the RPC finds the appropriate object wherever it is on the network. DCOM also supports several security services that are used when objects provide their services across a network. Chapter 10 will give you a complete understanding of DCOM applications and how to create them.

ActiveX Controls

In 1996, Microsoft introduced ActiveX controls; not a new creation, but rather a marketing-inspired transformation of existing OLE controls into Internet-transportable applications. ActiveX controls are also based on COM, but unlike OLE controls that require at least 15 different interfaces, ActiveX controls require only one interface: IUnknown. This reduction of the services ActiveX controls are required to provide makes them up to 75 percent smaller than comparable OLE controls and, therefore, easily transportable across the Internet at bandwidths as low as 14.4 Kbps.

ActiveX controls feature some added capabilities, such as support for asynchronous connections and incremental rendering, which make them well suited for Internet applications. ActiveX controls also feature the ability to create entries for themselves in the system registry of a computer system on which they have been loaded, thereby effectively installing themselves. ActiveX controls can be considered objects that feature three elements used to define what they are, what they do, and when they do it:

Properties. Characteristics or attributes of an object that detail what it is and how it looks. These properties include the object's name, height, width, default URL, caption, and just about anything else you can imagine.

Methods. Commonly implemented procedures of functions that a client calls from an object to have it perform a particular task. This is what the object does.

Events. Events indicate when an object performs some action or processing. For example, when you click your mouse on a commandButton control, this control typically performs some action or instructs another object to perform an action.

Although ActiveX controls are self-contained applications, they also need an Active client, or control container, in which to be instantiated.

Control Containers

ActiveX controls are not self-supporting applications: They must run in control containers. A control container is a program that can provide the support services required to host an ActiveX control. Although the interface requirements for ActiveX controls are quite lax, a control container must support the following interfaces to be able to host an ActiveX control:

IDispatch (events)

IDispatch (properties)

IOleinPlaceFrame

IOleinPlaceSite

IOleinPlaceUIWindow

IOleControlSite

IAdviseSink

IOleClientSite

IPropertyNotifySink

ActiveX control containers include applications such as Internet Explorer and Word.

When a user contacts one of your Web pages that contains an ActiveX control, Internet Explorer first checks the user's computer registry to see if the specified ActiveX control is already present. If the ActiveX control is present on the user's computer, Internet Explorer activates it in the Web page, downloading only the properties designated by the developer. When ActiveX controls are installed on a Windows 95 system they are placed in the C:/windows/Occachedirectory.

When the ActiveX control can't be found on the user's computer, Internet Explorer locates the ActiveX control on the Internet and downloads it to the user's computer system, then installs it after getting the user's approval. ActiveX controls feature this auto-download and transparent installation capability, much like Java applets.

Development Environments

FrontPage is a visual development environment that is ideal for incorporating ActiveX controls into your Web applications, and it serves as an excellent demonstration tool. Many developers have already had experience with the ActiveX Control Pad that was made available with the first ActiveX controls and used for inserting them in Web pages. All of the capabilities of the ActiveX Control Pad have been integrated into FrontPage, including the Script Wizard and the HTML Layout Editor. You can use FrontPage as a separate application or as part of the integrated Internet development environment of Visual InterDev. Some of the ActiveX control features found in the ActiveX Control Pad and FrontPage are also duplicated in Visual InterDev, such as the Script Wizard and the HTML Layout Editor. This chapter illustrates the different tools and options used to insert ActiveX controls into Web pages using both FrontPage and Visual InterDev.

Inserting ActiveX controls into a Web page couldn't be any simpler than it is in FrontPage. First load an existing or new Web page to which you want to add an ActiveX control, and place your cursor in the desired location for insertion. Choose the Insert|Other Components menu selection, and then select ActiveX Control, which results in the appearance of the ActiveX Control Properties Window, shown in Figure 2.1.

Click on the **Pick a Control** spinner box to open a drop-down menu box that displays all of the ActiveX controls currently available on your system. Choose a control, and designate properties such as border size and location on the Web page.

Figure 2.1 Select the ActiveX control you want to insert and specify its properties.

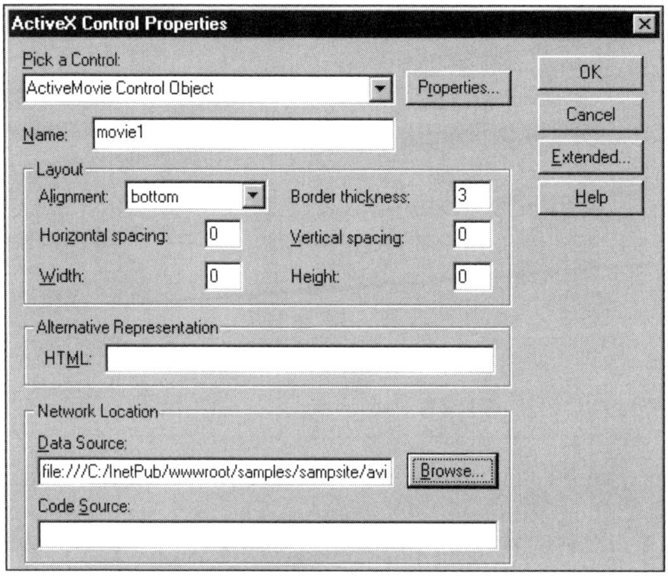

You can also specify alternative HTML content to be displayed to users who have browsers that don't support ActiveX controls. In the example shown in Figure 2.1, an Active Movie control was inserted, and so a data source file also needed to be specified; in this case, a video AVI file was chosen.

You can also click on the Properties button to customize the ActiveX control for your Web page. The window that appears depends on the ActiveX control. For a few ActiveX controls, the window shown in Figure 2.2 will appear.

The NAME|VALUE pairs that you enter for the ActiveX control in this window will be included within <PARAM> tags for the ActiveX control.

For most other ActiveX controls, the Edit and the Properties windows (see Figures 2.3 and 2.4) will appear when you click on the Properties button shown in Figure 2.1.

The Edit window allows you to use your mouse to designate the appearance of the ActiveX control that you are inserting in your Web page, in terms of width and

Figure 2.2 Remove or add NAME|VALUE pairs that you want to be included with the ActiveX control.

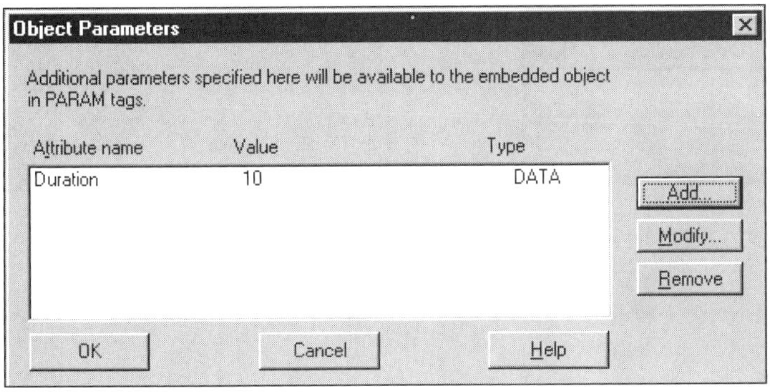

height. Simply use the drag-and-drop capabilities to quickly set the desired size of the ActiveX control, and the appropriate properties will be dynamically modified in the Property window.

Figure 2.3 Use the mouse's drag-and-drop capabilities in the Edit window to vary the appearance and size of the ActiveX control.

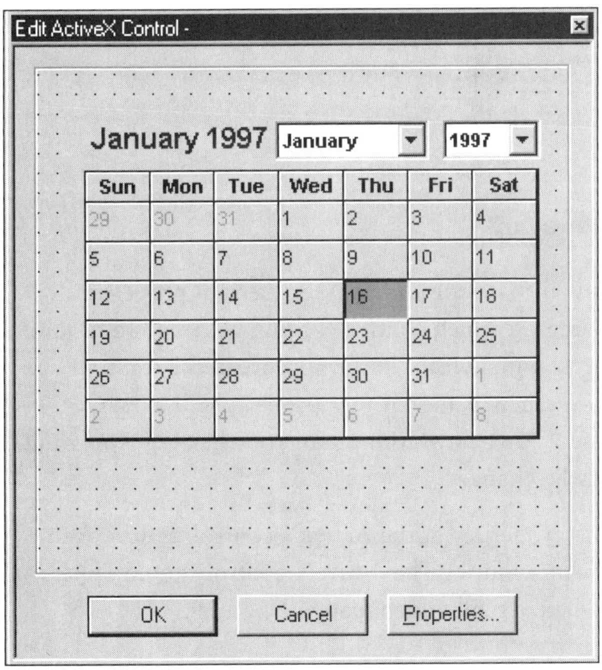

Figure 2.4 Use the Properties window to customize all aspects of the ActiveX control for your application.

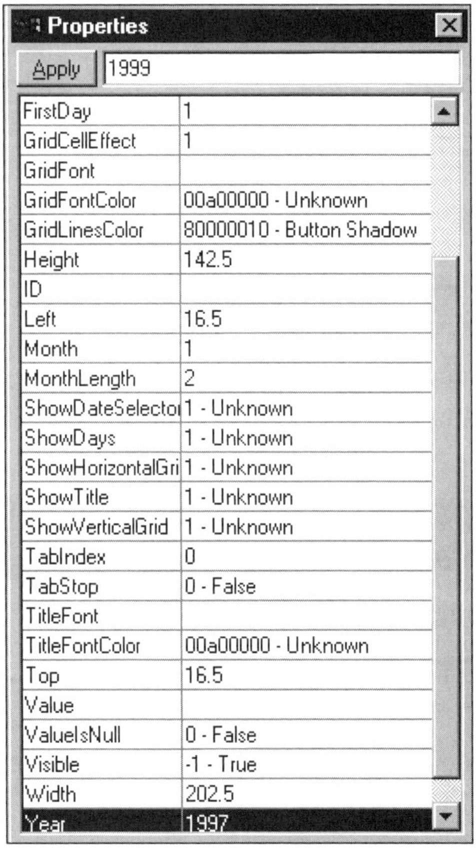

The Property window allows you to customize an assortment of properties, which significantly differ depending on which control is being inserted. To modify a property, click on it in the Property window; the value appears in the top text box next to APPLY. Type in or select the new value for that property and click the Apply button, which modifies the value below. Make sure you click the Apply button, or the value may not always be changed.

Once you have customized the properties of the ActiveX control, return to the main FrontPage visual development window. The ActiveX control should appear in the Web page as it will appear when actually downloaded by a user.

HTML Source Code

After you have inserted an ActiveX control in a Web page, you can view the actual HTML source code generated by FrontPage by choosing the View|HTML menu selection. Here is an example of the HTML source code generated by FrontPage to insert a Calendar control into a Web page:

```
<OBJECT

id=" Calendar1"

name=" Calendar1"

classid=" clsid:8E27C92B-1264-101C-8A2F-040224009C02"

border=" 0"

width=" 297"

height=" 187" >

</OBJECT>
```

In the window that appears you can make modifications to the HTML source code by simply placing your cursor in the appropriate place and inserting or deleting at will.

<OBJECT> Tag

Like any other Web components, ActiveX controls require the appropriate HTML tag for insertion into Web pages. Java applets require the <APPLET> tag, plug-ins require the <EMBED> tag, and ActiveX controls require the <OBJECT> tag, as shown in the HTML source code preceding.

Within the first <OBJECT> tag, assorted different attributes can be defined that indicate characteristics of the ActiveX control, such as its ID name or its WIDTH. Table 2.1 lists the attributes that can be defined for an ActiveX control.

In addition to the basic attributes that can be defined for an ActiveX control within the <OBJECT> tag, many ActiveX controls can be additionally customized by the inclusion of various NAME|VALUE pairs within the <PARAM> tag. Here is an example of the <PARAM> tag included within the <OBJECT> tag for inserting an ActiveX control into a Web page.

```
<OBJECT
ID=" RealAudio1"
WIDTH=148
HEIGHT=40
CLASSID=" CLSID:CFCDAA03-8BE4-11CF-B84B-0020AFBBCCFA" >
<PARAM NAME=" _ExtentX"  VALUE=" 3916" >
<PARAM NAME=" _ExtentY"  VALUE=" 1058" >
<PARAM NAME=" AUTOSTART"  VALUE=" 0" >
<PARAM NAME=" NOLABELS"  VALUE=" 0" >
</OBJECT>
```

> **NOTE** The different NAME|VALUE pairs that can be defined for a particular ActiveX control are determined by the programmer when the control is created. When you make modifications to the actual HTML source code to change the NAME|VALUE pairs you should be aware that many times the NAME|VALUE pairs are case sensitive.

There are additional attributes, known as VALUETYPE, that can be included within the <PARAM> tag to further specify the type of VALUE. The three possible VALUETYPE attributes are as follows:

REF. Indicates that the value specified is a URL.

DATA. Indicates that the value specified is a string that should be passed directly to the ActiveX control.

OBJECT. Indicates that the value specified is a URL for an OBJECT element located within the same document.

These VALUETYPE attributes are included in the <PARAM> tag, as shown in the following example:

```
<PARAM NAME=HomePage REF VALUE=" www.microsoft.com" >
```

Table 2.1 <OBJECT> Tag Attributes

Attribute	Description
ALIGN	Designates the alignment of the object on the Web page. The possible values for this attribute are those used when inserting images such as left, right, or center.
BORDER	Specifies the width of the border surrounding the object.
CLASSID	Designates the GUID, Global Unique Identifier, of the ActiveX control inserted into a Web page.
CODEBASE	Specifies the URL location where the browser can download the ActiveX control.
CODETYPE	Ensures that the viewing agent can display the object.
DATA	Specifies the URL and file name for the data that will be displayed by the ActiveX control, such as a .MIDI sound file or a .AVI video.
DECLARE	Indicates that the object is to be declared but not instantiated.
HEIGHT	Specifies the height of the object on the Web page, defined in standard units.
HSPACE	Indicates the vertical space between the inserted object and any other content on the Web page such as text. This value is defined using standard units.
ID	The name given to the inserted object, which can then be referenced by other objects or scripts within the Web page.
NAME	Used by the browser to determine if an object in the FORM block will participate in the "submit" process.
SHAPES	Indicates that the inserted object has one or more anchors defined on its visible area.
STANDBY	Specifies text to be displayed while the object is being loaded.
TYPE	Ensures that the viewing agent can recognize the program type of the inserted object.
USEMAP	Specifies a URL when a client-side image map is used.
VSPACE	Indicates the vertical space between the inserted object and any other content on the Web page such as text. This value is defined using standard units.
WIDTH	Specifies the width of the object on the Web page, defined in standard units.

Some of the attributes defined in Table 2.1 may not seem even to apply to ActiveX controls. The World Wide Web Consortium, commonly referred to as the W3C, which oversees the HTML open standards, recently designated that the <OBJECT> tag will be used for the insertion not only of ActiveX controls, but also of an assortment of Web objects:

- Java applets, replacing the <APPLET> tag
- Plug-ins, replacing the <EMBED> tag
- Images, replacing the <IMAGE> tag

The W3C's reasoning is that ActiveX controls, Java applets, and plug-ins are not going to be the last objects created for the Web: It seems appropriate now to designate the <OBJECT> tag as a generic tag that can be used on these existing objects and any other objects created in the future.

You can find more information about the W3C and keep up to date on the newest HTML specifications, by checking out:

www.w3.org.

CLASSID Attribute With many thousands of existing ActiveX controls you may be wondering, "When I include content in my Web page that must be viewed with an Active Movie control, how does the control container, such as Internet Explorer, determine whether the user has that control already installed?" When you include an ActiveX control within your Web page you must also include the CLASSID that specifies the CLSID number for the particular ActiveX control that you have selected. The CLSID number is often referred to as the GUID, Global Unique Identifier, for a control.

Whenever a new ActiveX control is created, a new GUID is generated for that control. The GUID is a 128-bit identifier number that is generated using a combination of data unique to the developer's computer and programming session. Each GUID generated includes a time stamp and is based on the unique machine identifier of the machine on which it was created. This ensures that the GUID generated for an object is unique in time and space. Whenever an ActiveX control is installed on your system, it records its GUID in the system registry. The system registry is then checked for a particular GUID before an Active Client downloads a particular ActiveX control. This system makes it highly improbable that two controls ever have the same GUID.

When a browser encounters the <OBJECT> tag, the browser searches for the value of the CLASSID attribute, and searches the user's computer to see if that particular ActiveX control is already present. If it is, the ActiveX control is instantiated with the characteristics specified within the <OBJECT> tag, and any specified data is downloaded and displayed.

CODEBASE Attribute In many cases, the user who attempts to view one of your Web pages will not have the designated ActiveX control installed on his or her computer system. The ActiveX-compatible browser can download the appropriate ActiveX control from anywhere on the Internet, but it needs to know where to look. When you place an ActiveX control in a Web page, the CODEBASE attribute that is included in the <OBJECT> tag is used to identify the URL and version number of the ActiveX control that should be downloaded.

You can use the CODEBASE attribute to specify the location of three different file types that are commonly used for ActiveX controls:

- .CAB.
- Portable Executable files such as .OCX, .EXE, .DLL.
- .INF.

Many of the Microsoft-created ActiveX controls don't require the CODEBASE attribute. These controls use the ActiveX Object Index, which is able to identify the proper URL for the control by referencing the CLSID number for the control that you have incorporated into your Web page.

HTML Layout Editor

Every Web designer has probably experienced the frustration of being able to define only three particular alignments for the position of ActiveX controls on a Web page. The HTML layout editor allows you to place ActiveX controls on a Web page in any orientation you want. It even allows you to overlap different ActiveX controls, giving Web pages a three-dimensional appearance. The HTML layout file is actually a text file that is saved with an .ALX extension.

You can create an HTML layout of your ActiveX controls using Visual InterDev. Choose File|New and, in the Files folder, select HTML Layout. Visual InterDev will create an HTML layout file with an .ALX extension, and it will open the windows shown in Figure 2.5.

Figure 2.5 Choose what ActiveX controls you want to place on your HTML layout, designate their size, and orient them three-dimensionally with respect to each other.

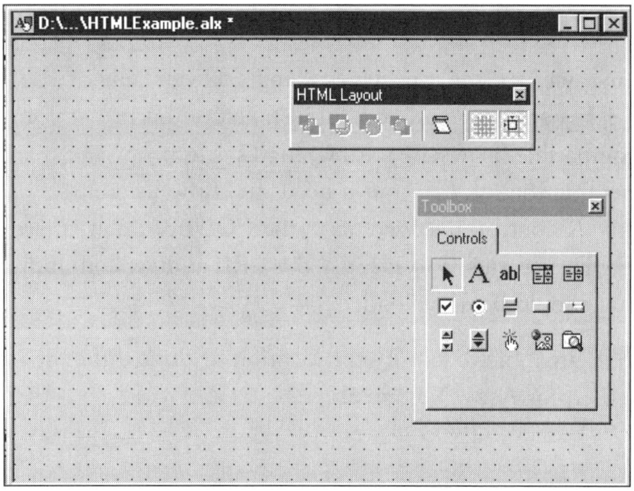

The HTML Layout window allows you to select ActiveX controls that you have already laid out and move them in front of or behind other ActiveX controls. Simply select the control you want to move, and click on the appropriate movement in the HTML Layout window. Once the ActiveX control is on the .ALX window you can resize it using drag-and-drop, and you can modify its properties by right-clicking on the control and selecting properties.

Here is an example of the script generated for an HTML layout .ALX file.

```
<SCRIPT Language=" VBS" >

     <!--

     ComboBox1.AddItem "Classical"

     ComboBox1.AddItem "Country"

     ComboBox1.AddItem "Rock'n Roll"

     ComboBox1.AddItem "Alternative"

     ComboBox1.AddItem "Elevator"
```

```
    ComboBox1.AddItem "Disco"


    -->
</SCRIPT>

<DIV ID=" Layout1"  STYLE=" LAYOUT:FIXED;WIDTH:400pt;HEIGHT:300pt;" >
    <OBJECT ID=" Label1"
     CLASSID=" CLSID:978C9E23-D4B0-11CE-BF2D-00AA003F40D0"  STYLE="
TOP:149pt;LEFT:58pt;WIDTH:74pt;HEIGHT:17pt;ZINDEX:0;" >
        <PARAM NAME=" Caption"  VALUE=" Choose a selection: ">
        <PARAM NAME=" Size"  VALUE=" 2619;583" >
        <PARAM NAME=" FontCharSet"  VALUE=" 0" >
        <PARAM NAME=" FontPitchAndFamily"  VALUE=" 2" >
    </OBJECT>
    <OBJECT ID=" RealAudio1"
     CLASSID=" CLSID:CFCDAA03-8BE4-11CF-B84B-0020AFBBCCFA"  STYLE="
TOP:50pt;LEFT:58pt;WIDTH:165pt;HEIGHT:83pt;TABINDEX:1;ZINDEX:1;" >
        <PARAM NAME=" _ExtentX"  VALUE=" 5821" >
        <PARAM NAME=" _ExtentY"  VALUE=" 2910" >
        <PARAM NAME=" AUTOSTART"  VALUE=" 0" >
        <PARAM NAME=" NOLABELS"  VALUE=" 0" >
    </OBJECT>
    <OBJECT ID=" ComboBox1"
     CLASSID=" CLSID:8BD21D30-EC42-11CE-9E0D-00AA006002F3"  STYLE="
TOP:149pt;LEFT:132pt;WIDTH:91pt;HEIGHT:16pt;TABINDEX:2;ZINDEX:2;" >
```

```
        <PARAM NAME=" DisplayStyle"  VALUE=" 7" >
        <PARAM NAME=" Size"  VALUE=" 3201;556" >
        <PARAM NAME=" MatchEntry"  VALUE=" 1" >
        <PARAM NAME=" ShowDropButtonWhen"  VALUE=" 2" >
        <PARAM NAME=" FontCharSet"  VALUE=" 0" >
        <PARAM NAME=" FontPitchAndFamily"  VALUE=" 2" >
    </OBJECT>
</DIV>
```

This example illustrates the different pieces of information that the .ALX file provides to the HTML layout control:

- ActiveX controls that should be displayed and their customized properties
- The orientation and spatial arrangement of these ActiveX controls on a layout
- Any scripting that is used to create interactivity between the different ActiveX controls within the layout

This HTML layout can then be placed in one or more different Web pages in your Web application. Open the Web page or Active Server page in which you want the HTML layout inserted, and place your cursor in the desired insertion location. Choose the Insert|Into HTML menu selection in Visual InterDev, select the HTML Layout option, and the window shown in Figure 2.6 should appear.

Here is an example of a Web page with an HTML layout file inserted. Where you are editing the Web page will also determine how you want the URL to the document to be included within the Web page.

Here is an example of the HTML source code generated to insert an HTML layout file into a Web page.

```
<OBJECT
CLASSID=" CLSID:812AE312-8B8E-11CF-93C8-00AA00C08FDF"
ID=" Html_Layout1"
STYLE=" LEFT:0;TOP:0" >
```

Figure 2.6 Select HTML layout to add it to a Web page.

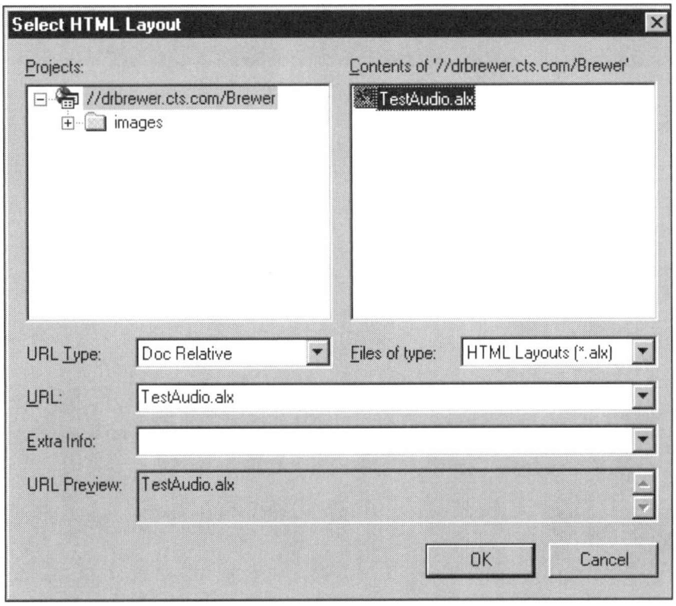


```
<PARAM NAME=" ALXPATH"  REF VALUE=" TestAudio.alx" >

</OBJECT>
```

This source code illustrates that the HTML layout file is really an HTML layout ActiveX control, which uses the .ALX text file as the data source.

The Web page that is one of the best, and definitely the oddest, demonstrations of the capabilities of the HTML Layout control is Mr. Eggplant Head, created by Microsoft. A sample of this Web page (see Figure 2.7) comes with Visual InterDev, or you can check it out at

www.microsoft.com.

BackStyle Property

When you place objects on a Web page in front of or behind other objects, you may also want to address the transparency of different objects. Some objects may be opaque, and any objects located behind them would not be visible to the user, while other objects could be transparent, thereby displaying any objects located behind them. Some ActiveX controls have a customizable BackStyle property that allows you to set the transparency.

Figure 2.7 Create your own Mr. Eggplant Head utilizing the features of the HTML Layout ActiveX control.

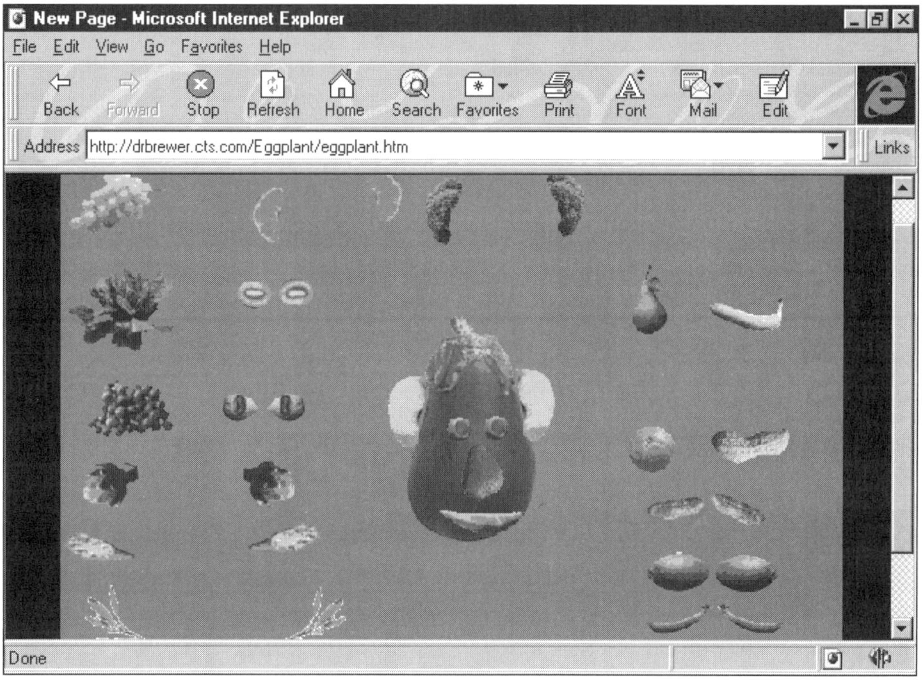

Toolbox

When you create your first HTML layout the Toolbox window that appears, shown in Figure 2.5, displays only the Microsoft-ActiveX and Microsoft-Forms related controls. It is worth mentioning that Microsoft has converted the familiar form components into Microsoft Form controls. Here is a list of the existing Microsoft 2.0 Form controls:

CheckBox

ComboBox

CommandButton

Label

ListBox

OptionsButton

ScrollBar

SpinButton

TabStrip

TextBox

ToggleButton

There are probably many other ActiveX controls installed on your system that you can also insert into an HTML layout file, but first you must add them to your Toolbox. To add ActiveX controls to a page in the Toolbox window, right-click on the desired Folder, and choose Additional Controls. Then select all of the ActiveX controls that you want added to that page in the Toolbox window.

Considering the endless number of available ActiveX controls and the cryptic icon representation of the ActiveX controls in the Toolbox window, you may want to create pages in addition to the standard Controls folder. Right-click on the Controls page or the area surrounding it within the Toolbox window. In the window that appears you can simply choose New Page to create a new page where you can add ActiveX controls. Now you can have distinct folders for form, multimedia, and even database-related controls.

ActiveX Scripting

Anyone even vaguely familiar with the Internet knows that the keyword is "interactivity." One of Netscape's first technological developments after its first Web browser was the creation of a scripting language known as JavaScript. Web developers needed a way to create interactivity with the elements found on a Web page. What they got was a simple, low-level, scripting language. Although JavaScript didn't have many of the features found in programming languages such as C++ and Java, it did provide a way for developers to build processing capabilities within the HTML source code downloaded to a browser. This replaced the old Web paradigm where every user action and input was transmitted back to a CGI (Common Gateway Interface) program running on the server, which determined the response to that action and transmitted this information back to the Web browser. Of course, in response to Netscape's development of JavaScript, Microsoft created Visual Basic Script, referred to as VBScript.

The <SCRIPT> tag was developed to allow the integration of scripting languages into Web pages, as seen in this example.

```
<SCRIPT LANGUAGE=" VBScript" >

<!--

Sub CommandButton1_Click()

Calendar1.Day = TextBox1.Text

end sub

-->

</SCRIPT>
```

This book is not meant to provide a complete description of the fundamentals of ActiveX scripting. You should consider reading books such as *ActiveX Sourcebook* by Ted Coombs, Jason Coombs, and Don Brewer; *VBScript Sourcebook* by Rod Stephens; or *JavaScript Sourcebook* by Gordon McComb (all published by John Wiley & Sons) to get a complete reference to using scripting language in your Web pages.

ActiveX controls are like any other objects in that they have key events, properties, and methods that can be accessed by other programs. ActiveX scripting is simply using either JavaScript or VBScript to create interactivity among ActiveX controls and other objects. Because you can use more than one scripting language in a Web page, you must specify the scripting language with the LANGUAGE attribute, as shown in the previous HTML source code.

You may also have noticed that the script is located between the <!-- start tag and the -- > end tag. These tags are included to prevent a Web browser that doesn't recognize scripting information from crashing.

With Active scripting, one ActiveX control can modify the properties of another ActiveX control or even have it execute a particular method upon some user action. For example, a user can enter a value into a text box ActiveX control, and that value could then be displayed in a scrolling message produced by the Marquee ActiveX control.

Script Wizard When you place ActiveX controls within a Web page, you can use the Script Wizard to link them together to create user interactivity. For example, you can let a user set the month in a text box ActiveX control that changes the displayed month of a calendar ActiveX control. The advantage of using the Script Wizard, rather than Notepad, for example, is that it illustrates the available properties, methods, and events for the controls that you have already placed in a Web page. It can also automatically generate code for you, while all you do is select the event and properties that you want to have interconnected.

You can open the Script Wizard (see Figure 2.8) in Visual InterDev by simply selecting View|Script Wizard. The Script Wizard allows you to quickly generate ActiveX scripting to tie together the ActiveX controls in a particular Web page.

The Script Wizard has three main windows. On the left, the Event window displays the events, such as OnClick or OnLoad, of the ActiveX controls. The methods and properties of the different ActiveX controls are shown in the Action window, on the right. The methods are denoted with an exclamation point icon

Figure 2.8 Select the desired event of one ActiveX control and connect it to a property or method of another.

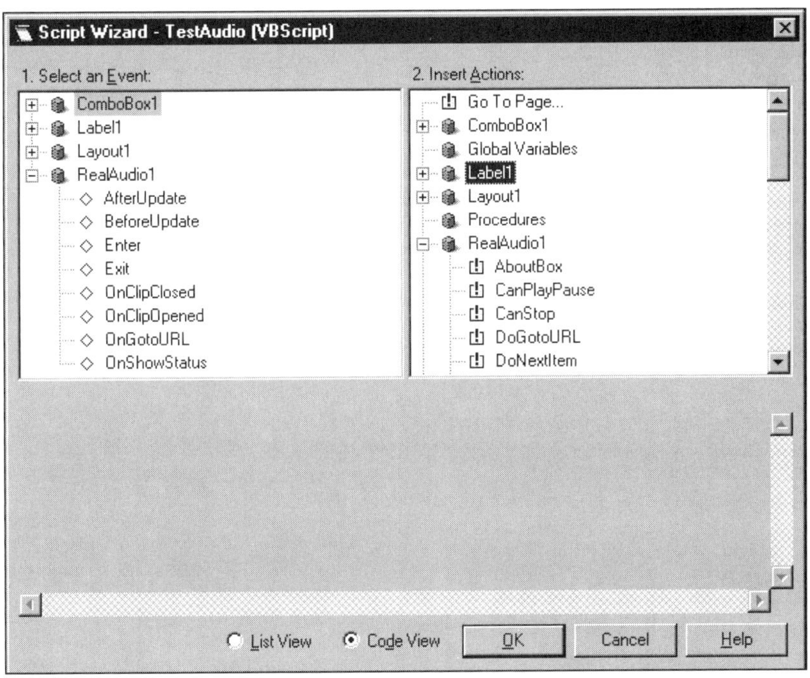

next to them, while an icon that looks like a page with script on it denotes a property. The bottom window can be used to display either List View or Code View of the script.

Code View. Displays the actual ActiveX scripting code that is generated.

List View. Displays a textual explanation of what object is to be affected and what action is supposed to take place based on the ActiveX script that has been written.

The following example illustrates how you can easily tie together numerous ActiveX controls. In this example a calendar, a command button, and a text control are placed on the same HTML layout from the Toolbox using Visual InterDev. The objective was to allow a user to enter a date in the text box that would then be selected in the calendar control whenever the user clicked on the command button. Users familiar with the calendar control may wonder why they can't just click on the desired date, and of course, the answer is that they just can't. Script Wizard was started by right-clicking on the HTML Layout window, and selecting the Script Wizard option.

In the Script Wizard, the click event of the command button was first selected, which generated the first line of script code. Then the Day property of the calendar control was selected, an = sign was typed into the bottom Code View window, and then the Text property of the TextBox1 control was selected. Here is an example of the source code for the HTML Layout control that was created, with the script that was generated by the Script Wizard shown at the beginning of the .ALX file.

```
<SCRIPT LANGUAGE=" VBScript" >

<!--

Sub CommandButton1_Click()

Calendar1.Day = TextBox1.Text

end sub

-->

</SCRIPT>

<DIV ID=" Layout1"  STYLE=" LAYOUT:FIXED;WIDTH:400pt;HEIGHT:300pt;" >
```

```
<OBJECT ID=" CommandButton1"
 CLASSID=" CLSID:D7053240-CE69-11CD-A777-00DD01143C57"  STYLE="
TOP:17pt;LEFT:149pt;WIDTH:66pt;HEIGHT:25pt;TABINDEX:0;ZINDEX:0;" >
    <PARAM NAME=" Caption"  VALUE=" Press Here" >
    <PARAM NAME=" Size"  VALUE=" 2328;882" >
    <PARAM NAME=" FontCharSet"  VALUE=" 0" >
    <PARAM NAME=" FontPitchAndFamily"  VALUE=" 2" >
    <PARAM NAME=" ParagraphAlign"  VALUE=" 3" >
</OBJECT>
<OBJECT ID=" Calendar1"
 CLASSID=" CLSID:8E27C92B-1264-101C-8A2F-040224009C02"
 DATA=" DATA:application/x-
oleobject;BASE64,K8knjmQSHBCKLwQCJACcAgAACABsHAAAVBMAAM0HAwAdAA8AAIAAAAAAAACg
ABAAAIAAAKAAAQABAAIAAAABAAAAAQAAAAEAAAABAAAAAQAAAAEAAAAAAAAA
AAAAAAAAAAAAAAAAAAAAAAAAAAAAAAAAAAAAAAAAAAAAAAAAAAAAAAAAAAAA
AAAAAAAAAAAAAAAAAAAAAAAAAAAAAAAAAAAAAAAAAAAAAAAAAAAAAAAAAAAA
AAAAAAAAAAAAAAAAAAAAAAAAAAAAAAAAAAAAAAAAAAAAAAAAAAAAAAAAAAAA
AAAAAAAAAAAAAAAAAAAAAAAAAAAAAAAAAAAAAAAAAAAAAAAAAAAAAAAAAAAA
AAAAAAAAAAAAAAAAAAAAAAAAAAAAAAAAAAAAAAAAAAAAAAAAAAAAAAAAAAAA
AAAAAAAAAAAAAAAAAAAAAAAAAAAAAAAAAAAAAAAAEAAAC8AkRCAQAFQXJp
YWwBAAAAkAFEQgEABUFyaWFsAQAAALwCwNQBAAVBcmlhbA==
"   STYLE=" TOP:50pt;LEFT:17pt;WIDTH:206pt;HEIGHT:140pt;TABINDEX:1;ZINDEX:1;" >
</OBJECT>
<OBJECT ID=" TextBox1"
```

```
    CLASSID=" CLSID:8BD21D10-EC42-11CE-9E0D-00AA006002F3"
STYLE=" TOP:17pt;LEFT:83pt;WIDTH:50pt;HEIGHT:26pt;TABINDEX:2;ZINDEX:2;" >
        <PARAM NAME=" VariousPropertyBits"  VALUE=" 746604571" >
        <PARAM NAME=" Size"  VALUE=" 1764;917" >
        <PARAM NAME=" FontCharSet"  VALUE=" 0" >
        <PARAM NAME=" FontPitchAndFamily"  VALUE=" 2" >
    </OBJECT>
    <OBJECT ID=" Label1"
    CLASSID=" CLSID:978C9E23-D4B0-11CE-BF2D-00AA003F40D0"
STYLE=" TOP:25pt;LEFT:25pt;WIDTH:50pt;HEIGHT:25pt;ZINDEX:3;" >
        <PARAM NAME=" Caption"  VALUE=" Enter Day:" >
        <PARAM NAME=" Size"  VALUE=" 1764;882" >
        <PARAM NAME=" FontCharSet"  VALUE=" 0" >
        <PARAM NAME=" FontPitchAndFamily"  VALUE=" 2" >
    </OBJECT>
</DIV>
```

This HTML layout control was then inserted into a .HTM file, generating the following HTML source code, is shown in Figure 2.9.

```
<META NAME=" GENERATOR"  Content=" Microsoft Developer Studio" >
<META HTTP-EQUIV=" Content-Type"  content=" text/html; charset=ISO-8859-1">
<TITLE>Document Title</TITLE>
</HEAD>
<BODY>
<OBJECT CLASSID=" CLSID:812AE312-8B8E-11CF-93C8-00AA00C08FDF"
```

```
ID=" Html_Layout1"  STYLE=" LEFT:0;TOP:0" >

<PARAM NAME=" ALXPATH"  REF VALUE=" D:\ActiveDesktop\Chapters\Ch2-

ActiveXControls\Layout1.alx" >

</OBJECT>

</BODY>

</HTML>
```

The code generated by the Script Wizard can be either Visual Basic Script or JavaScript. ActiveX controls can respond to either. You can set which scripting language the Script Wizard generates by selecting Tools|Options and then selecting the HTML folder. In the Default Languages window, select the radio button for either VBScript or JavaScript. Although the Script Wizard allows you to generate either Visual Basic Script or JavaScript, you can use only one scripting language per page.

Figure 2.9 Enter a value into the text box and click on the command button to select that particular day in the calendar.

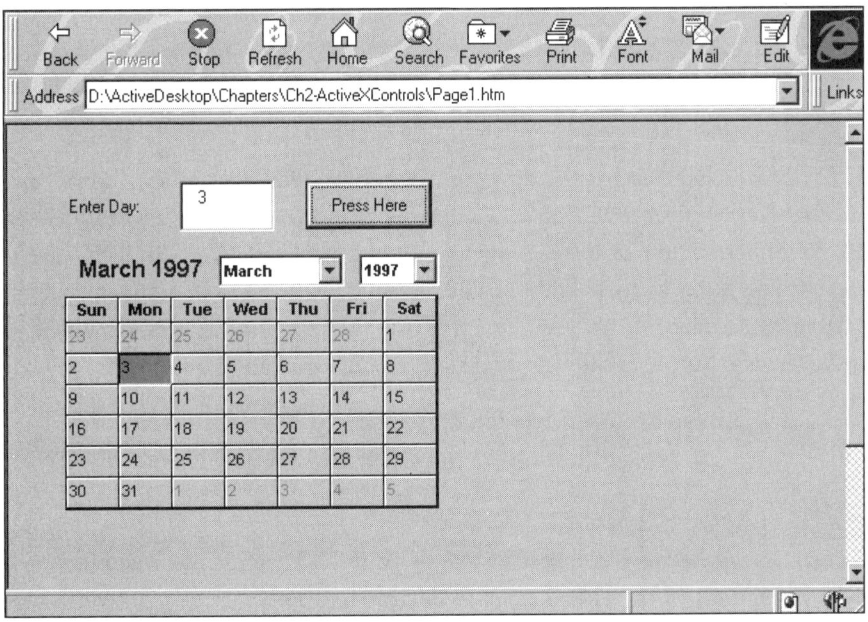

Design-Time ActiveX Controls

Design-time ActiveX controls differ from ActiveX controls; they are not incorporated in web page applications that a user can download. Design-time ActiveX controls don't have binary runtime equivalents like conventional ActiveX controls, but they are used to generate text. They can generate any text that any knowledgeable developer could have written in Notepad. The text that they generate is done only at the design mode, and it becomes static once the file has been saved. You can insert design-time ActiveX controls in your Web page while working in the Visual InterDev development environment. Design-time ActiveX controls run on the server and generate HTML source code that is actually downloaded to the user's Web browser. The main advantage of this is that as a developer, you don't have to worry that users accessing your Web application who don't have an ActiveX compatible browser won't be able to view the content you have created. In Web applications, design-time ActiveX controls are currently used for an assortment of different purposes:

- Conventional HTML tags
- Client-side and server-side scripting
- Java applets
- ActiveX controls
- ActiveX server components

The HTML insertion text for the design-time ActiveX control makes it invisible to a user's browser. Design-time Active X controls allow you to view and experiment with the functionality of these controls as you create your Web applications, but the real strength lies in their ability to generate HTML-based content that is then viewable by any type of browser, not just one that supports ActiveX controls. They can be used to automatically generate server-side or client-side script.

Chapter 7 will give you a more detailed illustration of how you can insert design-time ActiveX controls in the applications you create using Visual InterDev.

ActiveX Control Support

Before incorporating ActiveX controls in one of your Web pages, you might worry about what percentage of Internet users will be able to appreciate this ActiveX content. Internet Explorer 3.0 was the first browser to support ActiveX controls, and obviously that support has continued in Internet Explorer 4.0. Netscape has also added support for ActiveX controls in its Navigator 4.0 browser. Because Internet Explorer and Navigator make up at least 95 percent of the existing browser market, you can feel relatively comfortable about incorporating ActiveX controls.

Of course, the other concern about ActiveX control support is compatibility with users' operating systems. For intranet applications, you may know that most users accessing your application run the Windows operating system, but on the publicly distributed Internet users may also be using Unix and Macintosh platforms. Because OLE and COM, and so ActiveX control technology, was developed for the MS Windows operating systems, it is fair to ask whether ActiveX technology is supported by other operating systems. In response to this obvious concern, Microsoft has recently ported the ActiveX technology from Windows to both Mac and Unix. For more information on the porting of ActiveX to the Unix platform check out the following URLs:

www.bristol.com

www.mainsoft.com

For information about the porting of ActiveX technology to the Mac platform check out the following URL:

www.metrowerks.com

In addition to its own efforts to standardize ActiveX on various platforms, Microsoft has pushed ActiveX as an Internet standard and turned the control of ActiveX and DCOM over to an open standards committee. You can find additional information about this committee and the latest news about ActiveX technology as an Internet standard at The Active Group:

www.activex.org

Microsoft's efforts to make ActiveX technology ubiquitous should allay some of your concerns about creating applications with ActiveX controls.

Security

The only significant potential flaw with ActiveX controls involves security. On one hand, every Web developer has dreamed of having the ability to create an application that can do just about anything, so that when a user contacts a particular Web site the application is downloaded to his or her system, is installed, and then executes. Of course, for these applications to do anything useful, perform any significant functions, they must have access to users' files. That's where the problem starts. Any program that can access files to perform useful operations can just as easily perform mischievous operations.

Microsoft has developed an "accountability system," known as Authenticode, which is its security solution for ActiveX controls. Authenticode is based on trust and digital certificates. The model for this system is that after a developer has created an ActiveX control, he or she must apply for a certificate from a certificate authority, such as VeriSign. This company is supposed to check the code to ensure it doesn't do anything malicious, and then to provide a digital certificate for the code that indicates both the name of the developer and the name of the certificate authority.

Internet Explorer

When a user encounters an ActiveX control on the Internet, the Authenticode system built into Internet Explorer browser is supposed to display the details of this ActiveX control. You can set the desired safety level for your system in Internet Explorer by choosing the View|Options menu selection and then clicking on the Security folder (see Figure 2.10).

After selecting the kind of content you are willing to have downloaded onto your computer, click on the Safety Level button to indicate the actual security you want the browser to provide, as shown in Figure 2.11.

Now when your Web browser encounters an ActiveX control on a Web page it will open a window that indicates that whether the ActiveX control has the appropriate certificate (see Figure 2.12).

Assuming you want the ActiveX control loaded on your system, click the Yes button. You can see what certificate authorities your Internet Explorer browser currently accepts as issuing valid certificates. Click on the Advanced button to open the window shown in Figure 2.13.

Not every existing ActiveX control has the appropriate authenticated certificates. These are the ActiveX controls that you must diligently monitor—they have the highest probability of damaging your system. When your Web browser encounters an ActiveX control that doesn't have a certificate the window shown in Figure 2.14 will appear.

Figure 2.10 Check the appropriate boxes in the Active Content window.

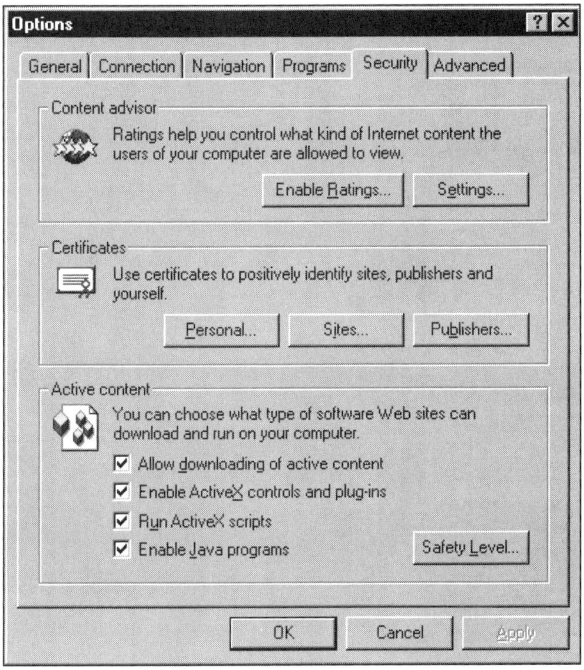

Figure 2.11 Indicate the security settings you want for your system.

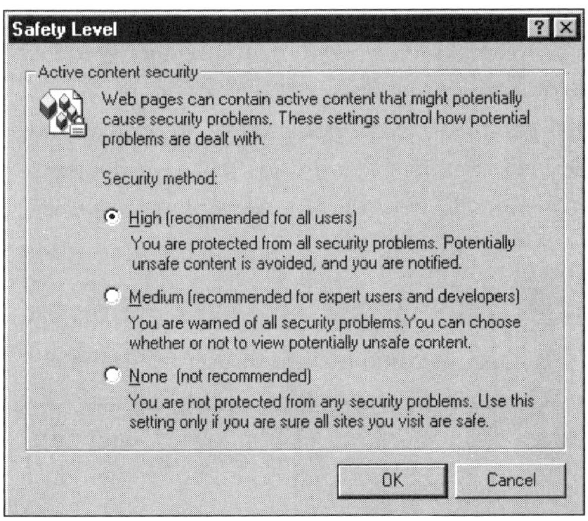

Figure 2.12 Here is the window that appears when an ActiveX control you are going to download has the appropriate certificate.

Of course, you can still choose to download an ActiveX control, even if it doesn't have the appropriate certificates issued to it, but then you are taking your life, and the life of your computer, into your own hands.

When it comes to security, most people have the attitude that a security problem could never happen to them. The first thing to realize is that developers have already created ActiveX controls that demonstrate the potential these controls have to damage a user's system. The following examples demonstrate that warnings about security concerns with ActiveX controls are not unfounded.

Down Goes the System

An innovative Seattle programmer, Fred McLain, was one of the first to demonstrate the potential security risk that ActiveX controls could present to users. He created an ActiveX control called Exploder. Whenever this control is downloaded and installed on a user's system it performs a clean shutdown of Windows 95 and turns off the power on any machines that have a power conservation BIOS. Not good.

Figure 2.13 You can add more or delete the current certificate authorities in this window.

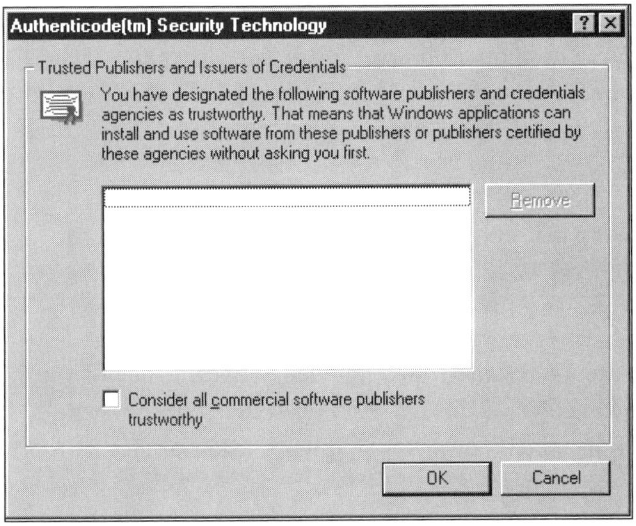

When Fred McLain first placed this ActiveX control on his Web site it was digitally signed with a certificate issued by VeriSign. McLain had obtained a software publisher's key from VeriSign, and anyone who attempted to download it would see that it was issued a proper certificate, the only protection built into Microsoft's Authenticode security system for ActiveX controls. Of course, in digitally signing the code, McLain had violated the pledge that all code signed with the software publisher's key would not be malicious. After the significant publicity that this ActiveX control generated, VeriSign demanded that McLain remove the signed version of the control from his Web site. In this instance, McLain made public the

Figure 2.14 Security window that appears when the ActiveX control doesn't have the appropriate certificate.

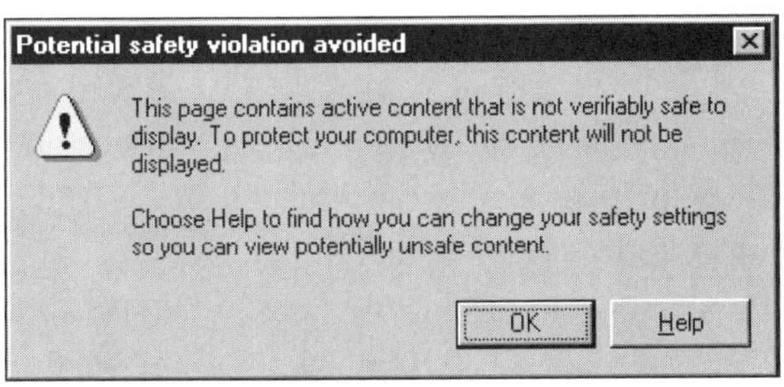

malicious capability of his ActiveX control, which obviously allowed VeriSign to enforce censure of it on the Web.

This should demonstrate that your only protection on the Web—even from certified ActiveX controls—is that the developer observes his or her pledge to VeriSign to be good. I somehow don't believe too many criminal-minded individuals would have a second thought in breaking a pledge.

> **NOTE** Remember, even if an ActiveX control has an issued certificate, it still could damage your system.

For those brave souls that are interested in the Exploder ActiveX control, you can check it out at www.halcyon.com/mclain/ActiveX/. Of course, I recommend that you don't agree to have it installed, but this is simply a suggestion.

Money Transfer

The Chaos Computer Club, from Hamburg, Germany, recently created an ActiveX control that demonstrated how mischievous code could hit you right in your pocketbook. This ActiveX control was designed to access information on computer systems that had Intuit's popular Quicken financial planning program installed.

Once the user had downloaded the ActiveX control, it would scan the system to see if the user had Quicken installed. Then it would trick Quicken into transferring funds from the designated bank account into another bank account the next time that the user logged onto his or her online banking service. This would all be done without requiring the user to enter a personal identification number (PIN), which is designed to prevent theft.

This particular example did not get a certificate so that when a user loads a Web page with this ActiveX control, he or she is notified of the potential security hazard (see Figure 2.14).

The problem is that it's easy for even experienced users to unwittingly accept an unsigned ActiveX control if they get lazy or frustrated by the Authenticode warning window. Many novice users simply don't know about or understand the potential security hazard, and they may unwittingly allow the malicious ActiveX control to be downloaded and installed on their systems. Once it is installed, the program is free to do its work.

This particular integration of a devious ActiveX control and online banking services can be quite disturbing considering the estimates in Chapter 1 of an expected 16 million households in the United States doing their banking online by the year 2000. This particular ActiveX control was created only as a demonstration of the potential dangers, but is it a harbinger of things to come?

Be Careful Out There

Microsoft's response to these demonstrations of ActiveX insecurity has been to create the Microsoft Web Executable Security Advisor site:

www.microsoft.com/security/

This site does little to improve the security associated with ActiveX controls—its message is simply "Bad things can happen." Microsoft also replies to many security critics by pointing at the security flaws that also exist in competitive technologies like Java.

A security system built on the theory of accountability, such as Authenticode, only ensures that you might possibly know who created an ActiveX control that did damage to your system, although you may have trouble even figuring that out if the deviant ActiveX control downs your system permanently. Of course, knowing who did the damage may be little comfort if he or she trashed your hard drive or took money out of your bank account.

Publicly Available ActiveX Controls

The GIGA Information group estimates that the ActiveX industry already generates more than $240 million in sales. There are already thousands of existing ActiveX controls that you can incorporate into your Web application to add multimedia and interactivity. Most of the applications that you have running on your Windows systems are already .OCXs. Because ActiveX controls are based on existing .OCXs there are already hundreds, if not thousands, of ActiveX controls already created. With the release of the Visual Basic Control Creation Editor developers around the world can create ActiveX controls in minutes. Microsoft already estimates that nearly 250,000 ActiveX controls have been created.

Here are just some of the locations you can check out on the Internet to find entertaining and useful publicly available ActiveX controls that you can integrate into your own Web applications. Microsoft has created the complete ActiveX resource page:

www.microsoft.com/activeX/gallery

This Web page contains the most current developments involving the ActiveX technology along with a gallery that lists an endless number of ActiveX controls that you can download and use within your own Web applications.

C|NET also provides a comprehensive library of ActiveX controls that you can download:

www.activex.com

Other ActiveX control resource Web pages include the following:

www.activexcontrols.com

browserwatch.iworld.com/activex.html

Licensing

Most major companies make a concerted effort to ensure that their employees don't violate the licensing agreements of software that they run on their computer systems. In this new ActiveX control world, users may be downloading new ActiveX controls, basically complete applications, into their systems. What occurs if these users then use these ActiveX controls in their own applications?

ActiveX controls include a mechanism to prevent the unlicensed use of controls in Web pages. Today, this mechanism is supported in development tools such as Visual Basic and Microsoft Access, and it is also supported in the beta 2 release of Internet Explorer 3.0. The licensing mechanism works by allowing controls to be distributed with either a developer license or with a runtime license. With a developer license, a user can use the control for development purposes in Visual Basic, the ActiveX Control Pad, and similar tools. With a runtime license, the user can only view the control within an existing application or Web page, but cannot insert the control into a tool for further development purposes. Supporting the licensing mechanism is up to the individual control vendor. Some control vendors choose not to implement the licensing mechanism, so their controls can be used for development purposes by anyone once they are installed on the computer. Other control vendors permit royalty-free redistribution of the runtime version of the control only, while charging for the developer license. Users should read the license agreement provided with the control to understand how they can distribute a control on the Web.

The only simple answer is to be wary. Not all of the ActiveX controls that are downloaded onto your system allow for complete redistribution. Read those license agreements; don't just click through them.

Conclusion

ActiveX controls form the center of the Microsoft Active Platform. They are the building blocks that will form all of the applications that you create for Internet or intranet deployment. Now you should be familiar with what ActiveX controls are and how to integrate them into your applications. Chapter 3 will take you through the next step, and demonstrate how you can create your own customized ActiveX controls. Then you will be on your way to creating complete ActiveX applications.

Chapter

3

Creating ActiveX Controls

The real power of ActiveX controls is not based solely on the large number of available ActiveX controls, but rather on the ease with which you can create new ActiveX controls customized for your own applications. Unlike Java applets that must be written using only the Java language, ActiveX controls can be created using a number of different programming languages and tools, such as these:

Visual C++

Visual Basic

Visual J++

The process of creating ActiveX controls involves not only determining their simple design and functionality, but also how you will deploy them in your Web applications. This decision includes how you will package the various files needed to execute a particular ActiveX control, and you will digitally sign the control to assure users that it does not contain any malicious code.

This chapter will describe how you can create ActiveX controls using one of the simplest development tools, Visual Basic Control Creation Editor, and how you can easily deploy your ActiveX controls in your Web applications.

Visual Basic Control Creation Editor

Microsoft created the Visual Basic Control Creation Editor (VBCCE), integrated in Visual Basic 5.0, to capitalize on the millions of existing Visual Basic programmers and to advance the ActiveX platform. Now any programmer who can create applications with Visual Basic, one of the simpler programming languages available, can create ActiveX controls. Although VBCCE is not capable of creating ActiveX documents and complete applications, as the full version of Visual Basic 5.0 can do, VBCCE still has the many new improvements made to Visual Basic 5.0. Some of these new features that you can find in VBCCE include the following:

- Multiple ActiveX controls can be inserted and debugged in the same test session.
- Intellisense provides syntax reference and assistance when you are writing code to inform you of the name of available objects in your current project or of complex, hardly used codes.
- Improved Object Browser allows you to search for objects and their properties and methods easily in various libraries.

When you decide to create your ActiveX controls you may find that you can create your own customized ActiveX controls in several ways. The three typical ways to create ActiveX controls using VBCCE are as follows:

- Create entirely new ActiveX controls.
- Use encapsulation to add functionality to existing ActiveX controls.
- Group multiple ActiveX controls into one ActiveX control.

As indicated in the previous chapters, ActiveX controls can be thought of as old OLE controls with a couple of Internet tricks up their sleeves. The ActiveX controls that you create with VBCCE are capable of utilizing any of the following Internet features:

- Hyperlinking
- Digital signatures
- Intelligent download
- Asynchronous reads

Although VBCCE is a component of the Visual Basic 5.0 development environment, Microsoft also provides VBCCE as a standalone application to be used solely for ActiveX control creation. You can download it for free from www.microsoft.com.

Look and Feel

When you first run VBCCE, the first window that appears provides you with three different types of applications that you can choose to create the following:

- ActiveX control
- Standard EXE
- CtlGroup

After you select any one of these, you can begin creating your application in the VBCCE integrated development environment (IDE). You will use several windows in the design, creation, and testing of the ActiveX control you create. You can access most of these windows simply by clicking on the desired button on the right side of the toolbar.

Project Explorer. Displays all the different files that constitute a particular project or project group (see Figure 3.1).

Controls Toolbox. Features all the constituent controls that you can add to the ActiveX control you are creating (see Figure 3.2).

Properties. Displays the properties and their values for the control that you have selected (see Figure 3.3).

Object Browser. Displays all the different object classes available on your system and the properties, events, and methods of any of the classes that you select (see Figure 3.4).

Figure 3.1 Click on a form in a particular project folder to instantly open it for further editing.

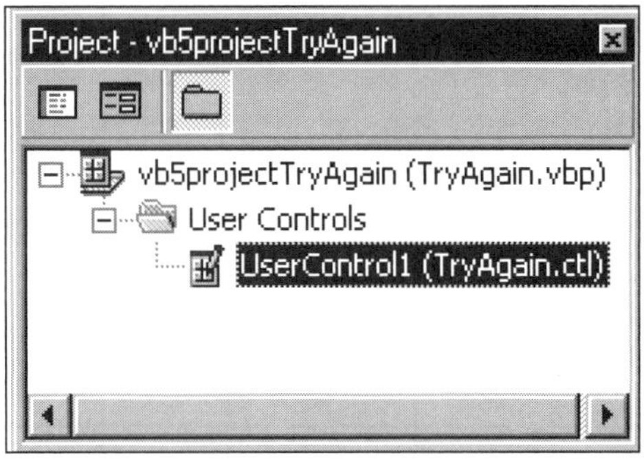

Form Layout. View the form layout that you want when the application is run (see Figure 3.5).

Event window. Allows you to write code that should be executed when a particular event occurs. Once you have written code for a particular event it will appear in bold whenever you use the drop-down menu box. This allows you to

Figure 3.2 Select the controls that you want to place in your ActiveX control from this window.

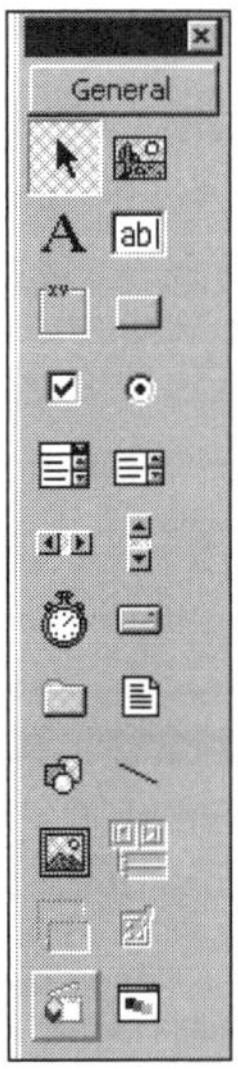

Figure 3.3 Select the property of a control in this window and make the necessary modification.

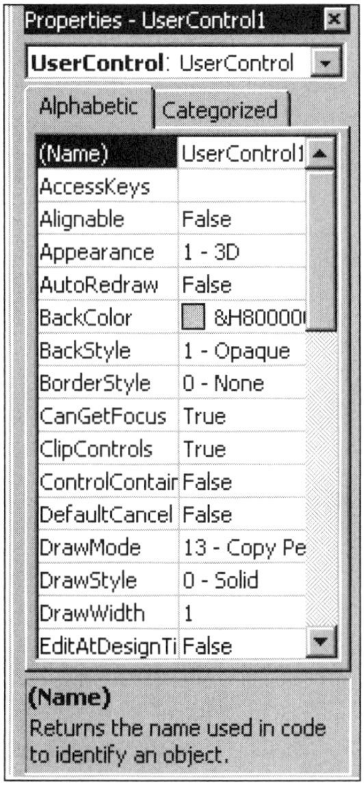

quickly identify what events have been coded as you develop your control. All of the event-related code is included in the same window whenever you select the Full Module View (see Figure 3.6).

Toolbox window. Add new tabs to the Toolbox window by right-clicking on the Toolbox and selecting Add Tab. You can add more controls to be used in your current project by selecting Components, similar to the Toolbox window described in Chapter 2. When you choose the Components menu selection the window shown in Figure 3.7 appears.

All of these individual windows constitute the main development window of the VBCCE, as shown in Figure 3.8.

In addition to understanding the various design and development elements of the VBCCE, you should also be familiar with a certain amount of terminology.

Figure 3.4 Select the object you are interested in and see its various properties, events, and methods.

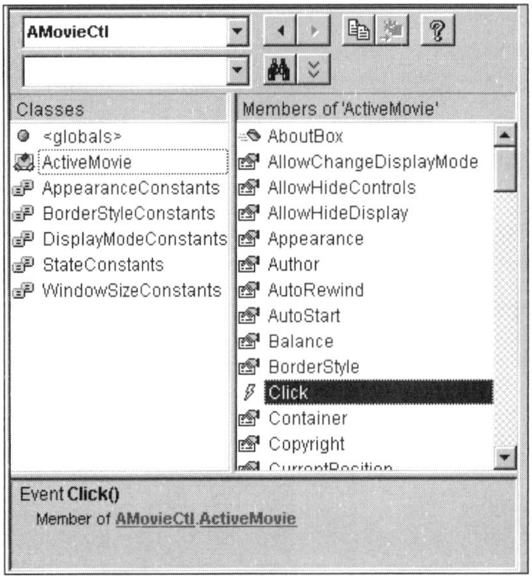

The ActiveX controls that you create consist of the basic UserControl that contains an assortment of *constituent* controls. The constituent controls are any of the controls added from the Toolbox window, which contains the available controls on your system.

An ActiveX control project can actually contain an unlimited number of other ActiveX controls. The ActiveX control projects are then compiled into binary files

Figure 3.5 Position the form on the computer screen exactly how you want it to appear when the application is running.

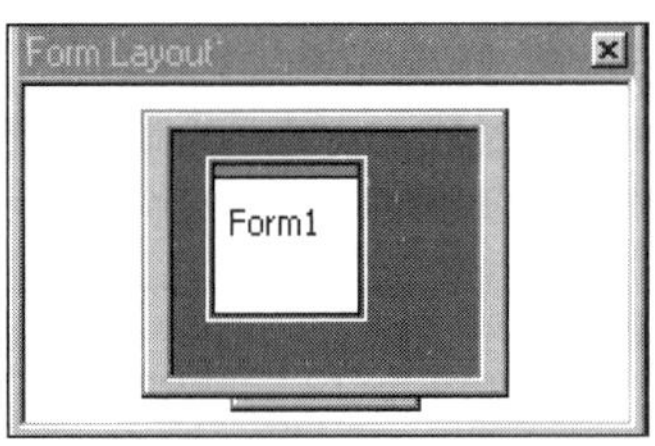

Figure 3.6 Type in the desired event code you want for a particular control in your application.

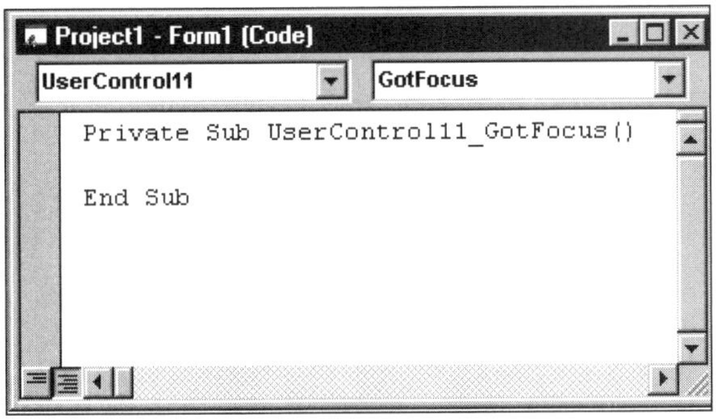

with the .OCX file extension. Of course, before you begin creating your ActiveX control you must have a clear design specification that identifies what you want the ActiveX control to do and how it should appear on a user's screen. Once you have this done you are ready to begin creating your ActiveX controls.

Figure 3.7 Select the controls that you want to appear in the Toolbox.

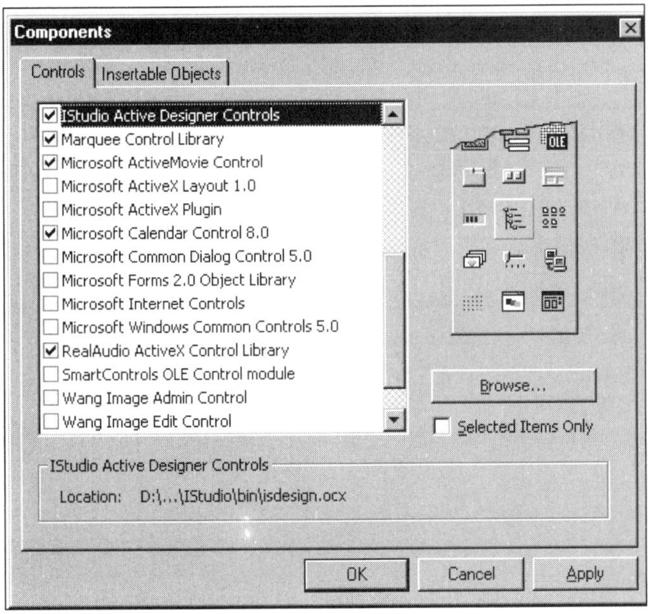

Figure 3.8 Visual Basic Control Creation Editor window.

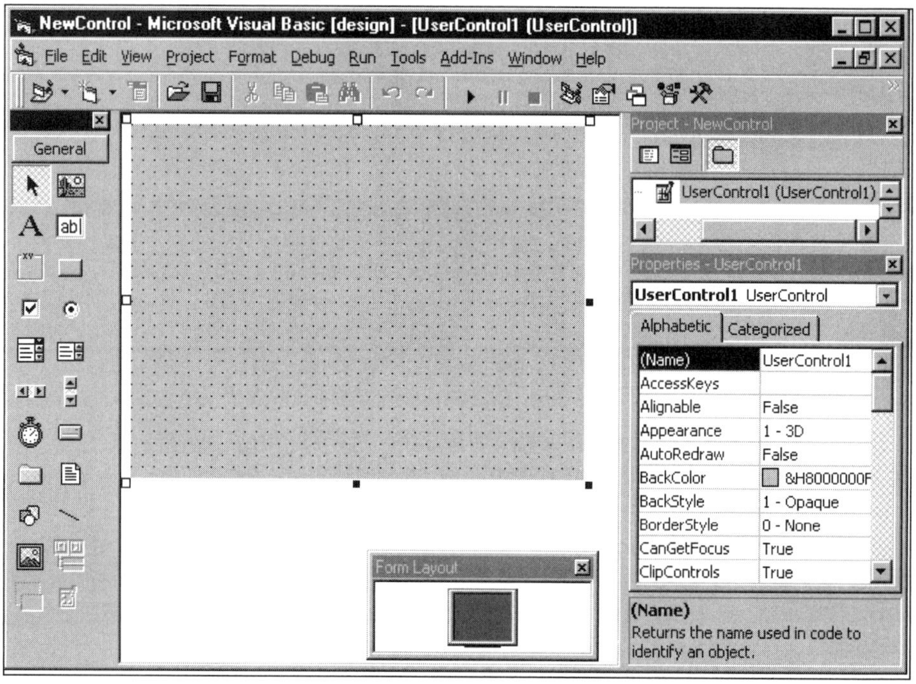

Getting Active

As with any programming application, the first step is to determine what this application will do, how it will function, and what it will look like. Once you have considered these design characteristics you can begin to create your own ActiveX controls in minutes using VBCCE.

The following example will be a useful demonstration of how to create an ActiveX control with VBCCE. In this example, you will place the following three constituent controls on the form:

Label

TextBox

CommandButton

This simple ActiveX application works this way: The Label will simply give instructions to the user, such as "Enter color guess below." The user will enter various text strings into the TextBox and click on the CommandButton. If the text string matches the color text string hard-coded in the Click event of the CommandButton a "correct" text string will appear in the TextBox; otherwise, a "guess again" text string will appear.

1. Click on **File|New Project** or select Standard .EXE when you first run VBCCE. Once you select the Standard .EXE and you name the various files that VBCCE will create, you will see a form loaded in the Project window. This project will be a container that will be used to test the ActiveX control that you create.
2. Select **File|Add Project**, and then click on the ActiveX control.
3. Several basic properties should always be set before you create an ActiveX control. You can designate these properties by choosing the **Project|Project1 Properties** menu selection and clicking on the General folder. The name of your project becomes the name of the component that is created, along with the name of the type library, used to identify the names of the different methods and interfaces of the control.
4. Proper versioning of the different ActiveX controls you create is important to ensure that the newest ActiveX control is being used in an application. Select the version number of the ActiveX control you are creating by clicking on the Make folder, which opens the window shown in Figure 3.9.
5. Choose the appropriate constituent controls that you will use to create your ActiveX control and lay them out by dragging-and-dropping in the proper location and dimensions. For this example, place a CommandButton, TextBox, and Label onto the form of your ActiveX control, as seen in Figure 3.10.
6. Modify any of the properties of the constituent controls by selecting the control, then making the changes in the Properties window.

   After the constituent controls have been laid out you can write the event-driven code that indicates how your ActiveX control will work.
7. Double-click on the constituent control for which you want to modify the code, as shown in Figure 3.11. Click on the top left drop-down menu button to display the various objects available in your ActiveX control, and click on the top right drop-down menu button to select the event you want.

Figure 3.9 Indicate the proper version of the control you are creating in this Properties window.

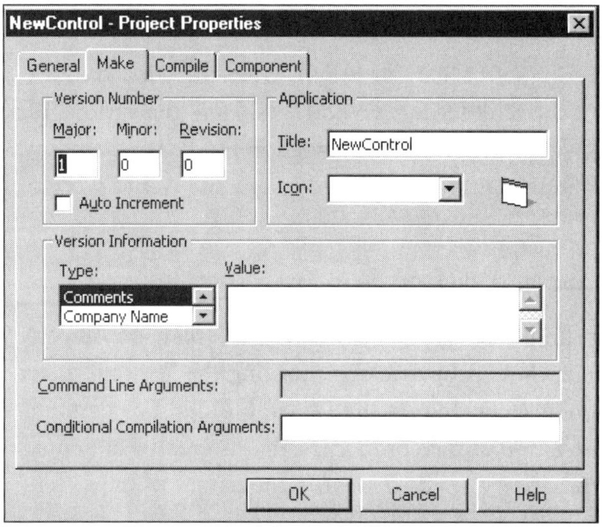

Events that have code written for them will appear bolded in the drop-down menu box.

In this window you can see either the Procedure View or the Full Module View, depending on the button you have selected in the bottom left corner of the window. In the Procedure View mode, you can see only the code for the current event you

Figure 3.10 In this example, the caption values for the three objects were changed from their object names.

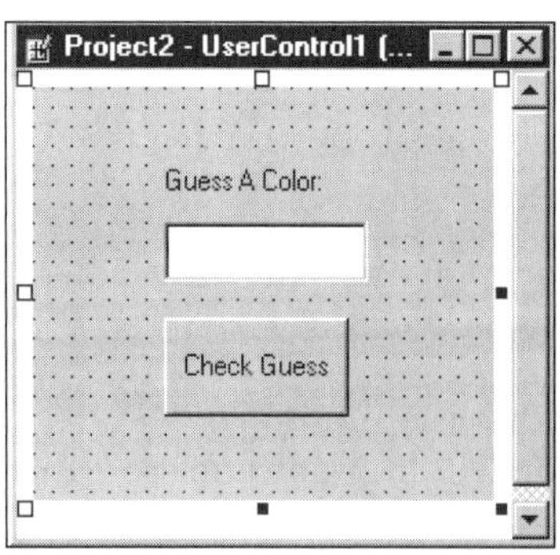

Figure 3.11 Write the appropriate code once you have selected the appropriate object and event.

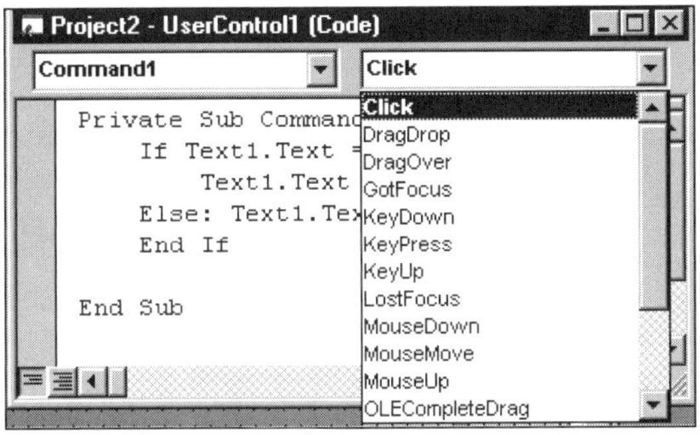

are viewing, whereas in the Full Module View, you can see all the code you have written for every object and event for this particular ActiveX control.

The window shown in Figure 3.12 clearly illustrates the Intellisense capability built in to VBCCE, which can make a programmer's life much easier. The Intellisense built in to VBCCE will illustrate available objects, attributes, or methods that you can select without the need to remember all the available possibilities.

8. For this example, you will make text in the text box, Text1 object; the system will return the message "try again" every time the user clicks on the Command button until he or she types the word "yellow." Then the value

Figure 3.12 Once you type an object and a "." the Intellisense capability will display available options.

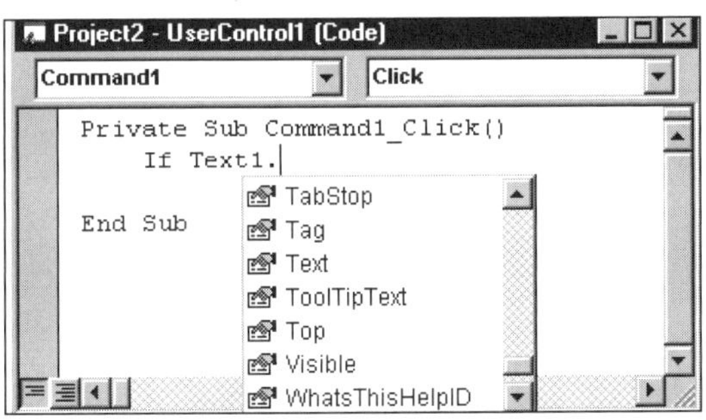

Figure 3.13 Type in the desired code and close the window to have it saved.

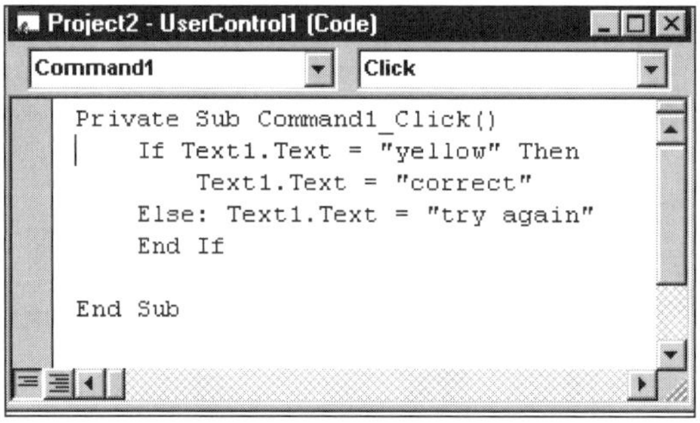

of the text box will become "correct." Type in the code as it is illustrated in Figure 3.13.

9. After you have completed the visual layout and added the appropriate code, you can close the window for your ActiveX control. Once you close the ActiveX control window it appears in your Toolbox window.

10. Select the ActiveX control from the Toolbox window and place it on the test container application that you created.

Figure 3.14 Type in different guesses and click on the Command button.

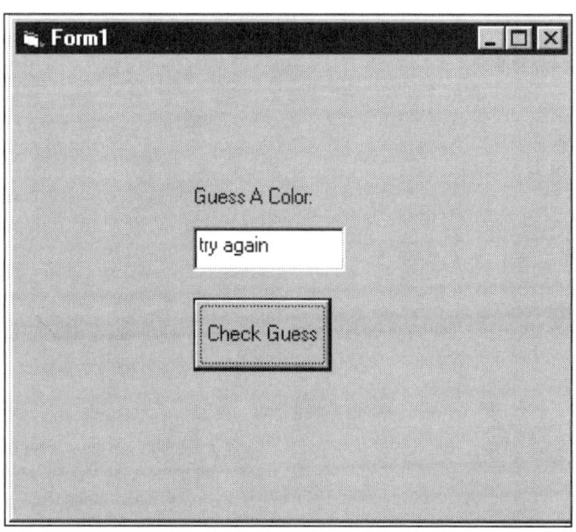

11. Press F5 or select the Start button on the Toolbar to test the ActiveX control that you just created. The container application you created opens a new window with the ActiveX control running in it, as shown in Figure 3.14.

After you have thoroughly tested your control in a form to ensure that its appearance and functionality meet your requirements, you can compile it into a binary .OCX control. Select **File|Make ControlName.ocx**, where ControlName is replaced by the name of your ActiveX control. The binary .OCX should be created and added to your registry. Now you can open one of your other applications, such as Visual InterDev, and place ActiveX controls in an Internet application. Simply add this new control to the Toolbox in any other application.

Not too shabby—you just created your first ActiveX control with VBCCE. You now have an ActiveX control, but you still need to place it in the proper package before you can easily distribute it in your Web pages.

Obviously, you must save your files as you work through this process. When working with VBCCE to create ActiveX controls you will find numerous saved files, including the actual control project, which is saved with the .VBP file extension, the binary .OCX, and .CTL. Here is an example of the .CTL file created for an ActiveX control in VBCCE; you can see how the file indicates the layout of the different constituent controls along with the Event code that was written.

```
VERSION 5.00
Begin VB.UserControl UserControl1
   ClientHeight    =   2580
   ClientLeft      =   0
   ClientTop       =   0
   ClientWidth     =   3000
   ScaleHeight     =   2580
   ScaleWidth      =   3000
   Begin VB.CommandButton Command1
      Caption         =   "Check Guess"
```

```
      Height          =   615
      Left            =   840
      TabIndex        =   1
      Top             =   1440
      Width           =   1215
   End
   Begin VB.TextBox Text1
      Height          =   375
      Left            =   840
      TabIndex        =   0
      Text            =   " "
      Top             =   840
      Width           =   1335
   End
   Begin VB.Label Label1
      Caption         =   "Guess A Color:"
      Height          =   375
      Left            =   840
      TabIndex        =   2
      Top             =   480
      Width           =   1815
   End
End
Attribute VB_Name = "UserControl1"
```

```
Attribute VB_GlobalNameSpace = False
Attribute VB_Creatable = True
Attribute VB_PredeclaredId = False
Attribute VB_Exposed = True
Private Sub Timer1_Timer()


End Sub


Private Sub Command1_Click()
    If Text1.Text = "yellow" Then
    Text1.Text = "correct"
    Else
    Text1.Text = "try again"
    End If


End Sub




Private Sub VScroll1_Change()
Text1.Text = VScroll1.Value
End Sub


Private Sub VScroll1_KeyDown(KeyCode As Integer, Shift As Integer)


End Sub
```

> **NOTE** It is very important to keep track of the names given to the the assortment of different files created as you develop and test your ActiveX controls.

Design-Time versus Runtime

In creating the previous ActiveX control example you should have noticed the two stages of control display: a design-time display and a runtime display. It is important to recognize the differences between these two different modes. When you place constituent controls on a form to create your own ActiveX controls, the constituent controls are in design-time mode. In design-time mode you can modify the constituent control's appearance and customize its properties, and you can even add Event code.

Once you have customized the controls to your specifications, you can check out how they will appear and function for a user in runtime mode. The next step is to close the window of your ActiveX control and place it on the form of a separate application for testing. When you have your ActiveX control laid out properly, click the F5 key or click the Start button on the VBCCE toolbar. Your ActiveX control will then be displayed in runtime mode.

ActiveX Control Interfaces

When you produce ActiveX controls you may choose to expose the properties or events of your ActiveX control so that developers who incorporate this control in a Web application can modify these characteristics. You can also create new methods for the ActiveX controls that you create. The interface you make to your ActiveX control's properties, methods, and events simply makes calls to the appropriate properties, methods, and events of the UserControl or any of the constituent controls. The IConnectionPointContainer is the interface your ActiveX control provides whenever the control has any events associated with it.

Here are the key events for most controls:

Initialize. This is the first event to occur for an ActiveX control, and it occurs every time a new instance of the control is created.

InitProperties. This event occurs the first time the control is instantiated on a form.

ReadProperties. This event occurs the second time the control is instantiated and for any other instantiations during the lifetime of the control. When this event occurs, the property values specified for the control in the <PARAM> tags are passed to this event using the PropertyBag object.

Resize. This event occurs whenever the control is created or resized.

Paint. This event occurs whenever the control's container has the control draw itself.

WriteProperties. This event occurs whenever the control's design-time implementation is destroyed and all of the properties set by the developer are retained.

Terminate. This event occurs whenever an instantiation of the control is destroyed.

In addition to the existing, standard properties and methods for your ActiveX control, you can add new properties and methods.

1. First open the ActiveX control you want to modify in the Designer Window, and open the Code Window for that control by double-clicking on the control.

2. On the Tools menu bar, choose the Add Procedure selection, which opens the window shown in Figure 3.15.

3. Indicate the desired name, select the Property radio button, and choose whether you want the property to be public or private.

4. Add the appropriate code to the control's Code window for the Let procedure, used when a new value is assigned to the control, and the Get procedure, executed when a value is retrieved from a control.

Here is an example of the code generated in the Code window after you have indicated information about the control's new property.

```
Public Property Get NewProperty() As Variant
```

Figure 3.15 Indicate the various properties of the procedure you are adding to a control in the Add Procedure window.

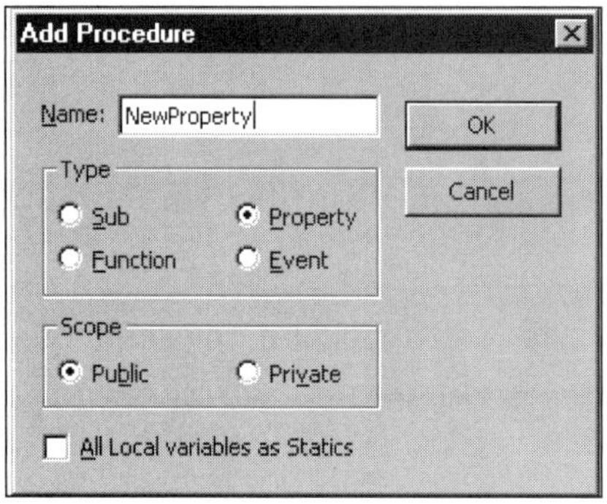


```
End Property
```

```
Public Property Let NewProperty(ByVal vNewValue As Variant)

End Property
```

Once you have completed this procedure the property will be added to the Properties window for that particular control. After you create an ActiveX control to meet your design specifications, you can compile it into an .OCX that you can distribute to other users.

1. Select your project in the Project Explorer window.
2. Choose the **File|Make YourProjectName.OCX** menu selection.
3. In the window that appears, indicate the location for the file.
4. You then need to insure that Visual Basic uses the newly created binary .OCX you have created rather than the open project. You can remove the project from the project group by choosing **File|Remove Project** menu selection.

Press F5 to test the binary component that you have created.

ActiveX Control Interface Wizard Of course a program such as VBCCE also provides a simple wizard to make various interfaces for your ActiveX controls accessible. The ActiveX Control Interface Wizard allows you to quickly and easily designate the properties, events, and methods that are exposed when a developer incorporates this ActiveX control in a Web page, and generates the underlying code. Start the ActiveX Control Interface Wizard by selecting **Add-Ins|ActiveX Control Interface Wizard.**

The first window that you use to customize your ActiveX control for deployment is illustrated in Figure 3.16.

Obviously there is an endless list of the various properties, methods, and events to which you can create interfaces for your ActiveX control. There are some basic properties for which you should definitely provide interfaces:

Appearance

BackColor

BackStyle

BorderStyle

Figure 3.16 Select additional properties, methods, and events that you want to make available to developers to customize this control.

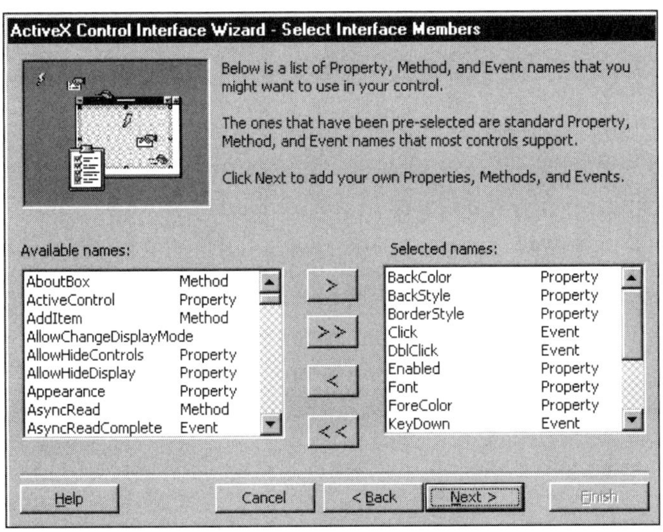

Enabled Font

ForeColor

The ActiveX Control Interface Wizard also allows you to provide accessible interfaces to any of the properties of the constituent control that are incorporated into your ActiveX control. You can allow developers to place other controls on your ActiveX controls by setting the ControlContainer property of the UserControl to True.

You can also make your control transparent by setting the BackStyle property of the UserControl to Transparent. Then any other controls that this particular UserControl is positioned in front of can still be visible. This proves ideal for creating Web sites with a three-dimensional feel.

Once you have selected the various properties, events, and methods and exited from the ActiveX Control Interface Wizard, choose File|Make YourControl.OCX. This will ensure that the most current binary .OCX is loaded in the registry of your computer system. Now the property values for the ActiveX control you just made, its interfaces available to be addressed, will be specified with the <PARAM> tags within the <OBJECT> tags.

Packaging

Once you have created your ActiveX control, you must complete several other steps before you can successfully incorporate it into one of your Web applications:

- Prepare the control for download by creating a downloadable file such as a .CAB.
- Digitally sign the ActiveX control so users will not have to worry about having the control downloaded and executed on their system.

You can create and distribute ActiveX controls in two different forms: as a publicly distributable .OCX or as a privately distributable control, denoted by the .CTL file extension and integrated as a component in a project or another control.

- Public controls can be used only in ActiveX control projects, but they can be used in other applications after the ActiveX control project has been compiled into a binary .OCX.
- Private controls can be used in a project of any type.

When you create a setup program for an .OCX file for your ActiveX control, it will contain the .OCXs for all of the constituent controls used along with the run-time .DLL of Visual Basic.

Catch a .CAB

Microsoft supplies a CAB Development Kit that provides the tools and information you will need to create .CAB files for your controls. The .CAB file contains all the other files necessary to install and register the ActiveX control on a user's system. Having one file that contains several others allows compression, results in faster download, and makes the operation more convenient. When you provide a control you have created to a user you can, and should, indicate the following three forms of protection.

Digital Signature. This gives the user the name of and information about the company that developed this control, as well as a way to find the company should the control perform any malicious acts on the user's system.

Safe for Initialization. This assures the user that this control will not harm his or her system.

Safe for Scripting. This assures the user that your control can't be scripted to perform actions that could be detrimental to his or her system.

You will find the CAB Development Kit in the following directory on your computer system, which is also where you should run the Setup Wizard. Figure 3.17 illustrates the first window that appears when you run the Setup Wizard.

C:\Vb5cce\Setupkit\Kitfil32

1. Enter the Project file name (.VBP) for the ActiveX control that you want to create the setup file, and click the Internet Download Setup radio button in the window shown in Figure 3.18.
2. In the next window that appears, specify the location on your local system where the .CAB files should be saved, and click Next.
3. Specify the directory on the Internet from which you want to download the run-time components, and indicate whether the ActiveX control is safe for download and scripting.

Figure 3.17 Use the Setup Wizard to prepare the .CAB file that will be used to distribute your ActiveX control.

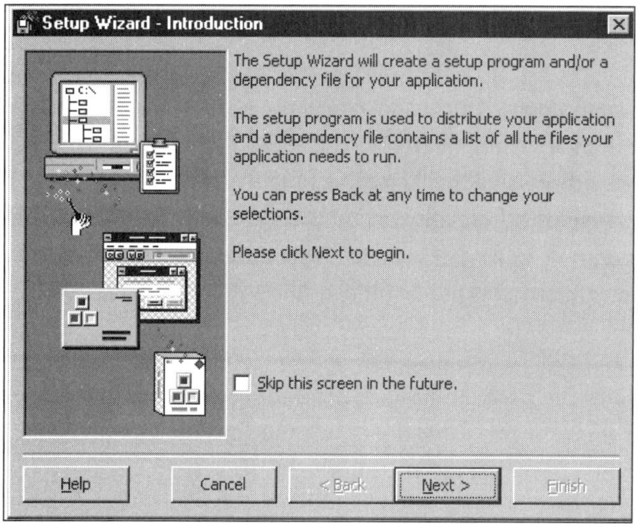

You should also determine if the control you created is safe for scripting. For example, a control that could save property information or user input data as a file on the user's computer would not be safe if the developer who incorporated it into a Web page could designate the file name. Using script, a conniving developer could easily incorporate script in the Web page along with your control to change the file name that is saved to CONFIG.SYS or some other significant system file, potentially damaging the user's computer. If you created an ActiveX control with capabilities such as this, it would definitely not be safe for scripting.

The Setup Wizard will then illustrate the files required to install your ActiveX control successfully on a user's computer system; these files should all be contained in the .CAB file (see Figure 3.19). Click Next to finish the compilation of the .CAB file.

The Setup Wizard will create the compressed .CAB file and an HTML Web page and place them in the directory you indicated; a separate Support subdirectory will contain some of the support files, such as the .OCX. The SetupWizard creates several different files, shown in Table 3.1, necessary for the successful installation of the ActiveX control onto a user's system.

Figure 3.18 Click Next after you select the ActiveX control for which the .CAB file will be created.

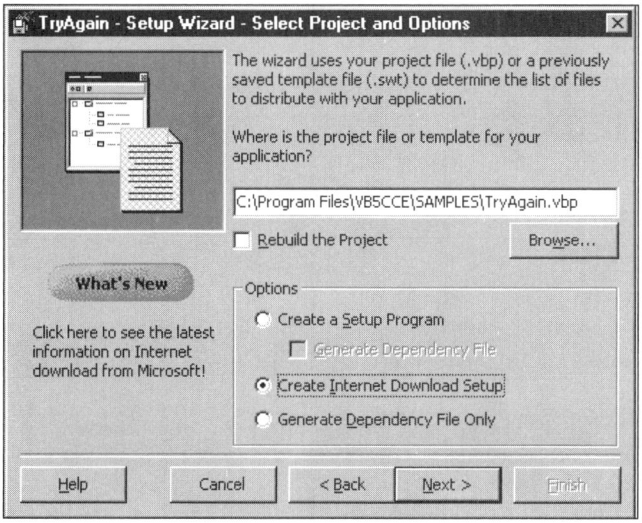

Here is an example of the HTML source code generated for the support HTML document that references the .CAB file created for your ActiveX control.

```
<HTML>

<!--    If any of the controls on this page require licensing, you must

        create a license package file.  Run LPK_TOOL.EXE to create the
```

Table 3.1 Files Created by the Setup Wizard

File Extension	Description
CAB	The "cabinet" file contains the various dependent files needed for installing the ActiveX control on a user's system.
.OCX	This is the ActiveX control file.
.INF	The setup information file indicates how the ActiveX control should be installed.
.DDF	Diamond Directives File is the project for .CAB files.
.HTM	This is a basic Web page that references the designated ActiveX control.

Figure 3.19 Select a particular file and click on File Details to see additional information.

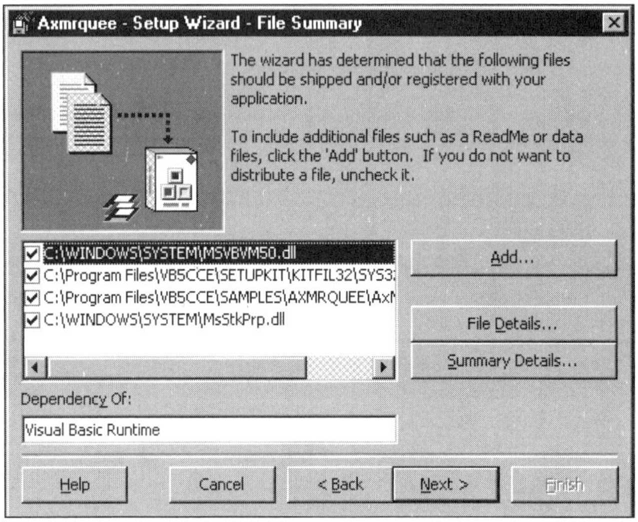


```
        required LPK file.  LPK_TOOL.EXE can be found on the ActiveX SDK,
        http://www.microsoft.com/intdev/sdk/sdk.htm. If you have the Visual
        Basic 5.0 CD, it can also be found in the \Tools\LPK_TOOL directory.

        The following is an example of the Object tag:

<OBJECT CLASSID="clsid:5220cb21-c88d-11cf-b347-00aa00a28331">
        <PARAM NAME="LPKPath" VALUE="LPKfilename.LPK">
</OBJECT>
-->
<OBJECT ID="AXMarquee" WIDTH=307 HEIGHT=182
CLASSID="CLSID:69B8D6F4-C6A1-11D0-A2E9-0000F663211A"
```

```
CODEBASE="AxMrquee.CAB#version=1,0,0,0">
</OBJECT>
</HTML>
```

The Application Setup Wizard also creates an .INF file used to indicate the .CAB file's various file dependencies. The following code was generated as the .INF file for the sample Marquee ActiveX control included with VBCCE.

```
;INF file for AxMrquee.ocx
;DestDir can be 10 for Windows directory, 11 for Windows\System(32) direc-
tory, or left blank for the Occache directory.

[version]
signature="$CHICAGO$"
AdvancedINF=2.0

[Add.Code]
AXMRQUEE.OCX=AXMRQUEE.OCX
MSSTKPRP.DLL=MSSTKPRP.DLL
ASYCFILT.DLL=ASYCFILT.DLL
MSVBVM50.DLL=MSVBVM50.DLL

[AXMRQUEE.OCX]
file-win32-x86=thiscab
RegisterServer=yes
clsid={69B8D6F4-C6A1-11D0-A2E9-0000F663211A}
```

```
DestDir=
FileVersion=1,0,0,0

[MSSTKPRP.DLL]
hook=MsStkPrp.cab_Installer
FileVersion=5,0,37,14

[MsStkPrp.cab_Installer]
file-win32-x86=http://activex.microsoft.com/controls/vb5/MsStkPrp.cab
InfFile=MsStkPrp.inf

[ASYCFILT.DLL]
hook=AsycFilt.cab_Installer
FileVersion=2,20,4056,1

[AsycFilt.cab_Installer]
file-win32-x86=http://activex.microsoft.com/controls/vb5/AsycFilt.cab
InfFile=AsycFilt.inf

[MSVBVM50.DLL]
hook=MSVBVM50.cab_Installer
FileVersion=5,0,37,24
[MSVBVM50.cab_Installer]
file-win32-x86=http://activex.microsoft.com/controls/vb5/MSVBVM50.cab
InfFile=MSVBVM50.inf
```

This file indicates both the various dependent files that you selected when you ran the Application Setup Wizard and the Internet location from which these dependent files can be downloaded, should they be needed.

> **NOTE** When you plan on placing several different ActiveX controls on the same Web page you should consider placing these controls in the same Visual Basic project so that you have to create just one .CAB file for that Web page.

Run-time DLL The ActiveX controls that you create with the Visual Basic Control Creation Editor are actually compiled as P-code .OCX files. Because the .OCX files are complied as P-code they are much smaller, making download across the Internet much faster. The P-code-compiled .OCX files require that the run time .DLL for Visual Basic is installed on the user's system before ActiveX controls created using the Visual Basic Control Creation Editor will execute. Whenever you create a .CAB file for the ActiveX controls you distribute you must include the MSVBVM50.DLL file. If it is already present on a user's computer the MSVBVM50.DLL file won't be downloaded, only the .OCXs that you created.

Figure 3.20 illustrates that the Visual Basic Virtual Machine is quite a large file, over 1.5 MB, but it is compressed to about 700Kbytes. Assuming that a user doesn't have it already installed, the MSVBVM50.DLL file can make an extremely large download to run what may be a very small ActiveX control. It is important to note that the typical ActiveX control created using VBCCE is about 20 Kbytes, small enough to download quickly.

The advantage of the .CAB file system is that this file needs to be downloaded only once onto a user's system. Once it is installed, all additional .CAB files will check for this file and will not download it again once it determines that it is already present.

Signing Your Controls

The ActiveX SDK provides the tools you need to add your company's digital signature to the ActiveX controls you create. The first step is to obtain a Software Publisher's certificate that you can use to sign your ActiveX controls. You can do this by visiting www.microsoft.com/workshop/prog/security/authcode/certs.htm.

Figure 3.20 File details on the Visual Basic Virtual Machine.

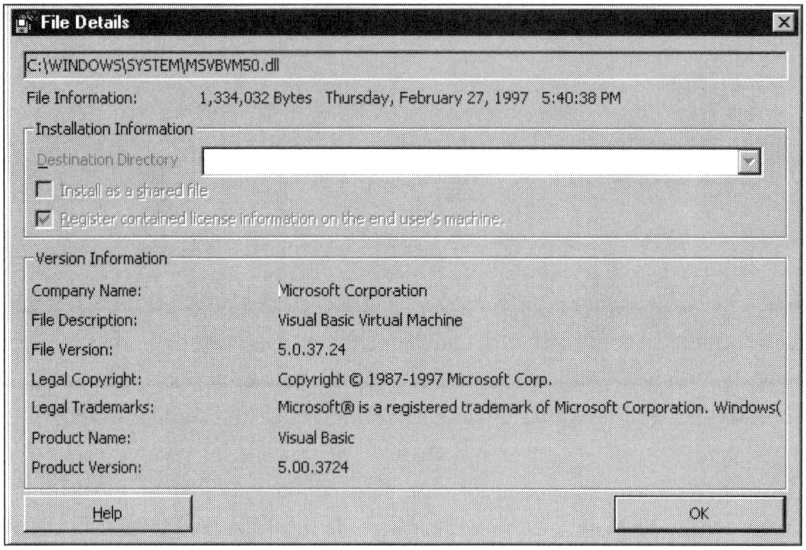

Once you have your Software Publisher's certificate you can digitally sign any of the following different file extension types, all necessary for your ActiveX control to run successfully on a user's computer:

.EXE

.CAB

.OCX

.DLL

If you do not have the SignCode.EXE file with VBCCE you will find it as part of the ActiveX SDK. Use this application to identify and digitally sign your files.

You can download the ActiveX SDK from Microsoft's Web site, and you can find additional information about code-signing at

www.microsoft.com/workshop/prog/sdk/.

Licensing

At this point, you have realized that ActiveX controls can be complete software applications that simply require a host container, such as Internet Explorer, in which to run. The software industry estimates that it currently loses several billion dollars every year to copyright infringement by pirate CD manufacturers, and nearly that much to consumers who load licensed software onto more than one computer. ActiveX controls are software applications designed to be easily distributable on the Internet, which opens up the concern about how software manufacturers can possibly control copyright infringements.

In this new software licensing environment, developers need to be concerned about several issues: protecting the software they create and preventing themselves from unlawfully violating someone else's software license.

Constituent Controls

When you create your own ActiveX controls using VBCCE you must ensure that the constituent controls you incorporate into your ActiveX control are freely available. You can include any of the constituent intrinsic controls that come with the VBCCE and are found in the Toolbox window, except the OLE container control. Here is a list of the intrinsic controls available for your use:

CheckBox

ComboBox

CommandButton

Data

DriveListBox

DirListBox

FileListBox

Frame

HScrollBar

Image

Label

Line

ListBox

OptionButton

PictureBox

Shape

TextBox

Timer

VScrollBar

For any other controls that you acquire by purchase or download, you must check the licensing agreements to be sure that you can include them in one of your ActiveX controls and distribute them. Not all of the ActiveX controls included in the Professional Version of Visual Basic are available for incorporation into other applications royalty-free. Typically, when you purchase an ActiveX control you should also be given the rights to distribute it royalty-free in any other applications or controls in which it is incorporated. Obviously, you should check your license agreement to ensure that you have these privileges.

Many controls, such as those supplied with Visual Basic 4.0, implement licensing. To distribute these controls over the Web, you must generate the appropriate runtime license file and include it with your Web page; otherwise, the controls will not display on users' machines. Only those with a valid developer's license for a given control can generate a runtime license for that control. For detailed instructions on including runtime-licensed controls in your Web pages, see the ActiveX SDK documentation on licensed controls (there is also an example in the new ActiveX Control Pad FAQ). Note that Microsoft and third parties are also supplying many ActiveX controls for royalty-free runtime use on the Web. No runtime license file is necessary to include these controls in a Web page.

Also remember that when you incorporate ActiveX controls into Web page that users can interact with, the Web server must have a license, just as you would get a license for a developer to use a particular control.

When considering licensing issues, you must also think about protecting your own investment. After you have spent many long hours creating the greatest control on earth, do you want to let everyone use it for free? Visual Basic has licensing protections built-in so that you can require users to have a license key before the control will execute on their system.

License Your Own Active Controls

You can easily add licensing protections to your ActiveX control. First, simply choose the Project|YourProjectName Properties menu selection, which opens the Project Properties window shown in Figure 3.21. Then select the General folder and check the Require License Key selection. Now when you compile your .OCX the VBCCE will also generate a .VBL file containing the license key needed for a license to the designated ActiveX control.

When a user purchases your ActiveX control and runs the Setup program, the registry key is added to the registry on his or her computer. Now if a user simply copies only the .OCX file for the control to a buddy's computer the control won't execute.

When the developer who purchased your ActiveX control places it within a compiled application your .OCX is included with the application, but your license key is not installed on the new application's users' systems. When a user runs this application the Visual Basic runtime .DLL causes your ActiveX control to create a runtime instance of itself.

Should users running the application that incorporates your ActiveX control then run another application, such as Visual Basic, they will find that your .OCX file is now available on their computers. When any of these users attempt to incorporate your .OCX into their applications Visual Basic will ask the ActiveX control to create itself on the form using the license key resident in the user's computer registry, which will be there only if they actually purchased your ActiveX control.

Figure 3.21 Select the Require License Key selection to prevent your ActiveX control from being freely distributable.

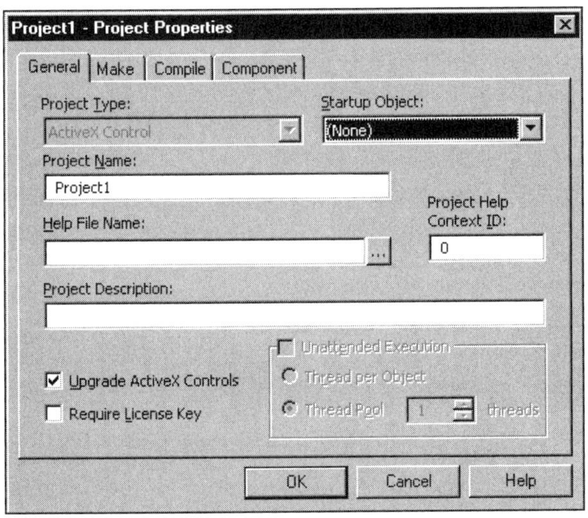

This license key system effectively prevents unlicensed proliferation and copying of your ActiveX control into an endless number of applications.

Conclusion

Microsoft estimates that there are already at least 250,000 existing ActiveX controls, a number that will grow exponentially with the power of VBCCE. As this chapter demonstrates, Microsoft has made creating ActiveX controls using the VBCCE just about as easy as developing Web pages. You don't have to learn C++ programming tricks, or complex Windows code. This chapter illustrates some of the capabilities and features of the VBCCE.

Previous chapters have shown the power and ease-of-use that ActiveX controls provide. Now you realize how easy it is to create entirely new ActiveX controls using VBCCE to match your specific application requirements. Microsoft has brought advanced Internet programming capabilities to average computer users with VBCCE.

You may also want to check out some books about Visual Basic 5.0, which will give you a complete guide to all of the programming features of VBCCE, plus advanced information about ActiveX controls. These Wiley titles include *Custom Controls Library* and *Advanced Visual Basic Techniques*, both by Rod Stephens.

For more information about VBCCE, check out

www.microsoft.com/vbasic/icompdown/

Part Two

Active Client

Chapter

4

Internet Explorer

Internet Explorer 4.0 represents the first step toward integration of the Internet and the personal computer operating system. In this new paradigm, the Internet is seamlessly integrated within your own computer system, just as if it were a local hard drive. Every resource available to your operating system is treated the same, whether it is found locally or on a remote FTP or HTTP server. Here are just a few of the exciting new capabilities possible with Internet Explorer 4.0:

- Personalized Internet content is pushed to the user without the need to search the Web endlessly.
- Autocomplete recalls Internet addresses so that you don't have to retype them.
- Offline reading capability allows you to review Web material without wasting connect time.
- Dynamic HTML, described in detail in Chapter 5, allows you to create an assortment of new multimedia and graphical displays not possible in conventional HTML documents.

- Active Desktop components can be created that can update themselves at periodic intervals.
- An integrated set of tools for communication, collaboration, and Web authoring is available.

Internet Explorer 4.0 turns your Windows operating system into the Active Desktop, the client that can interact with the powerful Active Server component, thereby creating the Active Platform environment.

New Features

When you first load and run Internet Explorer 4.0 you won't see much difference between it and Internet Explorer 3.0. Microsoft *has* made few changes to the user interface, as illustrated in Figure 4.1.

Although Internet Explorer 4.0 may not appear very different from previous Web browsers, it actually represents the first step toward an entire paradigm shift. Not only does Internet Explorer 4.0 let you browse the Internet for cool Web pages, but it also allows you to search your own local computer system for files and applications. Simply type C:\ in the Address window to display the folders and files found on your local hard drive within the Internet Explorer 4.0 window, as shown in Figure 4.2. As you would in Windows Explorer, simply select a file and it will be launched in the appropriate application.

When Internet Explorer 4.0 is loaded, several minor modifications to the user interface of the Windows operating system are made.

The first one you should notice is an addition to your Start menu. Click the Start button and you will see a Favorites folder displayed, which contains all the Internet sites that you have designated as Favorites in Internet Explorer. Now your favorite Web sites are just a few clicks away.

Some folders, such as the Control Panel and My Computer folders, have also been modified: They will now appear within Internet Explorer 4.0 whenever they are opened (see Figure 4.3).

Only a couple of folders are customized for this type of display. You can modify any other folder on your system to be displayed in this manner. Select a folder from

Figure 4.1 Little user interface change characterizes Internet Explorer 4.0 upon first examination.

within either Internet Explorer 4.0 or Windows Explorer and choose View|Customize This Folder, which will start the Customize This Folder wizard shown in Figure 4.4.

Once you have made a folder into an HTML file, you can place it on your Active Desktop to allow quick access to the files contained within.

When you install Internet Explorer 4.0, a new folder, the Downloaded ActiveX Controls folder, lists the ActiveX controls you have installed on your system. In the previous version of Internet Explorer, ActiveX controls were stored in the Occache directory. Once you have Internet Explorer 4.0 loaded on your system, the Downloaded ActiveX Controls folder will be created within your Windows directory. Figure 4.5 illustrates what you might see when you right-click on a particular control and then select Properties.

Figure 4.2 Click on a folder to display subdirectories and files contained therein.

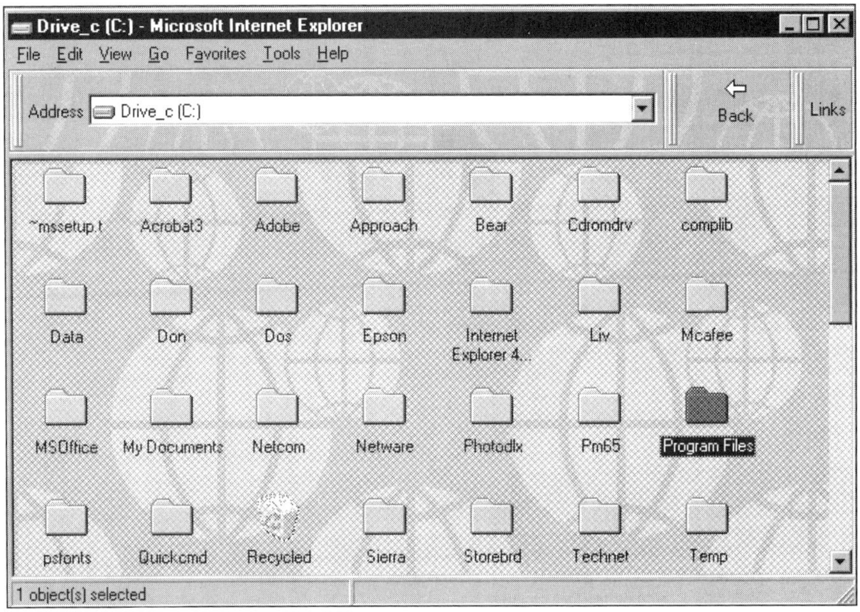

Because of ActiveX controls' usefulness—and their potential security risks—it is very important that you know how to find out what controls are loaded on your system and how to get rid of them.

Information Delivery

Microsoft has built two information delivery systems into Internet Explorer 4.0 to help you get the information you want with the least hassle:

- Subscription-based
- Webcasting

The manual client pull system that characterizes traditional Web access is not always the most efficient. You can choose either one of these push methods to provide the information you want with the least amount of effort on your part.

Figure 4.3 Select a desired application and it will be launched in its separate window.

Subscription-Based

In this new environment, information is not only all treated the same, regardless of its location, but it can be updated automatically. Internet Explorer 4.0 features the ability to gather periodic updates of information that you designate. Nearly every sophisticated user has searched through numerous Web sites packed with the most worthless information imaginable, trying to locate some vital information. You may have several Web sites that you want to check daily or weekly, such as www.cnn.com or www.news.com. Rather than your having to start your Web browser and navigate to these Web sites, Microsoft's Internet Explorer 4.0 uses a subscription-based system to locate and load the information you want without eating your time.

Internet Explorer 4.0 allows you to designate numerous Web sites that you want periodically updated, which you can then view offline. The key elements you need to designate are the Web sites to which you want a subscription and the frequency of updates. Set up a subscription to a Web site as follows:

1. Run Internet Explorer 4.0, go to the Web site you want to subscribe to, and choose Favorites|Add to Favorites.
2. Check the box labeled "Subscribe for downloading."
3. Once you have selected the appropriate folder in which to place the Web site, click the OK button, which opens the window shown in Figure 4.6.
4. Click on the Properties button to modify the subscription schedule; here you can designate how often you want the Web site updated, ranging from once every 15 minutes to once every day or week.
5. Internet Explorer 4.0 will then notify you when it has updated a particular Favorite Web site to which you subscribed. You can check your subscriptions by selecting Favorites|Subscription|View All, which opens the window shown in Figure 4.7.

Figure 4.4 Choose to create an HTML document, and you can then edit the HTML file that will be generated.

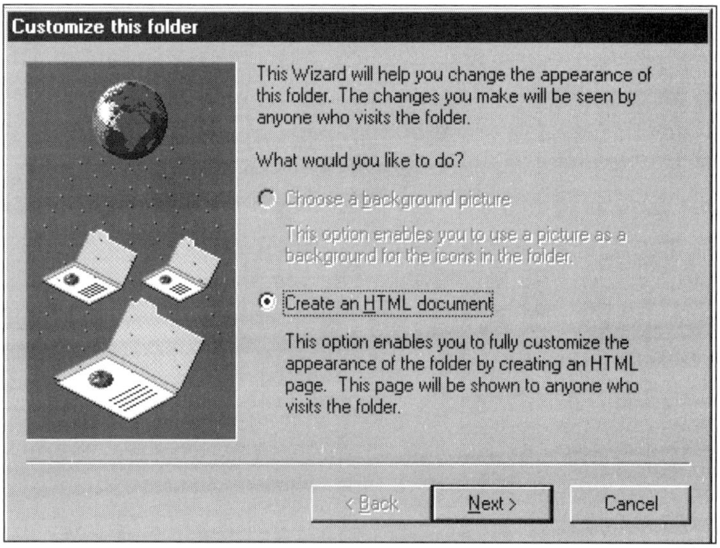

Figure 4.5 If the control is not shared, Windows will indicate that it is safe to delete this control.

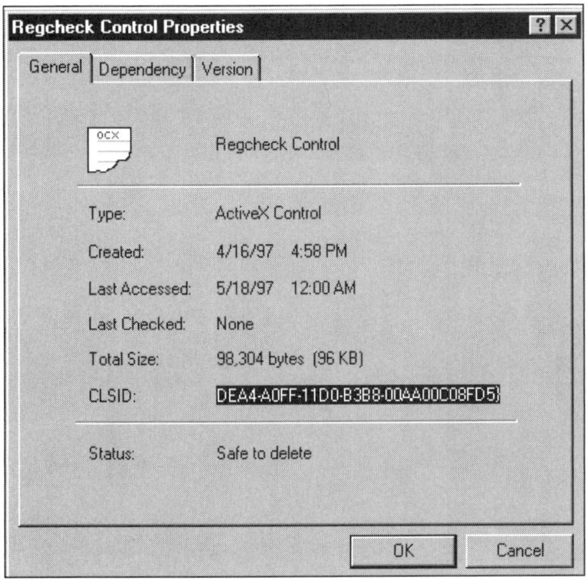

Webcasting

Anyone who has read the various computer magazines over the last year has heard the incessant references to "push" versus "pull" technologies. The Internet has been based on a client/server system where a client, typically in the form of a Web browser, makes a request for a particular document, such as a Web page, from a server that subsequently provides this information, obviously a client "pull" system. This approach has been extremely effective and usable, as demonstrated by the amazing growth and success of the Internet over the last couple of years. Although this client/server pull system has sufficed in most circumstances, it doesn't always prove to be the easiest for the user. This fact has led to the development of server-to-client "push" technology.

The Web site subscription system utilizes the familiar "pull" system, in which the user's client browser requests a Web page from a designated server, but Internet Explorer 4.0 also supports an exciting new "push" system, which is named "premium channels." This information delivery system allows you to select channels through which information is then pushed to your Active Desktop.

Figure 4.6 This window illustrates the characteristics of the subscription you just created.

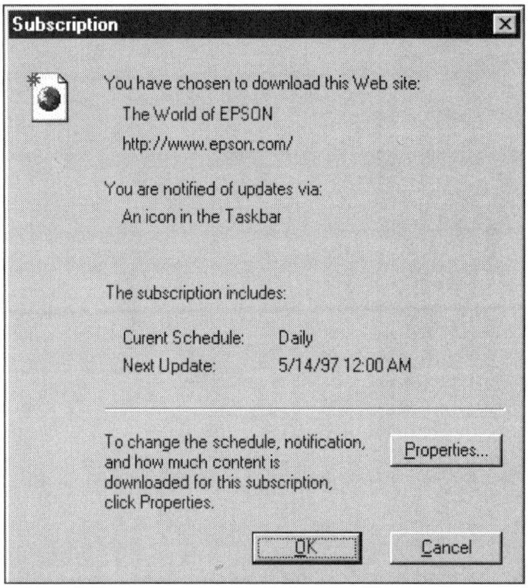

Active Desktop

The Active Desktop describes the integration of the Web with the desktop. In this new paradigm you can think of Internet Explorer 4.0 as the conduit that makes information or Internet components appear to be seamlessly available just as they would be if they were loaded on your system locally.

The Active Desktop allows a user to select numerous Desktop components that are links to specific content found locally or remotely. As you saw before, these components can even go out and request updated information at the periodic intervals you specify. Here are just some of the modifications that have been made within this new Active Desktop environment to improve performance:

- Windowless controls
- Quick component activation
- Asynchronous data download capability

Microsoft has also built a corporate lockdown option in the Active Desktop environment. Now IS managers can create a standardized Active Desktop for the employees in their corporation. They can create a desktop that provides easy access to such vital information as e-mail or the IS help desk. By activating the lockdown option, IS managers can prevent users from deleting necessary, critical information.

Desktop Components

When you add a desktop component to your Active Desktop environment, it appears as an icon on your desktop just as do any shortcuts to various software applications that you may have on your system. The difference is that desktop components are simply icons that connect to HTML content, or Active objects, when selected. Here are just some of the desktop components available:

- News headlines
- Tickers
- Pop-up broadcast messages
- Pictures

You can check out several demo desktop components at

www.microsoft.com/ie/ie40/gallery/

Should you find any desktop components that you like on this Web page, simply click on the link "Place this control on my desktop."

Figure 4.7 Right-click on a subscription and you can choose to copy it or delete it.

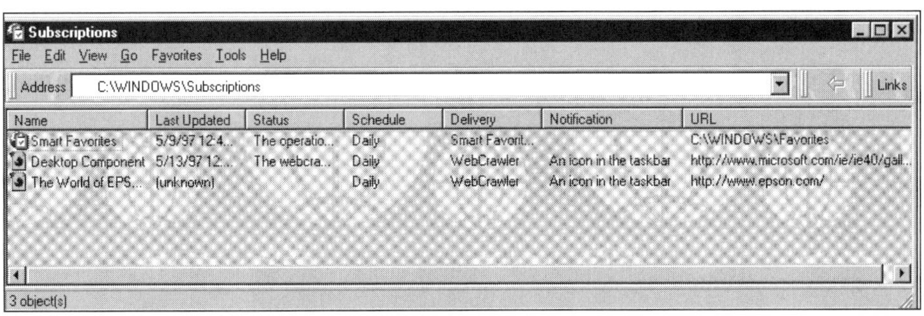

Figure 4.8 Enter new desktop components; choose to display in conventional Windows 95 mode or with the chosen desktop components displayed.

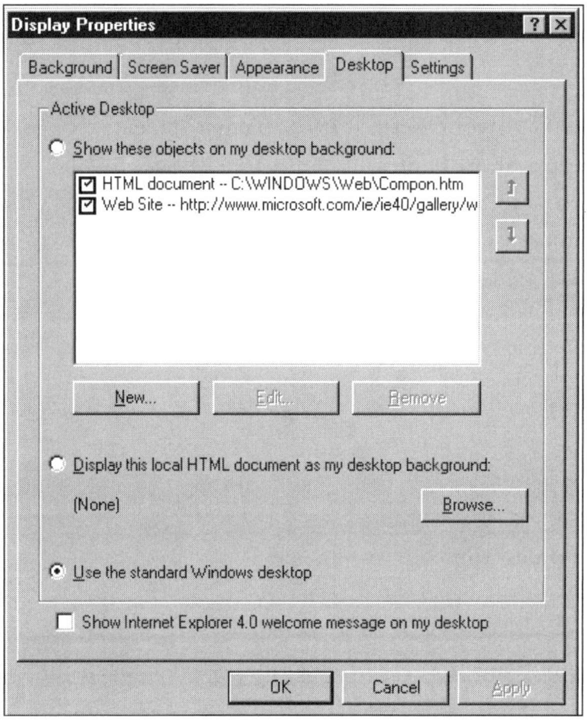

You also can create any desktop component that you want by following these steps:

1. Open your Control Panel and select the Display icon.
2. In the Display Properties window, select the Desktop folder, as shown in Figure 4.8.
3. Once you have added a desktop component you can modify various properties of this component:
   - Schedule
   - Delivery
   - Notification

4. After you have modified the chosen desktop component, the system will ask if you want the desktop component downloaded. You can place your system in Active Desktop mode by selecting the Show these objects on my desktop background, or you can click the Use the standard windows desktop radio button.

Figure 4.9 shows the Active Desktop environment with a desktop component added, which in this case is the C|NET news Web site.

Component Controls

In the Active Desktop environment, the power lies in the ActiveX controls, otherwise referred to as component controls. When you install Internet Explorer 4.0, an assortment of component controls is added to your system; they become available

Figure 4.9 Resize the desktop component and scroll down to review this Web page.

for incorporation in the Web applications you create. The component controls added to your system with the installation of Internet Explorer 4.0 are as follows:

ComboBoxEx

Custom Draw

Date and Time Picker

Flat Scroll Bars

Header Control

Image Lists

IP Address

Label

List View

Marquee

Menu

Month Calendar

Popup Menu

Popup Window

Preloader

Progress Bar

Property Sheets

Rebar

Status Windows

Stock Ticker

Tab Control

Timer

Toolbar

ToolTip

Trackbar

Tree View

Up-Down

Temporary Internet Files

After running Internet Explorer for some time, you may notice that you are starting to lose memory on your hard drive. No, the memory isn't actually disappearing. Internet Explorer has a handy little feature that saves the Web pages and the images loaded in them in a Temporary Internet File directory. The advantage of this feature is that whenever you click on the Back button to review previous Web pages, they are simply loaded from memory. Of course, if you don't know that these files are being saved you may be puzzled by your apparently disappearing capacity.

In the Win NT or Windows 95 directory, you will find the Temporary Internet Files directory. Open this up and see if it contains any files. Obviously, you can delete these files—unless you are a cyber-pack-rat who enjoys keeping a record of every image and Web page you've ever come across on the Internet.

If the automatic saving of Web pages and images to the Temporary Internet Files directory proves to be an annoyance, you can change Internet Explorer's default settings. Select the View|Options menu selection, and click on the Advanced folder. In the Temporary Directory Files window, click the Settings button; the window shown in Figure 4.10 will appear.

You can also choose View All to see all the temporary Internet files that have been saved on your system.

Still missing 5–10 MB on your system? Next, check out the C:\Windows\History or C:\Winnt\History folder depending on whether you are using Windows 95 or Windows NT, respectively. This folder should be noticeable—in Windows Explorer it contains the Internet Explorer icon, which consists of the world on a white page. This wonderfully useful directory keeps track of all the URLs you have visited. After some time that can represent a significant number of Web sites and consequently require a significant amount of memory.

Figure 4.10 Select the percentage of your hard drive to allocate for the Temporary Internet Files folder.

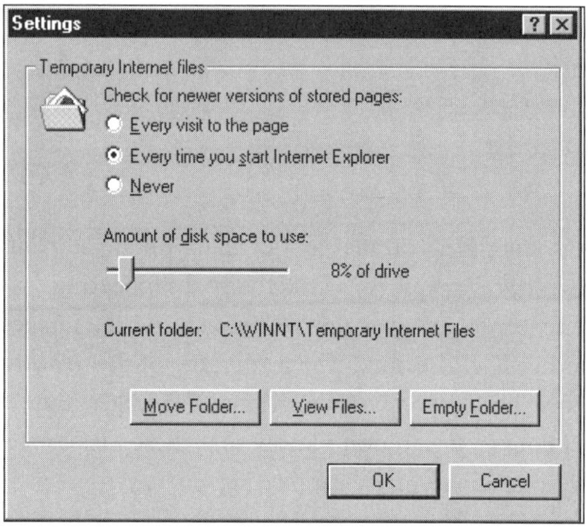

Security

Internet Explorer 4.0 has become the window from your desktop to the Internet and the rest of the world. Of course, the problem with windows is that you can see through them whether you are on the inside or outside. When you use Internet Explorer 4.0 to manipulate files and objects on the Internet as if they were on your local hard drive, you might wonder if your files could be just as accessible to other Internet users. Microsoft, of course, says there's no reason to worry, but we doubt that Bill Gates would send you a reimbursement check if someone should steal information or do damage to your system.

In Internet Explorer 3.0, a serious security flaw was discovered that gave a hacker access to files on your system using the shortcuts built into Windows 95 and Windows NT. Although this security problem was fixed, and occurred in Internet Explorer 3.0, not Internet Explorer 4.0, it should heighten your awareness. Keep in mind that other security flaws will most certainly be found.

Internet Client SDK

Microsoft provides the Internet Client SDK (Software Developer Kit) for Internet Explorer 4.0 so that you can create Web applications that fully utilize all its new capabilities and exploit the potential of the Active Desktop. You can download the Internet Client SDK from www.microsoft.com/sitebuilder/.

You can also view all the documentation found in the Internet Client SDK at www.microsoft.com/workshop/prog/inetsdk/docs/.

You will find that the Internet Client SDK addresses four main categories that include all the new Internet development features you can utilize:

Dynamic HTML. New HTML format that allows for real-time Web page updates along with new graphical and multimedia presentation capabilities.

Scripting. Describes programming information on how to use Visual Basic Script (VBScript) and JavaScript (JScript) within your Web pages.

Components. Details the properties and methods of the common components integrated in Internet Explorer 4.0.

Service. Multimedia functionality including sound, animation, and graphics.

Conclusion

Internet Explorer 4.0 is the first indication of the features that will be found in the operating system that succeeds Windows 95. It is truly an impressive Web browser that incorporates many of the modifications that sophisticated users want, yet does not diminish ease of use for the average user. Internet Explorer 4.0 effectively represents the new Active Desktop and complements the powerful Active Server component, which will be described in Chapter 9. Microsoft has worked to develop a solid client/server platform for Internet application development. And Microsoft has, once again, thoroughly documented all aspects of this new Active Platform environment, making it possible for developers to begin application development immediately.

One of the most attractive features of Internet Explorer 4.0 is its incorporation of the Dynamic HTML capabilities. Dynamic HTML will allow you to create the next generation of Web pages with faster, enhanced multimedia capabilities and with data binding on the client. Chapter 5 will detail Dynamic HTML so that you can quickly create the best Web applications on the Internet.

Chapter

5

Dynamic HTML

The typical Web page created today is a static, dull, graphic-and-text document produced with the often-cumbersome HTML source code. As most developers will attest, HTML simply does not provide the development and design capabilities needed to create the new Internet and intranet applications expected by users. Many developers have become accustomed to the sophisticated development tools used to create client/server applications; comparable Web application development environments simply cannot be made because of the inherent limitations of HTML. This is the premise behind Microsoft's new Dynamic HTML technology, a featured component of Internet Explorer 4.0.

Microsoft created Dynamic HTML to move from static Web applications to dynamic, multimedia extravaganzas. Dynamic HTML is based on an object model that is an extension to the existing HTML platform. Now developers can use interactive scripts to integrate the assortment of objects placed on a Web page, including the Web page object itself. You can also add sophisticated menus and animations to your Web pages without extensive programming.

The Internet community is fated to have bandwidth limitations well into the next century. Through such developments as cable modems and ADSL, many U.S. Internet users may have significant bandwidth within the next five years; however, the Internet user base will most certainly become a worldwide population, which means that universal access to higher bandwidth may be a long time coming. Obviously, the current model—every user's request is sent over the Internet to a server that then returns the requested information or Web page—is not conducive to this low-bandwidth scenario. Dynamic HTML provides ways to limit the need for constant communication with a remote server across the Internet. Here are some of Dynamic HTML's added features:

- 2D and 3D manipulation of objects on a Web page by a developer or user
- Dynamic styles
- Dynamic content
- Filter and transition controls
- Animation and multimedia controls
- Compatibility with the Cascading Style Sheet specification put forth by the W3C
- Data awareness

Development of Web applications using Dynamic HTML simply relies on incorporating and scripting a collection of scriptable objects, available in Internet Explorer 4.0.

Interactive Documents

The interactive documents feature of the Dynamic HTML object model supports more interactive and user-responsive documents. In the typical Web scenario, you may find a link to a Web site that you have some interest in; after you click on the hyperlink, the Web page is downloaded to your system. In a Dynamic HTML interactive Web page, when you click on a particular selection in a Web page more information can be displayed without the client's requesting information from the server. This feature obviously provides information to the user faster than if a request were sent to the server and new information were returned to the client. You can use several components of Dynamic HTML to create truly interactive documents:

Dynamic Styling. You can modify text elements on a Web page to change style based on mouse or keyboard actions. For example, to motivate a user to click a specific hyperlink, you could cause the text font to get bigger as the mouse approaches the hyperlink.

Dynamic Expansion. In the best example of Dynamic Expansion's usefulness, a user would conduct a keyword search of your Web site. The search results displayed could list the various Web pages; when the user performs some event, such as a mouse-over event, a summary of that particular Web page would be displayed. The user can now select the information that he or she wants to see, thereby creating a more interactive system, and one without any time delays as the request travels to the server and the information back to the client.

Dynamic Table Manipulation. Now when a user downloads database information in the form of lists or search results, he or she can use the built-in local database engine to sort and filter the requested information.

Dynamic HTML Multimedia Controls. Use these controls to produce graphical transitions between the displays of different information and to work with sprite images and sound files.

Dynamic Styling

Using Dynamic HTML, Web designers can dynamically change the style of every HTML element in a document. In HTML, styles are specified as element attributes or via Cascading Style Sheets (CSS). The Dynamic HTML object model exposes every HTML element in the document, including its attributes and CSS properties. Using simple scripts, Web page designers can dynamically read and change the values of these attributes and CSS properties. For example, dynamic styles can be used to do the following:

- Show or hide an element. For example, the detail text of a bullet point could be hidden until the user moves the mouse pointer over the bullet.
- Change the size, color, or other font properties of elements. For example, a title could be emphasized by enlarging the font and changing the color of text when the user moves the mouse over it.
- Change the X-, Y-, or Z- position of elements on a page.

Unlike other browsers, Microsoft Internet Explorer 4.0 uses Dynamic HTML to change the style and content of a page dynamically at any time, even after it has been loaded. Dynamic HTML supports intelligent recalculation to redisplay a page if sections of that page change, including reformatting text paragraphs as needed. For example, if list items are shown or hidden, Dynamic HTML adjusts the other related items and renumbers them where appropriate.

Here are just some of the text effects you can create in your Web pages:

- Colors
- Font manipulation
- Multichannel audio mixing

The ability to modify the attributes of text displayed on a Web page sounds good to developers, but the main feature of the dynamic styling capability is that these attributes can be modified while a user views a particular document.

Cascading Style Sheets

When you create a new Word document you get to select a particular style sheet. A style sheet can contain any or all of these styles: different headings, chapter titles, figure captions, among others. Each style's appearance is predefined using attributes such as point size and font appearance (bold, underline), plus the location and positioning for any text defined as that particular style.

Until now, developers who create Web pages have been limited to <H1>, <H2>, <TITLE>, and a few other styles. Creating Web pages that have the same advanced styling features available in a basic word processing application has not been easy. That problem has been eliminated by the W3C's acceptance of the Cascading Style Sheet specification. Now you can integrate advanced styling capabilities into your Web pages.

Why are they called Cascading Style Sheets? The styles that are displayed are determined in a descending, or cascading, order of precedence. For example, you may create a style sheet that indicates that a hyperlink should appear in blue when clicked, but the user may have configured his or her browser to display clicked hyperlinks in yellow. The Cascading Style Sheet uses predetermined precedence rules to determine which style to display whenever conflicts like this occur.You can check out the full Cascading Style Sheet specification at www.w3.org.

Of course, before you can view a style sheet in a Web page, you must make sure that you have the Use Style Sheets box checked in the View|Options menu selection on the Advanced Tab. Once it is selected, you can check out the several sets of style sheets that Microsoft provides at www.microsoft.com/gallery/files/styles/default.htm.

Using style sheets allows you to predefine the font sizes and layout for the various elements of your Web pages. You can define many characteristics of a Web document using style sheets:

Background

Color

Font-family

Font-size

Font-style

Font-weight

Line-height

Margin-left

Margin-right

Margin-top

Text-align

Text-decoration

Text-indent

The Cascading Style sheet capability can be integrated into a Web page in three different ways:

Inline. Make style specifications for specific HTML tags within the Web page itself.

Embed. Embed the entire style sheet specification within the HTML source code for the Web page you are creating.

Link. Link your Web page to a specific style sheet that you have created.

Inline Style Sheet Information Inline style placement is easy for those applications where you need to modify the style of a particular HTML tag quickly.

```
<H1 STYLE="font-size: 30 pt; color: blue">
```

In a couple of keystrokes you can modify the style of information displayed within your Web page.

Embed Style Sheet Information Embedding style sheet information in a Web page gives you a point where you can quickly modify the selected styles during design and development. Between the <HTML> tag and the <BODY> tag place the <STYLE> tag.

```
<HTML>

<STYLE  >

H1 STYLE="font-size: 30 pt; color: blue"




</STYLE>

<BODY>

….

</BODY>

</HTML>
```

All the tags defined in the embedded style sheet will then appear in the designated fashion throughout the entire Web page.

Link Style Sheet Information The advantage to linking to a particular style sheet is that you can use the same style sheet for several Web pages. Simply make the style sheet file easily accessible on your server. You can use the <LINK> tag to incorporate a style sheet with your Web page, as shown in the following HTML example.

```
<LINK REL= STYLESHEET HREF="http://myserver./stylesheet.css" >
```

As this example illustrates, simply indicate the location of the linked style sheet file with the HREF attribute of the <LINK> tag. The other issue is the actual creation of the text-based style sheet file itself.

In some cases you may even want to use different styles within a Web page that has an embedded style sheet or is linked to a style sheet file. Simply make your style modification within beginning and ending <DIV> tags.

```
<DIV   STYLE="font-size: 26pt">

<H1> No matter what content you place between these two tags, it will

appear the same.

</DIV>
```

Everything between the pair of <DIV> tags will have the same style, but after the </DIV> tag the styles will revert to the Web page's standard styles. Figure 5.1 shows a sample Web page with an assortment of fonts predefined in a style sheet.

Dynamic Expansion

"Keep it simple, stupid" is a premise that should resonate throughout the Web pages you create—and throughout nearly everything you do. Use minimal information with maximum impact. When you present information in your Web pages, the average user does not need to be confronted immediately with all the information you have. In fact, most users are probably interested in only a small subset of your information. Dynamic Expansion is a very useful capability that allows you to provide an outline of information, with additional information available upon some defined user-event.

Table Manipulation

As more and more Web pages become connected to databases and provide a display of other data information, the need to work with tables will grow. Dynamic HTML features several controls that assist the developer and user in the display and manipulation of data displayed in a table. The main advantage of these controls is that they work on the client without requiring the server to reconfigure or manipulate the information displayed in the user's Active Client.

Repeated Tables

One useful capability is the new Repeated Tables feature, which lets you include the DATASRC attribute with the typical HTML tables that you place in your Web applications. The DATASRC attribute allows you to retrieve information from a data source object included on the Web page and ties it directly with the HTML

Figure 5.1 Use style sheets to ensure uniformity in the many Web pages you create for a particular Web application.

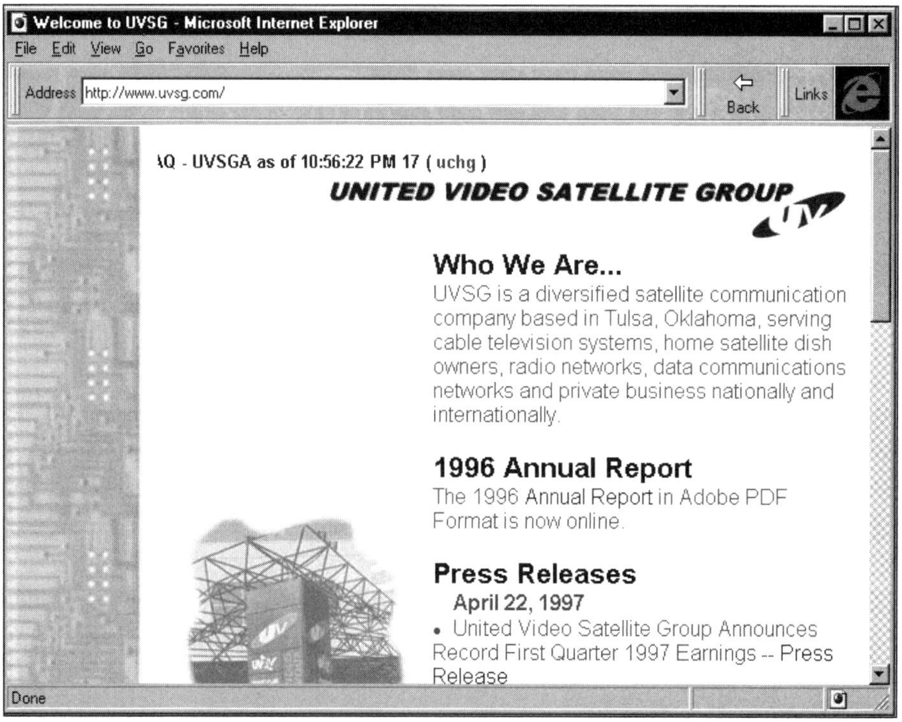

tables. This provides the data within the Web page that has been downloaded to the user's system, allowing him or her to manipulate the data without having to retrieve information from your end.

Microsoft features an example of this repeated tables capability in its gallery of demos of Dynamic HTML. In this example, when you click on any one of the titles in the HTML table, the data is sorted—without your having to send this request back to a server and download a new Web page. Here is an example of the HTML source code used to incorporate the repeated tables capability within a Web page:

```
<!DOCTYPE HTML PUBLIC "-//IETF//DTD HTML//EN">

<html>

<Body TOPMARGIN=0 LEFTMARGIN=40 BGCOLOR= "#FFFFFF" LINK= "#000066" VLINK=
```

```
"#666666" TEXT= "#000000">
<FONT FACE="verdana,arial,helvetica" SIZE=2>
<head>
<meta http-equiv="Content-Type"
content="text/html; charset=iso-8859-1">
<meta name="GENERATOR" content="Microsoft FrontPage 2.0">
<title>IE4 Preview Web Gallery Components - Repeated Table Data
Binding</title>
</head>
<H2>Repeated Tables</H2>
<hr>
<p><object id="quotelist"
classid="clsid:333C7BC4-460F-11D0-BC04-0080C7055A83"
align="baseline" border="0" width="0" height="0"><param
name="DataURL" value="quotes.txt"><param name="UseHeader"
value="True"></object></p>
<P>
Click on the Table headers to sort by that column. Note that the sort is
done on the client, without a round-trip to the server.
<P>
<table border="1" id="elemtbl" datasrc="#quotelist">
<THEAD>   <tr>
        <td><font color="#0000FF"><b><u><DIV
id=symbol>Symbol</DIV></u></b></font></td>
```

```
        <td><font color="#0000FF"><b><u><DIV
id=quote>Quote</DIV></u></b></font></td>
        <td><font color="#0000FF"><b><u><DIV
id=change>Change</DIV></u></b></font></td>
        <td><font color="#0000FF"><b><u><DIV
id=volume>Volume</DIV></u></b></font></td>
    </tr>
</THEAD><TBODY>    <tr>
        <td><SPAN DATAFLD="Symbol"></SPAN></td>
        <td><DIV DATAFLD="Quote"></DIV></td>
        <td><SPAN DATAFLD="Change"></SPAN></td>
        <td><DIV DATAFLD="Volume"></DIV></td>
    </tr>
</TBODY></table>
<script language="VBSCRIPT">
function symbol_onclick()
  quotelist.SortColumn = "Symbol"
  quotelist.Reset()
end function
function quote_onclick()
  quotelist.SortColumn = "Quote"
  quotelist.Reset()
end function
function change_onclick()
  quotelist.SortColumn = "Change"
```

```
  quotelist.Reset()
end function
function volume_onclick()
  quotelist.SortColumn = "Volume"
  quotelist.Reset()
end function
</script>
```

In this code you can see how the data source object is included along with the DATASRC attribute within the <TABLE> HTML tag.

Dynamic HTML Multimedia Controls

Standard HTML text on a Web page characteristically has been boring. For some time now, you could place text on a Web page and even vary the size and color of the displayed text. This limited feature hardly utilized the full range of multimedia capabilities of existing computers. Microsoft has created several multimedia controls, incorporated into Dynamic HTML, to assist you in developing impressive Web pages.

Fade Control. Vary the opacity of the Web page in front of text, images, or other objects on a Web page to make them appear or disappear when a user activates a particular event.

Outline Control. Use this control to display an informational outline that the user can expand and condense simply by clicking on the desired information.

Visual Filter Control. Change the appearance of objects on a Web page when a user performs a particular event.

Structured Graphic Control. Use this control to apply dynamic graphical modifications to the Web page that is displayed to a user.

Sprite Control. Modify the images that you insert within your Web pages.

Mixer Control. Mix several .WAV sound files using this control.

Transitions Control. Create unique transitions between displayed information.

Fade Control

Both kids and adults are enchanted with the appearance and disappearance of objects. The Fade control is just one of the Dynamic HTML Multimedia controls; it allows you to perform this amazing effect on your own Web pages.

Of course, you can offer fade as a button that a user could click, but you probably will incorporate it into your Web pages so that a particular user-event results in the disappearance or appearance of a particular message. The following HTML source code illustrates one of Microsoft's examples of the Fade control incorporated with a button on a Web page.

```
<!DOCTYPE HTML PUBLIC "-//IETF//DTD HTML//EN">

<html>

<Body TOPMARGIN=0 LEFTMARGIN=40 BGCOLOR= "#FFFFFF" LINK= "#000066" VLINK=

"#666666" TEXT= "#000000">


<!--TOOLBAR_START-->

<!--TOOLBAR_EXEMPT-->

<!--TOOLBAR_END-->

<body bgcolor="#FFFFFF">

<FONT FACE="verdana,arial,helvetica" SIZE=2>

<H2>FadeOut</H2>

<hr>

<BR><BR>


<INPUT name=ie4button onclick="fade();" type=Button value="Fade Out">


<DIV ID=FadeMe style="width: 100%; height:70px">
```

```
This is some HTML.<FONT size=+2> It can be <i>whatever</i> you
<b>want</B></FONT> it to be.<BR>
<DIV id=D1 onmouseover="D1.style.fontWeight='Bold'">It's totally
<i>LIVE.</i></DIV>
</DIV>

<OBJECT ID=Fader WIDTH=1 HEIGHT=8
 CLASSID="CLSID:DA9E9D23-3661-11D0-BDC2-00A0C908DB96">
       <PARAM NAME="Effect0.clsid" VALUE="{3EE8A933-4D3F-11d0-97D0-
00AA00BBB6E2}">
       <PARAM NAME="Effect0.opacity" VALUE="100">
</OBJECT>

<script language=VBScript>
FadeMe.filter = Fader
dim faded
faded = false

function fade()
  if (faded = false) then
     fadeout(100)
     ie4button.value = "Fade In"
     faded = true
  else
```

```
      fadein(0)
      ie4button.value = "Fade Out"
      faded = false
    end if
  end function

  function fadeout(i)
    dim v
    Fader(0).opacity = i
    Fader.refresh
    i = i - 10
    if (i>=0) then
      v = window.setTimeout("fadeout(" & i & ")", 100, VBScript)
    end if
  end function

  function fadein(i)
    dim v
    Fader(0).opacity = i
    Fader.refresh
    i = i + 10
    if (i <= 100) then
      v = window.setTimeout("fadein(" & i & ")", 100, VBScript)
    end if
```

```
end function

</script>


<HR>

<TABLE CELLSPACING=0 CELLPADDING=0 BORDER=0>

<TR>
<TD ALIGN=LEFT VALIGN=TOP COLSPAN=2><FONT FACE="Verdana, Arial, Helvetica"
SIZE="2"><B>Description</B></FONT></TD>
</TR>

<TR>
<TD ALIGN=LEFT VALIGN=TOP COLSPAN=2><FONT FACE="Verdana, Arial, Helvetica"
SIZE="2">This example shows the use of an Alpha Filter control applied to
some HTML text. When the button is clicked the first time, the text will
fade out. If the button is clicked again, the text will fade back in. The
fadeout effect is achieved by varying the opacity of the Alpha Filter over
time using a timer.

<P>The most important thing to understand about this demo is that
the multimedia effect participates in the rendering of the HTML,
```

```
and does not replace it. If the control was not present, the text
would still appear, but it would not have the capacity to fade
in or out.

<P>The ability to have controls modify the display of HTML
is a significant feature in Internet Explorer 4.0. Other multimedia con-
trols
reserve an area of the screen for their display. The information
displayed is often described in other proprietary formats, not in HTML.
The ability
to author the page in HTML and apply effects after the fact makes it eas-
ier to
create multimedia effects.</FONT>
</TD>
</TR>

<TR>
<TD ALIGN=LEFT VALIGN=TOP COLSPAN=2><FONT FACE="Verdana, Arial, Helvetica"
SIZE="2"><B><P><BR><B>Browser compatibility</B></FONT></TD>
</TR>

<TR>
<TD ALIGN=LEFT VALIGN=TOP COLSPAN=2><FONT FACE="Verdana, Arial, Helvetica"
SIZE="2">Other browsers would simply display the static HTML, without the
```

```
Fadeout behavior.</FONT></TD>
</TR>

<TR>
<TD ALIGN=LEFT VALIGN=TOP COLSPAN=2><FONT FACE="Verdana, Arial, Helvetica"
SIZE="2"><P><BR><B>Usage</B></FONT></TD>
</TR>

<TR>
<TD ALIGN=LEFT VALIGN=TOP COLSPAN=2><FONT FACE="Verdana, Arial, Helvetica"
SIZE="2"> The &lt;DIV&gt; tag can contain anything you'd like to fade:
images, controls, applets, text, tables. Use this page as a template when-
ever you want to create a fading effect.</FONT></TD>
</TR>
</TABLE>
<P>
<FONT FACE="MS SANS SERIF" SIZE="1" COLOR="BLACK">
&#169; 1997 Microsoft Corporation. All rights reserved. <A
HREF="/misc/cpyright.htm" target="_top">Legal Notices</a>.<P>
</FONT>

</body>
</HTML>
```

This example causes the text to fade in or out when the button is clicked.

Transitions Control

You have either created or seen slide presentations, produced in an application like PowerPoint, that featured impressive transitions between the different slides. This same sort of transition capability can be built into your Web pages using the Transitions control, part of Dynamic HTML. The Transition control features a number of predefined transitions, as illustrated in Table 5.1.

Table 5.1 Transition Effect and Number Used to Designate Use in Your Web Page

Transition Effect	Value
Box in	0
Box out	1
Circle in	2
Circle out	3
Wipe up	4
Wipe down	5
Wipe right	6
Wipe left	7
Vertical blinds	8
Horizontal blinds	9
Checkerboard across	10
Checkerboard down	11
Random dissolve	12
Split vertical in	13
Split vertical out	14
Split horizontal in	15
Split horizontal out	16
Strips left down	17
Strips left up	18

Table 5.1 *Continued*

Transition Effect	Value
Strips right down	19
Strips right up	20
Random bars horizontal	21
Random bars vertical	22
Random	23

Absolute Positioning of Objects

You were first introduced to the ability to lay out objects on a Web page in any two- or three-dimensional arrangement using the HTML Layout control. These same layout capabilities have now been integrated into the Dynamic HTML object model. Now there is no need for a separate layout control to be downloaded to a user's computer just to view the layout of the controls in your Web application.

Absolute positioning layout functionality was first available from Microsoft by using the HTML Layout Control. The absolute positioning functionality now built into Dynamic HTML uses native HTML, rather than the special ActiveX objects previously used to produce 2D and 3D layouts. Dynamic HTML supports X-, Y-, and Z-order positioning of HTML elements, as specified in the W3C Working Draft on Positioning HTML with Cascading Style Sheets. Using this positioning system, you can precisely lay out the location of images, ActiveX controls, and text on your Web pages. By designating the Z- position of these same objects, you can give your Web pages a three-dimensional feel, with some objects overlapping other objects from the user's point of view.

Data Awareness

Many HTML pages are based on data, whether that data is stored in databases or files. Dynamic HTML incorporates several features to integrate data with native HTML elements. These features make HTML a better environment for displaying and collecting data. Microsoft Internet Explorer 4.0 includes the following data awareness features:

- Binding of basic HTML tables to a data source contained within a Web page, so that tables can be generated automatically for each record in the data source
- Repeated HTML tables that can redisplay information based on the request of a user, allowing for sorting and filtering data without having to re-contact the server
- Binding of elements of a Web page to a specific database record
- Form fields in a Web page can be bound to fields in a record. This feature allows users to make entries that the data source object on a Web page can then connect to in order to update the database.

Dynamic HTML data awareness is implemented using an open architecture in which a data source control is placed within each Web page. A data source control is an invisible ActiveX Control or JavaBean that knows how to communicate with a data source, primarily a database. In fact, you can use data source controls that are generated using various computer languages:

Visual Basic

C++

Java

Data source controls display their information asynchronously, thereby allowing information to be displayed on the Web page incrementally as it is downloaded, rather than waiting for it to be completely downloaded to the user's system.

Dynamic HTML features the capability to bind various Web elements to fields in the data source control. Within every data-aware Web page is a data source ActiveX control that can communicate with a designated database. Dynamic HTML includes data source controls that can communicate with four different sources of data:

- Data in comma-delimited files
- Data in Microsoft SQL Server
- Open Database Connectivity (ODBC)-compliant data sources
- Java database connectivity (JDBC) data sources

Dynamic HTML's data awareness functionality lets you use native HTML to allow users to retrieve and input data in an environment that requires minimal contact with your server, thereby reducing server load and providing a faster, more responsive, data-aware Web application.

Dynamic HTML Data Binding

Dynamic HTML supports data binding—you can bind data on a server to tables or controls that appear in a Web page on the client computer. Microsoft provides two controls that simplify the process of creating data-aware Web pages: the Tabular Data Control and the Advanced Data Connector. The Tabular Data Control allows you to bind data stored in a delimited text file to a table. The Advanced Data Control is a component of the Advanced Data Connector that allows you to bind a record set to a text box, a grid control, or a combo box.

For more information about the Tabular Data Control, see "Tabular Data Control" in the Component Library section of the Internet Client SDK. For samples that use the Tabular Data Control, see the \samples\ directory of the SDK.

For more information about the Advanced Data Connector, see "Advanced Data Connector" in the Component Library section of the Internet Client SDK.

Dynamic HTML and W3C Standards

Dynamic HTML is a standards-based technology, enabling easy use in conjunction with today's software, tools, browsers, and other Internet components. Unlike other approaches, Dynamic HTML builds on and is completely consistent with the Cascading Style Sheets Specification recently ratified by the W3C consortium. Microsoft has submitted its object specification for HTML programming to the W3C for adoption as an open standard. Microsoft has been working closely with the W3C and will enhance future versions of Dynamic HTML and other Active Client technologies to conform to W3C specifications. Because of the open extensibility and the flexibility Dynamic HTML provides, Microsoft is adopting it across all of its tools and applications as its standard user-interface engine.

Cross Platform

When a developer creates a Web application for use across the Internet using a new technology platform, the most obvious concern is whether users of different platforms will be able to access the same content. Dynamic HTML is supported in Internet Explorer 4.0 and, most obviously, on the Windows platform. Microsoft is doing its best to ensure that cross-platform support for Dynamic HTML occurs on both the Macintosh and Unix platforms. Dynamic HTML is available as a no-cost component that can run on all platforms supported by Active Client, currently including Macintosh and Unix. One of the exciting elements of Dynamic HTML is that it is not limited to Web pages. The controls that make up Dynamic HTML can also be integrated royalty-free into any other applications that you choose to create.

Conclusion

Dynamic HTML takes HMTL to the next level. It expands the graphical and multimedia possibilities available to a Web developer for easy and quick integration into a Web site, but you must remember that it is not readable by all browsers. Companies like Microsoft and Netscape often describe new Web technologies as "submitted to the W3C." Of course, submission doesn't ensure acceptance. Companies are now creating proprietary technologies readable by only their Web browsers, and they are releasing the new technologies to the public before W3C can make any determination about accepting the technology as a standard. Remember, Dynamic HTML is great, but what you see may not be what your users will see; in fact, they may not see anything at all.

Chapter

6

Office 97

When Microsoft first released Microsoft Office the company sounded a wake-up call to the entire software industry. At this time, companies were charging hundreds of dollars for a single word processing or spreadsheet program, but now Microsoft was charging nearly the same amount for an entire suite of fully equivalent software products. The software industry experienced some momentous changes as significant applications, such as WordPerfect, changed from household names to red marks on several companies' balance sheets. Office became a flagship product for Microsoft; today it generates up to one-third of Microsoft's sales.

Office 97 is Microsoft's newest release of this classic product. With it, you can create Web pages in Word, provide database information on the Web using Access, and create impressive multimedia Internet presentations with PowerPoint. All of these functions and more make Office 97 an integrated component of the Active Desktop environment. Here is a list of just some of the new capabilities and features built into Office 97's applications:

- Insert hyperlinks into documents that link to content on the Web or other Office-related applications

- Create Web page content in any of the Office 97 applications
- Provide Access database information on the Web in Active Server Pages
- Insert ActiveX objects into documents to add live content such as audio, video, and animation
- Host content downloaded from the Internet or intranets in a Web browser as an ActiveX document

Office 97 does not promise to have the same revolutionary effect as the original release of Microsoft Office, but it clearly demonstrates that Microsoft has caught the Internet bug and is continuing to push ahead as ferociously as any young startup company. Years ago, Web developers charged significant prices to design Web pages using cryptic HTML source code. Now anyone familiar with Word can create Web pages as easily as writing a letter. Office 97 consists of the following applications, all of which feature numerous Internet enhancements:

Word. Word has become the de facto standard word processing application; with its enhancements in Office 97, it may become the de facto simple Web page creation tool. Word is an excellent example of the Active Desktop at work. Word has been Internet-enabled so that the lines that distinguish your computer system from the network have blurred.

Excel. Excel is the premier spreadsheet and graphing application.

PowerPoint. PowerPoint allows you to create multimedia-rich slide presentations, which you can now integrate into your Web site.

Access. Access is an ODBC-compliant, easy-to-use database that has been enhanced with an assortment of new Internet capabilities.

Outlook. Outlook is the only new application added to the Microsoft Office 97 suite. Using this application you can do calendaring and scheduling, save contact information, and, most importantly, send and receive e-mail. As e-mail clients go, Outlook is quite impressive. Of course, the integration of an e-mail client with the other business-related applications in Office 97 once again gives some indication of Microsoft's view of the Internet's significance.

This chapter will highlight the new Internet capabilities of the Office 97 applications and will instruct you on how to use them to create or enhance your Web applications.

Internet Content with Word

Not only can you create content for the Internet with Word, but the new features built into Office 97 allow you to retrieve files and information from the Internet just as if they were on your local system.

In several of the Office 97 applications, when you select the File|Open menu selection you can choose to open a document found on the Internet, at a particular Web or FTP site. You can add an FTP site, such as your local intranet, to the available Internet locations by choosing the File|Open menu selection, then clicking on the Look In box. Below the Internet locations selection, click on the Add/Modify FTP Locations selection to open the window shown in Figure 6.1.

Figure 6.1 Enter the name of the FTP site you want to add and whether you want to log in anonymously or with a particular user name and password.

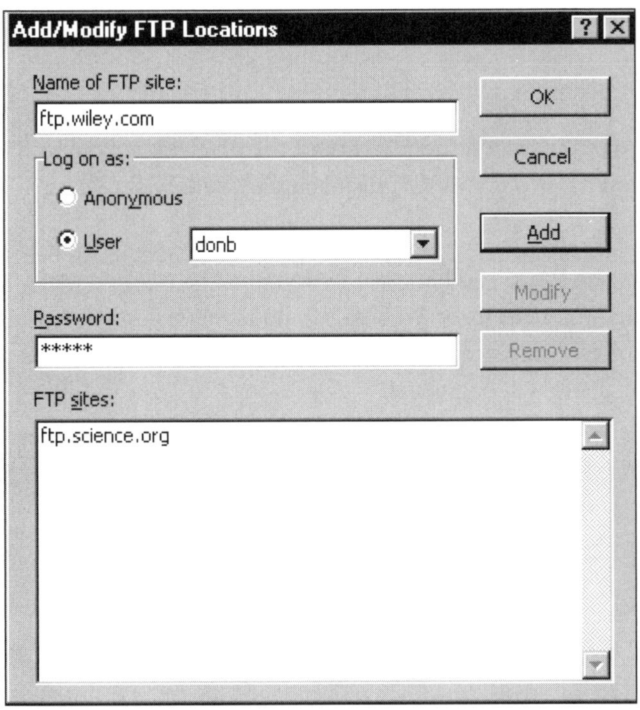

After you have entered in the appropriate information about the FTP site you want to add, simply click the Add button. Once you save the various FTP sites you can open files from the Internet as easily as you load them from your local hard drive. Adding a new FTP site in Word does not mean that this site will be added automatically to the other Office 97 applications as well; this information is saved separately for each application in the suite.

Creating Web Documents

The first step in using Word as your Web document creation tool is to install the Web Authoring Tools option. When you choose to create your Web page all the Word features that are available in HTML will be available for use. You should have installed the Web Authoring Tools option when you installed Office 97. If you didn't, you will have to install the Web Authoring Tools option separately.

Word provides two different ways to create a Web document:

- Create a new Web document using the Web page templates available when you have the Web Authoring Tools installed.
- Save an existing Word document as HTML using the File|Save as HTML menu command.

When you create new content that you plan to publish as a Web page, you should use the existing Web page templates. Simply choose the File|New menu selection and click on the Web Pages folder, which displays the window shown in Figure 6.2.

When you select a template the Word toolbars will be modified to provide additional features and tools needed to create your Web page, simultaneously making some of the features that Word typically provides but can't be converted to HTML unavailable. Here are some of the new features that will be added to your toolbar:

- Web Page Preview
- Form Design Mode
- Insert Picture

Word also allows you to insert into your Web page the same assortment of objects that any other HTML authoring tool allows:

Figure 6.2 Choose which type of Web page template you want to use for your new content.

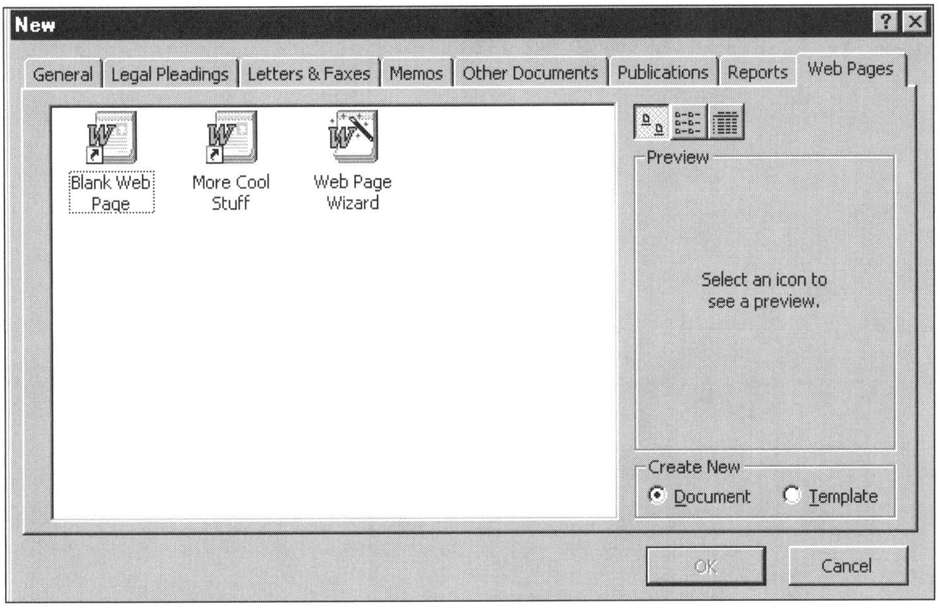

- Scrolling text
- Videos
- Forms and tables
- Background color or images

Like any of the other sophisticated Web page authoring tools, Word allows you to see the Web page you are creating exactly as it will appear to users when it is downloaded. While you are in Web Page Authoring mode, you can use different graphical images for the bullets used in lists. To display the images available, choose the Format|Bullets and Numbering menu selection, which will open the window shown in Figure 6.3, or click the More button to choose your own image for the bullet.

Defining the background color or fill pattern is critical to the impression your Web pages convey when users first download them. You can select a background color for your Web page by choosing the Format|Background menu selection. Click

Figure 6.3 Highlight the text you want as a bullet list and then select which image you want to use for the bullet.

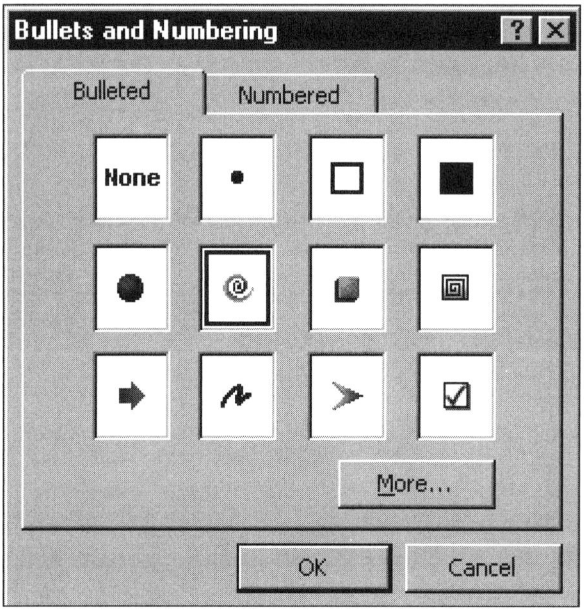

on the Fill option to display the variety of textures, such as white marble, or use an image you have created as a background texture by clicking the More button.

Every Web developer knows that one of the most time-consuming aspects of Web page creation is producing the proper graphics or images. Office 97 features an impressive number of clip art images for bullet points, textured background images, and high-quality photos. These files are found in the Clipart folder of the Office 97 CD-ROM, which you can copy to your local system for easy access.

Inserting Multimedia

Inserting pictures in a Web page using Word could not have been made any easier. Simply click on the Insert Picture icon on the toolbar and select the desired image file from your local system. Once the image is inserted in the document you can vary its size by selecting the image and then clicking on and dragging one of its corners to produce the desired dimensions. Additional modifications can also be made by first right-clicking on the image you want to modify, which will open the window shown in Figure 6.4.

You can insert video into your Web pages just as easily as pictures. Choose the Insert|Video menu selection to open the window shown in Figure 6.5.

The Video Clip window allows you to include alternate information and to select what event you want to trigger the playing of the video, if you want user controls to be visible, and how many times you want the video to be played.

Of course, true multimedia is more than just visual stimulation: It also includes audio. Word allows you to insert background sounds by choosing the Insert|Background Sound menu selection, then choosing Properties to open the Background Sound window; see Figure 6.6.

You can also preview the background sound file you are planning to place in a Web document by choosing Insert|Background Sound and selecting the Play option. Word even allows you to include scrolling text information. No, you don't have to work with a difficult Java applet; simply choose Insert|Scrolling Text to open the Scrolling Text window, as shown in Figure 6.7.

Figure 6.4 Modify the text layout around the image, or make the image a link to another Web document after selecting it.

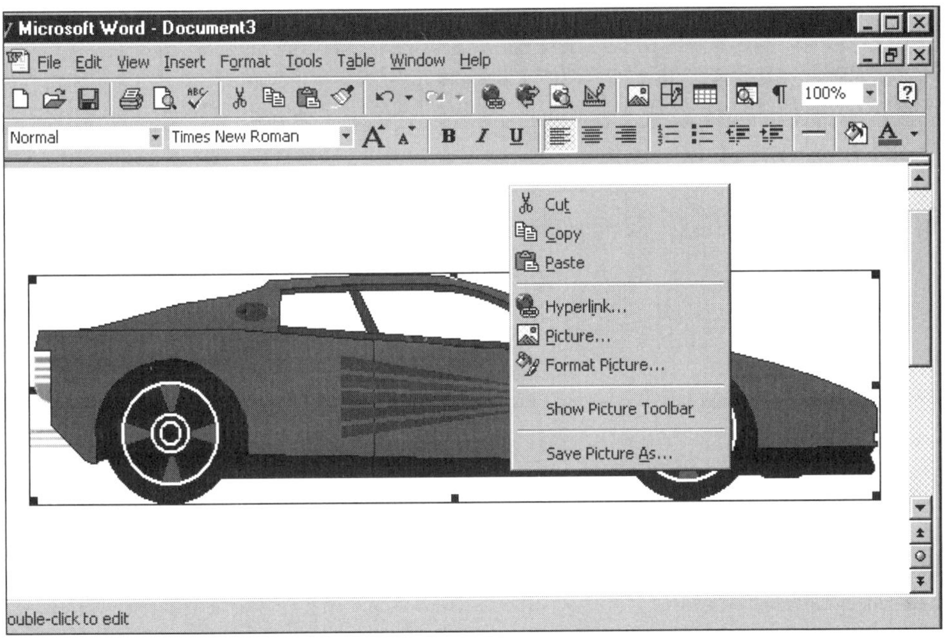

Figure 6.5 Select the video file and any alternate files that you want displayed in a browser that isn't capable of viewing video files or even pictures.

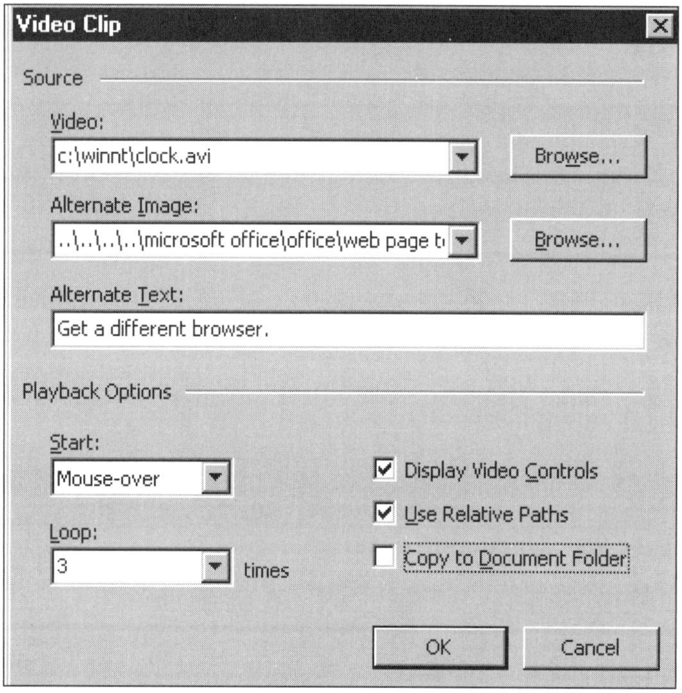

Inserting Forms

Forms are one of the key methods used to provide user interactivity in a Web page; they also provide a way for developers to obtain information from users visiting a particular Web page. Word provides the Form Design Mode, which is used to create forms for your Web page. Figure 6.8 displays the Control Toolbox window that appears when you click on the Form Design Mode icon on the toolbar.

This window features Exit and Properties icons and allows you to insert any one of the following form elements:

- Check box
- Option button
- Drop-down box

Figure 6.6 Select the audio file you want to have played and indicate how many times the file should loop.

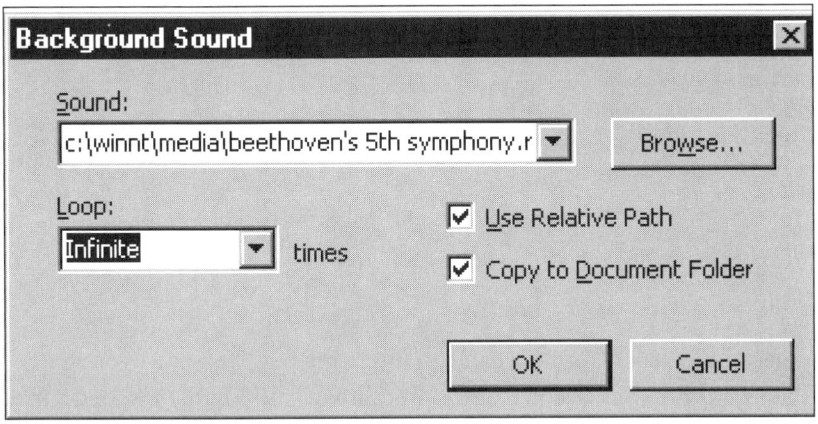

Figure 6.7 Type the text you want to scroll and customize for your application by indicating the direction from which it should scroll and its speed.

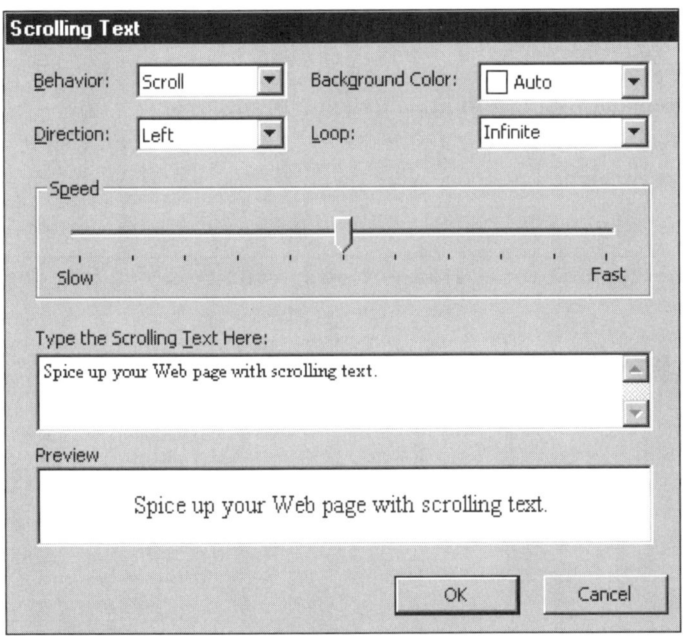

- List box
- Text box
- Text area
- Submit button
- Image Submit button
- Reset button
- Hidden
- Password box

After you select a particular form element to insert in your Web page you must then choose the Properties icon in the Control Toolbox to modify the inserted form element.

Inserting Hyperlinks

Office 97 also supports both text and image hyperlinks in documents. When users read your document all they have to do to retrieve the linked document from the local intranet or across the Internet is click on the hyperlink.

Many people consider hyperlinks as the essence of the Web, and Word wouldn't be much of a Web development tool if it didn't allow you to place them within your Web pages easily. You can select a section of text or an image in your Web page, then click on the Insert Hyperlink icon, which will open the window shown in Figure 6.9.

Figure 6.8 Choose the type of form element you want to place in your Web page.

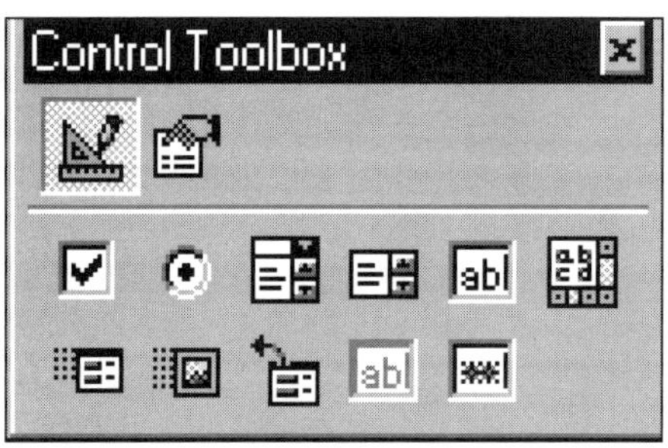

You can also insert a hyperlink without selecting any text or images; place your cursor in the Web page where you want the hyperlink to be created and click on the Insert Hyperlink icon. Choose the desired location that the hyperlink will contact, and the hyperlink will be placed in your Web document as a URL, such as http://www.microsoft.com. Once the desired link has been selected the hyperlink will be created. Text will change to a particular color, most often blue, to indicate that it is now a hyperlink.

You may have noticed the Use Relative Path for Hyperlink check box at the bottom of the window shown in Figure 6.9. When the box is checked, the hyperlink that is inserted will use a relative path to the desired link. This feature is useful if you plan to move the Web page you are creating from its current location before you publish it.

Figure 6.9 Choose the local or remote location to which you want the hyperlink to point.

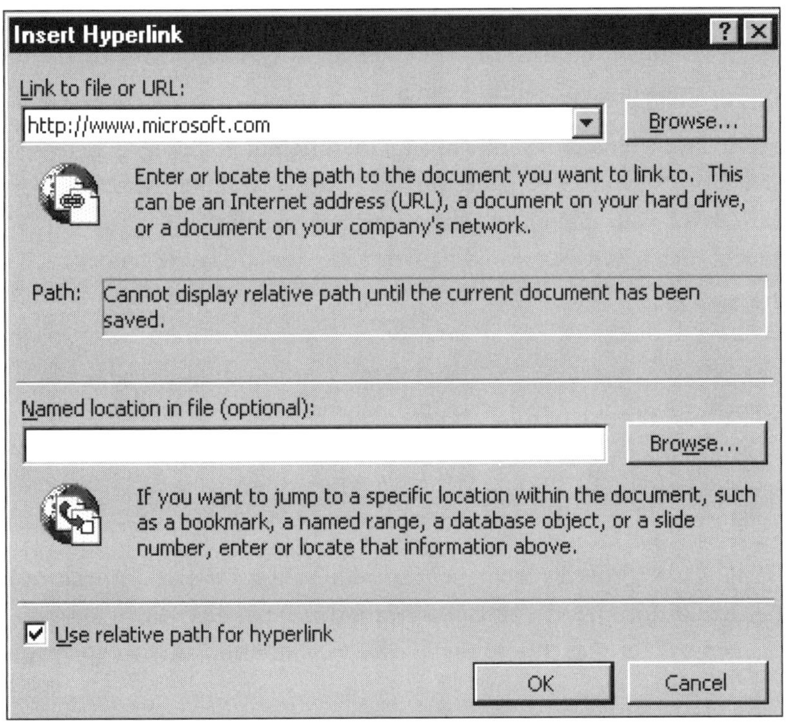

Inserting Toolbars

By choosing the View|Toolbars menu selection or by right-clicking on the Word toolbar you can display the additional toolbars available to simplify Web page creation. Some of these toolbars provide a variety of design capabilities, including database insertion, tables, and borders modification.

At any time as you create a Web document, you can view the actual HTML source code by choosing the View|HTML Source Code menu selection. Figure 6.10 illustrates an example of the HTML source code for a Web document created in Word, which may trigger terrible flashbacks for those developers who have already forgotten what HTML looks like.

> **NOTE** Always save your document before you choose to see it displayed as HTML source code. If you do not save the document, you will lose any changes you have made to the Web document since it was last saved.

After creating a document you can save it as HTML rather than in Word's .DOC file format. Word then allows you to save the document any place on the Internet, rather than limiting you to just your local system.

You can be assured that Internet users will employ different computer and display configurations to view your Web pages online. After you have painstakingly created the right look for your document you want to ensure that every user who views your document sees it as you created it. Word provides a way to embed TrueType Fonts within your document so that you can guarantee that users viewing your document will have the fonts used in your document, even if they do not have the True Type fonts already installed on their systems. To embed the TrueType fonts within your document, first select the Tools|Options menu selection and click the Save folder tab. Check the box for Embed True Type Fonts. You can check the box for Embed Characters in use only to reduce the size of the file; not every TrueType font will have to be embedded in the document file.

Word also allows you to protect a document by requiring a password to edit or even read that particular document. You can activate this capability when you save one of your documents. After you choose the File|Save As option, you can enter the

Figure 6.10 In this view you can modify the actual HTML source code, allowing you to add features to a Web page that aren't available in Word.

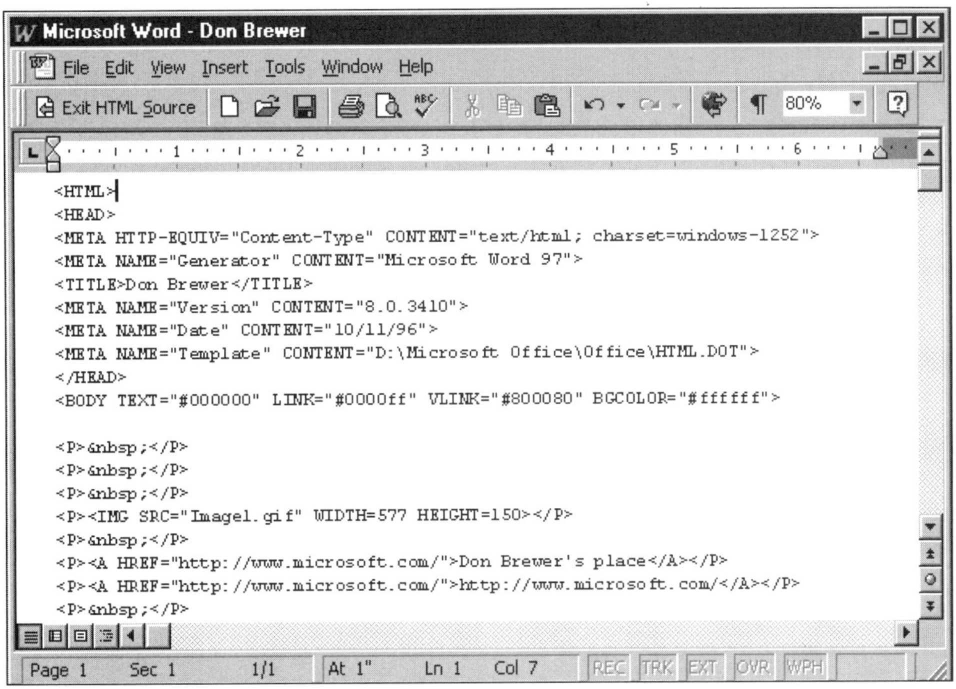

desired password in the available box. Don't forget your password because you will never be able to access that document again if you do forget it.

E-Mail Is King

When it comes to Internet content, Web pages may be interesting, but the number of e-mails sent every day far exceeds the number of Web pages downloaded. Outlook is Microsoft's way of recognizing the value of a sophisticated e-mail and calendaring application as part of its business suite of applications.

Outlook signals the end of simple, plain-text e-mail messages. In Outlook, you can make Word your e-mail editor. Once Word is selected, you can easily include any sort of font or style, in addition to including images, hypertext links, and other documents, such as Excel spreadsheets, in your e-mail messages. This feature is of significant value as e-mail is being used for more and more intranets.

You can turn Word into your e-mail editor by choosing the Tools|Options menu selection in Outlook, then clicking on the E-Mail folder tab. Indicate the appropriate choice in the Use Microsoft Word as e-mail editor check box to turn this option on or off. Now you are on your way to creating sophisticated e-mail content.

Hyperlinks

One of the Internet's most significant features is the almost unnoticeable incorporation of hyperlinks. Hyperlinks make the Internet a web of interconnected information. One minute you can retrieve content from a Web server in Kansas; click on a hyperlink and you can retrieve related information from Budapest.

Admittedly, many hyperlinks often take you to undesired or just plain worthless Web pages, which can drain that most precious of commodities, time. At the end of the day, however, most veteran Web users will agree that the hyperlink functionality makes finding desired content on the Internet an intuitive and simple procedure.

Hyperlink capability has now been incorporated into the Office 97 applications, allowing you to create dynamic links to content found on the Internet or an intranet. When you give a document to someone now, it won't have to be a paraphrase of other information; instead, it can include hyperlinks to that original information, which the reader can choose to check out.

You can specify a hyperlink within your documents by including one of two pieces of information:

- A valid URL (Uniform Resource Locator) to a resource on the Internet or an intranet
- A path to content found on the local hard drive or a drive found on the local LAN (local area network)

URL Hyperlink

Even the most novice Web developer has at one time created hyperlinks where a valid URL was specified, such as

http://www.microsoft.com.

You can also specify the exact content file or object that should accessed by including the name of the file after the URL:

http://YourServerName/Business.doc

In this sample hyperlink, an actual Word document was specified that, when accessed by someone who has both the Internet Explorer Web browser and either Office 95 or Office 97 installed, will appear in the browser as an ActiveX document.

Of course, the hyperlinks you create aren't limited to just the Web; you can also specify an FTP URL:

ftp://www.mycompany.com

Whenever you place the URL syntax shown in these examples into the documents you create with Office 97 they will typically appear in blue text and underlined, as they appear in a typical Web page. Clicking on them will launch the registered Web browser on your system, which will, in turn, attempt to contact that particular location.

Standard Path Hyperlink

Years ago, a business plan or similar report was a simple, typed, text document. Today, documents can consist of text, databases, spreadsheets, and even presentations, all generated by the Office 97 applications. Of course, in your documents you may want to include links to related files or content found on your local system or the LAN. Office 97 provides a convenient way to create a hyperlink to documents found on a LAN:

\\Server\SharedDir\FileName.xls

When other users with the same LAN access load your Office 97 document, which includes this hyperlink, they will be able to access these other files (in this case, an Excel spreadsheet). You can also specify a hyperlink by indicating the desired network mapped drive, directory, and file name on your local system:

D:\CompanyName\Financials\ProForma.xls

Should a user load this file on a system different from yours, he or she will not have access to this file.

Absolute Versus Relative

A dynamic intranet work environment is becoming a reality. In this type of environment, users access shared files, with each user adding his or her own expertise. Using hyperlinks successfully in documents that are shared by many intranet users requires a basic understanding of the difference between an absolute and a relative hyperlink.

An absolute hyperlink is to a fixed file or URL location, which includes C:\MyDrive\Filename or http://ServerName/file.html. Should anyone move this file or rename it, the hyperlink will be broken.

A relative hyperlink is a link to a file location relative to the file that is currently loaded. For example, you have a file found in the D:\Company\Financials directory, and you want to include a hyperlink to a particular document, D:\Company\Financials\1997.xls. The part of the path that the loaded file and the hyperlinked file have in common is called the hyperlink base. In this example, the hyperlink base would be D:\Company\Financials. To create a relative hyperlink, all you have to do is indicate the file relative to the hyperlink base.

You can also specify the desired hyperlink base for a document in its property sheet. In Word, PowerPoint, or Excel simply select File|Properties and click on the Summary Folder; in Access, choose the File|Database Properties menu selection.

The main advantage of using a relative hyperlink is that if the file is later moved around to different servers, its hyperlinks will not be broken when other users access it.

Hyperlinks in Access

As with any of the other Office 97 applications, Access features the ability to host Web pages and to have hyperlinks in documents. The hyperlinks can link to other Office documents or Web pages on your local system, your LAN, and even the Internet. You can place hyperlinks within forms or data sheets to allow users to move easily between other databases. Hyperlinks can also be placed in reports, but they will work only when the report is output to Word. You can also store active hyperlinks in tables. Figure 6.11 illustrates how you can create hyperlinks in a new or existing table by going to Design View and selecting the hyperlink data type.

When inserting hyperlinks in your forms and data sheets, you can indicate whether the hyperlink is an absolute or a relative link to the chosen document. As mentioned earlier, for files that you intend to copy or move around you should save the hyperlink as a relative link. The relative link that is created depends on the hyperlink base that you have selected for the particular database. You can modify the hyperlink base for a database by choosing the File|Database Properties menu selection, then selecting the Summary folder. Here you can indicate the hyperlink base you want for the relative links that you create within this database application.

Access the Web

One of the most powerful features of Office 97 is its integration of Access with new Web capabilities. When many people are considering connecting databases to the Internet, Access in Office 97 provides a simple, and inexpensive solution.

Figure 6.11 Select the hyperlink data type for a table entry.

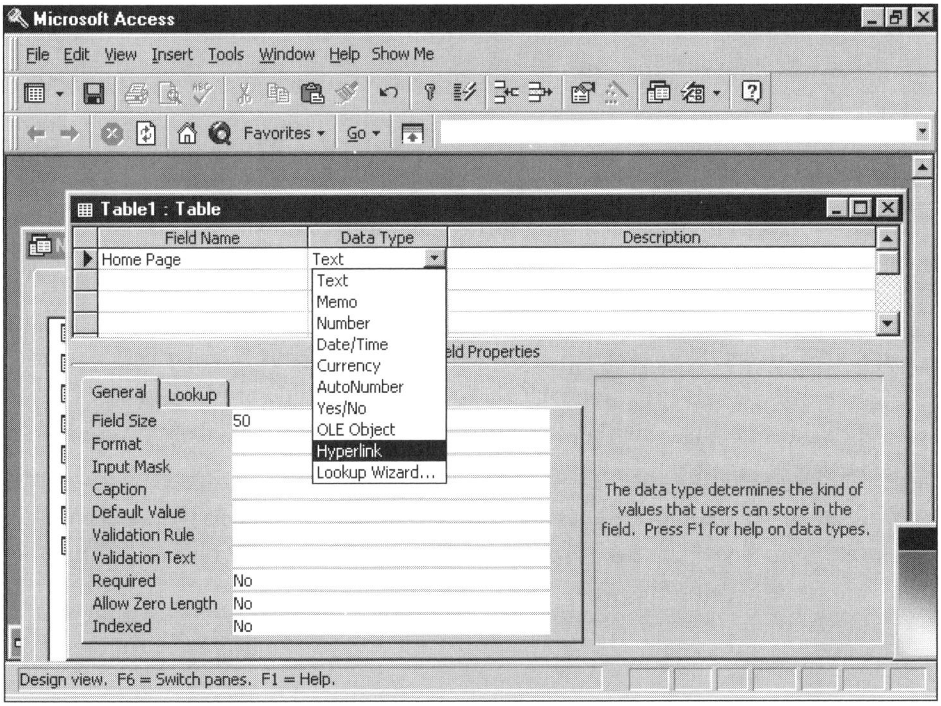

> **NOTE** At this point, it is important to note that this book assumes that you are familiar with Access and basic database concepts. For more information on this material, check out the online tutorial included with Access.

Although lacking in robustness compared to such sophisticated databases as Oracle or SQL Server, Access has created a niche due to its ease of use and low cost. Like any other database, Access allows you to create the assortment of different file types needed to make usable database applications:

- Table
- Query
- Report
- Form data sheet

Once you have created your database application and decided to provide this information on the Web, you are ready to explore some of Access's impressive features. Access provides several ways to save data and information as HTML content using the Publish to the Web Wizard:

Static HTML. Create a static HTML document that captures the information in a table, report, form data sheet, or query at that particular time.

Active Server Pages. Save tables, queries, and form data sheets as Active Server Pages, which can display current information from a database running on a Web server; they are described completely in Chapter 8.

IDC/HTX files. Save table, query, or form data sheets as Internet Database Connector/HTML extension (IDC/HTX) files. This type of files generates HTML documents from the data returned by querying a database running on a Web server.

You can run the Publish the Web Wizard by choosing the File|Save As HTML menu selection. The wizard that launches will inquire about the type of information you want to provide on the Web.

Static HTML

Although Web content is becoming more dynamic with spontaneously created Web pages, there will always be a need for some conventional, static content. Access makes it very easy to convert a table, report, query, or form data sheet into a static HTML document, effectively creating a snapshot of that database information at that moment in time. Here is the basic procedure you can follow to create a static HTML document of your current database information:

1. Select the particular database item that you want to save as a static HTML document.
2. Choose the File|Save As/Export menu selection.
3. Make sure that the radio button for To an External File or Database is selected and click on the OK button.
4. Indicate the desired location and file name, choose HTML document in the Save As Type text box, and then click on the Export button.

Here is an example of the source code generated for a static HTML document from the Customers Form found in the Northwind database sample included with the Access:

```
<HTML>

<HEAD>

<META HTTP-EQUIV="Content-Type" CONTENT="text/html; charset=windows-1252">

<TITLE>Customers</TITLE>

<META NAME="DocumentEn" CONTENT="windows-1252">

</HEAD>

<BODY LINK="#0000ff" VLINK="#800080">

<IMG SRC="NWlogo.GIF"> <FONT SIZE=4 FACE="Book Antiqua">Northwind

Traders</FONT>

<HR>
```

```
<TABLE BORDER=1 BGCOLOR=#ffffff CELLSPACING=0 RULES=none><FONT FACE="MS
Sans Serif" COLOR=#000000><CAPTION><B>Customers</B></CAPTION>

<THEAD>
<TR>
<TH BGCOLOR=#c0c0c0 BORDERCOLOR=#000000 ><FONT SIZE=2 FACE="MS Sans Serif"
COLOR=#000000>CustomerID</FONT></TH>
<TH BGCOLOR=#c0c0c0 BORDERCOLOR=#000000 ><FONT SIZE=2 FACE="MS Sans Serif"
COLOR=#000000>CompanyName</FONT></TH>
<TH BGCOLOR=#c0c0c0 BORDERCOLOR=#000000 ><FONT SIZE=2 FACE="MS Sans Serif"
COLOR=#000000>ContactName</FONT></TH>
<TH BGCOLOR=#c0c0c0 BORDERCOLOR=#000000 ><FONT SIZE=2 FACE="MS Sans Serif"
COLOR=#000000>ContactTitle</FONT></TH>
<TH BGCOLOR=#c0c0c0 BORDERCOLOR=#000000 ><FONT SIZE=2 FACE="MS Sans Serif"
COLOR=#000000>Address</FONT></TH>
<TH BGCOLOR=#c0c0c0 BORDERCOLOR=#000000 ><FONT SIZE=2 FACE="MS Sans Serif"
COLOR=#000000>City</FONT></TH>
<TH BGCOLOR=#c0c0c0 BORDERCOLOR=#000000 ><FONT SIZE=2 FACE="MS Sans Serif"
COLOR=#000000>Region</FONT></TH>
<TH BGCOLOR=#c0c0c0 BORDERCOLOR=#000000 ><FONT SIZE=2 FACE="MS Sans Serif"
COLOR=#000000>PostalCode</FONT></TH>
<TH BGCOLOR=#c0c0c0 BORDERCOLOR=#000000 ><FONT SIZE=2 FACE="MS Sans Serif"
COLOR=#000000>Country</FONT></TH>
<TH BGCOLOR=#c0c0c0 BORDERCOLOR=#000000 ><FONT SIZE=2 FACE="MS Sans Serif"
```

```
COLOR=#000000>Phone</FONT></TH>
<TH BGCOLOR=#c0c0c0 BORDERCOLOR=#000000 ><FONT SIZE=2 FACE="MS Sans Serif"
COLOR=#000000>Fax</FONT></TH>

</TR>
</THEAD>
<TBODY>
<TR VALIGN=TOP>
<TD BORDERCOLOR=#808080 ><FONT SIZE=1 FACE="MS Sans Serif"
COLOR=#800000>ALFKI</FONT></TD>
<TD BORDERCOLOR=#808080 ><FONT SIZE=1 FACE="MS Sans Serif"
COLOR=#800000>Alfreds Futterkiste</FONT></TD>
<TD BORDERCOLOR=#808080 ><FONT SIZE=1 FACE="MS Sans Serif"
COLOR=#800000>Maria Anders</FONT></TD>
<TD BORDERCOLOR=#808080 ><FONT SIZE=1 FACE="MS Sans Serif"
COLOR=#800000>Sales Representative</FONT></TD>
<TD BORDERCOLOR=#808080 ><FONT SIZE=1 FACE="MS Sans Serif"
COLOR=#800000>Obere Str. 57</FONT></TD>
<TD BORDERCOLOR=#808080 ><FONT SIZE=1 FACE="MS Sans Serif"
COLOR=#800000>Berlin</FONT></TD>
<TD BORDERCOLOR=#808080 ><FONT SIZE=1 FACE="MS Sans Serif"
COLOR=#800000><BR></FONT></TD>
<TD BORDERCOLOR=#808080 ><FONT SIZE=1 FACE="MS Sans Serif"
COLOR=#800000>12209</FONT></TD>
```

```
<TD BORDERCOLOR=#808080 ><FONT SIZE=1 FACE="MS Sans Serif"
COLOR=#800000>Germany</FONT></TD>
<TD BORDERCOLOR=#808080 ><FONT SIZE=1 FACE="MS Sans Serif"
COLOR=#800000>030-0074321</FONT></TD>
<TD BORDERCOLOR=#808080 ><FONT SIZE=1 FACE="MS Sans Serif"
COLOR=#800000>030-0076545</FONT></TD>

</TR>
```

The HTML source code obviously continues ad infinitum for each of the database entries placed in the HTML document table, but this sample illustrates how the appropriate tables are generated. All the information that is displayed in the form in Access is now displayed in the resulting Web page, but rather than just one entry, all the entries in the database are displayed, as shown in Figure 6.12.

Figure 6.12 Customer's Form as a static HTML Web page loaded in Internet Explorer.

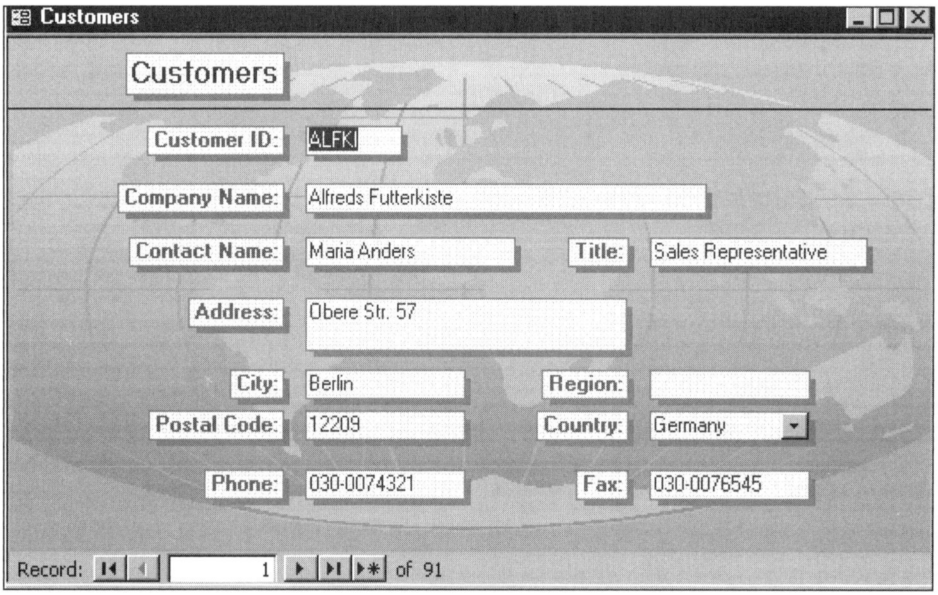

When you save datasheets as HTML documents they are saved as single files, but when you save reports as HTML documents they are saved in multiple files. Access automatically names the multiple HTML documents and simply attaches the _Page# to the name of the file you want saved. When most developers create HTML documents containing multiple pages, they want some navigation ability so the user can find desired information quickly. You can ensure that the desired navigation controls are added to the Web pages by merging the output with an HTML template that already provides support for navigation controls. Then, when you create a static HTML document for a report, for example, the navigation controls will feature hyperlinks to the various Web pages.

HTML Templates

When you use the Office 97 applications to create Web pages, you may want to create a consistent look and feel. For example, you may want the phone number and e-mail address to appear at the bottom of every Web page along with your company logo, all in a pleasing color pattern. Office 97 provides HTML templates that you can then merge with the HTML content generated by a particular application.

The HTML template also allows you to include placeholders. These placeholders indicate the type of information that should go in a particular location in the HTML document. Table 6.1 indicates all the placeholders you can include in a HTML template, where you can put the designated placeholder in an HTML template, and a description of the data that replaces the placeholder when the HTML document is generated. These placeholders are specific to the generation of HTML documents using Access.

Figure 6.13 Indicate the location of the template with which you want the HTML document to be merged.

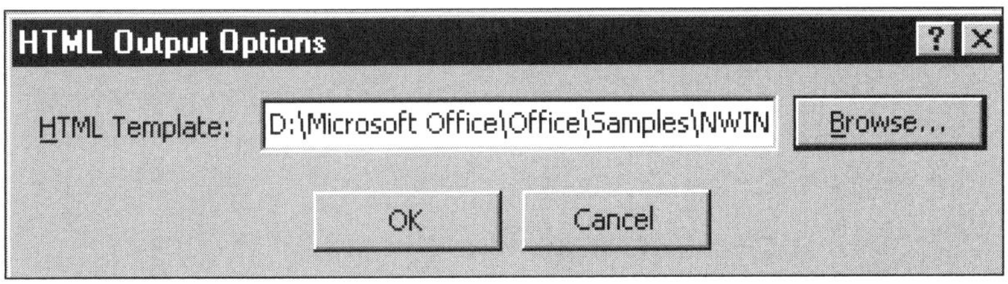

Table 6.1 Placeholders for Use in HTML Templates for Web Publishing Data Obtained from Access Databases

Placeholder	Location in Document	Description
<!--AccessTemplate_Title-->	<TITLE>Between </TITLE>	Name of the file that is saved
<!--AccessTemplate_Body-->	<BODY>Between</BODY>	Name of data or file that is saved
<!--AccessTemplate_ PageNumber-->	Between start <BODY> and end </BODY> tags or simply after the </BODY> tag	Page number of HTML document
<!--AccessTemplate_ NextPage-->	Between start <BODY> and end </BODY> tags or simply after the </BODY> tag	A hyperlink to the next page
<!--AccessTemplate_ PreviousPage-->	Between start <BODY> and end </BODY> tags or simply after the </BODY> tag	A hyperlink to the previous page
<!--AccessTemplate_ FirstPage-->	Between start <BODY> and end </BODY> tags or simply after the </BODY> tag	A hyperlink to the first page
<!--AccessTemplate_ LastPage-->	Between start <BODY> and end </BODY> tags or simply after the </BODY> tag	A hyperlink to the last page

When you save a form in Access, the window shown in Figure 6.13 appears, where you can indicate the location of the HTML template with which you want the data merged.

Here is an example of an HTML template that comes as a sample with Access 97 for the Northwind database:

```
<HTML>

<HEAD>

<META HTTP-EQUIV="Content-Type" CONTENT="text/html; charset=windows-1252">

<TITLE><!--ACCESSTEMPLATE_TITLE--></TITLE>

<META NAME="DocumentEn" CONTENT="windows-1252">
```

```
</HEAD>

<BODY LINK="#0000ff" VLINK="#800080">

<IMG SRC="NWlogo.GIF"> <FONT SIZE=4 FACE="Book Antiqua">Northwind

Traders</FONT>

<HR>


<!--ACCESSTEMPLATE_BODY--> <BR>

<A HREF="<!--AccessTemplate_FirstPage-->">First</A>

<A HREF="<!--AccessTemplate_PreviousPage-->">Previous</A>

<A HREF="<!--AccessTemplate_NextPage-->">Next</A>

<A HREF="<!--AccessTemplate_LastPage-->">Last</A>


</BODY>

</HTML>
```

When Access compiles the data information that you choose to export into static HTML format, the appropriate information replaces the various <! -- AccessTemplate_XXXX -- > placeholders, which in this example would simply be the actual body of data and links to first, next, and last Web pages created.

IDC/HTX Files

Like the Active Server pages, an IDC/HTX file is dynamically created with the content that resides in the database at the time that the HTML document is requested, rather than being a static snapshot of the database information at a previous moment.

The IDC/HTX dynamic HTML model is based on the capabilities built into Microsoft Internet Information Server (IIS). IDC stands for Internet Database Connector, a component of IIS. The .IDC file is created from the data source information that you enter in one of the several Publish to Web Wizard windows. This file indicates the data source with which the Web server needs to connect, along with the security passwords if they are required. The following source code is an example of the type of content that can be found in a .IDC file:

```
Datasource:testa

Template:Customers_1.htx

SQLStatement:SELECT * FROM [Customers]

Password:donb

Username:donb
```

In addition, information about accessing the data source includes the SQL statements that should be executed and the .HTX file where the returned information should be output. The .HTX file that Access creates is an HTML extension file that contains several data placeholders that the Web server should later replace with the data obtained when the data source is queried by a Web browser accessing the published site.

```
<HTML>


<TITLE>Customers</TITLE>


<BODY background = gray.jpg>


<TABLE BORDER=1 BGCOLOR=#ffffff CELLSPACING=0><FONT FACE="Arial"

COLOR=#000000><CAPTION><B>Customers</B></CAPTION>


<THEAD>

<TR>

<TH BGCOLOR=#c0c0c0 BORDERCOLOR=#000000 ><FONT SIZE=2 FACE="Arial"
```

```
COLOR=#000000>Customer ID</FONT></TH>
<TH BGCOLOR=#c0c0c0 BORDERCOLOR=#000000 ><FONT SIZE=2 FACE="Arial"
COLOR=#000000>Company Name</FONT></TH>
<TH BGCOLOR=#c0c0c0 BORDERCOLOR=#000000 ><FONT SIZE=2 FACE="Arial"
COLOR=#000000>Contact Name</FONT></TH>
<TH BGCOLOR=#c0c0c0 BORDERCOLOR=#000000 ><FONT SIZE=2 FACE="Arial"
COLOR=#000000>Contact Title</FONT></TH>
<TH BGCOLOR=#c0c0c0 BORDERCOLOR=#000000 ><FONT SIZE=2 FACE="Arial"
COLOR=#000000>Address</FONT></TH>
<TH BGCOLOR=#c0c0c0 BORDERCOLOR=#000000 ><FONT SIZE=2 FACE="Arial"
COLOR=#000000>City</FONT></TH>
<TH BGCOLOR=#c0c0c0 BORDERCOLOR=#000000 ><FONT SIZE=2 FACE="Arial"
COLOR=#000000>Region</FONT></TH>
<TH BGCOLOR=#c0c0c0 BORDERCOLOR=#000000 ><FONT SIZE=2 FACE="Arial"
COLOR=#000000>Postal Code</FONT></TH>
<TH BGCOLOR=#c0c0c0 BORDERCOLOR=#000000 ><FONT SIZE=2 FACE="Arial"
COLOR=#000000>Country</FONT></TH>
<TH BGCOLOR=#c0c0c0 BORDERCOLOR=#000000 ><FONT SIZE=2 FACE="Arial"
COLOR=#000000>Phone</FONT></TH>
<TH BGCOLOR=#c0c0c0 BORDERCOLOR=#000000 ><FONT SIZE=2 FACE="Arial"
COLOR=#000000>Fax</FONT></TH>

</TR>
</THEAD>
```

```
<TBODY>
<%BeginDetail%>
<TR VALIGN=TOP>
<TD BORDERCOLOR=#c0c0c0 ><FONT SIZE=2 FACE="Arial"
COLOR=#000000><%CustomerID%><BR></FONT></TD>
<TD BORDERCOLOR=#c0c0c0 ><FONT SIZE=2 FACE="Arial"
COLOR=#000000><%CompanyName%><BR></FONT></TD>
<TD BORDERCOLOR=#c0c0c0 ><FONT SIZE=2 FACE="Arial"
COLOR=#000000><%ContactName%><BR></FONT></TD>
<TD BORDERCOLOR=#c0c0c0 ><FONT SIZE=2 FACE="Arial"
COLOR=#000000><%ContactTitle%><BR></FONT></TD>
<TD BORDERCOLOR=#c0c0c0 ><FONT SIZE=2 FACE="Arial"
COLOR=#000000><%Address%><BR></FONT></TD>
<TD BORDERCOLOR=#c0c0c0 ><FONT SIZE=2 FACE="Arial"
COLOR=#000000><%City%><BR></FONT></TD>
<TD BORDERCOLOR=#c0c0c0 ><FONT SIZE=2 FACE="Arial"
COLOR=#000000><%Region%><BR></FONT></TD>
<TD BORDERCOLOR=#c0c0c0 ><FONT SIZE=2 FACE="Arial"
COLOR=#000000><%PostalCode%><BR></FONT></TD>
<TD BORDERCOLOR=#c0c0c0 ><FONT SIZE=2 FACE="Arial"
COLOR=#000000><%Country%><BR></FONT></TD>
<TD BORDERCOLOR=#c0c0c0 ><FONT SIZE=2 FACE="Arial"
COLOR=#000000><%Phone%><BR></FONT></TD>
<TD BORDERCOLOR=#c0c0c0 ><FONT SIZE=2 FACE="Arial"
```

```
COLOR=#000000><%Fax%><BR></FONT></TD>


</TR>

<%EndDetail%>

</TBODY>

<TFOOT></TFOOT>

</TABLE>


</BODY>


<BR><BR>


<IMG SRC = "msaccess.jpg">


</HTML>
```

The dynamic (.IDC/.HTX) HTML publishing methods work in the following fashion. A Web browser contacts a Web server and effectively requests certain data; the Web server then processes the information in the .IDC file to get the exact SQL request and data source information. The Access database is queried, and the resulting data is then merged with the .HTX file to result in an HTML document that is then supplied to the Web browser, thereby creating a dynamic HTML file based on whatever data was in the database at the time of the query. This method of publishing HTML information has obvious advantages over the static HTML publishing method, since the information provided is always the most current information stored in the database, and not just at the time that the static HTML page was generated. Even more important, since the users are directly accessing the database, they can even be allowed to add or delete information present in the database.

Here is the simple procedure to create an IDC/HTX file:

1. Select the desired table, form, or query.
2. Select File|Save As Export.
3. Make sure that the radio button for the To an External File or Database option is selected, and click on the OK button.
4. In the Save dialog box, type in the file name you want saved, choose Microsoft IIS 1-2 in the Save as type list box, and click on the Export button, which opens the HTX/IDC Output Options dialog box.

Specify the data source for the database, a user name and password to access the database if you want to limit access, the desired HTML template to use in the generation of the dynamic HTML documents, and then click the OK button.

Import and Link

That Access in Office 97 is "Internet-enabled" not only allows you to provide database information easily on the Internet, but also features the ability to import or link to data across the Internet. First, it is important to distinguish between import and link. Import occurs when you grab data in the form of a table, for example, and place it within your database application. When you link to data from your database application, you are actually retrieving current data. Typically, when you link to data, any changes you make to that data within your database application should also modify the data source to which you are linking, but when you link to data found on an HTTP or FTP server you have read-only capabilities.

Here is the basic procedure to use to import data found on an FTP or HTTP server:

1. Go to the Database window in the open database that you want to import or link to external data.
2. Choose the File|Get External Data menu selection, and choose the Import option.
3. To import data from an HTTP server, simply enter the name of the HTTP server along with the desired file name into the FileName box that appears; for example, enter http://www.mycompany.com/AdBudget.html. This will initiate the Import HTML Wizard.

Internet Replication

In this new paradigm where different users may access the actual Access database or their own version, *replication* become an issue. Replication indicates the process in which a database is updated to represent the most current information found in two copies of the same database. Replication is designed to ensure that one user doesn't make a change to the database while another user enters contrary information into the same database file. Replication becomes more and more of an issue as more users work on database files using their laptops (which means their systems are not connected to the main database). Access's Replication Manager allows you to create replicas, schedule regular updates, and set the properties of the replicas you create. To complete replication, all a remote user needs is FTP access to the main Access database.

The combination of Import, Export, and Replication Internet capabilities in Access make it an ideal choice for many small businesses that need to provide valuable database information for external or internal use. Within minutes, you can now make selected database information accessible from anywhere in the world. For those developers who worked extensively with the age-old CGI back-ends on Web applications, Access's capabilities may seem like magic.

PowerPoint

PowerPoint has become the de facto standard in corporate America for generating slide presentations. Now PowerPoint features some new Internet capabilities as part of Office 97.

Just like the other Office 97 applications, PowerPoint allows you to include active hyperlinks in your slides that can point to an assortment of document types found on your local machine, corporate intranet, or the Internet. Insert hyperlinks by typing the hyperlink or selecting the Insert Hyperlink option. You can even create image maps by selecting a PowerPoint shape and clicking on the Insert Hyperlink option.

PowerPoint also features the simple import or export file capability to a designated HTTP or FTP site, but the most significant Internet capability integrated within PowerPoint is its ability to create presentations designed for viewing across the Internet.

Save as HTML

If you have any experience with PowerPoint 95, you may have already used Internet Assistant, a helper application that could be downloaded from Microsoft's Web site; once installed, it allowed a PowerPoint presentation to be exported in an Internet-ready format as static .GIF and .JPEG files, which could contain links to the previous or following slides.

This simple HTML conversion capability has now been built into PowerPoint 97, and it can be utilized by choosing File|Save As HTML. Once this option is chosen, PowerPoint launches a wizard that guides you through the process of converting your PowerPoint presentation into a series of Web pages, allowing you to choose a variety of selections that determine the final appearance of your presentation in a user's Web browser. Here are some of the characteristics that you can customize in this process:

Browser layout. Select a simple Web page or one that features frames.

Graphical type. Select a static JPEG or GIF file format, or display it as an animated PowerPoint presentation.

Graphic resolution. Size the graphics for a particular display resolution.

Miscellaneous Information. Add miscellaneous information, such as your e-mail address, home page URL, button graphic to link to other Web pages, and several other useful features.

Once you have selected the desired HTML characteristics, PowerPoint will do the conversion on your existing presentation and make it Web-ready. Then all you have to do is include the HTML documents and images on your Web server; see Figure 6.14.

When you save a presentation using the built-in capabilities of Internet Assistant to create static slide presentations, several features are removed from the original PowerPoint presentation:

- Transitions between slides
- Multimedia effects, such as synchronized audio
- Animation of the display of text and graphics

Figure 6.14 Click the arrow buttons to move through the HTML PowerPoint presentation, or click on any of the links in the frame on the left side to advance to a particular slide in the presentation.

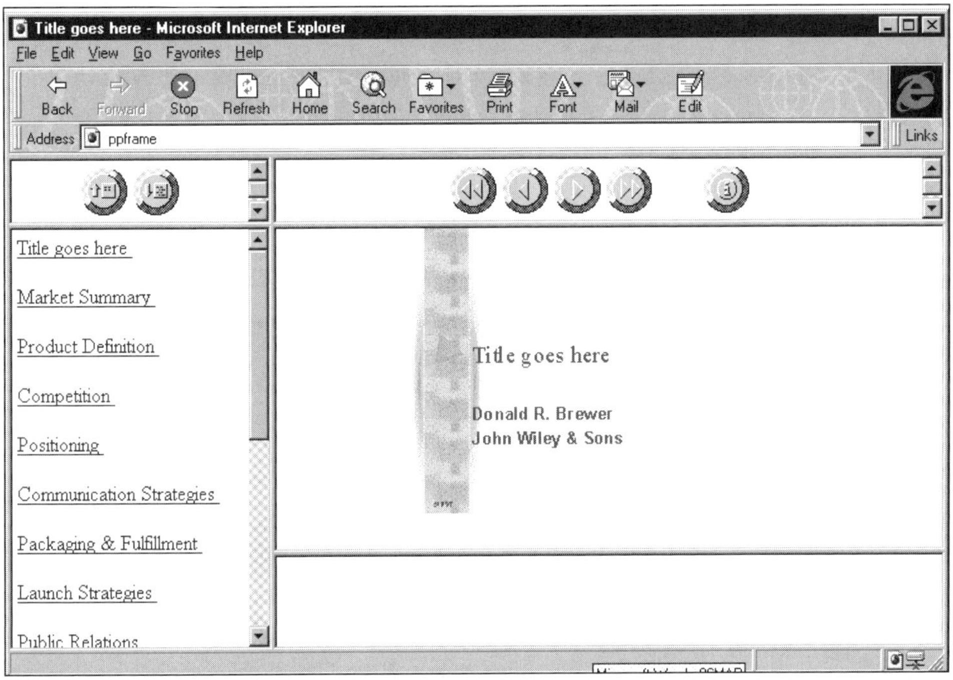

You can incorporate all the exciting multimedia features found in a typical PowerPoint presentation in a Web presentation by utilizing the capabilities of the PowerPoint Animation Player.

PowerPoint Animation Player

PowerPoint not only allows you to create a series of static slides, but it lets you produce Web presentations that incorporate the numerous animation and slide transition effects found in PowerPoint 97. When you publish your PowerPoint presentation on an intranet or the Internet, users can view the animation effects by using the PowerPoint Animation Player in combination with their Web browser. The PowerPoint Animation Player is an add-on feature that works with both Internet Explorer as an ActiveX control and Netscape Navigator as a helper application.

Here are just some of the features of the PowerPoint Animation Player that you can incorporate into the presentations you publish on an intranet or the Internet:

- Place image maps and links to other Web pages and slides within your presentation
- Allow for animated effects, such as moving text and dynamic screen changes
- Compress the presentation file for easier download and rendering
- Add streaming audio, such as RealAudio

With the old PowerPoint 95 application, you could download the PowerPoint Animation Player ActiveX control that, once installed, allowed you to view multimedia-rich PowerPoint presentations from within a Web browser. When the PowerPoint Animation Player was installed, the PowerPoint Animation Publisher could also be installed on a user's system, which modified the File menu of the PowerPoint application by adding the selection File|Export as PowerPoint Animation.

In PowerPoint 97, the capabilities and features of PowerPoint Animation Publisher have been built in and can be accessed using the File|Save As HTML menu command. When you choose this selection, you will go through the wizard to the screen illustrated in Figure 6.15.

Figure 6.15 Choose PowerPoint Animation to create multimedia-rich, Internet-ready presentations.

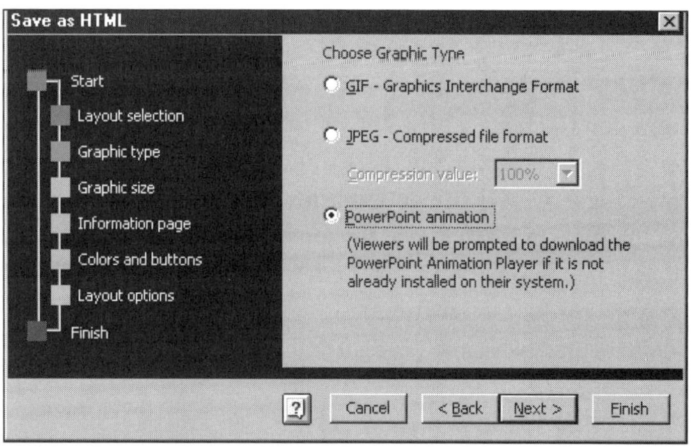

When you select PowerPoint Animation, the built-in PowerPoint Animation Publisher capabilities will then create two files: a .PPZ file and an .HTM file for this presentation. The .PPZ file is a compressed file that can be six times smaller than an uncompressed PowerPoint presentation, although this compression rate is significantly lower if the file includes audio or video. In addition to creating a compressed .PPZ file for the presentation, PowerPoint also creates an HTML document that contains the proper source code for the insertion of the .PPZ file; any user who has the PowerPoint Animation Player loaded will be able to view the presentation within his or her browser. Here is an example of the HTML document created, which defines the insertion of the PowerPoint Animation Player ActiveX control with the <OBJECT> tag:

```
<!-- Presentation generated by Internet Assistant for Microsoft PowerPoint
97 -->


<HTML>

<HEAD>

<META HTTP-EQUIV="Context-Type" CONTEXT="text/html;charset=windows-1252">

<meta name="GENERATOR" content="Microsoft Internet Assistant for Microsoft

PowerPoint 97">

 <TITLE>Title goes here</TITLE>

</HEAD>


<BODY    >


<CENTER>

<TABLE WIDTH=100%>

     <TR> <TD WIDTH=100% ALIGN=CENTER>

         <IMG SRC="space.gif" BORDER=0>
```

```
        <A HREF="index.htm"><IMG SRC="info.gif" BORDER=0 ALT="Index"></A>
        <A HREF="tsld001.htm"><IMG SRC="text.gif" BORDER=0
ALT="Text"></A>
    </TD> </TR>
    <TR> <TD WIDTH=100% ALIGN=CENTER>
        <OBJECT CLASSID="clsid:EFBD14F0-6BFB-11CF-9177-00805F8813FF"
WIDTH=400 HEIGHT=300>
        <PARAM NAME="File" VALUE="pres0.ppz">
        <EMBED WIDTH=400 HEIGHT=300 SRC="pres0.ppz"> </EMBED>
<NOEMBED>
This page contains an ActiveX Animation that your browser was unable to
view. <A HREF="pres0.ppz"> Click here to open pres0.ppz fullscreen.</A>
</NOEMBED>
        </OBJECT>
    </TD> </TR>
</TABLE>
</CENTER>
<!-- <UL>
<H2>Title goes here</H2>
<BR></UL></P>
<P><UL>
<H2>Donald R. Brewer
</H2>
<BR></UL><UL>
<H2>John Wiley & Sons</H2>
```

```
</UL></P>

<P>  -->

</Body>

</HTML>
```

You can piece some of this HTML information, which includes the description of the PowerPoint Animation Player ActiveX control, into an existing HTML document or simply publish it on the Web in its current form.

Users will need to have the PowerPoint Animation Player ActiveX control loaded on their system to view your presentation. On the INDEX.HTM file is an icon that links to the Microsoft Web site, where a user can download the PowerPoint Animation Player ActiveX control:

www.microsoft.com/powerpoint/internet/player/default.htm.

Animations The average PowerPoint user has not fully utilized all the animation and multimedia capabilities of PowerPoint 97. Some of the simplest and most eye-catching modifications involve slide transitions and preset animations that occur in the display of the various text and graphics on the slide. To add some of the animations, choose the Slide Show|Preset Animations menu selection. Here are some of the predesigned animations that you can immediately incorporate in your existing presentations:

- Camera
- Dissolve
- Flying
- Drive-in

In PowerPoint 97 you can also add an assortment of multimedia content to a slide presentation, including clip art, audio clips, and video clips. Microsoft has even included numerous multimedia files in the Multimedia Clip Art Gallery on the CD-ROM.

Web Server Once you have generated the compressed .PPZ presentation file and the .HTM file, you can publish them on your own Web server. To ensure that your Web server is capable of providing the PowerPoint presentation content to users, you must modify the MIME.TYPES file found on your Web server. In the root directory of a Web server such as Netscape Communicator or Internet Information Server, you can find the MIME.TYPES files, as illustrated by the following example code:

```
#-Netscape Communications Corporation MIME Information

# Do not delete the above line. It is used to identify the file type.

type=applications/octet-stream       exts=bin

type=application/oda       exts=oda

type=application/pdf       exts=pdf

type=application/postscript         exts=ai, eps, ps

type=application/rtf       exts=rtf

type=application/x-mif       exts=mif

type=application/x-csh       exts=csh

type=application/x-dvi       exts=dvi

type=application/x-hdf       exts=hdf

type=application/x-latex       exts=latex


type=audio/basic       exts=au, snd

type=audio/x-aiff       exts=aif, aiff, aifc

type=audio/x-wav            exts=wav


type=image/gif       exts=gif

type=image/jpeg       exts=jpeg

type=image/tiff       exts=tiff, tif

type=text/html       exts=htm,html
```

```
type=plain       exts=txt
```

```
type=video/mpeg       exts=mpeg,mpg,mpe
```

To ensure support of your PowerPoint presentation within a Web page, you must add the following lines of code to the MIME.TYPES file of your Web server to guarantee that no MIME conflicts exist. Simply open the MIME.TYPES file in a text editor like Notepad, and type in the following additional application MIME file types.

```
type=application/vnd.ms-powerpoint       exts=ppt

type=application/ms-powerpoint       exts=ppz

type=application/ms-powerpoint       exts=pps

type=application/ms-powerpoint       exts=pot
```

Conclusion

Office 97 has matured as an essential business tool, found in almost any company in the United States and around the world. While it effectively handles the typical desktop user's needs, Microsoft Office 97 also integrates the user's work with the corporate intranet or the Internet. Now all Office 97 applications allow you to publish spreadsheet, slide presentation, database, and even word processor content as universally readable Web pages.

Part Three
Active Server

Chapter

7

Visual InterDev

The significant differences among the technologies that can now be incorporated in Web applications have made creating Web applications a time consuming process. Creating a Web application in the old days required that a developer have only an application such as NotePad and familiarity with the basic HTML syntax. It was a welcome improvement when HTML editors allowed developers to construct their Web pages as if they were using an application such as Microsoft Word to bold text, make hyperlinks, or insert images.

Today, a developer can choose from an assortment of technologies, and each one seems to require its own tools for working with a Web application. For example, when you want to create Java applets, you need Visual J++. When you want to create ActiveX controls, you need the Visual Basic Control Creation Editor tool, and you need FrontPage for final editing and insertion into a Web page. Of course, we haven't even mentioned the numerous editors needed to capture and modify any images, sound, and multimedia that you want to insert in an application. The incorporation of database functionality in a Web application has also become a critical component.

Relief from the unending deluge of applications needed to create sophisticated Web applications comes with Visual InterDev. Formerly known as Internet Studio, Visual InterDev is an integrated development and deployment environment that allows you to create database-driven Web applications that incorporate the most popular Internet technologies. You can then deploy your Web application on an intranet or the Internet and use Visual InterDev as your site manager tool.

Visual InterDev is a Web development tool designed specifically for programmers, unlike FrontPage, which was developed for nonprogrammers. Visual InterDev is actually a component of Microsoft's suite of visual development tools, which includes Visual Basic, Visual C++, and Visual J++. Just some of Visual InterDev's capabilities and features are as follows:

- Allows the development of Active Server pages to be published on the Internet Information Server
- Provides visual script editor so you can include VBScript and JavaScript for server-side or client-side scripting
- Allows connections to be made to any ODBC-compliant database system
- Supports the insertion of an assortment of Internet technologies including Java applets and ActiveX controls
- Provides site manager capabilities that allow for quick and easy checking of hyperlink integrity
- Supports a multideveloper environment for creating and modifying Web applications running on the server
- Provides for easy insertion of Active Server Components into Web applications

Out of the Blocks

Remember that the Active Platform consists of both the Active Client and the Active Server. When you develop Web applications you need to address both elements of the Active Platform. During the installation, you will notice that Visual InterDev consists of both client-side and server-side components. The client-side consists of the following components:

- Internet Explorer

- Visual InterDev Client
- FrontPage
- Microsoft Music Producer
- Microsoft Media Manager
- Microsoft Image Composer

Several of these tools and editors allow you to generate the content that you will incorporate in your applications. The server-side components include an actual server, plus extensions to existing Web servers. The server-side components that you should install before running Visual InterDev are as follows:

- Personal Web Server
- Active Server Pages
- FrontPage Server Extensions
- Visual InterDev Server

The Personal Web Server gives you an environment in which to test your applications before posting them on your commercial server; it is meant to run on Windows 95. If you are running Windows NT and have existing Web servers on which to test your Web applications, you may not be interested in installing the Personal Web Server. Before you can run Visual InterDev (and create a Web project), you must ensure that the following components have been successfully installed:

- Web server, ideally the Internet Information Server
- FrontPage Server Extensions
- ODBC-compatible database, ideally Microsoft SQL Server 6.5 or Microsoft Access

Elements of Web Applications

The days of Web projects that consisted only of HTML files are long gone. Now, a typical Web project not only has numerous HTML files, but also contains images, sound files, and even scripting pages that run applications on the server. Visual InterDev provides a complete integrated development environment that recognizes the ever-growing assortment of files used to create a Web project. Here is a listing of the files that Visual InterDev supports:

- HTML files (.HTM or .HTML)
- Active Server Pages (.ASPs)
- ActiveX Layout files (.ALX)
- Global files (.ASA)
- Multimedia files (.GIF, .JPG, .AVI, .WAV, etc.)

Although most developers are already familiar with most of these file types, Visual InterDev introduces several other file types that you may not have seen before, such as Global files and Active Server pages.

Global Files

As a developer, you must recognize that Web sites are no longer a conglomeration of HTML files connected by hyperlinks, but instead are complete applications. In any type of Web application, you need some direction regarding when certain activities and tasks are completed. The global file (.ASA) acts as the director of a particular Web project's activities. Whenever you create a new Web project with Visual InterDev, a global.asa file is generated. The global.asa file contains four different event procedure stubs:

Application_OnStart. Event occurs when a Web project is started on a Web server.

Session_OnStart. Event occurs when a user contacts a particular Web project.

Application_OnEnd. Event occurs when a Web project is stopped on a Web server or when the Web server itself is stopped.

Session_OnEnd. Event occurs when a user leaves a particular Web project or is timed out.

The Session_OnEnd and the Application_OnEnd events do not have access to any objects; the Session_OnStart and Application_OnStart events have access to several objects. When these events occur, you can have certain properties of the following objects accessed. You can use these five objects to do everything from establishing a database connection to retrieving information about the user's browser:

Application

Session

Request

Response

Server

You can control the Web application by adding script to the various event procedures. These scripts are then executed when the designated event occurs. For example, database connections are typically established with a script in the Session_OnStart event, which tells the server to establish a database connection once the session is started. Here is an example of the global.asa file generated for a particular Web project:

```
<SCRIPT LANGUAGE=VBScript RUNAT=Server>

Sub Session_OnStart

	'==Internet Studio Generated - DataConnection startspan==

	'--Project Data Connection

		Set CustomerDB = Server.CreateObject("ADODB.Connection")

		CustomerDB.Open "DSN=Friendship Customer

Database;DBQ=C:\InetPub\wwwroot\Database\customers.mdb;DriverId=25;FIL=MS

Access;MaxBufferSize=512;PageTimeout=5;", "userID"

		Set Session("CustomerDB") = CustomerDB

	'==Internet Studio Generated - DataConnection endspan==

End Sub

</SCRIPT>
```

Request

One of the keys to producing dynamically generated Web pages is to obtain certain user-specific information, such as which Web browser the user has chosen. The Request object obtains this information from the Active client that contacts one of your Web applications.

The Request object has four collections that you can use to retrieve useful information quickly and easily. A collection is an assortment of related pieces of information that are accessed similarly to a data array. Here are the four collections that constitute the Request object:

Cookies

ServerVariables

QueryString

Form

Active Server Pages

Until now, you have been limited to creating static HTML-based Web pages. You would add the appropriate images and text, and maybe even some scripting, but in the end the HTML Web page that was displayed to users would consist of the same content. This is obviously a poor way to create Web applications, considering that now many Web applications incorporate database information. Most developers

> **NOTE** The following syntax illustrates how within your Web page you can script the Request object along with the desired collection name.
>
> ```
> Request.collectionname("variableName")
> ```
>
> In some cases you can simply include the Request object with the designated variable name.
>
> ```
> Request("variableName")
> ```
>
> When you search in this fashion, the collections are sequentially searched in the order ServerVariables, QueryString, Form, and Cookies for a variable with the names specified in your command. The first variable to match the name is returned. Obviously, it is recommended that

you use this code for variables that exist in only one of the collections. These variables are available in the ServerVariables collection:

ALL_HTTP

AUTH_PASS

AUTH_TYPE

CONTENT_LENGTH

CONTENT_TYPE

GATEWAY_INTERFACE

PATH_INFO

PATH_TRANSLATED

QUERY_STRING

REMOTE_ADDR

REMOTE_HOST

REMOTE_IDENT

REMOTE_USER

REQUEST_BODY

REQUEST_METHOD

SCRIPT_NAME

SERVER_NAME

SERVER_PORT

SERVER_PROTOCOL

SERVER_SOFTWARE

The ServerVariables collection is most often used to retrieve vital end-user information, which you can then use to customize the information displayed to the user.

would like to customize the content displayed based on the information they have about their user.

In response to this obvious need, Microsoft created Active Server Pages (.ASP file extension) as part of the Visual InterDev environment. Visual InterDev allows you to write client-side or server-side scripting in the HTML documents you create. When an HTML document features scripting that runs on the server, it is referred to as an Active Server Page.

Here is how the typical Active Server Page works: A user will unknowingly select a link to an Active Server Page. The Web server will be contacted with the request and will execute server-side scripting within the selected Active Server Page and then provide the resulting Web page to the client with the server-side scripting removed. When you create Active Server Pages with Visual InterDev you can use either VBScript or JavaScript. Here are just some of the capabilities possible with Active Server Pages:

- Allows you to obtain information from users and submit it to the server for processing
- Retrieves from or posts information to a database
- Dynamically generates HTML pages that are customized to the particular preferences of a user

Here is a basic example of the HTML code generated when you choose to create a new Active Server Page:

```
<%@ LANGUAGE="VBSCRIPT" %>


<HTML>

<HEAD>

<META NAME="GENERATOR" Content="Microsoft Internet Studio 1.0">

<META HTTP-EQUIV="Content-Type" content="text/html; charset=ISO-8859-1">

<TITLE>Document Title</TITLE>

</HEAD>
```

```
<BODY>

<% Insert Server-side script here %>

<!-- Insert HTML here -->


</BODY>

</HTML>
```

As you can see in this example, the <%....%> HTML tags are used to indicate to the Web server that a server-side script is contained therein. You should place most of the server-side script within the <BODY> tag of your HTML document. Here is an example of the HTML source code for an Active Server Page, one where you can see the server-side scripting.

```
<%@ LANGUAGE="VBSCRIPT" %>


<HTML>

<HEAD>

<META NAME="GENERATOR" Content="Microsoft Internet Studio 1.0">

<META HTTP-EQUIV="Content-Type" content="text/html; charset=ISO-8859-1">

<TITLE>Hello World</TITLE>

</HEAD>

<BODY>


<% FOR i= 3 to 7%>

<Font Size=<% =i %>>

Hello World <BR>

<% Next %>
```

```
<!-- Insert HTML here -->

</BODY>
```

WARNING Of course, as was indicated before, when a user requests a Web page that is an Active Server Page, the server-side script will be processed on the Active Server and then the Web page will be delivered to the user. Here is an example of the HTML source code that is actually delivered to the client when he or she requests the Activex Server Page that was previously illustrated, server-side scripting removed.

```
</HTML>

<HTML>

<HEAD>

<META NAME="GENERATOR" Content="Microsoft Internet Studio 1.0">

<META HTTP-EQUIV="Content-Type" content="text/html; charset=ISO-8859-1">

<TITLE>Hello World</TITLE>

</HEAD>

<BODY>



<Font Size=3>

Hello World <BR>
```

```
<Font Size=4>
Hello World <BR>


<Font Size=5>
Hello World <BR>


<Font Size=6>
Hello World <BR>


<Font Size=7>
Hello World <BR>
<!-- Insert HTML here -->


</BODY>
</HTML>
```

Active Server pages can also create and manipulate Active Data Objects to send requests for information to a database server. Active Server Pages are one of the most significant elements of Visual InterDev and of the Active Platform environment. Chapter 9 will describe how you can fully utilize the power of Active Server Pages within your Web applications.

Getting Started

Working with Visual InterDev is similar to working with other programming development environments, such as Visual C++ and Visual Basic. In the Visual InterDev environment, you use a Web development tool no longer to create Web pages, but rather to create Web projects. A Web project contains the assortment of files that constitute the Web application that you will publish on the Internet or your local intranet. As with any other development environment, the only way to understand and appreciate Visual InterDev's capabilities is to get your hands dirty. The following quick tutorial will demonstrate how you can easily create a Web project with Visual InterDev.

To begin, simply choose the File|New menu selection, select the Projects folder, and click on the Web Project Wizard icon. Then enter the name of the Web project file and the location where you want the files saved on your local system, as shown in Figure 7.1.

In the next window that appears, enter the name of the server where the Web project will reside. Visual InterDev must be able to contact the Web server to complete the initial generation of the Web project file. After Visual InterDev successfully contacts the server, it must verify that you have the proper permissions to create a Web project on the specified server. You can then choose either to generate a new

Figure 7.1 Indicate the name of the Web Project you want to create and the location where the files should be saved.

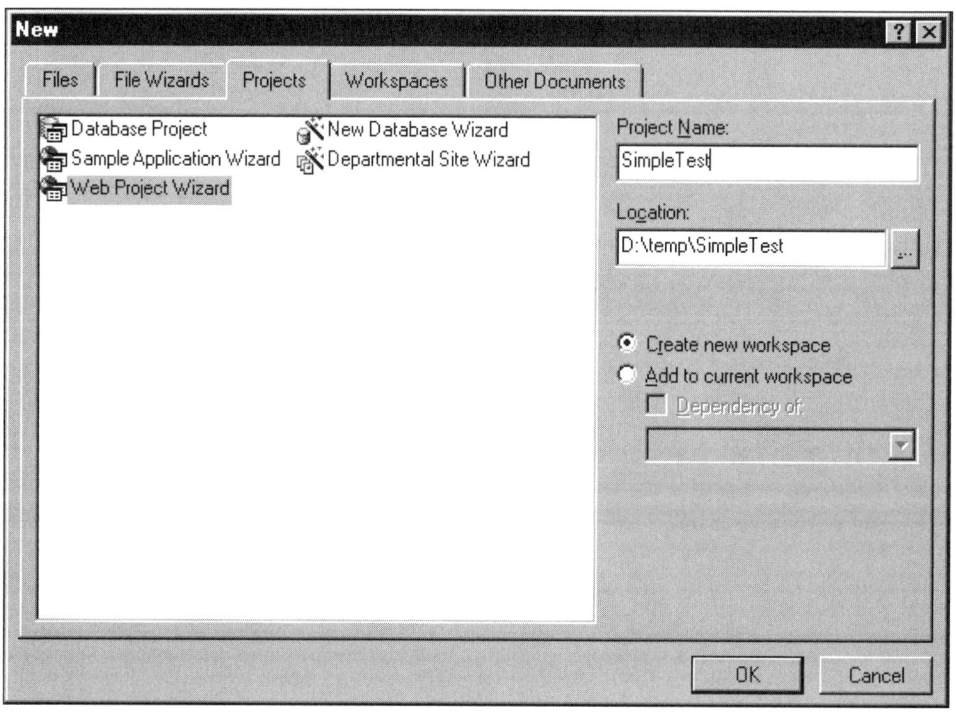

Web project or to connect to an existing Web project running on the Web server. Once these steps are completed, the Web project will be created in the root directory of the Web server.

After you have created your Web project, you will find the following organization of the Visual InterDev project workspace. Most developers who have used Visual C++ or any of Microsoft's other development environments will be familiar with this environment. In the left pane of the application you can see one of three views:

File View. Displays a listing of all of the files contained in the Web project.

Info View. Shows all the documentation available for review about Visual InterDev.

Data View. Indicates all the ODBC data sources in the particular Web project you are working on.

When you select a file in the left pane, it is displayed in full in the right pane of the Visual InterDev window. When you are working with a file that you have selected in File View, you should notice that it becomes colorized; the remaining files in the Web project are still grayed out. When a file is colorized it indicates that a working copy of it is currently on your local drive; when a file is grayed out it indicates that the file still remains on the server.

After you have edited or created a Web page, you must release it to the server so that it can be updated. Simply right-click on the file, and choose the Release Working Copy option. The file will then be uploaded to your server, and it will be made available to anyone contacting your server. You will know that the file has been updated by the file icon, which will turn gray upon updating.

Files Generated by Visual InterDev

If you are creating very basic Web applications, you may not want a global.asa file generated when you start a new Web project. You can prevent Visual InterDev from producing a global.asa file when a new Web project is created; choose the Tools|Options selection, and click on the Internet Studio folder, as shown in Figure 7.2.

Figure 7.2 Uncheck the box for generation of a new global.asa file.

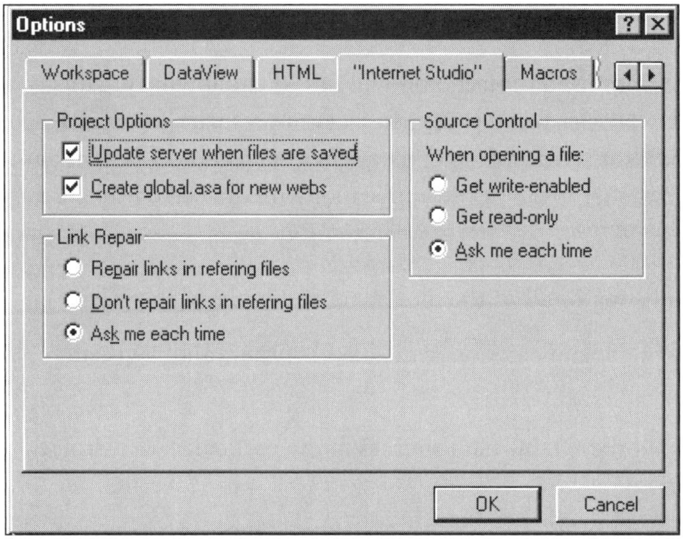

When creating a Web project, you can also indicate if you want a search.htm file included in the Web project. The search.htm file allows users to do full-text searches when contacting your Web site. Whenever you create a new Web project, Visual InterDev automatically generates a global.asa file, a search.htm file, and an images directory, used to place images later.

On the server, several other directories and files are placed in your new Web project besides the global.asa, search.htm, and images directory. They include the following:

_private

_vti _bin

_vti _cnf

_vti _pvt

_vti _txt

search.htm

You have already been introduced to some of the files generated when you create a Web application in Visual InterDev, such as the global.asa file and the search.htm file. The Web's immensity has catalyzed the need for search engines, which allow users to quickly identify Web sites that contain a reference to a particular word. This search capability is a desirable feature for users even on individual Web applications, many of which have become extremely large themselves.

The search.htm Web page that is created allows users to do keyword searches quickly when they contact your Web application. Here is an example of the source code of the search.htm file generated by Visual InterDev when you first create a Web application.

```
<!DOCTYPE HTML PUBLIC "-//IETF//DTD HTML//EN">

<html>

<head>
<title>Text Search</title>
<meta name="FORMATTER" content="Microsoft FrontPage 2.0">
</head>

<body>

<h1><a name="top">Text Search</a></h1>

<hr>

<p>Use the form below to search for documents in this web
containing specific words or combinations of words. The text
search engine will display a weighted list of matching documents,
```

```
with better matches shown first. Each list item is a link to a
matching document; if the document has a title it will be shown,
otherwise only the document's file name is displayed. A brief <a
href="#querylang">explanation</a> of the query language is
available, along with examples.</p>
<!--webbot bot="Search" s-link s-fields="TimeStamp,DocumentK,"
s-index="All" s-dsn="default" tag="FORM" s-text="Search for:"
i-size="20" s-submit="Start Search" s-clear="Clear" startspan -->

<form action="_vti_bin/shtml.dll/search.htm" method="POST">
    <input type="hidden" name="VTI-GROUP" value="0"><p><b>Search
    for: </b><input type="text" name="search" size="20" value></p>
    <p><input type="submit" value="Start Search"><input
    type="reset" value="Clear"></p>
</form>
<!--webbot bot="Search" endspan i-checksum="34878" -->

<hr>

<h2><a name="querylang">Query Language</a></h2>

<p>The text search engine allows queries to be formed from
arbitrary Boolean expressions containing the keywords AND, OR,
and NOT, and grouped with parentheses. For example:</p>
```

```
<blockquote>
    <dl>
        <dt><strong><tt>information retrieval</tt></strong></dt>
        <dd>finds documents containing 'information' or
            'retrieval'<br>
            <br>
        </dd>
        <dt><strong><tt>information or retrieval</tt></strong></dt>
        <dd>same as above<br>
            <br>
        </dd>
        <dt><strong><tt>information and retrieval</tt></strong></dt>
        <dd>finds documents containing both 'information' and
            'retrieval'<br>
            <br>
        </dd>
        <dt><strong><tt>information not retrieval</tt></strong></dt>
        <dd>finds documents containing 'information' but not
            'retrieval'<br>
            <br>
        </dd>
        <dt><strong><tt>(information not retrieval) and
WAIS</tt></strong></dt>
        <dd>finds documents containing 'WAIS', plus 'information'
            but not 'retrieval'<br>
```

```
          <br>
      </dd>
      <dt><strong><tt>web*</tt></strong></dt>
      <dd>finds documents containing words starting with 'web'<br>
          <br>
      </dd>
  </dl>
</blockquote>

<h5><a href="#top">Back to Top</a></h5>

<hr>

<h5>Author information goes here.<br>
Copyright © 1995 Your Company Name. All rights reserved.<br>
</h5>
</body>
</html>
```

Figure 7.3 illustrates the search.htm Web page as it appears when loaded on a user's browser.

The text search engine automatically created for your Web application is just one of the many features of Visual InterDev that allow you to produce the most powerful Web applications with the least effort.

Editors

Visual InterDev features an assortment of editors that can be used to create and edit the different files you can integrate into your Web project.

Figure 7.3 Type in the keyword on which you want to search the Web application and click on Start Search.

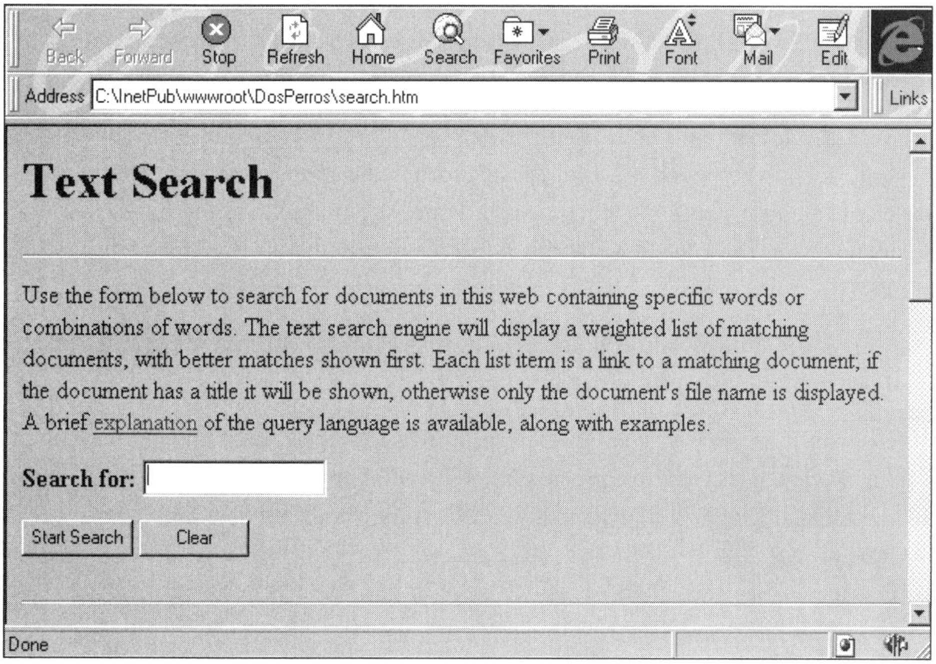

HTML Source Editor. For those developers who still use Notepad or another text editor for most of their development, this feature lets you see and edit the actual HTML text for a Web page. The HTML Source Editor color-codes the HTML source code in a Web page. Server-side script is indicated with yellow text.

FrontPage Editor. Most Web developers now prefer visual Web page environments—FrontPage Editor is one of the best. Now you can modify text and insert hyperlinks and other objects with a few clicks of your mouse without having to actually write the HTML source code.

Script Wizard. Use the Script Wizard to add VBScript or JavaScript to your Web pages by simply clicking on the desired object and linking it to the desired event.

Object Wizard. With the increasing use of objects in Web pages, you can use the Object Wizard to modify the properties of the objects you place in your Web pages.

HTML Layout Editor. With this editor, you can control the exact placement of objects on your Web page.

Those developers who have used the ActiveX Control Pad to insert ActiveX controls into their Web pages will find their favorite editors in Visual InterDev. When you want to edit a particular document in your Web project, simply right-click on the document in the File View of Visual InterDev, and choose the Open With option; see Figure 7.4.

In the Open With window, you can add other editors that you may prefer by simply clicking on the Add button.

After you have created your Web page, Active Server page, or any other element of your Web project, you can preview it as it would appear in a client's Web browser. Visual InterDev provides three different ways to preview Web pages:

Preview in Browser. Places the Web page in your default browser.

Figure 7.4 Select the type of editor in which you want the document to open.

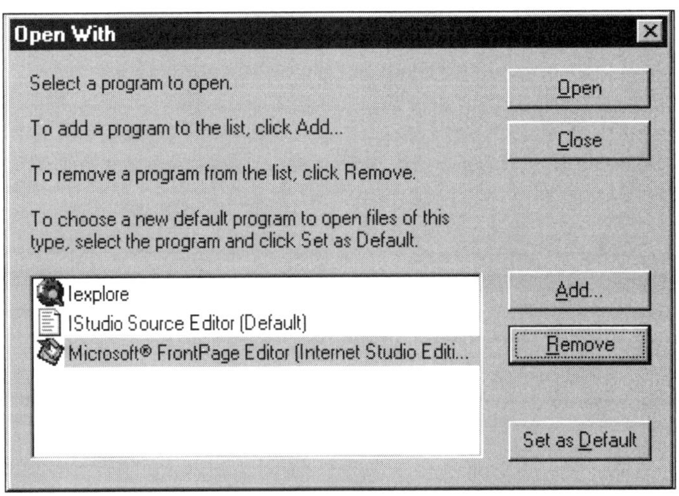

Browser Select. Allows you to choose the application or Web browser in which to preview the Web page.

Browser Info Window. Opens the Web page within Visual InterDev itself, as it would appear in a client's Web browser.

ActiveX Layout Creation

Designers have asked a simple question: "Why do all objects on the Internet have to be next to each other; why can't one object be in front of or behind another?" The days of two-dimensional Internet design are over, given the introduction of ActiveX's layout capability. Now you can position numerous ActiveX controls on your Web pages in overlapping configurations. This design capability, introduced in Chapter 2 as a component of the ActiveX Control Pad and then FrontPage, is now a part of Visual InterDev. To create your own ActiveX layout files (.ALX) in Visual InterDev, select File|New and choose HTML Layout in the Files folder.

Database Connection

The next generation of Web applications provide user interaction with powerful existing databases. Obviously, before you can use any of the information available on a database server, your Web application must first establish a database connection.

Network Sharing

Before you can create or modify a Web project that uses a database you must use a Windows NT feature that allows you to share directories with other computers on the network.

1. On your Web server, create a directory for your database, such as C:\MyDatabase.
2. In Windows Explorer, right-click on this directory and choose the Sharing option, which opens the window shown in Figure 7.5.
3. In the Properties window, click the Shared As radio button and indicate the directory name that you want to be recognized for this shared directory. Users will then be able to access this directory as //YourWebServer/SharedDirectoryName.

Figure 7.5 Select the parameters for sharing the directory you selected.

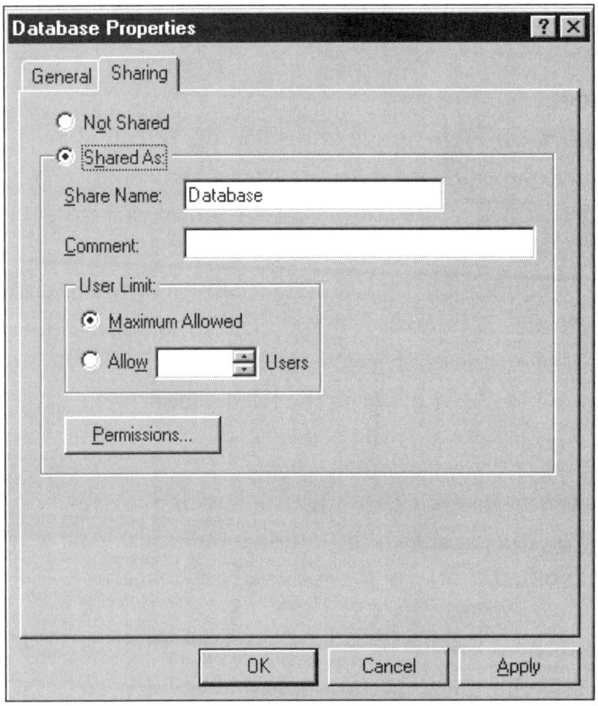

4. Before you accept this modification, click on the Permissions button, opening the window shown in Figure 7.6, and modify the access privileges for this directory.

5. Click on the OK button to finalize the shared directory configurations.

Here is one significant security concern: Whenever you choose to share a directory in Windows NT or Windows 95, the default privileges automatically give everyone unrestricted access to the shared directory. Anyone who doesn't modify these permissions could be in for a serious security breach in the future. All any enterprising hacker needs to do is contact your Web server with his or her Windows Explorer application.

DataSource

A Web application can contact a database only if the computer system on which it is running has ODBC 3.0 and the correct ODBC driver installed. To allow your

Figure 7.6 Select the permissions and access restrictions for your shared directory.

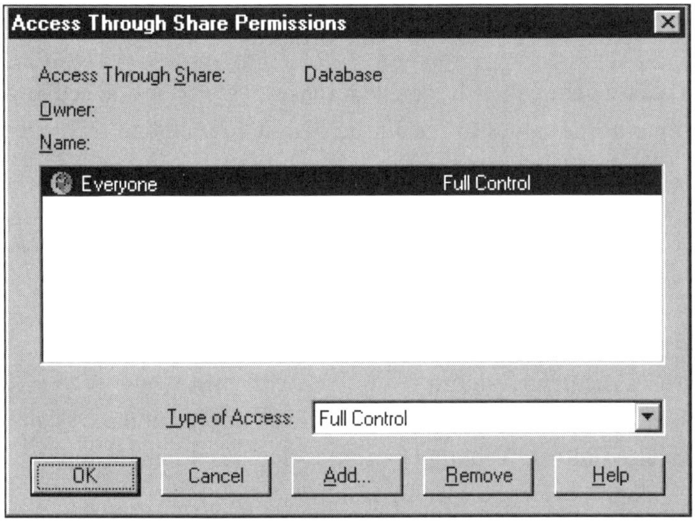

Web application to contact a database you must first set up a data source. First choose a data source name, typically a file with a .DSN extension, and then follow this procedure:

1. In FileView, right-click on the root of your Web project, and select the Add Data Connection option.
2. Choose Machine Source Data, and select the database file to which you want to establish a connection.
3. In the Properties window, you can add a login user name and password to access the database by selecting the RunTime folder.

You will notice that the database connection icon is connected to the global.asa file. When a Web project is first loaded on the Web server, the global.asa file is loaded first. The global.asa file contains all the initialization information required for the Web project, such as variables. In most Web projects, you want the database connection established as soon as the Web project is loaded; this is why it is directly connected to the global.asa file.

Once you add a database connection to an application, the DataView folder becomes available in the Project window. You can select the DataView folder and see the name and location of the database that is now connected to your Web project. Click on the + symbol next to any of the folders to expand and view its contents. Visual InterDev allows you to see all the tables, queries, and other database objects contained in the database you have added to your Web project.

You can even expand each of the tables in your database to see their respective columns. Right-click on one of the tables to see all the data it contains. In this window, assuming you have the necessary privileges, you can add, delete, or modify any record in any table, all within the same Visual InterDev development environment. Visual InterDev provides a plethora of data tools that let you modify tables, queries, and other information.

Design-Time ActiveX Controls

Visual InterDev also features the new design-time ActiveX controls, which are another powerful way to expand the capabilities of your Web applications. Design-time ActiveX controls, inserted into a Web application during development time, generate HTML source code to perform a specific task.

One of the problems with ActiveX controls is that not all browsers recognize them. Some content you would like to display to visitors will not be seen. Design-time ActiveX controls do not exist as ActiveX controls within a Web page; they simply generate the often lengthy HTML source code on the development side, saving much time for the developer. Visual InterDev provides several design-time ActiveX controls that come pre-installed.

Form Control. Generates HTML forms.

Data Range Header Control. Builds Web pages out of the data returned from a query, which allows users to browse back and forth through the returned information.

Data Command Control. Allows simple and complex SQL (Structured Query Language) statements to be generated and executed.

The data controls are integrated with the Query Designer to allow you to create SQL statements that can produce dynamically generated Web pages. The following example illustrates how you can insert the Data Range Header design-time ActiveX control into a Web project:

1. Open the Web page in which you want to insert the Design-Time ActiveX control, and place your cursor in the exact location.
2. Select the Insert|IntoHTML|ActiveX Control option, which opens the window shown in Figure 7.7.
3. In the Insert ActiveX Control window, select the Design-Time folder, and choose the desired ActiveX control.

Here is an example of the HTML source code generated by the Data Range Header Control; as you can see, the code consists of the various properties of the Design-Time ActiveX control, followed by the server-side scripting, which appears with a yellow highlight in the Visual InterDev HTML Source Editor window.

You should note that the code that specifies the various properties of the Data Range Header Control is actually contained within <!--METADATA --!> tags. This means that the client will be able to execute this Web page even if the browser does not support ActiveX controls.

```
<!--METADATA TYPE="DesignerControl" startspan

    <OBJECT ID="DataRangeHdr1" WIDTH=151 HEIGHT=24

     CLASSID="CLSID:F602E721-A281-11CF-A5B7-0080C73AAC7E">

        <PARAM NAME="_Version" VALUE="65536">
```

Figure 7.7 Choose which Design-Time ActiveX control you want to insert into your document.

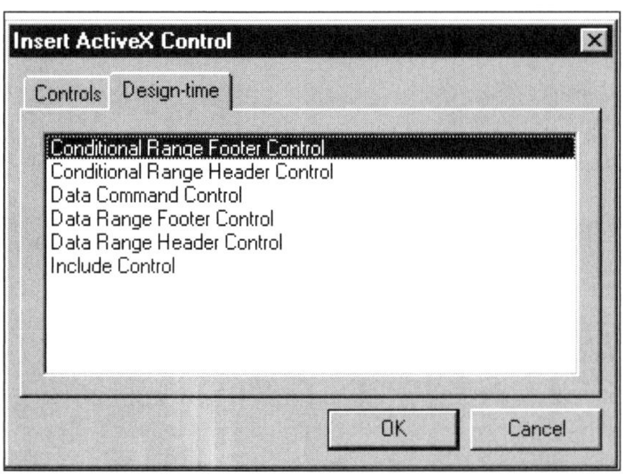

```
            <PARAM NAME="_Version" VALUE="65536">
            <PARAM NAME="_ExtentX" VALUE="3969">
            <PARAM NAME="_ExtentY" VALUE="635">
            <PARAM NAME="_StockProps" VALUE="0">
            <PARAM NAME="DataConnection" VALUE="CustomerDB">
            <PARAM NAME="CursorType" VALUE="1">
            <PARAM NAME="RangeType" VALUE="2">
            <PARAM NAME="BarAlignment" VALUE="2">
            <PARAM NAME="PageSize" VALUE="10">
        </OBJECT>
    -->

    <!--METADATA TYPE="DesignerControl" startspan
        <OBJECT ID="DataRangeHdr1" WIDTH=151 HEIGHT=24
         CLASSID="CLSID:F602E721-A281-11CF-A5B7-0080C73AAC7E">
            <PARAM NAME="_Version" VALUE="65536">
            <PARAM NAME="_Version" VALUE="65536">
            <PARAM NAME="_ExtentX" VALUE="3969">
            <PARAM NAME="_ExtentY" VALUE="635">
            <PARAM NAME="_StockProps" VALUE="0">
            <PARAM NAME="DataConnection" VALUE="CustomerDB">
            <PARAM NAME="CommandText" VALUE="SELECT Customers.Customer_ID,
    Customers.First_Name, Customers.Last_Name, CustomerDetail.Agent,
```

```
CustomerDetail.Claims FROM Customers, CustomerDetail WHERE
Customers.Customer_ID = CustomerDetail.Customer_ID ORDER BY
Customers.Last_Name">
        <PARAM NAME="CursorType" VALUE="1">
        <PARAM NAME="RangeType" VALUE="2">
        <PARAM NAME="BarAlignment" VALUE="2">
        <PARAM NAME="PageSize" VALUE="10">
    </OBJECT>
-->
    <% tEmptyRecordset = False
    fFirstPass = True
    tPageSize = 10
    tRangeType = "Table"

    fNoRecordset = False
    If IsObject(Session("DataRangeHdr1")) Then
        Set DataRangeHdr1 = Session("DataRangeHdr1")
        If IsEmpty(Request("PagingRequest")) Then
            PagingMove = "Refresh"
        Else
            PagingMove = Trim(Request("PagingMove"))
            If Request("PagingRequest") <> "DataRangeHdr1" Then
                PagingMove = "Refresh"
            End If
        End If
```

```
        Else
            fNoRecordset = True
        End If

        tRecordsProcessed = 0
        tHeaderName = "DataRangeHdr1"
        tBarAlignment = "Center"

        If fNoRecordset Then
            Set cmdTemp = Server.CreateObject("ADODB.Command")
            Set DataRangeHdr1 = Server.CreateObject("ADODB.Recordset")
            cmdTemp.CommandText = "SELECT Customers.Customer_ID,
    Customers.First_Name, Customers.Last_Name, CustomerDetail.Agent,
    CustomerDetail.Claims FROM Customers, CustomerDetail WHERE
    Customers.Customer_ID = CustomerDetail.Customer_ID ORDER BY
    Customers.Last_Name"
            cmdTemp.CommandType = 1
            Set cmdTemp.ActiveConnection = Session("CustomerDB")
            DataRangeHdr1.Open cmdTemp, , 1, 1
            DataRangeHdr1.PageSize = tPageSize
            If DataRangeHdr1.BOF or DataRangeHdr1.EOF Then
                tEmptyRecordset = True
                fHideNavBar = True
                Response.Write("No Records Available <br>")
            Else
```

```
            Set Session("DataRangeHdr1") = DataRangeHdr1

            Session("DataRangeHdr1AbsolutePage") = 1

        End If

    Else

        If DataRangeHdr1.PageSize <> tPageSize Then

            tCurRec = ((Session("DataRangeHdr1AbsolutePage") - 1) *
DataRangeHdr1.PageSize) + 1

            tNewPage = Int(tCurRec / tPageSize)

            If tCurRec Mod tPageSize <> 0 Then

                tNewPage = tNewPage + 1

            End If

            If tNewPage = 0 Then tNewPage = 1

            DataRangeHdr1.PageSize = tPageSize

            Session("DataRangeHdr1AbsolutePage") = tNewPage

        End If

         Select Case PagingMove

             Case "Requery"

                     DataRangeHdr1.Requery

             Case "<<"

                Session("DataRangeHdr1AbsolutePage") = 1

             Case "<"

                If Session("DataRangeHdr1AbsolutePage") > 1 Then

                    Session("DataRangeHdr1AbsolutePage") =
Session("DataRangeHdr1AbsolutePage") - 1
```

```
                    End If
                Case ">"
                    If Not DataRangeHdr1.EOF Then
                        Session("DataRangeHdr1AbsolutePage") =
Session("DataRangeHdr1AbsolutePage") + 1
                    End If
                Case ">>"
                    DataRangeHdr1.MoveLast
                    Session("DataRangeHdr1AbsolutePage") =
DataRangeHdr1.PageCount
            End Select
            DataRangeHdr1.AbsolutePage = Session("DataRangeHdr1AbsolutePage")
            If DataRangeHdr1.EOF Then
                Session("DataRangeHdr1AbsolutePage") =
Session("DataRangeHdr1AbsolutePage") - 1
                DataRangeHdr1.MovePrevious
            End If
        End If
        Do
            If tEmptyRecordset Then Exit Do
            If tRecordsProcessed = tPageSize Then Exit Do
            If Not fFirstPass Then
                DataRangeHdr1.MoveNext
            Else
                fFirstPass = False
```

```
        End If

        If DataRangeHdr1.EOF Then Exit Do

        tRecordsProcessed = tRecordsProcessed + 1 %>

<!--METADATA TYPE="DesignerControl" endspan-->
```

NOTE This long passage of HTML source code was automatically generated by a design-time ActiveX control; the time it can save in development is obvious.

To edit an existing design-time ActiveX control, right-click on the server-side script for that control while in the HTML Source Editor, and choose the Edit Design Control option.

Obviously, you can have the returned database information displayed in the user's browser in several ways. When you want the returned database information to be placed in a table you must modify the table you created in the Active Server Page. Of course, every table needs a description of the information in the columns. The Database Range Header Control can copy the variable information for the database that will be retrieved by the SQL statement. In the Properties window for the Database Range Header Control, click on the Copy Fields button, then select the fields that you want copied. The variable names will then be copied to the clipboard, and you can insert them in the proper location within the HTML source code for the desired Web page. Here is an example of the variable information that is copied to the clipboard when the Copy Fields feature is executed.

```
<%= DataRangeHdr1("Agent") %><br>

<%= DataRangeHdr1("Claims") %><br>

<%= DataRangeHdr1("Customer_ID") %><br>

<%= DataRangeHdr1("First_Name") %><br>

<%= DataRangeHdr1("Last_Name") %><br>
```

In addition to these pre-installed design-time ActiveX controls, you can create your own. The Visual Basic 5.0 Control Creation Editor can be used to build both design-time and standard ActiveX controls. A complete description of what must be done to create design-time ActiveX controls can be found in the ActiveX SDK (Software Developer's Kit), which you can download from www.microsoft.com/workshop/.

Database Footer Control

The Database Footer design-time ActiveX control is used to indicate the end of the database information that has been retrieved. When you have displayed database information retrieved by using the Database Range Header control in a table you must also include the Database Footer control to end it. Insert the Database Footer control before the ending </TABLE> tag. Here is an example of the HTML source code for the Database Footer control.

```
<!--METADATA TYPE="DesignerControl" startspan

    <OBJECT ID="DataRangeFtr1" WIDTH=151 HEIGHT=24

     CLASSID="CLSID:F602E722-A281-11CF-A5B7-0080C73AAC7E">

        <PARAM NAME="_Version" VALUE="65536">

        <PARAM NAME="_ExtentX" VALUE="3969">

        <PARAM NAME="_ExtentY" VALUE="635">

        <PARAM NAME="_StockProps" VALUE="0">

    </OBJECT>

-->

    <% Loop

    If tRangeType = "Table" Then Response.Write("</TABLE>")

    If tPageSize > 0 Then %>

        <HR>

        <% If Not fHideNavBar Then %>
```

```
            <TABLE WIDTH=100% >
            <TR>
                <TD WIDTH=100% >
                    <P ALIGN=<%= tBarAlignment%> >
                    <FORM ACTION="<%= Request.ServerVariables("PATH_INFO") &
stQueryString%>" METHOD="POST">
                        <INPUT TYPE="Submit" NAME="PagingMove" VALUE="   <<   ">
                        <INPUT TYPE="Submit" NAME="PagingMove" VALUE="   <    ">
                        <INPUT TYPE="Submit" NAME="PagingMove" VALUE="    >   ">
                        <INPUT TYPE="Submit" NAME="PagingMove" VALUE="   >>   ">
                          <% If Not fHideRequery Then %>
                              <INPUT TYPE="Submit" NAME="PagingMove" VALUE="
Requery ">
                          <% End If %>
                          <INPUT TYPE="Hidden" NAME="PagingRequest" VALUE="<%=
tHeaderName%>">
                    </FORM>
                    </P>
                </TD>
                <TD VALIGN=MIDDLE ALIGN=RIGHT>
                    <FONT SIZE=2>
                    <% If Not fHideNumber Then
                        If tPageSize > 1 Then
                            Response.Write("<NOBR>Page: " &
```

```
Session(tHeaderName & "AbsolutePage") & "</NOBR>")
                                  Else
                                     Response.Write("<NOBR>Record: " &
Session(tHeaderName & "AbsolutePage") & "</NOBR>")
                                  End If
                              End If %>
                              </FONT>
                          </TD>
                      </TR>
                      </TABLE>
                  <% End If
                  fHideNavBar = False
                  fHideNumber = False
                  stQueryString = ""
              End If %>
<!--METADATA TYPE="DesignerControl" endspan-->
```

Data Forms

In addition to using database connectivity to return a series of records from a database, many Web applications require the user to modify the data residing in a particular database. To create a data form, select New and select the Data Form Wizard. Follow the steps provided by the wizard, and make sure that in the first window you have specified the appropriate database connection. After you have completed the various wizard creation steps, Visual InterDev generates three Active Server pages that contain the code necessary to perform the specified SQL interface to your database:

FORM.ASP. The Web page that allows users to view database entries and make modifications to the database, such as adding new records, deleting existing records, or modifying existing records.

ACTION.ASP. The Web page that allows users to make a change to their database.

LIST.ASP. The Web page that allows users to view a list of all records.

You can open any one of these Active Server pages to make additional modifications to its appearance or functionality, as shown in Figures 7.8 and 7.9.

Users can also use the filter feature to view only those records that have a particular feature in common.

Managing Web Projects

Visual InterDev is truly the complete Web creation and management environment. When it comes to Web application management, you will find that Visual InterDev is a distributed development tool that allows one or more developers to access a Web project running on a Web server and to make any new creations or modifications on their own workstations.

Web sites are becoming ever larger and, in many cases, require teams of developers to keep content current—and working. Visual InterDev allows you to control the permissions of all individuals who can access the files to edit them and then repost them on the Web server. Visual InterDev also supports details of developer access. For example, you may not want two different people to access the same document simultaneously for editing. If two people edit the same document and then upload their revised versions to the server, only the changes made by the second will be preserved.

Management is controlled using Visual InterDev's Source Control option. You can access this option by selecting Tools|Options and clicking on the Visual InterDev folder. Two different accesses are allowed for multiuser authoring:

Figure 7.8 In the Form Web page you can make modifications to the various entries for each record.

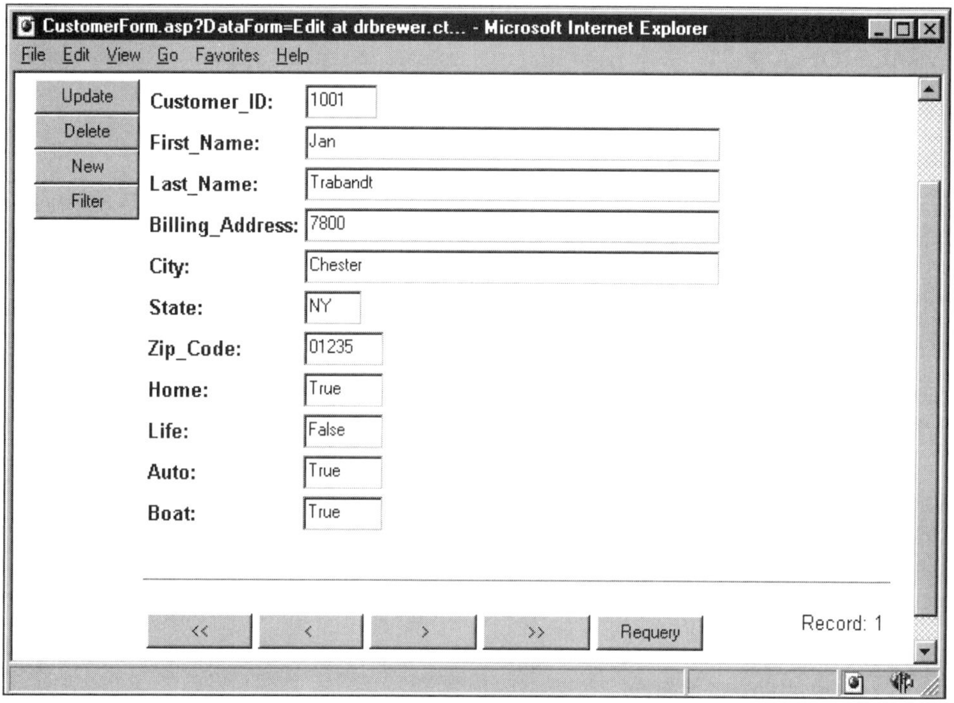

Free-for-All. Access to editing files available to anyone.

Source Controlled. The administrator can designate which developers can have access to edit the files.

Copy Web

As recommended, many organizations run several Web servers. For example, development and experimentation typically are done on one server; the commercial Web server, which should never go offline, is run on another machine. Many times you will complete a Web project on the development server, and you will need to transfer that project to the commercial server. Visual InterDev provides a Copy Web command for just that purpose:

1. Under the File menu selection, click on the project.
2. Click on the Tools menu selection, and select Copy Web.

Figure 7.9 The List Web page displays a list of all the records in a particular database.

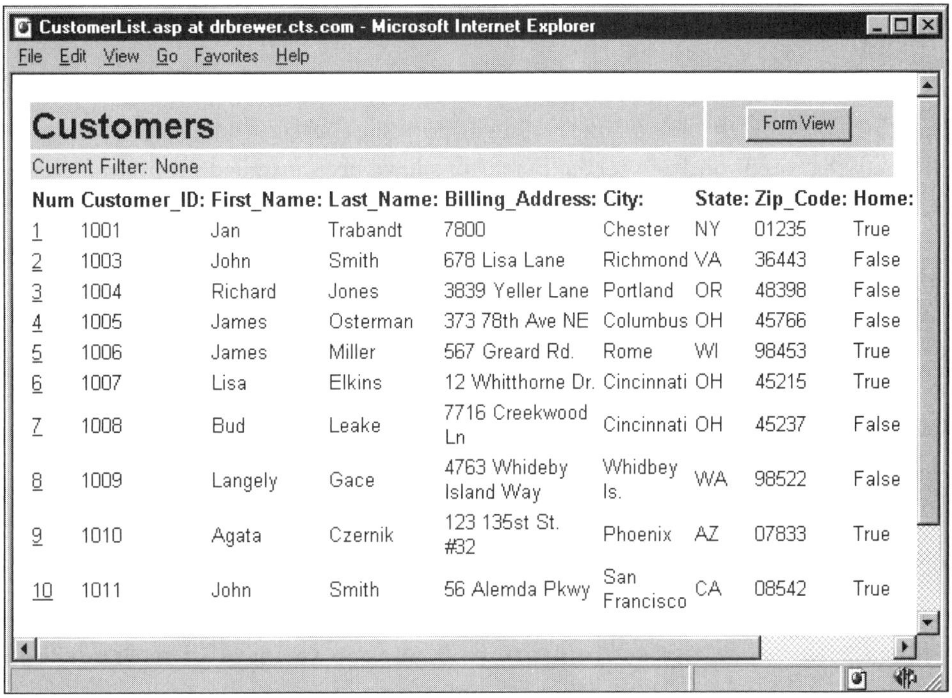

3. Indicate the name of the destination Web server and its host name, then click on the OK button.

Everything in the Web application will be copied to the new Web server. The only things that may not be the same are the security settings. The copied Web application will assume the same security settings as those set for the root directory of the Web server to which it is copied.

Problems with Visual InterDev

When you first try to create a Web project, Visual InterDev may return an error indicating that it is having difficulty contacting the specified Web server. This error often occurs because the FrontPage Server Extensions are not properly installed on your server.

You can check to see if the FrontPage Server Extensions are properly installed by running the fpsrvwin.exe program, which can be found in the \Microsoft FrontPage\bin directory. When this application runs it opens the window shown in Figure 7.10.

If the FrontPage Server Extensions were correctly installed, a port 80 should appear in the top-left dialog box. Highlight port 80, and click on the Check button to verify that the FrontPage Server Extensions have been installed properly. If this works, you should have no problem creating a Web project.

Link View

Content management on a Web site is nearly as important as content creation. With constant change in your Web site and other sites to which your site may be linked, ensuring that no links are broken is critical. Visual InterDev provides an impressive link management tool that you can activate by choosing the Tools|View Links on the WWW menu selection.

Once you select a particular host name, Visual InterDev will open a window that displays the home page and the links from it. You can view all objects linked to the

Figure 7.10 Check the configuration or choose to install the FrontPage Server Extensions if they are not installed.

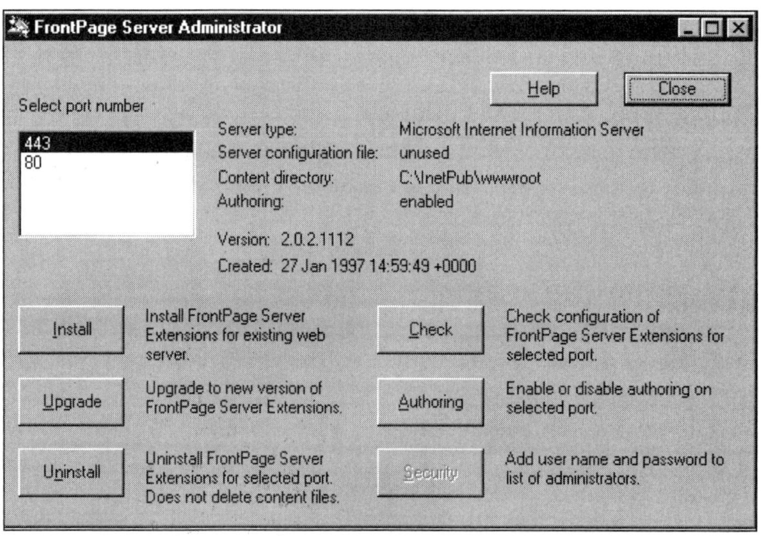

home page, including multimedia files (images and sound files), along with the Web pages, or you can choose to see just the Web pages linked to the home page.

Working on your Web page often involves modifying its contents. If you haven't modified any default settings, the window shown in Figure 7.11 appears.

You can select how you want Visual InterDev to automatically update modifications to links in your Web project by choosing the Tools|Options menu selection, and clicking on the Visual InterDev folder. In the Repair Links box, you can choose one of three options:

- Repair links in referring files
- Don't repair links in referring files
- Ask me each time

Whenever you work with a particular Web project, you may want to inspect both what it is linked and the integrity of each link. Right-click on the file in the File View folder of Visual InterDev, and select the Visual Links option. In this window, shown in Figure 7.12, the broken links are displayed with a red outline.

Multimedia Editors

Content, content, content. The key to creating interesting Web applications is the content. In a world obsessed with stunning animation effects in the movies and TV

Figure 7.11 Choose yes to update the links in the other Web pages in this particular Web project.

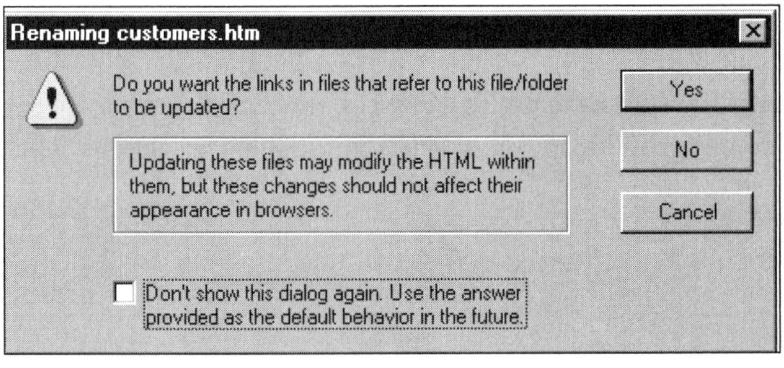

Figure 7.12 Use this window to determine which links reside in a Web page and to verify link integrity.

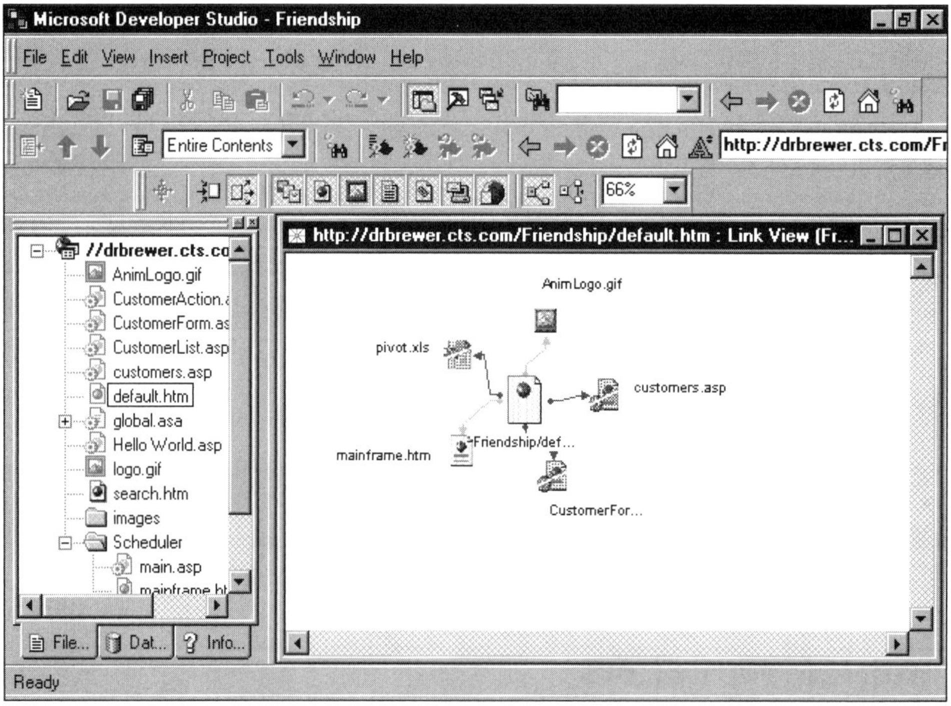

we view and the video games we play, it is clear that we are hooked on multimedia. If you can't make something dynamic and eye-catching, you probably won't keep users' attention more than 20 seconds.

The Web has not escaped the requirement to captivate. In fact, the Web revolution began with the simple integration of images with text. Web content has since blossomed into streaming audio, animation, and video. Web developers must now make an effort to produce stunning content.

To assist in this chore, Microsoft has developed several multimedia editors to create and manage the content you incorporate within your Web applications. This assortment includes the following:

- Image Composer
- Music Producer

- Media Manager

Using these editors allows you to create stunning multimedia content that you can integrate into applications deployed on the Microsoft Active Platform.

Image Composer

The frenzy over the Internet had its humble beginnings with the simple combination of images with text. Although streaming video and audio Internet content seem to get the most press today, almost everyone recognizes the importance of image content in a Web page. Most developers are familiar with several of the image editor programs currently available, including the popular Paint Shop Pro shareware program. To produce impressive content requires an image editor program that allows you to modify and work with content that comes from a variety of sources:

- Digital photographs
- Scanned images
- Screen captures

Image Composer is the Cadillac of image editors—it allows you to do everything from applying different art effects to an image to modifying the transparency of the background surrounding an image. Any developer who has searched the Web for hours looking for just the right image will also greatly appreciate the images bundled with Image Composer:

- More than 700 royalty-free images
- More than 500 tools

The 700 sample sprites consist of two different types of content:

- Photos (223 MB needed)
- Web art (17 MB needed)

When you install the Image Composer, you may want to leave the sample images on the CD, rather than install them on your computer system due to their space requirement (240 MB).

Image Composer, compatible with Office 97, allows you to cut, copy, and paste images easily from Image Composer to any of the other Office 97 applications, or vice versa. Figure 7.13 illustrates the window that appears when you first run the Image Composer.

Within Image Composer you deal with images as *sprites*. A sprite refers to any image object that has both shape and transparency attributes. A sprite consists of the actual image itself, along with the bounding box that contains it. The 700 sample sprites that come with Image Composer have the .MIC file extension, the standard file format for Image Composer. When you select a particular sprite to include in your Web page, you can user the Image Composer to convert the image to a .JPG or .GIF file format.

The position of a sprite in your composition depends on both where you place it and when you place it. When you place more than one sprite on a composition, they create a stack. The stack of sprites has a three-dimensional representation. The X and Y dimensions are determined by the width and height of the various sprites

Figure 7.13 Use Image Composer to create and edit the images you place within your Web applications.

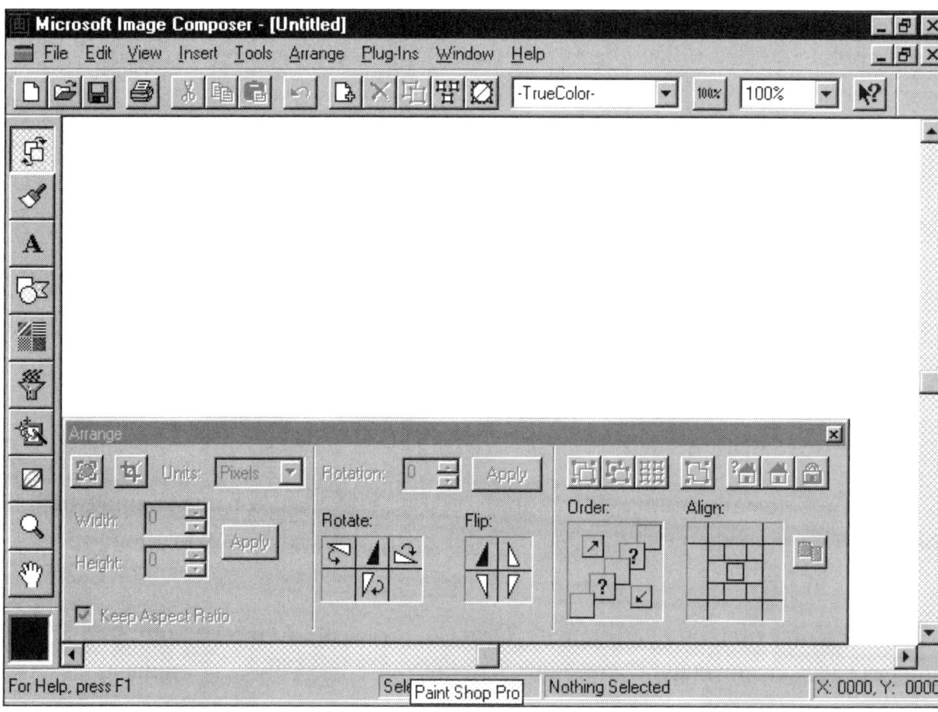

in a composition; the Z dimension for a particular sprite depends on when it was placed on the composition. For example, when you place three different sprites on a composition, the first sprite placed in the composition appears closest to the viewer and, therefore, would overlap both the second and third sprites placed in the composition.

Whenever you add a new sprite it is added to the top of the stack. You can cycle through the stack of sprites by pressing the Tab key. Of course, once you place several sprites in a composition you do not have to maintain their particular order in the stack; Image Composer allows you to modify the order of the sprites in the stack.

Music Producer

Multimedia is here today—and here to stay. Nearly all the desktop computer systems sold today include a sound card and speaker system. Some systems include Intel's MMX Pentium chip for multimedia. Today's computer user expects to be informed and entertained with both visual information and audio information.

Although most developers are probably familiar with the numerous image applications, relatively few have worked with audio, much less created and deployed it within their Web applications. To assist in this task, Microsoft has created Music Producer, which allows you to create musical compositions to include in your Web applications. You can design your musical compositions based on five elements:

- Style
- Personality
- Instrument
- Key
- Tempo

Once you have created a composition you like, you can save it as a MIDI file (.MID) and insert it in one of your Web pages.

Media Manager

Media Manager allows you to manage all types of multimedia files that you may include in your Web applications. Here are just some of its useful features:

- Periodically indexes the properties of a collection of various content files
- Plays multimedia files such as sound .WAV files and video .AVI files
- Searches specific files
- Offers thumbnail previews of images

Before you use Media Manager, create a Media Manager root folder where you will place all the other files that you want to manage. When you create other files in the Media Manager root directory, they will appear as metal briefcase icons, rather than as the common folder icon used for directories in the Windows Explorer window. You will find that this application provides a useful way to manage the multimedia content you integrate into your various Web applications.

Conclusion

This chapter has introduced you to the basics of the Visual InterDev development environment. This environment allows you to leverage all the capabilities of the Active Platform and design both client-side and server-side components of your Web applications. Chapters 8 and 9 will go into further detail to instruct you on how to fully utilize Active Server Pages and Active Server Components within your Web applications. After you have spent some time using Visual InterDev, you will probably choose to use nothing else to design and develop your Web applications. Visual InterDev is simply the best. For once, Microsoft created a great application the first time, rather than the third.

Chapter

8

Active Server Pages

Technologies such as ActiveX controls and Active Desktop have been created to provide a robust user experience, but most organizations need advanced solutions for their servers as well. To address the need for advanced Web-based solutions on the server, Microsoft has introduced Active Server Page (ASPs) and Active Server Components (ASCs). ASP makes server-side programming a reality, and ASC can be used by ASP for both local server and distributed object support.

Organizations deploying any type of Web solutions using the Microsoft Internet Information Server (IIS) will quickly reach the limits of static server solutions. The ASP and ASC technologies fill this critical gap with a solid and robust implementation. Based on Windows NT, whose scalability and reliability are making great strides in the mission-critical enterprise market, ASP and ASC help a designer to create enterprise solutions in a fraction of the time previously required.

Cornerstone of Active Platform

Active Server Page (ASPs) turn your ordinary Web server (either Internet Information Server or Personal Web Server) into a server that can dynamically generate HTML files. ASP allows you to provide customized information to different users based on the specific requests of a particular browser or client. Here are just some of the server's capabilities when it employs ASP:

- Generate an HTML page from a database query
- Test the type or features of the browser used to access a page; dynamically modify HTML content accordingly
- Test conditions including passwords or any user-entered information
- Allow complete database access including retrieval, insertion, deletion, and record updates
- Access server-side components including ASC, ActiveX controls, or complete OLE-enabled applications
- Execute script code in VBScript, JavaScript, or third-party scripting languages such as PerlScript

For critical deployment, the Active Server platform requires the power of Windows NT and Microsoft Internet Information Server. ASP is featured in all versions after IIS 3.0, and it allows for server-side construction of HTML content. The technology is available for Personal Web Server, but we do not recommend this server for anything but the simplest solutions or core development work.

How It Works

The first step to understanding how ASP works is to forget everything you know about conventional Web-based client/server systems. Figure 8.1 illustrates the basic operation of a Web server when an ASP file has been requested from a browser such as Internet Explorer or Netscape Navigator. When the browser first requests the page, the .ASP file is requested from the server. The .ASP file extension tells the server that this file needs to be interpreted by the Active Server engine before anything is sent to the client.

Figure 8.1 Basic ASP document processing.

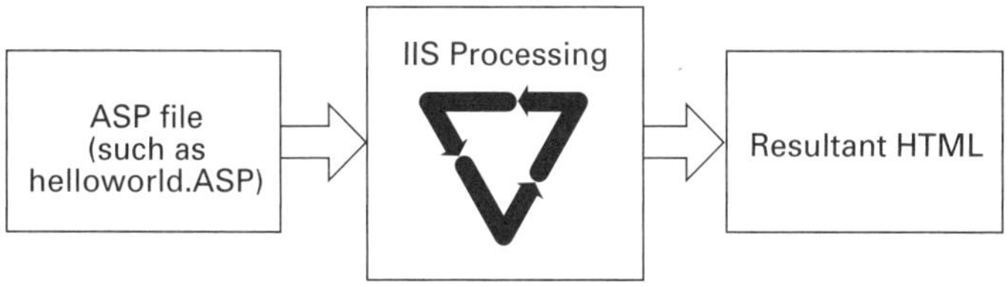

The original file request for an .ASP file type sets off a chain of processes. On the server, the file is sent through the Active Server Page processor, which has already been installed either in the Internet Information Server or the Personal Web Server. The ASP processor outputs a static HTML file, which is then sent to the browser. The Web browser never actually sees the contents of the ASP file, only the resultant output from the processed ASP.

Of course, all the processing that occurs on the server can be quite complicated. Figure 8.2 shows an overview of how the process actually occurs. The Active Server processor is actually an ISAPI filter installed on the Web server. Any file with the .ASP extension that is requested by the Web server is intercepted by this Active Server ISAPI filter. It is then processed, executing any script contained within the ASP file. The script engine may also have compatible script processors installed. By default, processors for both VBScript and JScript, Microsoft's version of JavaScript, are also included.

The script engines can execute any commands contained within their code and can connect to any ASC (described in detail in Chapter 9). For example, database access occurs through the Active Data Object component, which retrieves or manipulates information from the database file or database server through an ODBC driver. The scripting engine can also be used to activate distributed data objects, which are components located on other computers across the network or the wide area network.

Advantages of ASP

Several difficulties have plagued the creation of real Web solutions for businesses and organizations:

Figure 8.2 Overview of ASP.

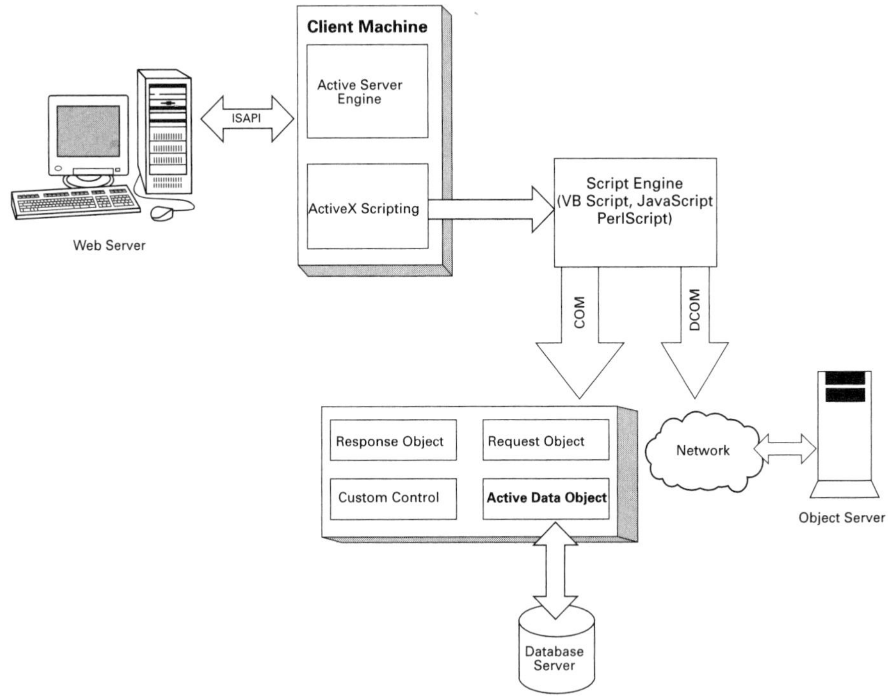

- Limited browser capabilities
- Administration problems with proliferating Web pages
- Centralized control of data access

By providing programmatic control on the Web server, ASP allows system administrators to solve these problems. ASP's inherent structure also permits allocation and control of the environment and necessary resources.

Other technologies, such as Allaire System's Cold Fusion, have provided partial solutions by allowing some server-side logical functions and generalized database access. These solutions, however, often lacked the complete scripting capabilities of server-side components. ASP remedies these shortcomings and also supports the VBScript scripting language that is already familiar to millions of Visual Basic programmers. The advantages of using ASP can be neatly broken down into a Top 10 list.

Top 10 Reasons to Use ASP

1. Client- (browser-) independent Web content (if desired)
2. Database connectivity
3. Centralized administrative control for data server and security
4. Server-side logic capabilities using VBScript or JavaScript
5. Active Server Component access for both local and distributed object usage
6. Content adjustment based on browser type
7. Server-side access to cookies stored on the client
8. Integration with Microsoft Access or SQL Server
9. Server tracking of user sessions
10. Server-side execution of Java components

The core pieces of the Active Server provide a script-hosting engine, which allows any script language to be used and gives the scripting code access to objects. These two factors make the Active Server Platform infinitely expandable and allow you to exploit numerous advantages.

Client Independence

When the World Wide Web began its dramatic growth, the HTML standard that defined what a browser would display became more of a foundation document than a realistic example of what could be done with a Web browser. The explosion of Web-enabled applications and technologies, which range from client-side Java processing to ActiveX installation, has left the HTML standards committee unable to keep up with innovation.

Even accepted standards, such as the <TABLE> tags supported by many browsers, did not make it into the HTML specification until long after their widespread adoption. This delay left numerous features that would have enhanced the Web experience almost unused. After all, Web designers seek to reach the widest possible audience in their target markets. The wide diversity in browser capabilities made it uncertain whether a majority of users visiting a Web site could take advantage of any HTML tags not included in the HTML standard. Those users who lacked a particular feature or used an older version of a browser were unable to view part of the Web site, and visitors who could not use a site effectively left.

The solution to this problem is simple: Include advanced processing on the server. Now the server can provide data access, form submission error-checking, and other advanced services without the client's needing to support any special tags. Because the content can be actively generated on the server, even more complete solutions can be built by checking the client browser for functionality and automatically conforming to its capabilities. With this technology in place, Web developers don't have to fear that users who lack browsers supporting advanced capabilities will not be able to experience the content they create.

Before ASP, the solutions available for server Web processing were fairly meager. Server-side processing through the use of CGIs (Common Gateway Interfaces) or Perl scripts tended to be difficult to use, processor- or resource-intensive, and uneven in their capabilities. Because most Web serving originated on the Unix platform, most of these tools were ported to the Windows platform in very rough and rudimentary form. Despite these problems, however, server-side control did allow a great deal of security and data access capability that would be very difficult to achieve on the client.

ASP is a technology that finally enables content creation that is browser-independent. Dynamically creating HTML files gives all the power of a robust server-side processing engine to any browser. If the browser is extremely simple, pure HTML code can be generated. A more powerful browser, one that can accept Java, client-side JavaScript, or VBScript, will see content that can include these features. By using the ASP file to perform preprocessing on the server, the resultant HTML pages can be made independent of the client browser.

Centralized Administrative Control

As Web site construction and the return on investment (ROI) provided by the Internet and intranets have grown, data centralization has become an increasing problem. The ease with which Web sites can be set up and HTML pages posted has helped content to flourish. A good deal of this data is retrieved from databases and output as simple HTML files. All types of documents have been placed on Web servers, ranging from personal Web sites to secure sales information and interoffice memoranda.

Just as distribution of data has become decentralized, the collection of data has also become haphazard. The HTML standard included the ability to create forms. The easiest way to submit information included in a form was not to write the information into a proper database, but to encapsulate it within an e-mail message. This approach caused the proliferation of ad hoc systems. Until now, there has been no effective solution to this problem because even a simple CGI solution was expensive to implement and required sophisticated programming skills.

Traditionally, all the data dispersed and received funneled through custom-designed programs using the client/server model. These systems consisted of a client program installed on each individual machine, communicating with a central server. Although such solutions provided all the user interface elements and security needed for entering, retrieving, or manipulating data, they also required professional construction and expensive distribution.

Client/server systems require a separate client application to be installed on each machine. All subsequent updates must also be installed on every machine. Updating can be extremely time-consuming and costly, especially in large organizations. Most data entry and access applications do not require the rich user environment that a separate client application provides.

An HTML file can be created by nearly anyone with a little coding knowledge and a Web site development application like FrontPage or a text editor like Notepad. Even though client/server applications are indispensable for mission-critical, interface-rich programs, many solutions require quick and cheap construction and instant distribution.

Using ASP, you can create an application on the Web server. You can then use any Web browser to access the corporate applications on the server with nothing other than a browser installed on the client machine. To update the application, only the central page on the Web server must be updated; any browser that subsequently accesses that page will instantly see the new application.

Before ASP, many Web providers used utilities that created a series of formatted Web pages containing all the information stored in the database. For example,

Access 97 can output all report data as HTML files, which are then stored on a Web server. These pages can then be placed on any Web server and accessed by a browser.

Of course, there were several problems with this scenario. First of all, the data was not very current. It was output into static HTML pages; therefore, frequent manual updates were required to keep the pages current. This process was tedious and expensive, and the data was only as current as the last update.

Far worse, the data, perhaps highly confidential information, was held in unsecured, individual HTML pages—thereby creating an administrative and security nightmare. With ASP, HTML is created on the fly, generating Web pages directly from the database as the user accesses the page and makes a request. The data displayed upon request is current.

Server-side applications also provide central administrative control. Rather than leaving the data unsecured on the Web server, it remains in the secure database. Rather than thousands of individually generated Web pages, instead there can be a single ASP file used for data access.

Database Access

Server-side database access dramatically simplifies the deployment of an application because the client does not access the server data directly, but rather through the application located on the server. In this situation, data connections can be easily maintained because the connection is invisible to the client machines. If the data source were changed in a client/server solution, each client program would have to be redirected to point at the new data source.

Client/server solutions also have a hard time keeping data current. Many client applications download data, and data that remains on the client gets older: Data currency is impaired. By the time the client application sends an update of the information to the server, the data records on the server may have been changed by other users. Retaining all the data on the server and providing access through an ASP ensure consistent data.

Object Access

With previous server-side tools, implementing objects was nearly impossible. Without object relations, server solutions were limited to using the equivalent of

10-year-old technology without the benefits of modern component solution creation. Object access for all key information access is the basis of ASP.

The ability to create self-contained, reusable components has been the goal of the development community for decades. The success of the Visual Basic development environment and the explosion of a commercially viable market for Visual Basic components have finally brought this dream to fruition. A developer can now purchase a component or control that has the functionality needed and simply plug it into the application being developed.

Now, ASP allows controls known as ActiveX controls to be used by the Web server. ActiveX controls have been shown for use by a client program, but these same controls can also be used on the server to enhance the Web pages being generated. How to effectively use these server-side components, called Active Server Components, will be covered in great depth in the next chapter. For now, it is important to understand that these controls can be accessed and used on the server through ASP.

ASP is even more powerful than traditional object systems. Using distributed computing technology such as Distribute Component Object Model (DCOM), ASP can manipulate objects located across a local or a wide area network. Distributed computing uses objects or components that are self-contained pieces of code and information that can be located anywhere. This approach allows particular processing tasks to be performed where they arise or by deploying objects to resources that can best cope with the task at hand.

Installation

Now that you have some appreciation for ASP's capabilities and features, it is time to begin creating your own dynamic applications. You need to install several components on your machine before you can begin ASP development. ASP is available for both the Microsoft Internet Information Server, version 2.0 or later, and the Personal Web Server. IIS 2.0 requires the IIS 3.0 upgrade kit to use the ASP capabilities; IIS 3.0 and above include the Active Server extensions pre-installed and enabled. IIS also requires Windows NT.

To use the Personal Web Server, you must install the Active Server extension. Once these applications are installed, you can begin your ASP development. The one disadvantage of the Personal Web Server is its lack of compatibility with the

Visual InterDev advanced loading and versioning features. The FrontPage extensions that provide Visual InterDev with site maintenance and automatic site update features are not available for Personal Web Server. Therefore, if you need to use Visual InterDev for team development or site maintenance, you must use the IIS.

When you begin creating your own ASP files, make sure that the folder in which you place the ASP files has Execute capabilities. The Execute property is available in both IIS and PWS when you set security for individual folders. If Execute privileges are not present or if ASP is not installed on the Web server, the server will most likely send the ASP file untouched to the client browser. This possibility is a definite security concern because ASP files may contain user name, password, and other database information. Make sure to deploy ASP solutions with care.

Example of an Active Server Page

The best way to understand ASP files is to construct one; simply put, learning is doing. To create your first ASP file, you need either Visual InterDev or the Notepad application. Even though the use of Visual InterDev is essential for any large-scale project and its wizards will save a great deal of time, ASPs can be constructed using any text editor.

Let's begin your journey into the world of ASPs with a simple "Hello World" file. Enter the following code either in Notepad or using Visual InterDev.

```
<HTML>

<BODY>

<% For i = 1 To 5 %>

Hello World!<P>

<% Next %>

</BODY>

</HTML>
```

Now save this file as helloworld.asp in a directory on your Web server. All ASPs must have the ASP file name extension. It is important to remember that when you save a file in Notepad, the program by default adds the TXT extension— even if you include another extension, such as ASP, in your file name, unless you change the Save As Type combo box during a save. If you select the All Files option instead of the default Text Documents, the file will save with the extension you included in the file name box.

Once you have saved your page, you will need a Web browser to test it. If you are using Visual InterDev, you can view the results within the InterDev environment. When you open your helloworld.asp file in a Web browser, you should see five "Hello World!" strings on the screen (with a URL such as "http://cdnet/ASPExample/helloworld.asp"). Most important, you can open this file in any browser! Because the processing is done on the server, the browser can be anything from the simplest text-based browser to the latest version of Internet Explorer or Netscape Navigator.

Remember, you cannot open this file using the standard file-based browsing available in either Netscape Navigator or Internet Explorer. Using an option such as Netscape's Open File in Browser effectively bypasses any server processing, and the Active Server engine never has a chance to parse the ASP file.

The HelloWorld ASP page uses VBScript to create a loop that writes the five strings into the final HTML file. The first line of the body text begins with a <% %> clause. The brackets enclose code to be processed by the ASP scripting engine. In this case, it's a For...Next loop that increments the variable from 1 to 5. The next line in the code is standard HTML, but it occurs within the loop. Therefore, every time the loop cycles as it is processed by the ASP, this text is added to the static HTML file that is sent to the client browser.

The final script line, *Next*, completes the loop. When the Web server processes this ASP file, the browser is actually sent the following HTML source code:

```
<HTML>

<BODY>

 Hello World!<P>

 Hello World!<P>

 Hello World!<P>

 Hello World!<P>
```

```
Hello World!<P>

</BODY>

</HTML>
```

Notice that none of the script is included, only the HTML constructed from the code. The client browser will never see the script code that executes on the server. All scripting is processed out of the ASP file before the HTML is sent over the Web.

The "Hello World" example shows how the script is processed and even demonstrates how additional HTML is inserted, but it does not demonstrate how variables are added to appear in the resultant HTML. Change one line of code to insert the variable that contains the current number of the loop into the Web page so that it appears as follows:

```
Hello World! <% = i %><P>
```

Now reload or refresh the page in your browser. All five of your "Hello World!" strings should be followed by a number that is the value of the variable *i* through each cycle of the loop. This is one example that illustrates how loop structures can be used to generate any HTML source code. To create truly useful applications, your ASP solutions will most certainly need to access external data.

Creating a Simple Database Query

Although the "Hello World" example introduces you to the basic concepts of using scripts within an ASP file, most of the power of ASP lies in its ability to access database information. ASP allows data to be easily read and displayed from any common ODBC data source, ranging from Access databases to Excel files to ordinary text files.

In this example, you will create a page that allows users to be added to an e-mail list that will be stored in Microsoft Access 97. Users can then query the data after several simple examples have been recorded:

1. Open Microsoft Access, and create a new database named *email.mdb*. Within the database, create a table titled *emailtable*. This table will store all the information about users who wish to be added to the list.

2. Now add the fields shown in Table 8.1.

Table 8.1 Data for Creating a Table Named *emailtable* in Microsoft Access

Field	Type	Size	Description
uniqueid	AutoNumber	Long Integer	Unique record id
catid	Number	Long Integer	Category of stored e-mail
email	Text	50	E-mail address
computertype	Text	15	Type of computer
comments	Text	255	Comments from the user
browsertype	Text	20	Type of browser
version	Number	Double	Version number of browser
versionmajor	Number	Long Integer	Major version number # of browser
versionminor	Number	Long Integer	Minor version number # of browser
frames	Yes/No		Does client support frames?
tables	Yes/No		Does client support tables?
cookies	Yes/No		Does client support cookies?
bgrndsounds	Yes/No		Does client support background sound?
Vbscript	Yes/No		Does client support VBScript?
javascript	Yes/No		Does client support JavaScript?

3. Once you have all these fields entered, your Access table design screen appears, as shown in Figure 8.3. Be sure to set the Allow Zero Length property of the Text fields to Yes so that if the user leaves any of the fields blank on entry, an error is not generated.

4. Now that you have a database file created, open the table and add some dummy data. Create three records, and make sure you fill the e-mail, computertype, and comments fields with recognizable values. In just a moment,

Figure 8.3 Microsoft Access display of the emailtable file.

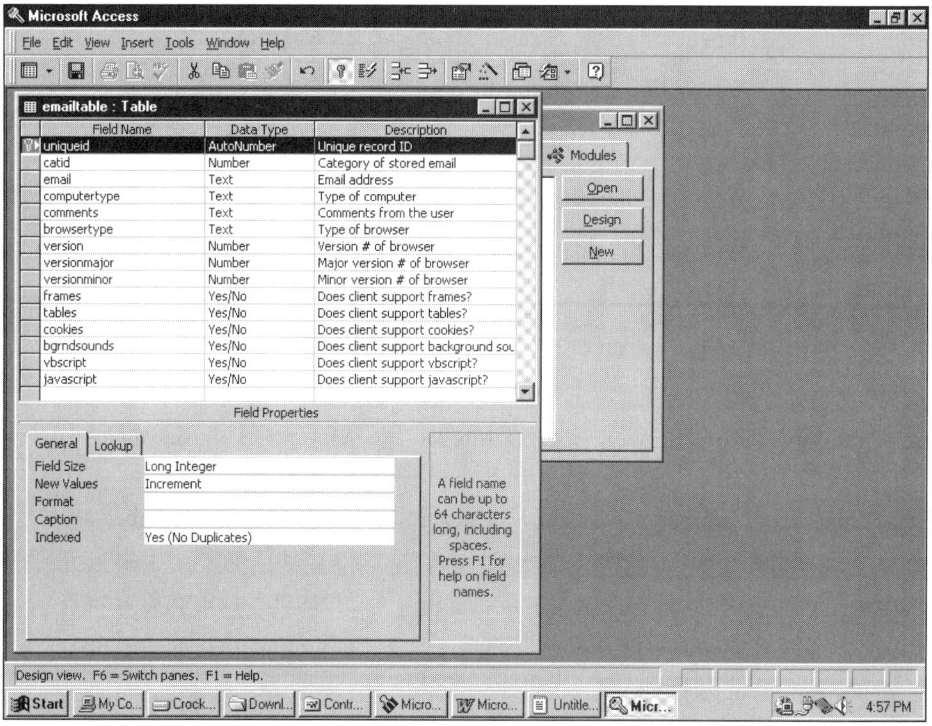

we will create an ASP file to retrieve and display this information in a table.

5. Once you've added the data, close the database file in Access. If you leave it open, the Web server will generate an error when it attempts access.

   Now you need to create an Open Database Connectivity (ODBC) connector to point at your database. As we said previously, all access between an ASP and a database occurs through the ODBC middleware layer.

6. To create a data source, open the Control Panel folder from the Settings menu on the Windows Start menu. In the Control Panel folder, you will see a control labeled 32-bit ODBC. If this control is absent from your system, go to the database you plan to use (Access or SQL Server) and execute the

ODBC Setup program. Once ODBC is installed, you will be able to create data sources on the machine.

7. Double-click the 32-bit ODBC control to show the main dialog. Select the FileDSN tab and click on the **Add** button. A FileDSN is a new type of data source that can be contained entirely within a file. Older ODBC implementations required that the ODBC connections be configured separately on each machine. A FileDSN contains all the important properties of a DSN, so it may be installed quickly and easily to separate machines or shared by a team.

8. Select the Microsoft Access Driver from the list, and click the Next button. Type the name of the data source as *emailODBC*, and click the Finish button. Now you have a database that contains some data and a data source to reach that table.

9. All you need now is the ASP code to display the list of information. Type in the following code:

```
<HTML>

<HEAD>

<TITLE>Sample Query</TITLE>

</HEAD>

<BODY>

<H2>Show the data held in table: emailtable</H2>

<%

' Create an ADO object

Set Conn = Server.CreateObject("ADODB.Connection")

' Connect to the emailODBC data source

Conn.Open "emailODBC"

' Select all of the fields and records from the table
```

```
sql="SELECT * FROM emailtable"
' Execute the query
Set EM = Conn.Execute(sql)
' Set a variable to count the number of records
mycount = 0
%>
Here are the results from the query: <I><B> <%=sql%></I></B>
<P>
<P>
<TABLE BORDER=1>
   <TR>      <TD><B>Email Address</B></TD>
      <TD><B>Computer Type</B></TD>
      <TD><B>Comments</B></TD>
   </TR>
<% Do While not EM.eof%>
        <TR>
      <TD><% = EM("email") %></TD>
      <TD><% = EM("computertype") %></TD>
<TD><% = EM("comments") %></TD>
   </TR>
      <%
   ' Move to next record and increment variable
   EM.MoveNext
```

```
   mycount = mycount + 1
Loop
' Finished with loop, close data sources
EM.close
Conn.close
%>
</TABLE>
<P>Number of records in table: <% =mycount %>
<P>
</BODY>
</HTML>
```

10. Once you have entered the code, save the file as *query.asp*. Store this ASP file on your server so that it can be accessed. The ASP code actually creates an Active Data Object, which is the control used for database access. A query in the SQL language (see the section "SQL Overview" later in the chapter) is used to retrieve all the records from the database.

11. Each row contains three columns of data. You can see within the <TD> tags the command EM("fieldname") where the *fieldname* parameter returns the data contained in the specified field. Each column is used to display a different data field stored in our emailtable.

12. Open your browser now, and execute the ASP. You should see a three-column table showing your data. It is that simple. Your browser should appear like the one shown in Figure 8.4. Notice that the final line shows the total number of records displayed. At the beginning of the ASP, a variable named *mycount* was set to zero. Every cycle through the record loop increments this value, resulting in the total number of records.

Figure 8.4 Netscape Navigator displaying data in e-mail list.

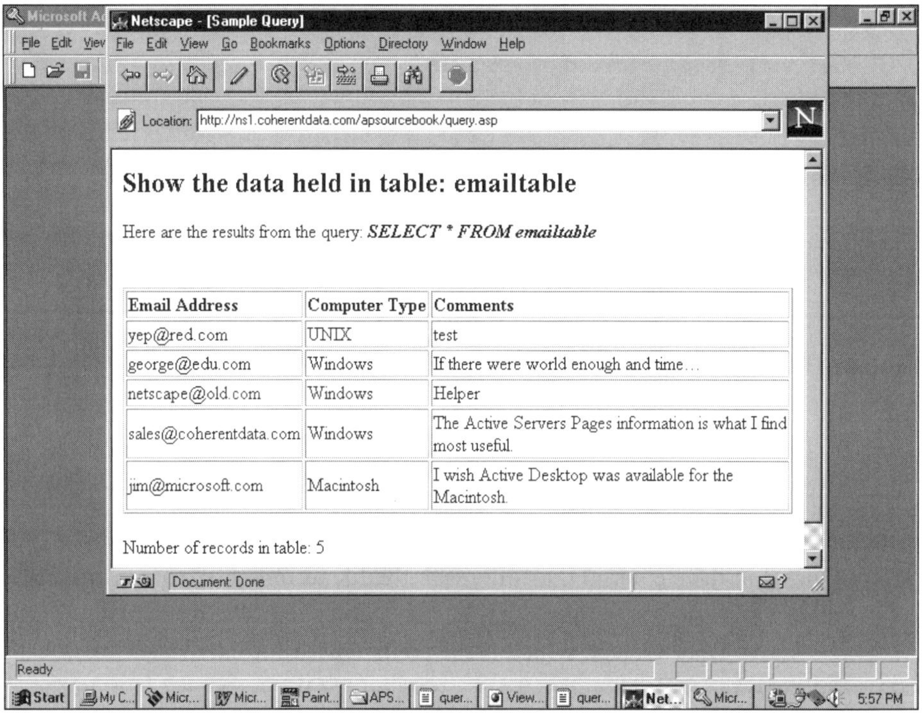

Creating an E-mail Address Storage

Web sites often have numerous visitors but no way to track who they are. For an organization, this can mean missing potential customers. For a personal Web site, getting the e-mail addresses of visitors allows you to compile a list of people with similar interests. A common application required of server-side technology is the storage of data entered into an HTML form in a database.

ASP lets you easily create a form for data entry and storage. The next example could easily be modified to ask for a mailing address for addition to a newsletter mail list, for example. This example uses ActiveX Data Objects to write the incoming data into the Access database we've just created. You will create three separate files:

> **emailAdd.ASP.** The emailAdd file presents the user with a data form for entry of information.

emailDone.ASP. When the form is submitted, the emailDone ASP is executed. The emailDone file is the code that actually inserts the data into the Access database.

emailList.ASP. The file emailList is used to view a list of all the records entered into the database. Different from the query.ASP that you previously created, this file buffers 50 records at a time for display. It demonstrates a solution if the number of records is very large. Rather than waiting for each set of data to be loaded, the records can be buffered in specific intervals.

1. To create this application, start a new ASP file in Visual InterDev or Notepad, and enter the code below:

```
<HTML>

<HEAD><TITLE>Email List Addition</TITLE></HEAD>

<BODY>

<H3>Add yourself to the email list</H3>


<%

On Error Resume Next


   ' This part of the script allows a person

   ' to enter data on an HTML form.

%>


<P>Please enter your email address to be added to our mail list.

<FORM METHOD=POST ACTION="emaildone.asp">


       <P>Email address (i.e. myemail@mycorp.com) :

        <INPUT TYPE=TEXT SIZE=50 MAXLENGTH=50 NAME="name"><BR>
```

```
        <P>Computer you're using:
        <SELECT NAME="computertype" MULTIPLE SIZE=3>
        <OPTION SELECTED> Windows
        <OPTION> Macintosh
        <OPTION> UNIX
        </SELECT>

        <P>Comments:
        <TEXTAREA NAME="comments" ROWS=5 COLS=35></TEXTAREA><BR>

        <P><INPUT TYPE=SUBMIT VALUE="Add me to the email list"><INPUT
TYPE=RESET VALUE="Reset Form">
        </FORM>
<P>
<A HREF="default.htm">Return to home page</A>

</BODY>
</HTML>
```

2. Save this file as emailAdd.ASP. When the user enters the information into the form and clicks the Submit button, the data is taken from the form and inserted into the table. You can see that the name parameter given to each field (name, computertype, and comments) will store the information entered in these fields. These parameters will be passed, using these names, through the Request object to the next ASP file.

3. Now create the new file that will be named emailDone.ASP. In this file, you will use the SQL *Insert* command to write the data to the table. This application writes more than just the data supplied by the user. You will also include information about the user's browser. This information is stored within the table to provide better service to the Web site's primary users.

```
<HTML>

<HTML>

<HEAD><TITLE>Email List Addition Successful</TITLE></HEAD>

<BODY>

<H3>Adding your name...</H3>

<%

       ' Create BrowserType object to retrieve & store browser info

       Set bc = Server.CreateObject("MSWC.BrowserType")

       ' Create ODBC connection to emailODBC data source

       Set Conn = Server.CreateObject("ADODB.Connection")

       Conn.Open "emailODBC"

       ' Store a SQL Insert statement to writes all data into the db

       sql = "Insert into emailtable (email,computertype,comments,browser-

type"

       sql = sql + ",version,versionmajor,versionminor,frames,tables,cook-

ies,bgrndsounds,VBScript,JavaScript) VALUES ("

       ' First store fields user provided

       sql = sql + "'" & Request.Form("name") & "'"

       sql = sql + ",'" & Request.Form("computertype") & "','" &

Request.Form("comments") & "'"
```

```
        ' Now store browser info about user
        sql = sql + ",'" & bc.Browser & "'," & bc.Version  & ""
        sql = sql + "," & bc.Majorver & "," & bc.Minorver & ""
        sql = sql + "," & CBool(bc.Frames) & "," & CBool(bc.Tables) & ""
        sql = sql + "," & bc.cookies  & "," & bc.BackgroundSounds & ""
        sql = sql + "," & bc.VBScript & "," & bc.Javascript & ")"
        ' Execute the Insert statement
        Set RS = Conn.Execute(sql)
%>

<H3>You've been added to the email list</H3>
<P>
        <%  If Request.Form("name") = "" Then %>
    <P>You did not provide your email address.
        <%  Else %>
            <P>Your email address is <B><%= Request.Form("name") %></B>
            <%  End If %>

            <%  If Request.Form("computertype").Count = 0 Then %>
    <P>You did not select a computer type.
        <%  Else %>
    <P>The computer you use is: <B><%= Request.Form("computertype") %></B>

    <%  If Request.Form("comments") = "" Then %>
```

```
  <P>You did not enter any comments.
  <%  Else %>
     <P>Your comments are:
     <B><I><%= Request.Form("comments") %></B></I>
   <%  End If %>
      <%  End If %>
<P>
<A HREF="default.htm">Return to home page</A>



</BODY>
</HTML>
```

4. Save this code as emailDone.ASP. After the data is written to the database, the user is shown a page with the information that he or she had entered.
5. Building on the previous example, you can create a page that displays all the data gathered by this form. The previous query example displayed only the first three fields contained in the table, displaying every value. This new file displays all the fields, but only 50 records at a time. This way the user does not wait for a large HTML page to be constructed with all the available entries. Enter the code below and save it as emailList.asp:

```
<HTML>
<HEAD>
<TITLE>Email List</TITLE>
</HEAD>
<BODY>
<H2>All of the email addresses added to the list</H2>
```

```
<%

' Create connection to the emailtable through ODBC

Set Conn = Server.CreateObject("ADODB.Connection")

Conn.Open "EmailODBC"

' Select all of the field of the table

sql="SELECT * FROM emailtable"

Set RS = Conn.Execute(sql)

%>

Here are the results from the query:<BR><I><B> <%=sql%></I></B>

<P>

<P>

<TABLE BORDER=1>

<TR>

<%  For i = 0 to RS.Fields.Count - 1 %>

      <TD><B><%  = RS(i).Name %></B></TD>

<%  Next %>

</TR>

<P>

<%

      ' Get 50 records into the array

      eArray=RS.GetRows(50)

      RS.close

      Conn.close

%>
```

```
<%

      ' Loop through all of the loaded records

      For row = 0 to UBound(eArray,2)

%>

      <TR>


      <%   ' Loop through all of the fields

            For col = 0 to UBound(eArray,1) %>

                        <TD><%  = eArray(col,row) %>  </TD>

      <%  Next %>

      </TR>

<%  Next %>

</TABLE>

<P>

</BODY>

</HTML>
```

6. Save this code as emailList.ASP. The query.asp file displayed the specific data for three fields of the table. This code is more useful because it uses the basic record set to determine how many rows and columns to display. It then loads the information into a sample array.

This code is a better model if you assume that a great number of records will be stored in your database. If the user has to wait for all the records to be added to the HTML file, the wait time could be prohibitive. Instead, a specific number of records is retrieved at a time and stored in an array. With the addition of a simple Next button, the user is allowed to page through the data 50 records at a time.

Why Use ASP Files?

Now that you've created some ASPs and understand the fundamentals of how they are used, it is important to know that ASP is only one possible solution to server-side development. You may have heard of two other primary technologies:

- CGI applications
- ISAPI drivers

Both provide excellent environments but have some serious disadvantages when compared with ASP solutions.

Most of the development on server-side Web solutions has involved the implementation of CGI-based scripting. Because CGI won't disappear any time soon, it is important to understand the disadvantages of deploying a CGI-based site. Already mentioned is the difficulty in programming these solutions because they must be created in a complete programming environment (such as C), thereby making creating, debugging, and testing a lengthy and expensive process.

CGI programs are far more dangerous than ASP to your server system in these three areas because they are written primarily in compiled languages:

- Server performance
- Server stability
- Security

When a CGI is called, it runs in its own memory space. Therefore, if your CGI application uses 4 MB of memory when it is run, then this amount of memory must be allocated for each user who activates the particular CGI simultaneously. If 10 users activate your CGI at once, 40 MB of memory are required. The potential server performance problems are significant.

ASP are multithreaded, which means that multiple processes can run in the same service memory space. The memory savings and speed increases gained by not requiring complete load and shutdown of an application can be several orders of magnitude. These savings can preserve precious server resources and provide for a more stable system.

Worse than the performance problem is the basic stability of the application itself. Because the program is most likely written in a low-level language like C++ and therefore has access to core system functions, a malfunctioning program could crash the server. Using Active Server scripting largely protects the developer from creating a bug that can affect system services. A compiled CGI offers no such protection and could lead to erratic behavior or system faulting on your server.

Finally, the issue of security is potentially troubling. A CGI script could conceivably have access to the full range of system resources, including the memory within the server. There are few ways to protect against full server system observation by an executing CGI application. Compared with the relatively benign abilities of ASP, this security issue is a significant consideration. Servers, including Windows NT Server, are essentially designed to provide security against outside access. Placing a CGI on your server requires a great deal of trust that the CGI itself will perform only those actions for which it is intended.

ISAPI drivers have many drawbacks in common with CGI applications. They do not suffer the performance problems because they can be designed to be multithreaded, but they can very easily crash the server system or breach server security. Actually, ASP is an ISAPI filter!

Microsoft designed ASP to be a safe and effective middleware between the programmer and the raw ISAPI interface. Therefore, if you need to access the server in ways not provided by the ASP system, you could construct a custom ISAPI filter to supply the needed features.

Active Server Scripting

The key to the construction of ASP is scripting. The scripting available in the ASP is an interface to a scripting engine that can allow you to use any language. At this time, however, only the three most significant scripting languages are available for ASP:

JavaScript

VBScript

PerlScript

JavaScript is a language created and owned by Netscape Communications Corporation. It is popular on the client side of Web applications because of its broad availability with every Navigator browser, but it has suffered because of Netscape's numerous and incompatible implementations. When Navigator made the transition from version 2.0 to version 3.0, a substantial amount of the JavaScript simply would not function on the newer browser.

Netscape has promoted JavaScript as a key development tool on the server by making it its core server-side language. Netscape servers feature a JavaScript compiler to create compiled applications to execute on the server. With the introduction of its new tool, Visual JavaScript, Netscape obviously intends to make JavaScript a center piece of its future strategy.

The scripting language that you choose to incorporate into your Web applications is an important consideration if your organization plans to deploy both Microsoft and Netscape servers. The code base, although not strictly compatible, could be designed for core function translation. JavaScript also resembles C/C++ in its programming construct so that programmers accustomed to the C-based environment will face a smaller learning curve moving to JavaScript than VBScript.

JavaScript is implemented in ASP through Microsoft's JScript. JScript is a JavaScript-compatible script engine that acknowledges code denoted as either JavaScript or JScript. Microsoft keeps JScript updated in its compatibility with the most current Netscape version. Be warned that Microsoft's Jscript seems to lag approximately three to six months behind the current Netscape JavaScript implementation, so make sure all the commands you need are in the released JScript version.

Perl (an acronym for Practical Extraction and Reporting Language) is a legacy scripting language from the Unix platform. Once again, if you are planning a mixed deployment of servers, this time Microsoft and Unix-based, Perl may give you the advantage of standardizing on a single scripting language. ActiveWare creates the PerlScript implementation that runs with ASP (see "Related Sources" at the end of the chapter).

The primary and default scripting language for the Active Server Platform is definitely VBScript. Most of the examples available are presented only in VBScript, largely because it provides the greatest transparency and, therefore, functionality with the Web server.

Overview of VBScript

Microsoft has focused most of ASP's capabilities on using VBScript. This decision is both a competitive one—Microsoft controls VBScript while Netscape controls JavaScript—and a strategic one—VBScript allows designers and programmers to leverage their existing knowledge. There are approximately 3 million Visual Basic programmers in the world and an uncounted number of VBA (the Visual Basic-compatible language included in the Microsoft Office applications) programmers. By providing VBScript to Web server creators, Microsoft has allowed many users to create solutions with knowledge they already have rather than by learning a new language such as JavaScript.

Microsoft is attempting to make VBScript the basic scripting language of the Internet. It is supported in the Internet Explorer browser, Outlook, and ASP. Through Outlook, Microsoft intends for VBScript to be used extensively in group-ware solutions. By positioning it as the language for intranet/Internet development, VBScript may become the dominant language for server-based information systems development.

Although Microsoft supports both the JScript and the JavaScript tags within its products, it certainly favors the JScript tag for obvious reasons. When using JavaScript in server-side scripting with Microsoft solutions, you most definitely should use the JScript tag. Although detailing the entire VBScript language is beyond the scope of this book, the next part of this chapter will provide an overview of the language for those unfamiliar with it. This guide is primarily for those who already understand Visual Basic or Visual Basic for Applications.

VBScript lacks the traditionally strong debugging features available for the Visual Basic platform. Microsoft currently features only VBScript debugging for client-side browser applications, but in the near future debuggers will most likely appear in all the VBScript development environments, particularly Visual InterDev.

List of Available Commands

VBScript is a subset of VBA, so many commands have been removed to simplify access. In VBScript, the type of a variable cannot be defined. All variable types are automatically set to variant. Some of the conversion commands are missing, such as

Val and Str. For specific data conversion, the data convert commands (such as CInt) are still available. The object construct With...EndWith is missing. For collections, the Add, Remove, Count, and Item commands are not included. Objects and database fields cannot be addressed using the exclamation (!) operator.

The Date, Time, and Timer keywords have been excluded. For error handling, only On Error Resume Next has remained. All line numbers and : operators have been removed. Basic file input and output have also been removed. ASP, however, can access files through the FileSystem object. The Mid string manipulation command is not available. All arrays must have a lower bound equal to zero.

The server-side implementation of VBScript is even somewhat more limited than traditional VBScript. Exceptions for the ASP version of VBScript include both the InputBox and the MsgBox commands. Because these commands stop execution to elicit user feedback, and because the ASP VBScript will execute on the server, these commands have no practical use.

If you are familiar with VBA, you recognize that a number of these missing keywords are essential commands. Not to worry. Most of the missing functionality can easily be implemented either by using the Active Server Components (see Chapter 9) included with IIS or by creating your own component with Visual Basic, which has the entire language dictionary.

Within the Active Server Page file, VBScript code is encapsulated between a <% and a %> tag. This convention lets the script interpreter know that the enclosed code is actually script. This script will never appear in the final HTML file with one exception: when the = operator is used. For example:

```
Hello, I'm standard HTML<P>

<% =mystr %><P>

Back to standard HTML<P>
```

When inserted into an ASP file and loaded into a browser, this code would print three lines, the middle line being the value stored in the variable mystr. You already experienced this use with the “Hello World” example and the other database samples.

Commands such as If...Else...Then and For...Next can be broken into several different code groups. In our first HelloWorld.ASP example, you saw the For command separated from the Next command by HTML text.

The IIS script processing engine uses the VBScript engine as the default scripting language. Notice in the earlier HelloWorld.ASP example that we didn't have to add a tag that determined which scripting engine would be used. If the code had been written using JavaScript, we would have needed a <SCRIPT> tag to specify a language to the engine. For example, if you wanted to use server-side JavaScript (the one included with IIS is Microsoft's version, JScript), your script tag would look like this:

```
<SCRIPT RUNAT=SERVER LANGUAGE=JSCRIPT>
```

The RUNAT attribute is used to let the IIS engine know that the Script tag is meant for it. Otherwise, this Script tag would be included in the resultant HTML for client-side execution. The LANGUAGE attribute must match the name of the requested language. Languages JScript and VBScript are included with IIS. Other language engines may be purchased and added.

The scripting language used may also be set for an entire page. For example, to allow the entire ASP file to use JavaScript, an ASP tag could be added at the top of the file that looks like this:

```
<%@ LANGUAGE=JSCRIPT %>
```

SQL Overview

Traditional programming languages such as Basic or C are not very elegant when accessing data. The reason for this shortcoming is primarily structural. These languages are known as procedural—they execute step by step, telling the computer exactly how to do something. A database language, on the other hand, is results oriented. A database programmer is not concerned with exactly how the data is retrieved, but wants to specify the data needs and let the database determine the most efficient way to retrieve that data.

The most popular database language or query language is SQL (Structured Query Language). The SQL language is handed a request for data that match certain characteristics, and the data is returned. The simplest SQL query looks like this:

```
Select * From customer
```

The *Select* statement is the command to select records from the database. The * command that follows it is a wildcard character requesting all the fields from the queried table. Instead of using the wildcard character, we could have specified particular fields for the query to return. For example:

```
Select lastname, firstname From customer
```

This query would return the values stored in those fields for all the records. To specify the table that the Select command will search, use the *From* command. As you have probably seen in Microsoft Access, any database is made up of one or more tables. Each table is used to hold a particular type of information. For example, a sales database might contain two tables, one to hold customer names and addresses and a second to record any items purchased by the customers.

Database access from ASP occurs through the Open Database Connectivity (ODBC) connector. ODBC provides a database-independent way to retrieve data. ODBC works in a way that is similar to printer drivers. A program that needs to print a drawing, for example, is designed to print to the Windows printer drivers. It can then print to any printer with an available driver for use with the Windows system.

Therefore, an application written to retrieve data from a Microsoft Access database through ODBC can also, without any change to the code, be used to retrieve data from an Informix database server. An Active Server Page that accesses data from a particular data source can be pointed at any ODBC data source and can retrieve from the new one.

ODBC uses SQL as its standard query language. Data access through an ODBC driver occurs using SQL query statements. In a later section of this chapter, we will construct a SQL query using Visual InterDev's Query Builder tool.

With only a basic *Select* statement, SQL might seem somewhat limited. There are many modifiers, however, to a standard SQL *Select* clause. The most common construct is the *Where* clause, which allows specific records to be chosen that meet particular criteria. For example, to retrieve all the Windows users from our e-mail list, you might use a *Select* statement that looks like this:

```
Select * From emailtable Where computertype ='Windows'
```

The set of records that would be returned in this data set would contain only those whose computertype field matches the value specified in the *Where* clause. The more database access that is required, the more powerful a tool the SQL language becomes in a solution provider's tool kit.

In addition to the *Select* statement used to display the information contained in the emailtable, the *Insert* statement was used to enter the data provided by the user and the browser object. You can examine the emailDone.ASP file to see how data can be inserted into a table using only SQL commands.

Using InterDev for ASP Creation

As you have already seen in Chapter 7, Visual InterDev is an extremely powerful solution for creating Active solutions. The primary focus of Visual InterDev is use with ASP and Web-based database solutions.

SQL Builder, one of the most powerful database tools in recent memory, is included with Visual InterDev. The SQL code demonstrated in the previous section can be created in SQL Builder in a drag-and-drop environment. You can build a few solutions using the built-in wizards included with every copy of Visual InterDev to illustrate how easy it is. Because development within InterDev is so simple, many supplementary tools will be available soon to allow customization for a particular task.

Visual InterDev has two labor-saving features. Even though they serve essentially the same function, they are typically used in two different areas of an application:

Wizards. A wizard is used at the beginning of a project or to add complete pieces. A wizard generally asks a series of questions and then generates one or more files, if not an entire project.

Server-side components. Server-side components, on the other hand, are used to insert code into your actual HTML or ASP file. Therefore, server-side components are used primarily to enhance your current application, while wizards can construct entire chunks of your intended solution.

Data Form Wizard

Let's begin with the most powerful wizard included with Visual InterDev. At a recent developers meeting, the speaker claimed that the Data Form Wizard actually generated about 1600 lines of ASP code. Once you look through your project, you may think that estimate is a little on the conservative side.

1. You'll need to create a new project. Make sure that you have access to either Personal Web Server or Internet Information Server. The Web server must have the FrontPage extensions installed to use the Data Form Wizard. The project will have to be connected to the Web server in order for everything to function properly. The easiest way to create a new Web project is to select the Web Project Wizard from the Projects tab. Because you already have a database created as well as an ODBC connection, you need to create just an interface for the database so that records can be viewed, added, deleted, and changed.

2. Name the project *emailProj,* and click on the OK button. The wizard will appear and request that you enter the name of your Web server. The combo box does not search the network for possible Web servers; it only presents servers that you've used in the past. If this is the first time you've used the wizard, enter the name of the server. For this example, we wanted to access our server named CROCKET, so that is what we entered in the box. Click on the Next button; the wizard connects then to the designated Web server.

3. After the wizard has established the connection and checked the site, you are given the option of creating a new Web site or using an existing one (see Figure 8.5). Click on the Finish button to accept the defaults. You now have a Web page that will be the basis of this database application. Your project should contain the basic files: the global.asa and the search.htm. All the pages created by the Data Form Wizard will be ASP files and will be added to this project.

4. Select the New option under the File menu again, but this time we want the File Wizards tab. Select the Data Form Wizard option, and enter *dfwEmail* for the file name. At this point, the wizard will begin and will present a screen asking for a database connection.

Figure 8.5 Creating a new Web site.

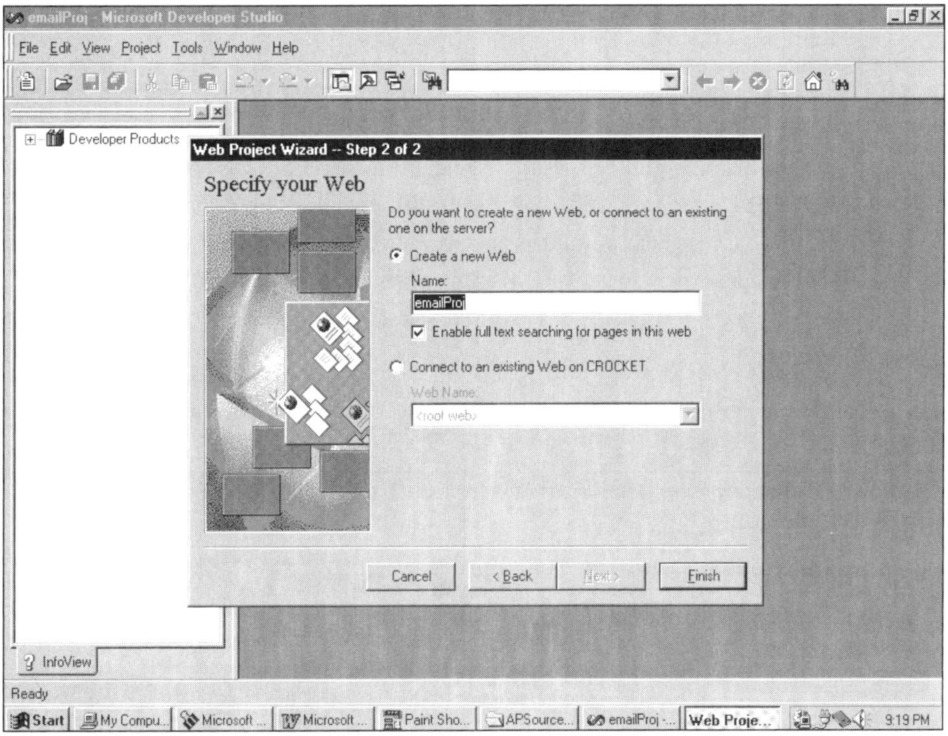

5. You've already created an ODBC data source for the e-mail database. By clicking the New button you will be allowed to select an existing data source. Select the emailODBC data source, and click the OK button. In the combo box, the word DataConn will appear, indicating the pointer to your

> **NOTE** Notice that several of the fields are already in the right box with asterisks preceding them. The asterisks identify them as required fields. Of course, the obvious question is "Why does this occur?" The fields in the right box are all Yes/No fields, also known as Boolean fields; they must contain a value. Other fields, such as Text fields, can contain a Null value to indicate that nothing has been placed within the field. Boolean fields cannot hold Null values; they must be either Yes or No (True or False). Therefore, to prevent a new data entry from attempting to save Null values to these fields, the Data Form Wizard requires that they be included on the form.

ODBC source. The title of your pages should be *Email Editor*, so enter that title in the text box. Your screen now appears like the screen shown in Figure 8.6.

6. The next step allows you to select where you want the data form to represent a Table, a View, or a SQL statement. We want to leave the default (Table), but in the future you may need to create a form from either a view or a SQL statement. A view is essentially a virtual table that uses logic on the database server to make a specific set of data within a table or multiple tables appear as if they were a single physical table. The SQL statement allows selective filtering of the data accessible on the form.

7. Click the Next button, and you will presented with the fields available for inclusion in the form. The two list boxes display the available fields (on the

Figure 8.6 Setting up the connection and the title in the first step of the Data Form Wizard.

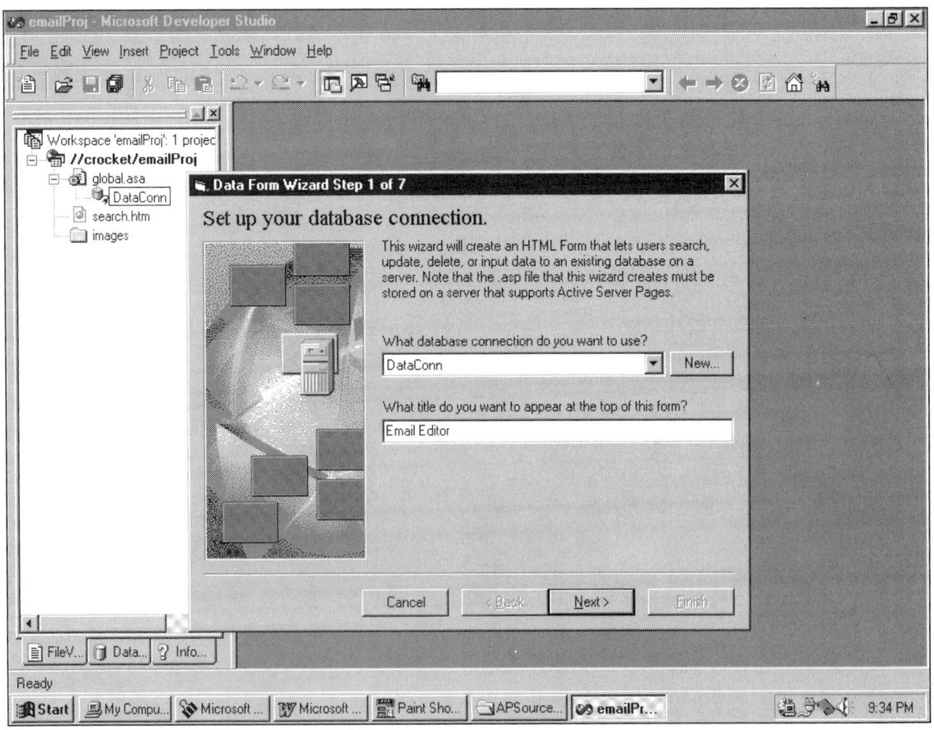

left) and the fields that will appear on the finished form (on the right). You can select the fields for display on the form one at a time and click the single arrow (>) to move to that particular field. You want all the fields, however, so clicking the double arrow (>>) will move all the fields to the right box. Click the double arrow now.

8. The order in which the fields currently appear is the order in which they will appear on the form. Therefore, use the up and down arrows that appear under the box to order the fields. We moved all the Yes/No fields to the bottom of the list so that they would appear at the bottom of the form (see Figure 8.7). You can place them in any order you wish. Click the Next button when the fields appear as you want them to appear.

Figure 8.7 All the fields are order-selected for construction on the form.

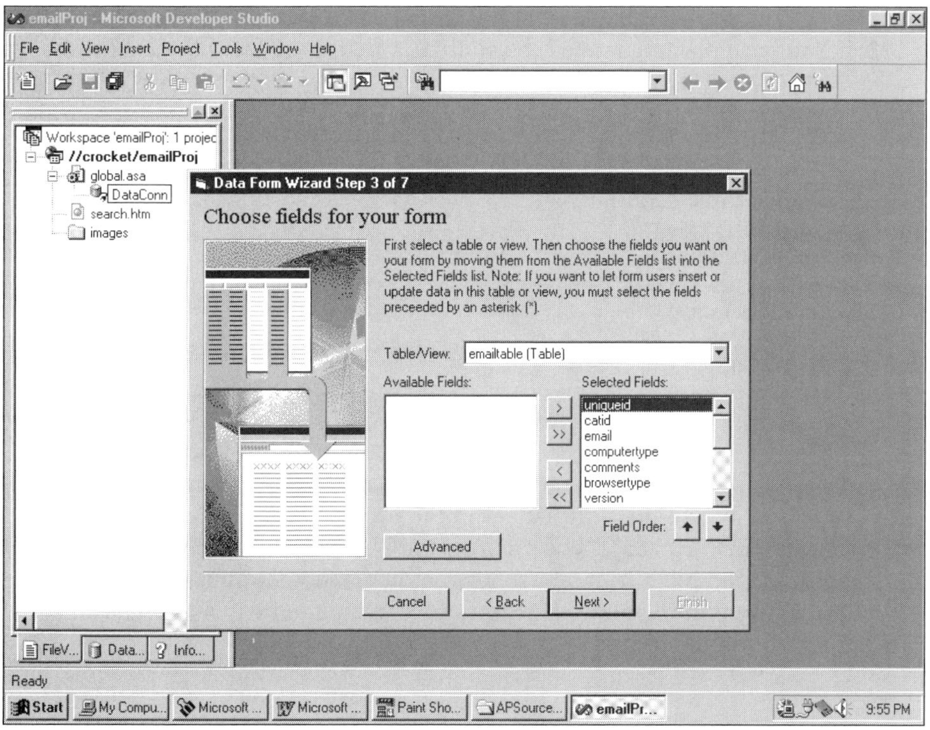

9. At this step, you can see the power of the Data Form Wizard. You can create a Web-application that allows simple database browsing, all the way to complete editing and deletion functions. You might have noticed the amount of code in the emailDone.ASP file used to add a simple database record to the table. Editing, modification, and presentation are far more complex. The Data Form Wizard provides a prototype and creates the foundation for almost any database application you'll need for an Internet/intranet solution.

10. Because you want a complete application, press the Next button to advance to the next step in the wizard. Once again, the defaults (displays in both List and Form view) are fine for this project. Click the Next button.

11. Now you have arrived at the step that allows you to select how the final application will appear to your users. Once the wizard has generated the code, you can freely modify the appearance to match your corporate logos or any other design needs. Choose one of the appearance themes, and click the Next button to reach the final step.

12. You have now completed the configuration of the Data Form Wizard. Clicking the Finish button will construct all the ASP files needed for the data form. After the status boxes finish informing you of your form's construction, your project now has some additional files. These files should include three ASP files:

dfwEmailAction.asp

dfwEmailForm.asp

dfwEmailList.asp

> **TIP** You can use the buttons along the top to modify, delete, update, or create new records. If you click on the List View button, the first 10 records stored in your database will be displayed. If you have more records, the buttons along the bottom of the screen will allow you to page through the records.

13. Use the right mouse button and click on dfwEmailForm.asp. Select the Preview in Browser option. When these files were created, they were also automatically loaded onto the Web server. In this case, the name of our Web server is ns1.coherentdata.com. Therefore, from the Web browser, we can access the page by typing:

    http://ns1.coherentdata.com/emailProj/dfdEmailForm.asp.

    Your editing form now appears as shown in Figure 8.8.

Figure 8.8 Data Form Wizard's completed form editing page for E-mail Editor.

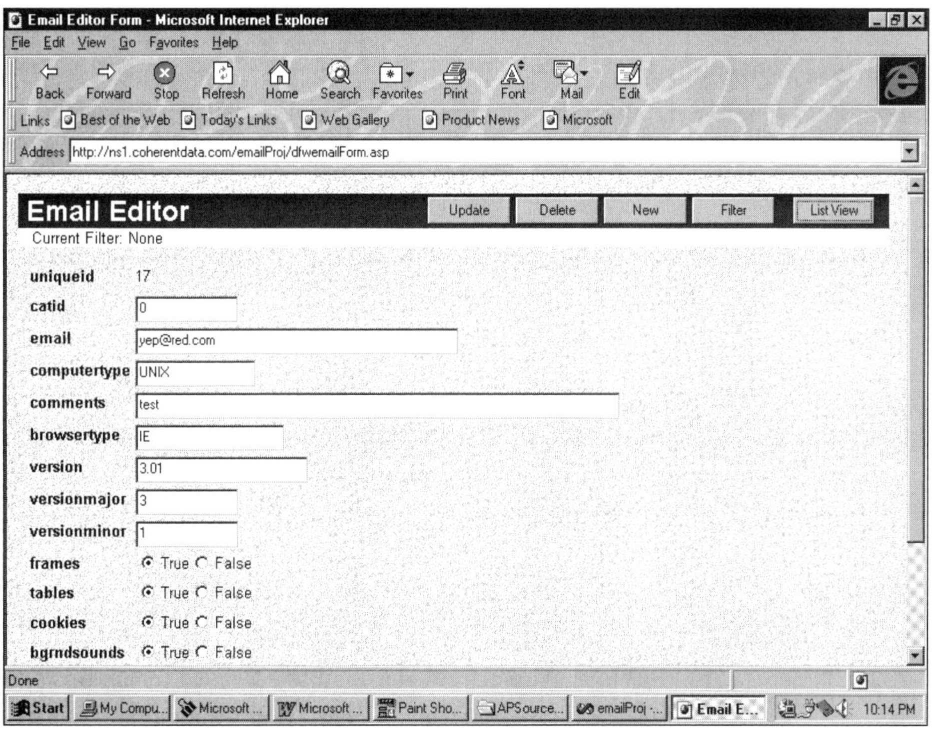

Your organization can now use this amazingly powerful application. It can be accessed by any Web browser because all the processing takes place on the server. If your Web server is hooked to the Internet, you now can modify or update your database from anywhere in the world!

The Data Form designer is the best tool for quickly creating server-based database access. Because all the files are stored as individual ASP files, you can freely edit the code to add necessary features and user interface elements. The first addition might be to provide a simple login screen to verify that the people who have access to the database need that access. You might also execute the Data Form Wizard again to provide a view that could view but not modify the data source. The new files would be added to the project along side the existing ASP files.

When you examine the ASP files the wizard generated, you might notice that all the scripting code is written in VBScript. Unfortunately, this wizard will produce only VBScript for the Data Form. Therefore, you would have to convert all the code to JavaScript or avoid using this wizard for your site construction.

Database Connection

Now that you have a database project, you can add another data source so that you can access more than one table. The Data Form Wizard, you might remember, automatically added a database connection previously. You can easily add another one to the existing project, but instead you will create a new project. This approach will create your own database application from scratch instead of having the Data Form Wizard create it. In this way, you will become more familiar with the actual structure and ASP code used to generate an application.

1. Use the Web Project Wizard again, but this time name the project *second*, for your second database project. Select the Web server where the project needs to be created. Click on the Finish button to open the second project. Notice that a few tabs appear at the bottom of the workspace shown in the window on the left. Currently, the FileView tab should be selected. When a data source is added, an extra Data tab is added. Watch for this tab after the data connection is created.

2. Select the Add to Project submenu under the Project menu. From this submenu, select the Data Connection option. The ODBC dialog that you've used before appears. Select the emailODBC data source, and click the OK

button. You will be returned to your project and a connection, labeled *DataConn,* has been added to your project. With the data connection in your project, you can use any wizard to access this data source.

3. Notice that the Data tab has been added to the bottom of the window. Click on this tab, and expand all the collapsed levels to see your entire table structure, as shown in Figure 8.9. You are now ready to create a database project. Return to the FileView tab by clicking on it to see all our files.

4. You can now add a new ASP file where the code will be located. Select the New option under the File menu, and create a new Active Server Page named *list* that will contain our code. Your document window will show the basic HTML starting code; the "Insert HTML here" text should be

Figure 8.9 The complete data connection expanded in the Data View tab.

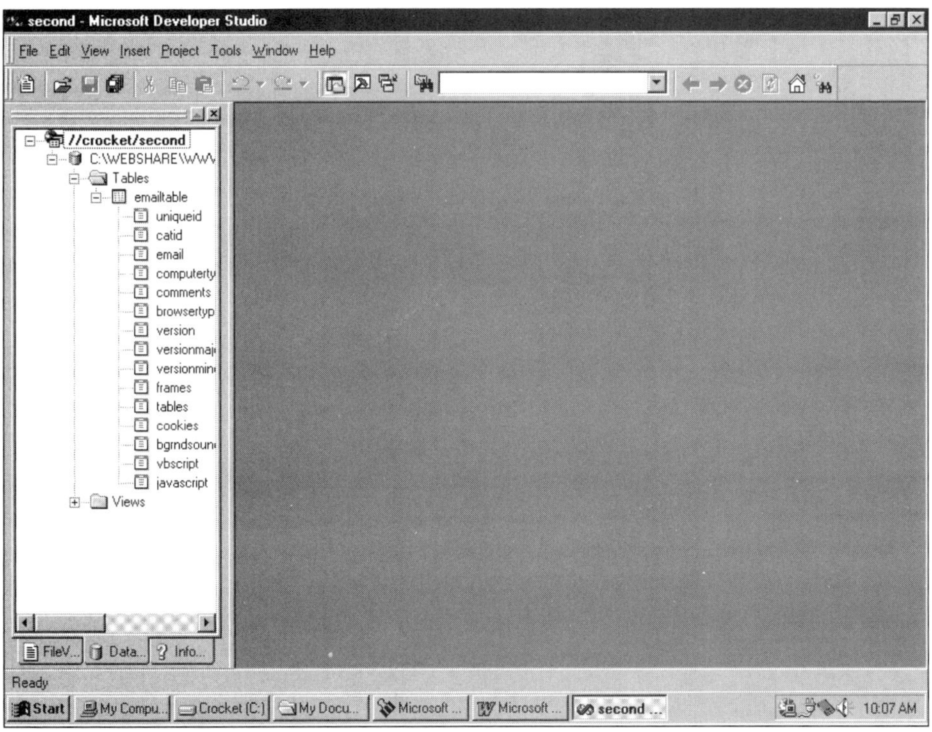

highlighted. Now you will begin using the Design-time controls included with Visual InterDev to create an application.

5. Right-click in the document window, and select the Insert ActiveX Control option. The window that appears will show the tab labeled Controls; you will see all the ActiveX controls that you are accustomed to seeing. Click on the Design-time tab (see Figure 8.10), and all the registered Design-time controls appear.

Data Range Header and Footer Controls

The Data Range Header and Footer controls are a matched pair. The Header control creates the necessary objects to access a data source and begins a Do...Loop to iterate through each record in the database. The Footer control provides all the code to complete the loop. What you put in the middle is up to you. You will create a simple demonstration that adds all the data held in the emailtable to an HTML

Figure 8.10 Select the Design-time tab to show the InterDev controls.

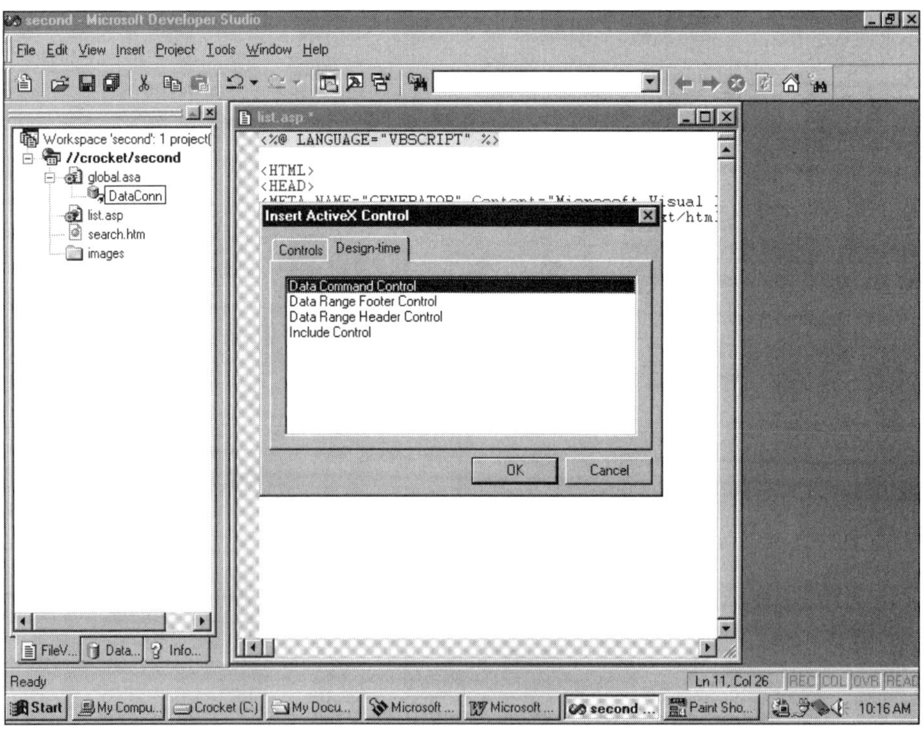

page. This task can be accomplished using just the Header and Footer controls without typing any code ourselves.

SQL Builder In the section "SQL Overview," we described the basic code structure of a SQL statement and showed how values could be inserted into tables. SQL takes a great deal of time to master and often requires a complex query to create the resultant data set. The SQL Builder tool included with Visual InterDev allows you to do as much or as little coding as you like.

With a graphics interface, you can drag a table onto the form and select any necessary fields. Tables can be joined, criteria can be set, and numerous other query options that would take hours to code by hand can be created instantly. SQL code that the Builder generates is not static. The code may be freely edited; the Builder reinterprets the code to allow continued use of the graphical front-end.

The following example illustrates an application that uses both the Data Range controls and the SQL Builder.

1. From the Design-time tab, click on the Data Range Header control, then click the OK button. Two windows appear on your screen, one labeled DataRangeHdr1 and the other labeled Properties. The DataRangeHdr1 window shows the visible component of the control you are inserting into your Web page. Because the control in this example is active only in design-time, nothing will appear on the screen. Therefore, you do not need this window. The only time you will interact with the window is to close it, thereby updating the code in your document window.
2. The Properties window contains information about the data connection you will use. Right now, the Data Connection combo box should be empty. Click on the right arrow to show the available data sources. You can see that the DataConn we added to the project earlier is available. Select the DataConn connection.
3. To access the proper data from our table, you must build a query to determine what data will be available to the ADO we are creating on our form. You will now use one of the most powerful tools contained within the Visual InterDev package, the SQL Builder tool.

4. Use the SQL Builder to construct the query we need for the data control. Click on the SQL Builder button in the Properties window. A new window appears, labeled Query Builder: DataRangeHdr1. Also, the Properties window changes to reflect the newly activated builder. Notice also that the window to the left that normally shows the FileView tab has automatically switched to show the Data View tab.

5. The Query Builder window is currently empty because no tables have been added to access. Drag-and-drop editing is a commonly used feature within the Builder. In this case, you need to add the emailtable, shown in the window on the left, to the query. In the Builder window, the gray area at the top is where accessible tables are shown. Click on the emailtable item in the left window, and drag it onto this gray area. The emailtable appears in the table workspace area, as shown in Figure 8.11.

Figure 8.11 The emailtable has been added to the table workspace area.

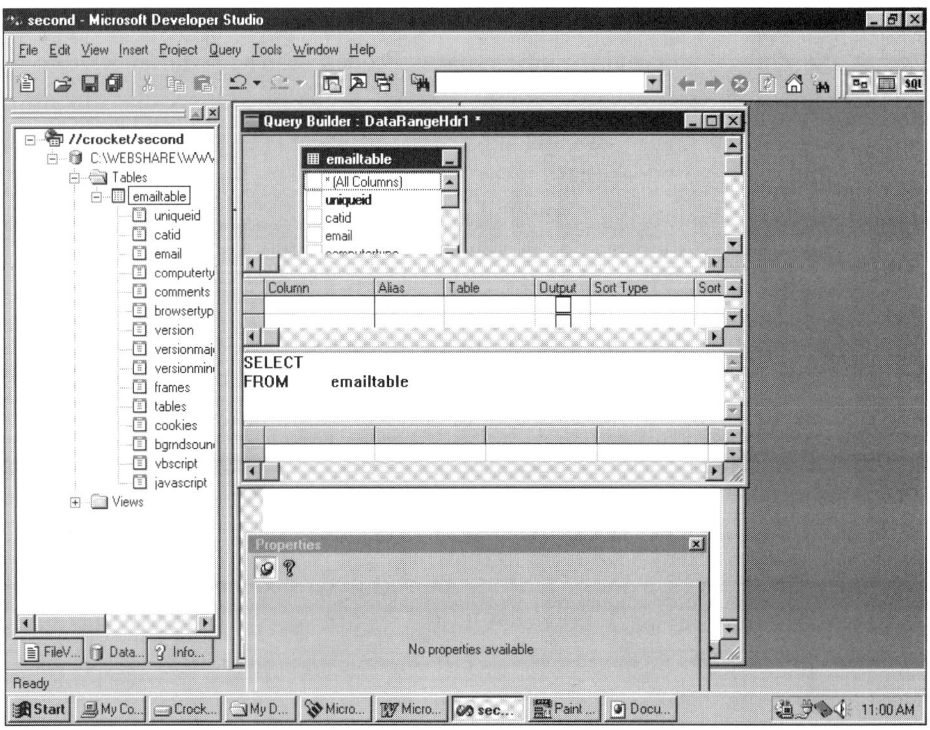

TIP In this query, you simply want to return all the fields and records contained within the table. In the emailtable window within the table workspace, the first option is labeled "* (All Columns)" and has a check box to the left. Click the check box to select all the columns. Notice that the SQL code pane automatically updates to reflect this change.

6. There are four separate areas to the Query Builder window. The table workspace shows all the tables currently available in the query. The second area shows all the columns specifically selected in the query and allows specific conditions to be set. For example, the query might display only the e-mail addresses of Macintosh users based on the computertype field. In the next area, you see the identifiable SQL code. As the query is generated, code is automatically added to the instructions contained within this pane. The final pane is called the Query Results pane. You can actually execute the query shown to test it to make sure the data returned is as you intended.
7. Now test the data to ensure that the query returned what you want. Click the right mouse button within the Query Results pane, and select the Run option. The query will run and return the data retrieved from the table, as shown in Figure 8.12.
8. Now that you've verified that everything works, close the Query Builder window. Click the Yes button to accept the changes made to the DataRangeHdr1 control. The SQL code for the query that was just constructed appears in the Command Text box. You are almost finished with the Data Range Header control.
9. Click the Copy Fields button. Because the header and footer wizards were created to provide a framework from which an application could be constructed, they do not explicitly create a finished application to display any data. The Copy Fields button is provided to generate simple display code for the fields within a query. Paste this code into your ASP file to show the data stored in the fields.
10. When the Copy Fields windows appears, click on the double arrow to select all the fields for storage in the clipboard. Click the OK button to save

Figure 8.12 After the query runs, the Query Results will be displayed in the table.

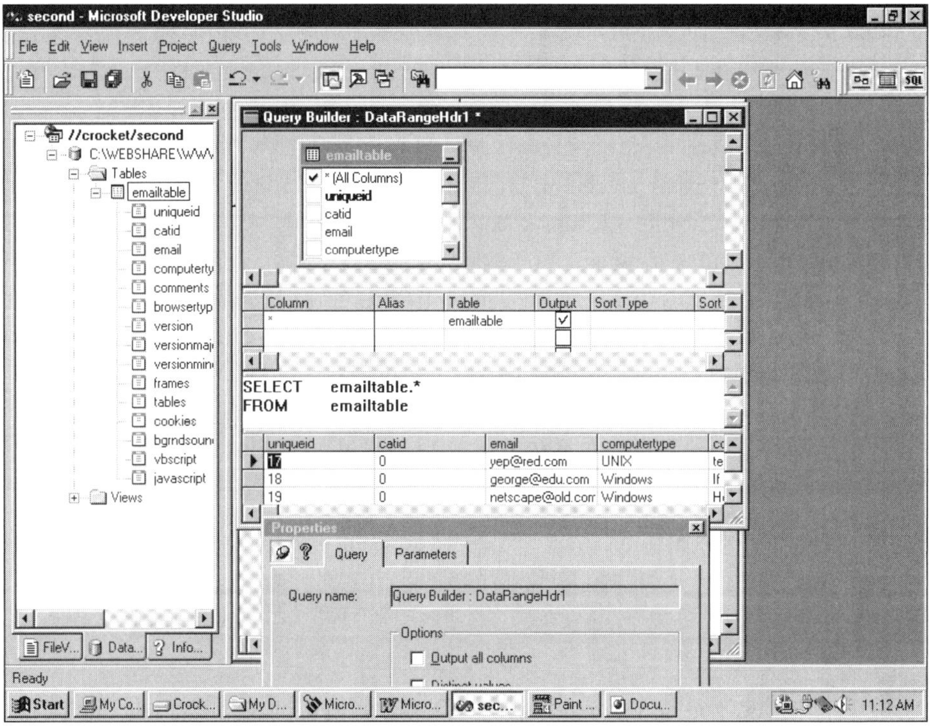

the sample code. Now close the DataRangeHdr1 window, automatically activating the design-time control and inserting all the necessary code into your application.

11. The code generated by the control is divided into three sections—the header, the body, and the footer. Scroll to the top of the document to reveal a set of code in green text: the header. The header contains information about the control inserted into the ASP file. Uncommonly with most available wizards, a design-time control may be reactivated for further editing. If you'd like to test this, right-click anywhere within the code generated by the control, and select the Edit Design-time control option.

The body contains all the actual code to connect to the database. Error checking here ensures that your solution executes effectively. Most programmers heartily admit that error checking, although vital, is time-consuming and tedious and is therefore rarely well implemented. Using these controls may create more solid programs in the future.

Finally, the footer is a single line that denotes the end of the control. You should see something like this:

```
<!--METADATA TYPE="DesignerControl" endspan-->
```

12. Place your cursor on the line that follows this footer. Here, you need to place the actual field code that was copied earlier onto the clipboard. Select the Paste option under the Edit menu to insert the code into the file. The code should appear like this:

```
<%= DataRangeHdr1("bgrndsounds") %><br>

<%= DataRangeHdr1("browsertype") %><br>

<%= DataRangeHdr1("catid") %><br>

<%= DataRangeHdr1("comments") %><br>

<%= DataRangeHdr1("computertype") %><br>

<%= DataRangeHdr1("cookies") %><br>

<%= DataRangeHdr1("email") %><br>

<%= DataRangeHdr1("frames") %><br>

<%= DataRangeHdr1("javascript") %><br>

<%= DataRangeHdr1("tables") %><br>

<%= DataRangeHdr1("uniqueid") %><br>

<%= DataRangeHdr1("vbscript") %><br>

<%= DataRangeHdr1("version") %><br>

<%= DataRangeHdr1("versionmajor") %><br>

<%= DataRangeHdr1("versionminor") %><br>
```

This VBScript code will insert into the HTML generated by the Active Server each of the fields available to the DataRangeHdr1 ActiveX Data Object. This code is simply ASP code that the control generates automatically. It can be changed freely to reflect how the data should appear in the final HTML page. For example, this code could be easily modified to display the output data in a table format.

13. Now that you have the Data Range Header control and all the fields, you need to close the loop with the Data Range Footer control. Make sure that your cursor appears on the screen following the fields you just inserted. Click the right mouse button again, and select Insert ActiveX Control.

14. Select the design-time Data Range Footer control now. The control should appear on the screen. All defaults are acceptable, so close the control window. You're done! We just created a database solution without any hand coding, yet all the code is available for easy modification.

15. Save the file and preview it in your browser. It may not be the most attractive layout, but all your data should now be visible. Try changing the <BR> commands in the field code to a comma (,) with a <P> on the final line. Then add a horizontal rule <HR> command to separate the various records. Your code should now look like this:

```
<%= DataRangeHdr1("bgrndsounds") %>,

<%= DataRangeHdr1("browsertype") %>,

<%= DataRangeHdr1("catid") %>,

<%= DataRangeHdr1("comments") %>,

<%= DataRangeHdr1("computertype") %>,

<%= DataRangeHdr1("cookies") %>,

<%= DataRangeHdr1("email") %>,

<%= DataRangeHdr1("frames") %>,

<%= DataRangeHdr1("javascript") %>,

<%= DataRangeHdr1("tables") %>,

<%= DataRangeHdr1("uniqueid") %>,

<%= DataRangeHdr1("vbscript") %>,
```

```
<%= DataRangeHdr1("version") %>,

<%= DataRangeHdr1("versionmajor") %>,

<%= DataRangeHdr1("versionminor") %><P>

<HR>
```

Now when you save and preview the page again, it will appear formatted as it is in Figure 8.13. Making changes to design-time code is very easy. Be warned that if you change the code dramatically, the design-time control will not allow you to edit it within the Control Wizard. Therefore, make sure that the modifications you need cannot be done from within the control before you reformat the code itself.

New Database Wizard In the previous example, you used the database already created in Microsoft Access to create an application. If you are designing with SQL

Figure 8.13 Formatted output of the database created by modifying the Design-time code.

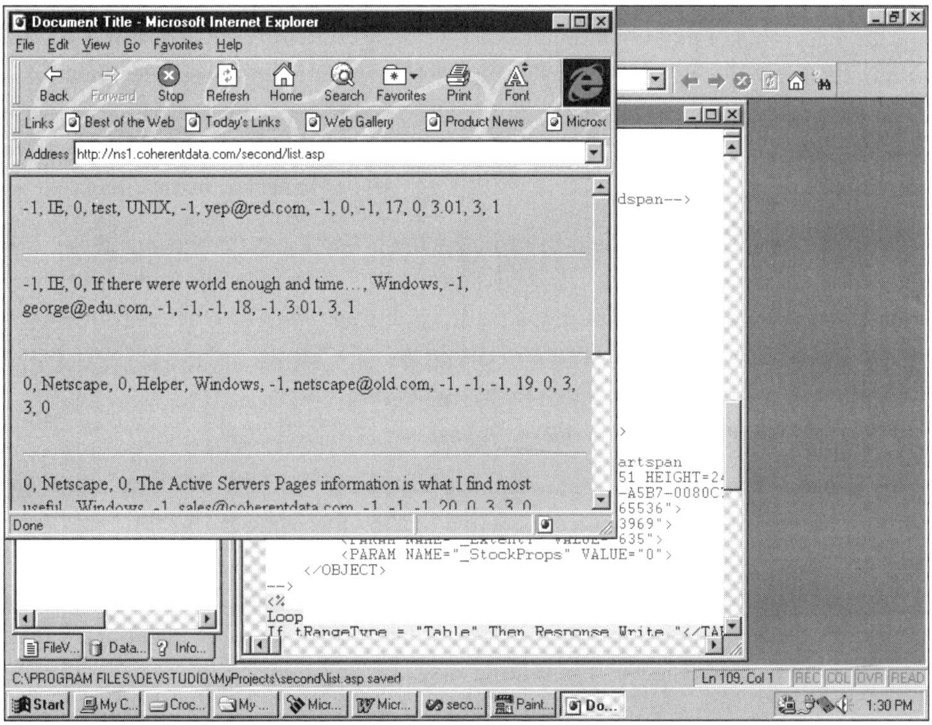

Server, you have another option when you begin a project. The New Database Wizard allows you to create a database on your database server without leaving Visual InterDev.

Rather than having to set up a database locally using the server-based database tools, you can do so remotely, even over the Internet. Future versions of Visual InterDev will more closely integrate with database development tools such as Visual Modeler so that all development and maintenance can take place from within the environment. The New Database Wizard provides a sample of future potential.

Active Server Components

Active Server Components are crucial to the effective use of ASP. In the previous ASP example files, two controls were used primarily, the Active Data Object control and the Request control. Although the Active Server Components will be covered in great detail in the next chapter, having an overview of how the ASCs function within the Active Server framework is a good idea.

You are probably already familiar with ActiveX controls. Active Server Components are essentially ActiveX controls that execute on the server. They can also be much more than that. They can be designed for specific server-side activities such as providing business rules, completing such business processes as routing documents or doing credit card checks, or storing user information in various files.

When a component is created in memory, the process is called *instantiation*. The object itself, created in memory, is called an *instance*. Instancing is important to understand and consider as you implement a solution. Each instance consumes a certain amount of memory and system resources. Therefore, components are best used in place of script code when a great number of actions can occur within the control, thereby minimizing the instantiation and destruction of components.

To create Active Server Components, use Visual Basic 5 Control Creation Edition. Server-side components are created in the same way that traditional ActiveX controls are made. Special considerations must be made in the design because, unlike ActiveX controls that typically have only a single instance executing at any one time, server components will most likely have multiple instances, one for each user currently accessing the ASP file that uses the component.

ActiveX Data Objects

The most important component included with the ASP system is undoubtedly the ActiveX Data Object (ADO), used in both the e-mail addition and the e-mail editor examples. Through this object you can access your database information.

ADO parallels the data access capabilities of Visual Basic and VBA by the Data Access Objects (DAOs) and the Remote Data Objects (RDOs). In fact, the programming of each is very similar. ADOs can be set to use keyset, dynaset, and various cursor configurations depending on the data source to be accessed. For each record set needed, an instance of the ADO must be created using the CreateObject command. An object may be created at the Application object level so that it can be used only for the duration of the user's session.

You might have noticed that in the e-mail example, to insert a record into the database, you used the SQL Insert command to create the record by hand. Much of the data access you will do in the future will use ADOs to insert and manipulate records. We included the example using SQL Insert as a sample of the use of additional SQL.

Connection to Access 97

You can export an Access table or report in three different forms, as shown in Figure 8.14.

- Multiple static pages
- Reports
- ASP files

The first two options are useful if you need to export Access data to a non-ASP-enabled server or if you need data to remain static. The third, ASP, allows you to export the access to your database through an ASP file.

One of the most powerful features of this wizard is its ability to export a report as a query or an HTML page. You can construct reports in Excel and make them instantly accessible on the Web. Although Access cannot be substituted for Visual InterDev when creating ASP database files, it does provide wizards to create core code that a designer can modify as needed.

Figure 8.14 Access Export as HTML Wizard providing three types of export.

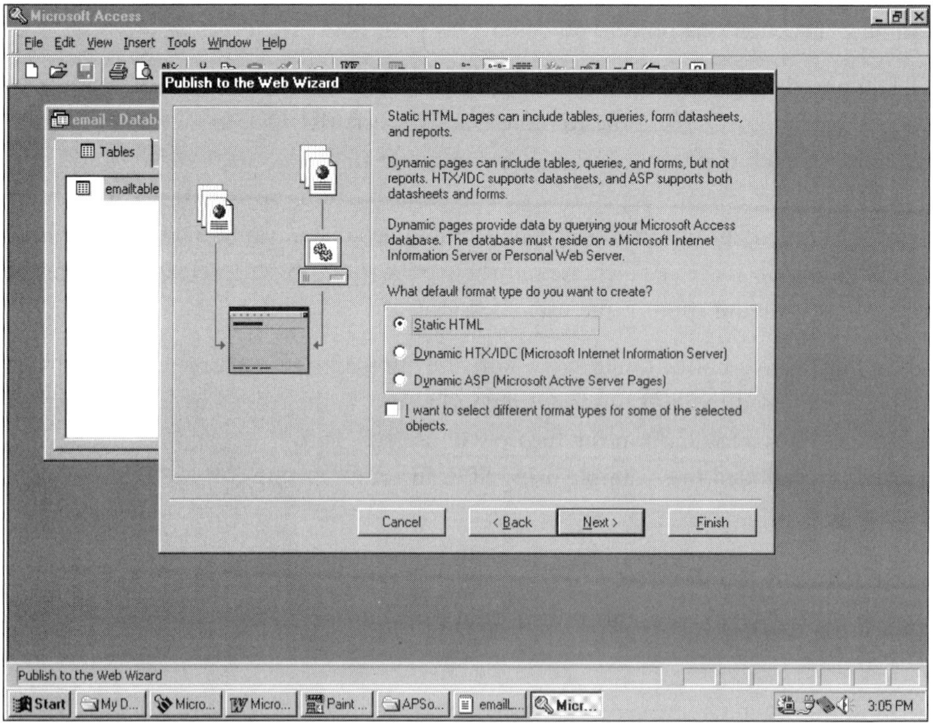

Intranet versus Internet Deployment

ASPs provide the ideal foundation for development of both Internet and intranet Web sites. The factors to consider for implementing ASP on an intranet or the Internet are fairly different. Typically, an Internet application has the following limitations:

- Low bandwidth availability with most users connecting with 28.8K modems
- Wide variety of possible browsers accessing the system
- Variable browser support for Java, JavaScript, VBScript, and so on
- Visitors who lack a vested interest in your site

When you design an intranet site, you can control the choice of browser used to access the site within an organization. If you watch the log files, however, you may be surprised by the number of "nonsanctioned" browsers in use. Whatever your audience, make sure your site can address their needs.

When you design a site for access by remote users, you must be aware that even though browsers can handle scripting code, the code may never reach some browsers. Many proxy servers used as gateways to an organization strip any scripting code from the HTML file as it passes through the server. Therefore, your script may never arrive at the destination machine. This limitation is another good reason to keep all critical processing on the Active Server, where simple HTML is sent after all processing is complete.

Debugging Your ASP

Debugging an Active Server Page can be more difficult than traditional program testing. Many different elements come together in each Active Server Page, including the following:

- Server-side scripting (possibly in multiple languages including VBScript and JavaScript)
- Client-side scripting
- Database connection
- Database integrity

Of course, each of these elements requires special tools and techniques.

Server-side script debugging can be fairly tricky. If your core VBScript routines that do not access data sources can run under Microsoft Internet Explorer, you can use the free Script Debugger to watch variables, set breakpoints, and track errors.

Another tool that prevents the user from seeing an error screen is the *On Error Resume Next* statement. Many of the examples included in this chapter use this command to prevent server-side script faulting. When an error occurs at a particular line, this command simply makes the execution skip that line and continue from the next line. This command prevents a complete halt of the code for a minor problem, but it is not available in JavaScript and JScript. There is no parallel command in the JavaScript language.

If you are programming in JavaScript, be aware of incorrect capitalization—both JavaScript and JScript are case-sensitive. The number of hours developers waste trying to find capitalization errors is staggering. Therefore, adopting a particular capitalization standard that you always use when naming variables is a good practice.

Client-side scripting can also be debugged with the free Microsoft Script Debugger. This task will be far easier than server-side debugging because the client-side code can be isolated. If you use ActiveX controls, be sure to test on a virgin system to make sure all controls download properly.

Using Visual Test for Automated Testing

Because Active Pages are constructed on the fly, traditional Web tools, such as those that check for broken links, will not effectively test your ASP solution before you deploy it. Automated testing can be the solution to this Web dilemma. Automated testing is essentially a group of macros that can simulate particular keystrokes, mouse clicks, and other events. The program can then watch the tested system's responses, compare them with expected results, and record the final report. Therefore, a set of tests can be run against a program and a simple report output that details where the program failed to act as expected.

Many people feel that Web creation tools are so new that advanced tools for automated testing are unavailable. A tool named Visual Test, was originally developed by Microsoft and later sold to Rational Rose. Visual Test allows sets of hierarchical tests to be created and run. Many of the tests can be created using a "watch-me" system as you perform the actions (such as user keystrokes, mouse clicks, and so on) that execute the process you need to test. The recorded macro is stored in a custom macro language for editing.

Visual Test's comprehensive nature allows you to create an entire automated test for your Web site. Before you invest the time and money to construct these tests, you must first determine whether testing would be effective for your organization. If your site is often redesigned from scratch, it would probably not be a good candidate for testing this way. The macros would have to be reconstructed every time a change is made.

If you frequently make slight modifications to your site and many users access it, you should seriously consider Visual Test. Malfunctioning Web sites do not inspire confidence in customers or other visitors. A Web site is an organization's public face, and users' problems often go unreported for a long time. The damage done to your public image may be far more expensive than the time invested for automated testing.

Basic Data Warehousing/Data Mining

Data warehousing is the process of providing commonly accessed, high-level data in a data source separate from the place where the data is stored. For example, if a company needs to check quarterly sales every day, a query that compiles this data from the main server used by the sales force would slow down the system. If 50 people needed to compile various figures from the main server every day, the load on the server would increase exponentially.

Therefore, data warehouses were invented to retrieve summary information from the main server at regular intervals. The data warehouses could then be queried without affecting the time-critical main server.

You can use data warehousing techniques easily when you build your Active Platform system. Replicating frequently used data from the main database to a custom database accessed by the ADO to build Web pages may improve both Web performance and the allocation of resources for your mission-critical database.

Staging Server and Deployment Server

Before you start development, you should consider how you will keep your primary Web site functioning as changes occur. Doing development work on your primary server is seldom a good idea, given performance restraints, the possibility of new technology crashing the server, or errors in your current Web site caused by not-ready-for-prime-time content.

Two servers are recommended: a staging server and a deployment server. A staging server can be placed on a corporate intranet for internal testing until the site is solid. Once the primary bugs have been eliminated, you can move the Web solution to the deployment server that the outside world will access. The outside world may still be on the corporate intranet, but it includes users who are not affiliated with the development effort.

For some organizations, dedicating a separate staging server may be prohibitively expensive for certain development projects. For these projects, you can use the Microsoft Personal Web Server with Active Server extensions to run on a far less powerful machine than the full IIS implementation requires. For example, a complete prototype could be built on a single Windows 95 machine with Access 97 data source connected to the Personal Web Server via ODBC. When the application is ready for deployment, it could be moved to a SQL Server database and IIS Web server.

Related Sources

The resources for ASP on the Web are significant. The following is a list of resources to supplement the information found in this chapter.

ASP Developers Site (www.genusa.com/asp/) presents developer resources on ASP, including an Active Server Page FAQ, troubleshooting tips, breaking ASP news, and sample source code.

Client/Server Central (www.coherentdata.com/cscentral) is our site that contains documents and articles about developments in the information systems industry. Also, we will post all the source code in Chapter 8 and 9 for free download.

15 Seconds (www.signmeup.com/online.asp?Publication_Id=36) is an online magazine that features articles on ASP, IIS, ODBC, and other relevant topics.

Microsoft IIS home page (www.microsoft.com/iis) contains information and downloads related to ASP technology. Microsoft also has a news group (news://msnews.microsoft.com/microsoft.public.inetserver.iis.activeserverpages) devoted to ASP issues.

John Wiley & Sons Web site (www.wiley.com/compbooks/) contains numerous books relating to Active Platform development, including *The ActiveX Sourcebook: Build an ActiveX-Based Web Site.*

Related books from John Wiley & Sons include books on VBScript, ActiveX Controls, IIS, and Visual Basic 5 and/or VB 5 Control Creation Edition.

Visual Test (www.rational.com/vtest) is an automated testing utility available from Rational Rose. Automated testing is becoming more necessary on Web pages than it has been with traditional programs. In the past, if something didn't work, at most several thousand people might see it. With the Internet, *tens of thousands* might see your mistake.

The PerlScript script engine (www.activeware.com) is a site created by ActiveWare that allows Perl scripts to be embedded in ASP. The scripting engine is available for free download.

Summary

We covered a lot of material in this chapter, the one point you should take away is how easy it is to create and deploy applications using the ASP technology. The following is a brief summary of the key topics you should follow as you continue your application development.

Active Server functioning overview. Active Server processes any files with the ASP extension through the specified scripting engine. After the script executes and any Active Server Components are activated, an HTML file is generated and sent to the client.

Client independence. With all processing occurring on the Web server, ASP files can easily generate content that, although dynamically created on the server, is simple HTML, usable by any browser.

Centralized administrative control. Control of data access, objects, processing, and the Web pages themselves can be centralized on the server. Although not perfect for all solutions, central control reduces management costs, especially as compared with those of diverse systems.

Basic installation. Either Internet Information Server 3.0 or Personal Web Server with Active Server extensions is required to process ASP files. Make sure that all folders that use ASP files have Execute rights.

Sample ASP file creation. You created several ASP examples including a simple e-mail storage application and a complete data form by using the Data Form Wizard included with Visual InterDev.

SQL overview. The basics of the SQL query language were covered as well as their use for database access. The emailList.ASP file demonstrated a SQL *Select* statement; the emailDone.ASP file demonstrated inserting record information using the *Insert* command.

Using the Data Form Wizard. Visual InterDev includes a wizard that, from a data connection, will create an entire Web-based data entry system including inserting, modifying, and deleting records. You created a solution using these tools.

Design-time components. Using the Data Range Header and Footer controls, you created a list of all data contained within the e-mail database without writing a single line of code. Using the SQL Builder tool, the data displayed the records returned from the SQL data set.

Access 97 HTML output. Access 97 includes a Save as HTML option that can be used to generate both static HTML pages and complete ASP files. These can be created from a table, a query, or even an Access report.

Conclusion

Active Server pages are key components of the Microsoft Active Platform. The features of ASPs answer the call that Internet developers have been placing for the past couple of years. This chapter has illustrated the potential applications of ASP ranging from creating dynamic Web applications to interfacing a database with your Web application. Now that you have the tools at your disposal, the rest is up to you.

Chapter

9

Active Server Components

Now that you understand how Active Server technology is used, you can begin to experience some of the true power of Active Server Components (ASCs). ASC lets you create server-based solutions that take advantage of a plug-in environment for inexpensive, robust, and reusable application development. Visual Basic has become popular because of the many components available within its programming environment. Active Server Components promise to bring the same popularity to the Active Server platform.

This chapter will demonstrate not only the power of the components included with Internet Information Server (IIS), but also how to use alternate components, both commercial and those you construct, to empower your server with the solutions your organization needs.

Advantages of Using Components

In the last chapter, the advantages of using Active Server Pages over designing a custom CGI program or building an ISAPI filter were demonstrated. CGI and ISAPI filters have to be created from scratch, and their implementation is difficult and time-consuming. ASP files are meant to be used in conjunction with components, so each provides a strength the other lacks. ASC can be used to fill most any gaps left in the functionality of the ASP implementation.

Like traditional client/server work, the ASP/ASC partnership allows particular programmers to focus on what they do best. Many people who begin to use ASP or HTML are accustomed to the Visual Basic environment. Active Server solutions provide both FrontPage and Visual InterDev development environments to allow you to create simple solutions.

A designer can create ASCs within any of a number of programming environments, allowing them to be built in the language most familiar to those already within an organization. If C++ is the language of choice and the language with which business logic has been constructed, designing components in C++ leverages knowledge.

Creating AS Components is no longer the purview solely of C++ programmers. ISAPI filters must be created using C, C++, or another complex language. With Active Server Pages with Active Components, any languages that can create OLE servers can be used for component creation. These include Visual Basic 5 and Visual Basic 5 Control Creation Edition, as well as languages such as Java that allow system-independent implementations.

The advantages of using components over a strictly script-based system are many:

- Better performance obtained from a compiled component
- Availability of features missing from the script language
- Reusability of components
- Use of legacy business code in a compiled language
- Programmatic access to the operating system
- Separation of user interface from core code
- Sealed code access for commercial production of components
- Distributed access to objects

As you have probably guessed by now, we believe the Visual Basic language is an effective standard for an organization to use. Visual Basic can be used to create several types of applications:

- Client applications
- Office applications
- Client-side applications
- Groupware applications
- ASP Web-based applications

Now we can add the creation of server-side components to the list. An organization can substantially leverage its investment in the Active Server Platform by adopting Visual Basic in its several forms to create Web-based solutions.

Here is a general rule of thumb for determining if you should create a component: If there is more script code on the server than simple HTML, it is probably time to create a control that contains some of the core logic. This approach will optimize performance because, unlike interpreted VB Script code, compiled components centralize important routines. Their use will also create an opportunity to reuse functions across multiple projects.

Active Server scripting is ideal for most tasks but when too much scripting runs, the server may become hard to administer and slow. Microsoft recommends that if this occurs, a server component should be created to contain the most commonly used functions. Encapsulating this code within a compiled control will allow it to execute more quickly, make it more reusable, and simplify bug testing.

Aspects of Components

Any OLE Automation Server can be used as an Active Server Component. Although in most cases using Excel as an Active Server Component would be inefficient, you will see how significant the breadth of application can be with this capability implemented. The execution of components can occur in two ways; see Figure 9.1.

In-process. In-process components actually load and execute in the same memory space as the calling application. In the case of Active Server Pages, components execute within the memory of the Active Server engine. In-process execution is very fast for two reasons: No separate memory must be allocated, and calls and exchange of information can occur between the application and the component without any translation.

Out-of-process. Out-of-process servers require their own memory space to execute. Therefore, every time an out-of-process server is used, an instance must allocate its own memory and application space. This process is the equivalent of double-clicking an application to begin its execution. Once the component is opened, all interaction between the calling application and the component must occur through the operating system. This significantly slows execution of any data exchange or command calls.

In order for ASP to access out-of-process OLE components, Microsoft requires you to enter a change to the Web server's registry and reboot the machine. By default, Microsoft discourages the use of any out-of-process server by the Active Server platform. Changing the registry entry *AllowOutOfProcCmpnts* from 0

Figure 9.1 In-process and out-of-process components.

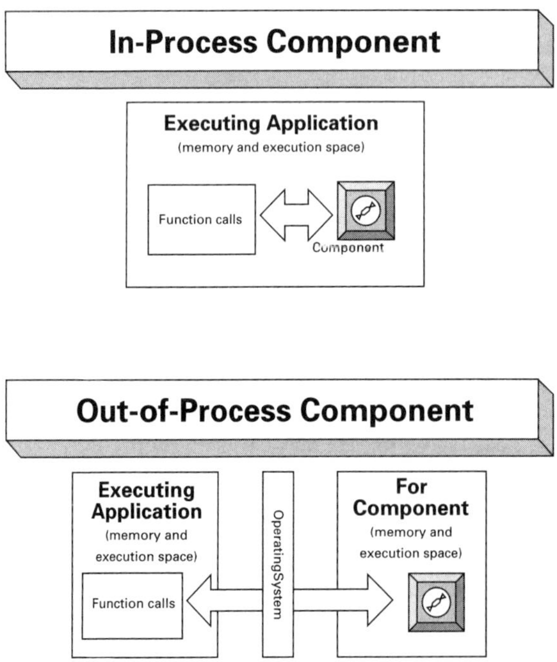

(false) to 1 (true) will allow the ASP engine to correctly process out-of-process object creation.

> **TIP** Besides resource and speed concerns, there are very real dangers to security. When an instance of an out-of-process server is created, it can be accessed by multiple sessions. A new calling function can inherit the security context of the previous calling application, creating a dangerous security loophole. Therefore, consider carefully before setting up an out-of-process component.

Object Declarations: ClassIDs and ProgIDs

Every ActiveX control installed on the system is identified by a unique *ClassID* value. You may have noticed that in any client-side code that uses ActiveX controls, there is a long single number like the following one:

```
asd0122-12123123
```

On the client side, ClassID values are used to prevent the possibility of the wrong ActiveX control being used if two or more were named identically. On the server side, where the system administrator has control over the components installed, the *ProgID*, or the component name, may be used. The ProgID format is vendor.component.version, although the vendor prefix and the version suffix are optional. Code that accesses a control by its ProgID will look like this:

```
CreateObject("Excel.Application")
```

On the server-side, ClassIDs may be used as well. When you use programs like Visual InterDev or ActiveX Control Pad, they will automatically insert the necessary IDs into your HTML code. You may consider using ClassIDs instead of ProgIDs on the server if there is a possibility of conflict. ClassIDs can also be used to great advantage if multiple versions of a control are being developed for use on the server. There will then be no danger of the prototype interfering with the operational control.

Overview of the Intrinsic Controls

Intrinsic controls are part of the Active Server Pages themselves. These components provide information on the state of the Web connection and the server. Intrinsic controls are always loaded into memory with the ASP engine so there is no additional memory or loading overhead. The intrinsic controls do not have to be created using the *CreateObject* method as do other Active Server Components.

Variables can be added to any of the Intrinsic controls and will remain active as long as the object itself remains. For example, the Session object remains in existence until the user no longer uses it; therefore, any variables stored in the Session object will remain as long as the session is active. Variables may be added to the object itself or to collections within the object. A variable added to a collection may be addressed by the collection name.

In the following example, you get the value of a variable named *filename* from the collection Form. The necessary collection is specified using the dot (.) command like this:

```
<% myVar = Request.Form("filename") %>
```

The same variable could be retrieved without the collection name. For example, to retrieve the same value, you could use this code:

```
<% myVar = Request("filename") %>
```

> **Tip** If there are multiple variables of the same name, the value of the first one found by that name is returned. Therefore, if there are similar variables in several collections, be sure to add the collection prefix.

The collections are searched in the following order:

1. QueryString
2. Form
3. Cookies
4. ClientCertificates
5. ServerVariables

If the variable is not held in any of the collections, the value is returned as Empty. The VB Script function IsEmpty() can be used to check this condition.

The five intrinsic controls include the following:

Server object contains central routines such as the *CreateObject* method to instantiate objects, routines to encode both URL addresses and HTML, and the MapPath routine to find the physical path to files on the server.

Application object is a key object in the total server solution because it provides a global staging area for methods and properties of an application.

Session object creates a "virtual session" to allow simplified tracking of a user through your Web site. Sessions are maintained while the user continues to request pages within a certain time period.

Request object is used for interaction with the Web user when an HTTP request is received from the browser.

Response object can be used to receive input (such as the Responses from form fields) and send HTML code to the browser.

The Server object is the primary object of the Active Server Components, representing the actual server. The Application object sits at the root directory for an application. Session objects may be created once the Application object has been created, while Request and Response objects occur from user interactions through the session. Before the application is executed, the ASP reads the Global ASA file to provide core variables and methods before it executes the first *Application* method.

Global ASA file

When using ASP, you can create an actual application that begins at a particular root directory. The application is made up of all project files contained in subdirectories within this hierarchy. The application can share files, variables, common methods, and information among simultaneous users. The *global.asa* file must exist in the root of the hierarchy; it is used to store event and object information available globally to all the ASP files that make up the application.

The global.asa file can contain application events such as Application_OnStart, session events such as Session_OnStart, and <Object> declarations. All script placed within the global file must be enclosed within <SCRIPT> tags. Multiple events or object tags can be combined within a single set of <SCRIPT> tags.

The global.asa file holds the event code for both the application and the session open and close events. When a user begins an application, the *Application_OnStart* method executes. This method can create any necessary application variables and instantiate required Active Server Components. The *Session_OnStart* method is executed before the opening of a session. Only the Server and Application intrinsic objects are available to scripts within the event code. The Request, Response, and Session objects are created later. An *OnStart* method might appear like this:

```
<SCRIPT LANGUAGE="VBScript" RUNAT=Server>

Sub Application_OnStart

      Application("homeURL") = "http://www.coherentdata.com/cscentral"

End Sub

</SCRIPT>
```

In this example code, we define a stored variable *homeURL* that we can use in any later ASP files. This allows us to centralize key variables at the beginning of an application. If the homeURL were to change and all of our ASP files referenced this variable to create a home link, we would need only to change this single variable reference for it to propagate automatically through the application.

Active Server Components can also be created in the Application object so other pages can have access to it. The following code creates an ASC on the server that may be globally referenced by the application through the myASC variable:

```
<% Set Application("myASC") = Server.CreateObject("ASP.ctlWrapper") %>
```

This script could be placed within the global.asa file to allow the application to instantiate the ASP.ctlwrapper when execution first begins. Events methods are also triggered when a process completes. When the Session has completed, the *Session_OnEnd* method is activated. After the application has completed execution, the *Application_OnEnd* method is called; see Figure 9.2.

Any changes made to the global.asa file are not used until all current sessions have been terminated. If a new user requests a session after changes to the file have been made, but not all sessions have been ended, the user will receive the message "The request cannot be processed while the application is being restarted." As soon

Figure 9.2 Process execution of an application.

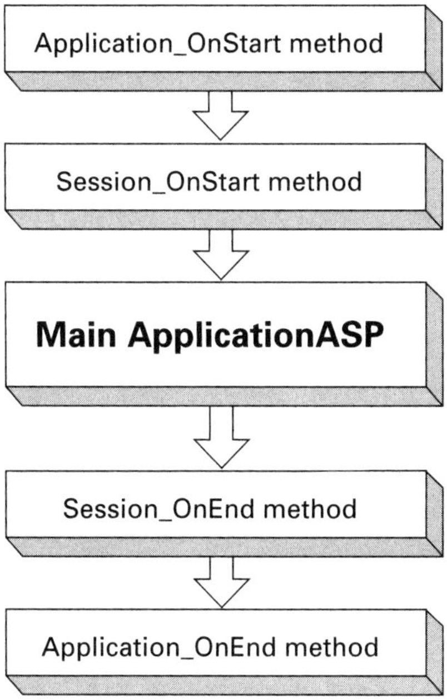

as all users have completed their sessions, the changes will take effect and the application will restart.

Server Object

The Server object can be used to manipulate the actions of the Active Server. All objects created in individual ASP files are actually created and stored on the server. These include components such as the Ad Rotator, Browser Capabilities, ADO, and other objects.

The *CreateObject* method is central to instantiation of Active Server Components. Use the Set command to create a reference variable to a new object. In the code below, we use the Set command with the *CreateObject* method to create a new instance of the MyComponent ASC:

```
<% Set myInstance = Server.CreateObject("MyComponent") %>
```

Programs often need to generate text for HTML, dynamically generating the HTML code that will be sent to the user's browser. The *HTMLEncode* method provides an additional way to do this. Using the *HTMLEncode* method writes a given string into the resultant HTML file.

For example, say you want the user to see the following text in a browser:

```
<B>Hello</B><P>
```

If this code were inserted into the HTML, the HTML tags would be processed and the user would see the world Hello in bold type. If you want the user to view the actual HTML source code, or if the text on your page uses a syntax that would erroneously be interpreted as HTML, you can use the = operator as follows:

```
<% = "<B>Hello</B><P>" %>
```

Using the *HTMLEncode* method ensures that the text will not be interpreted and will appear in the browser as you have sent it. Here is an example of the text string that might be sent by using the previous line of code:

```
<%= Server.HTMLEncode("<B>Hello</B><P>") %>
```

For file access, the actual directory path of a virtual directory must be used. The *MapPath* method will take a virtual directory URL address and convert it to a physical directory. Either complete or virtual paths may be passed to the *MapPath* method for conversion; for example,

www.coherentdata.com/cscentral

might be converted to the physical path

D:\inetsvr\wwwroot\cscentral.

Methods used by the FileSystem object require a physical path for execution, making the *MapPath* method essential for text or other file movement. Some of the demonstration code presented later will illustrate the use of the *MapPath* method to append text to a file.

The *URLEncode* method takes a normal string and encodes it for use in a URL. There are no spaces allowed in a URL string. When using the *QueryString* method in the Request object, a user search entry might be added to the *QueryString* by processing through the *URLEncode* method.

Application Object

The Application object heads the object hierarchy while an ASP application executes. It provides a medium through which various ASP files can exchange information and call unified methods.

The Application object is automatically instantiated when the central ASP file within the folder is accessed. Both variables and objects can be stored within an Application object. Objects stored within an application can be used by multiple users simultaneously. It is recommended, however, that objects be instantiated within a Session object.

A variable can be added to the Application object by defining it. When it is set to a value, it is automatically added to the collection. It will remain available until the Application object finishes or the server is stopped and restarted. Here is an example of the source code needed to create a new variable:

```
<% Application("myVar") = "Welcome" %>
```

An array may be stored within the Application object. Each array element value must be accompanied by an index value. For example, to set the fourth element in an array (the element index numbers begin at 0) you would use the index value of 3:

```
<% Application("myArray")(3) = "The fourth value" %>
```

Because variables remain accessible to multiple users at the application level, a particular user can reserve permissions. The *Lock* and the *Unlock* methods are used to allow only one user at a time to modify the Application-level variables.

```
<%

Application.Lock

Application("NumVisits") = Application("NumVisits") + 1

Application.Unlock

%>
```

Locks are not permanent. A Lock will automatically release at the end of a Script segment or when the script has a timeout.

When you design an application, it is usually a good idea to copy variables from the Application object into local storage. Because variables at the Application level are shared, it is possible for one user to lock the Application from modifications or change a variable that another user is relying on to stay constant. Copying into a local variable, such as a Session object variable, gives a particular instance independent access.

Session Object

Every time a user accesses the Application object, a Session object is created. The Session object is used to track the user through the site. The protocols of the Web do not lend themselves to a session in the traditional sense, where the user logs into the system and a constant connection is kept open until a logoff sequence occurs. With HTTP, a user can jump from page to page and even leave the Web site without giving any notification to the server.

Microsoft created the Session object to reduce the difficulty in tracking an individual user. Whenever an HTTP request occurs, the user's IP address is sent with the request, similar to CallerID service on phone lines. The Session object creates a new session based on a new request ID and includes a timeout value. When no accesses from that IP are received within a certain period of time, the Session is deleted.

It is important to note that a Session state can be created only for users who have a browser that supports Cookies.

Variables are created using the = operator. Adding an object to another object collection requires the *CreateObject* method. If you store an object in the Session object and use VB Script as your primary scripting language, you must use the Set keyword, as illustrated in the following script:

```
<% Set Session("MSC") = Server.CreateObject("MySessionComponent")
```

You can then call the methods and properties of the component MSC on subsequent Web pages, by using the following:

```
<% Session("MSC").MyObjMethod %>
```

You can also extract a local copy of the object and use the following:

```
<%

Set MyLocalObject = Session("MySessionComponent")

MyLocalObject.MyObjMethod

%>
```

When the Session is originally created, it is assigned a SessionID. The SessionID is sent to the client's browser as a cookie and stored in the SessionID property. Programs can use the SessionID to track the user and record preferences. The data type of the SessionID property is long integer. Note that you should not count on the uniqueness of a particular SessionID number for any length of time. If the Web server is stopped and restarted, the SessionID mechanism is reset so that a SessionID could be a duplicate of one created earlier.

Because a Session is really a loosely defined concept in the world of HTTP, ASP must rely on tracking the requester's IP address and the length of time between requests to define a session. The Timeout property can be set to any value that is reasonable. The Timeout period is stored in minutes. The default amount of idle time before a session is discontinued is 20 minutes.

A Session may be eliminated in script code by using the *Abandon* method. The *Abandon* method queues the session for deletion but does not actually eliminate the session until the scripts on the current ASP page have finished executing. Any variables stored in the session will be eliminated when it is abandoned. Use the *Abandon* method as follows:

```
<% Session.Abandon %>
```

As mentioned in the global.asa section, sessions also have two events that can execute starting and ending code. Session_OnStart and Session_OnEnd events are executed when the Session begin and when it ends.

Request Object

The Request object returns any information passed to the ASP by an HTTP server request. It also adds the functionality of variables to the ASP system. Parameters that need to be used on the server side of the solution can be stored within the Request object.

Because there are multiple instances of each of each object within the Request object (for example, there can be multiple cookies for a single user), the main Request object contains a series of collections for each type of object; see Figure 9.3.

The Request object contains the following collections:

ClientCertificate

Cookies

Form

QueryString

ServerVariables

Each of these collections contains multiple objects that pertain to the HTTP request made by the user.

Figure 9.3 The Request object with all its object collections.

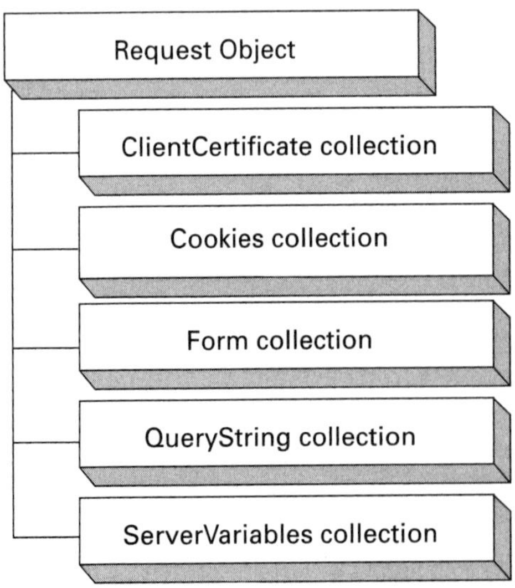

Form Collection

The Form collection holds the values of all the fields that the user entered on a form. When a form is submitted, an HTTP POST command is activated and ASP store the values of the fields as Form objects in the collection. Form values can be accessed by their name:

```
<% myVar = Request.Form("filename") %>
```

Each value also has an associated index value. To retrieve the value of the second parameter, code like this could be used:

```
<% myVar = Request.Form(2) %>
```

Multiple values can be stored in each parameter. For example, a list box could let the user select all the newspapers he or she reads daily. Here is an example of how the HTML source code might appear:

```
<HTML>

<FORM ACTION = "submit.asp" METHOD = "post">

<P>Select all of the newspapers you read daily: <SELECT NAME = "newspa-

per">

<OPTION>Union Tribune

<OPTION>Wall Street Journal

<OPTION>USA Today</SELECT>

<p><INPUT TYPE = SUBMIT>

</FORM>

</HTML>
```

When the user clicks the Submit button, all the selected values are stored in the *newspaper* field. A second level of specification is used if a parameter has multiple values. It comes in the form of following the parameter itself with an index value. The first newspaper parameter could be addressed by selecting the Form("newspaper")(1) value. To show all the newspapers that the user selected, you add the following code:

```
<%
  For I = 1 To Request.Form("newspaper").Count
    Response.Write Request.Form("newspaper")(I) & "<P>"
  Next
%>
```

You could also use the VB Script command structure For Each...Next:

```
<%
  For Each item In Request.Form("newspaper")
    Response.Write item & "<P>"
  Next
%>
```

This code would produce the same output as did the For...Next loop.

Client Certificate Collection

For security, a browser and a server can exchange digital certificates. Once the certificates are exchanged, all communication between the two is encrypted with these certificates. The ClientCertificate collection in the Request object contains all the information passed with the certificate to the server.

Only the IIS can be configured to provide server certificates. The Personal Web Server cannot be set up to exchange secure information. A server that provides certificate security uses "https://", rather than the traditional prefix of "http://", to signify that it is using a secure connection.

Cookies Collection

A cookie is a piece of information that a server can store on a client's machine, as long as the client's browser supports cookies. Typically, a server will store a user ID so that each request from a browser can be identified with the current user. Several electronic commerce applications use cookies to hold information, such as items added to a shopping cart.

When a Web server sends a cookie for the browser to store, the cookie is stored along with identification of the current server. Every HTTP request sent by the browser contains all the cookies that belong to that site. Sending only the cookies written by that site prevents one site from retrieving data that was written by another site.

QueryString Collection

When a QueryString is passed through a URL, all the parameter values are stored in the QueryString collection as separate objects.

```
http://www.coherentdata.com/search.asp?s=Active&s=Server&s=Pages
```

This particular command might activate a search engine stored in the script of the search.asp file. The command has requested a search with three words: Active, Server, and Pages. Each of these strings is stored as a separate object in the QueryString collection. To display the three values, you would use the following HTML source code:

```
<%
  For I = 1 To Request.QueryString("s").Count
    Response.Write Request.QueryString("s")(I) & "<BR>"
  Next
%>
```

With many of the ASPs, there is a problem if you'd like the user to bookmark a dynamic page in your site. The QueryString property eliminates this problem.

One real-world example of the effective use of the parameters passed in the URL string is provided by the online bookstore, amazon.com. It allows a Web page to reference a particular book within its catalog by including the ISBN number in a passed parameter. For example, the *Teach Yourself Visual Basic 5.0* book could be included as a link by putting an HREF in your HTML code:

```
<A HREF="http://www.amazon.com?ISBN=12345">TYVB book</A> xxx
```

Here is an example file that uses the parameters held in the QueryString collection:

```
<HTML>
<HEAD><TITLE>Request Query String</TITLE></HEAD>
<BODY>
<H1>Sample of a query string</H1>
<A HREF="qstring.asp?Value1=Active&Value2=Platform">Click here for a
demonstration.</A>
<P>
The current value of Value1 is <%= Request.QueryString("Value1") %><BR>
The current value of Value2 is <%= Request("Value2") %>
</BODY>
</HTML>
```

One of the best reasons to use Query Strings in certain parts of your site is to allow the user to record the request string in a bookmark. Parameters may be easily passed from one Active Server Page to another as the user moves through the Web site, but these parameters appear only in the background on the server. When the user selects the bookmark to return to a particular area of the site, he or she will instead return to the first page where the URL is acknowledged. Parameters passed as a request string are automatically saved in the URL of the bookmark. When the user reselects the bookmark, this information is once again passed to your site.

ServerVariables Collection

The ServerVariables collection contains all the variables that the server stores about the current client and the state of the server. Many of these variables are recorded in the Web server's log file written to disk.

Parameters such as the RemoteHost parameter, which gives the IP of the current user, can be used to examine information about the current user. Most of these variables are common to HTTP protocol variables.

The values contained within the variables can be read and used either for internal scripting, to check the complete URL for example, or for display to the user. The following code will add the QUERY_STRING value to HTML code:

```
<HTML>
<BODY>
The following example shows accessing an object in the ServerVariable col-
lection.
The variable QUERY_STRING:
<%= Request.ServerVariables("QUERY_STRING") %> <P>
</BODY>
</HTML>
```

Modifying the ServerVariables in a collection has no effect.

Response Object

The Response object will often be used by Web developers. The Response object holds all information provided by the user after a form has been submitted. Therefore, any collected data will be present in the collection of the Response object.

In this chapter, we demonstrate the response object by allowing the user to enter address information into a form that the Response.ASP file will then use to construct an HTML page containing the data.

Because the client may enter and exit a site at will, it is often difficult to track the user's identity or individual preferences. Cookies are small pieces of data stored on the client machine through the browser.

ASP can create and store cookies on the client machine to contain information such as the last page accessed by the user, a user ID, options selected by the user, the last item the user searched for, and other things.

In the Response object, ASP provide full access to setting the values of cookies using a collection named *Cookies*. A Cookie in the collection is referenced in the following fashion:

```
Response.Cookie("myLunch")( "Fruit").Value = "Apple"
```

This code creates a hierarchy of cookies stored on the browser. Known as a dictionary, myLunch would become the top level. The category Fruit within the myLunch dictionary would be set to Apple. When the user logs onto the site at another time or enters a different part of the site, this value can be retrieved.

If the Buffer property is FALSE, HTML can be sent to the user's browser prior to lengthy processing, so that the user knows he or she is not being ignored. This HTML could include a response table format, with the values to be inserted once the query is processed.

When the Buffer property is set to TRUE, use the *Flush* method to send the HTML contained in the buffer to the user's browser. If the *Flush* method is invoked but the Buffer property is not set to TRUE, ASP will generate a runtime error.

The ContentType property determines what content type will be sent for a particular HTTP request. The most common content type returned is "text/HTML". What if you needed to send back the data of a GIF file, or if, instead of processing the HTML code for a page, you wanted the browser to display the source code? The ContentType property tells the user's browser how to process the files it receives. Here are some common ContentType properties:

```
<% Response.ContentType = "text/plain" %>

<% Response.ContentType = "text/HTML" %>

<% Response.ContentType = "x-world/x-vrml" %>

<% Response.ContentType = "image/GIF" %>

<% Response.ContentType = "image/JPEG" %>
```

The Expires and ExpiresAbsolute properties are used to tell the browser when to eliminate the page from the cache. For example, you would never want an ASP file to be read from a cache because the ASP file is dynamic and may have changed every time it is accessed. An online newspaper, on the other hand, is renewed only once a day. Therefore, a cached version may be current today, but old tomorrow.

The Expires property sets the time in minutes before the page expires. Setting the property to 0 makes the page expire from the cache as soon as it is received. ExpiresAbsolute allows setting an exact date and time for the file to expire. The property must be set using the RFC-1123 date and time format. If our online newspaper has a new edition coming out on the first of January, we set the ExpireAbsolute property:

```
<% Response.ExpiresAbsolute=#January 1,1998 00:00:00# %>
```

Also, you can specify either the date or the time, or both. To make the page expire at 2:00 P.M., the code might look like:

```
<% Response.ExpiresAbsolute=#14:00:00# %>
```

The Status property contains the status code sent by the server. For example, almost everyone on the Web has, at one time or another, received a "404 Access denied" status code. The Status property, which holds the code returned by the server, may be retrieved and, possibly, modified in the ASP file. For example, an access denied error might be changed to:

```
<% Response.Status = "401 Unauthorized Access Denied" %>
```

Response Methods

AddHeader adds a header to HTML sent to the browser. Of course, it must be sent before any other information. The one exception to this involves the Buffer property. If the Buffer property is set to TRUE, nothing is sent to the browser until the *Flush* method is called. In this case, the *AddHeader* method may be called anytime before the *Flush* method.

AddHeader Method

AddHeader is used to send specific information to the browser. It is not a header like that on a document or even the <HEAD> tags in HTML. For example, to request that the browser use BASIC authentication, the ASP file might include the following HTML source code:

```
<% Response.Addheader "WWW-Authenticate", "BASIC" %>

<HTML>

Hello World! <P>

</HTML>
```

AppendToLog Method

AppendToLog is one of the most powerful methods included in ASP; you can use it to track usage of a Web site. This method appends a string to the current entry in the Web server log. By including your own information, you can store information in the log such as the referring Web page and anything else you can think of.

BinaryWrite Method

The *BinaryWrite* method can be used to send direct binary information to the client's browser. This method is useful if binary data is generated within the ASP that can be sent for display, but it should not be interpreted as HTML. For example, an Active Server Component could be created that generates a GIF of the current time in a special font. If this component were called GIFTime, the ASP code to send the GIF to the browser might look like this:

```
<%

Response.ContentType = "image/GIF"

Set gt = Server.CreateObject(ASP.GIFTime)

pict = gt.MakeGIF

Response.BinaryWrite pict

%>
```

The response type is set to send a GIF, and the component generates the binary data for the GIF. The *BinaryWrite* method then sends the GIF data in a binary stream to the browser.

Clear Method

The *Clear* method is used in conjunction with the Buffer property. If the Buffer is set to TRUE, the Clear command will eliminate anything held in the buffer. If the Buffer property is set to FALSE, activating this command will generate a runtime error. The *Clear* method does not clear anything contained in the header (see *AddHeader* method, discussed previously).

End Method

Executing the *End* method will halt the processing of the ASP file and return control to the user. If the Buffer property is set to TRUE, whatever is currently stored in the buffer will be sent to the browser. To eliminate the return of any currently buffered output, use the *Clear* method before the *End* method.

Flush Method

The *Flush* method sends any currently buffered information to the browser. Also see the Buffer property and the *Clear* method for direct buffer manipulation.

Redirect Method

The *Redirect* method sends the browser a command to redirect itself to another URL. This is often invoked when a page has moved because this method can automatically send the user to the new site. You will use this method later in this chapter when you construct the Banner advertisement demo using the Ad Rotator Active Server Component. In this application, when the user clicks on an ad, the user is sent to a page that records which ad is selected and then redirects the user's browser to the actual site the banner represents.

Write Method

The *Write* method is one of the most commonly used methods in the Response object. It can be used to programmatically output HTML from within a script. The *Write* method is limited to a single line or variable output per statement. The *Write* method will allow any amount of HTML to be sent to the browser; for example:

```
<%

Response.Write "<HTML>"

For i = 1 to 10

      Response.Write i + "<P>"

Next

Response.Write "</HTML>"

%>
```

Unless the Buffer property is set to TRUE, the HTML created using the *Write* method is sent to the browser as it is generated by the script: Be careful that the HTML you send is appropriate for viewing by the client in the order in which it will be received.

Base Components Overview

The Intrinsic controls provide information regarding the Web server itself. IIS also includes a number of controls that allow full-featured Web sites to be constructed easily and quickly. Examples of the use of each of the following functions made possible with ASC are given in this chapter:

- Allow database access
- Allow access to a filing system
- Retrieve client-side variables
- Rotate advertisements for automated banner ad implementation

The Base components will most likely be upgraded over time. As Microsoft refines the ActiveX Data Objects and more fully integrates them with both OLE DB and ODBC drivers, installation of new controls will obviate upgrading the entire IIS or PWS engine.

Active Data Connector

One technology that often creates some confusion among Active Server developers is the Active Data Connector. Although it is included with the Active Server Platform, it is important to recognize that it does not execute on the server *at all.* The ADC is a client-side data control that allows caching of data retrieved from a server, usually through the Active Data Objects, which do function on the server. After caching information on the client, the Web user can manipulate the data in simple ways, such as sorting, without having to request the data again.

Additionally, the Active Data Connector is an ActiveX control that requires an ActiveX-enabled browser that supports client-side scripting. The ADC is of primary interest to those deploying intranet solutions where users are best served by enabling simple client-side manipulation of server-provided data.

ActiveX Data Objects (ADO)

ActiveX Data Objects (ADO) will undoubtedly be the most used components included with IIS. ADO can communicate with any server-side ODBC data source. Through the use of ADO, you can construct entire Web/database applications. These applications are important to Internet Web deployment and crucial to intranet deployment.

ADO will supplant the Data Access Objects (DAO) and the Remote Data Objects (RDO) included with Visual Basic 5. ADO provide a thinner layer between the data access itself and your script. This makes data access faster and less memory-intensive. Microsoft plans to make ADO the standard way for all programs that in the past have used the DAO and RDO technologies to access database information. ADO provide a simple interface to the underlying OLE DB interface that connects to the data source.

Figure 9.4 OLE DB connection through a native driver and through an ODBC driver.

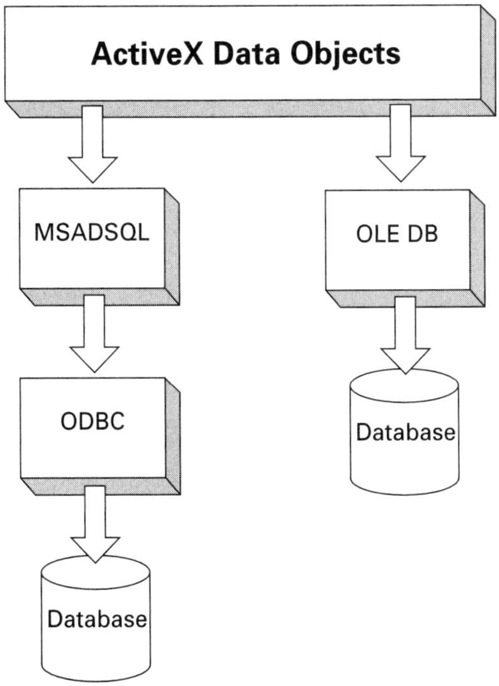

If there is a native driver, OLE DB can provide extremely fast access to the data. If the required data source uses ODBC, then the MSMDASQL driver is used to make the ODBC connection and translation; see Figure 9.4.

The Active Data Objects framework consists of Command objects, Connection objects, and Recordset objects, as shown in Figure 9.5. Unlike DAO and RDO, various ADO objects can be created and linked separately rather than having to construct an elaborate object hierarchy to create a simple query.

Data sources in ADO are most often queried using SQL statements. The following code creates a Recordset object to access a customers table:

```
Set tempRecordset = CreateObject("ADODB.Recordset")

tempRecordset.Open "SELECT * FROM customers",

"DATABASE=sales;UID=sa;PWD=;DSN=CustomerODBC"
```

The Recordset object is created using the *CreateObject* method. The *Open* method is then issued to return information to the Recordset object based on the SQL query criteria. In this case, the Open command is told to return all the records

Figure 9.5 ADO object model.

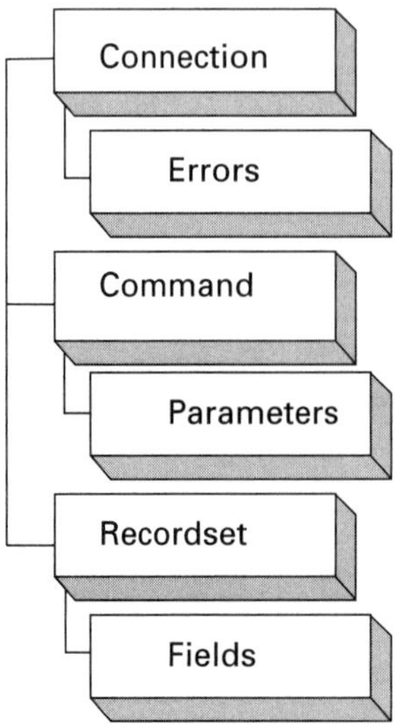

in the customer table that is accessed by the ODBC data source named CustomerODBC. The database that contains the requested table is named Sales.

Data is inserted into a database using the *Update* method. First the particular fields of a given record are set to new values. When the *Update* method is called, the ADO process the updates and send them through OLE DB to be synchronized in the main table.

The constants for the ADO data model are not included in VB Script. Therefore, to allow your ASP solution to use constant names rather than their numeric values, you must include a constant definition file in your ASP. If you are using Visual Basic Scripting Edition, include the file Adovbs.inc. If you are using JavaScript, include the file Adojavas.inc. Enter the following line of script to execute the include at the top of your ASP file:

```
<!--#include file=" Adovbs.inc "-->
```

ADO Object Model

For users already familiar with the DAO or RDO data models, it should be clear that ADOs are far simpler. Three main objects are used in the creation of an ADO object:

Connection object. The Connection object is used to make the connection to the data source including all the necessary base parameters such as the user name, password, default table, and timeout values.

Command object. The Command object holds the definition of a command that will be sent to execute against a particular data source. The commands stored in the Command object may include queries, stored procedures, record deletions or updates, or other SQL-based commands. When the *Execute* method is used with the Command object, it will return the number of records affected by the command.

Recordset object. Using the Recordset object requires essentially the same code structure as that available in DAO or RDO. The type of recordset may be a dynaset, a keyset cursor, a dynamic cursor, a static cursor, or a forward-only cursor.

Connection Object The Connection object keeps an open connection to an OLE DB data source. Configuration of the Connection object occurs through three properties:

Mode

ConnectionTimeout

ConnectionString

These configuration properties determine how the connection will react both to the connection established and to other users of the data source. A connection to the data source may be opened with the *Open* method, which requires three parameters:

ConnectionString

UserID

Password

The Connection string indicates the data source that will be used. This will most often be the name of an ODBC data source. The ConnectionString can also contain the data provider, the file name of the connection data, and the user name and password for transmission when the connection is opened.

If the user name and password are not supplied to the source through the ConnectionString, they are passed through the UserID and Password parameters to identify the user for login.

The *Close* method will disconnect the data source connection. Note that the *Close* method does not eliminate the Connection object—it merely closes the open data source connection.

The Attributes property stores the mode in which commits take place. By default, the Attributes property is set to 0. If the value is set to 131072, then the connection will perform retaining commits. This mode starts a new transaction automatically when the Recordset object *CommitTrans* method has been called. Setting the Attributes property to 262144 will start a new transaction automatically after the *RollbackTrans* method has been called. These two values can be added together to enable both options. Not all data sources provide these options.

The CommandTimeout property is set to the number of seconds that a command may run before the command is aborted and an error is issued: A process is aborted if the server use is too heavy or if the network traffic causes excessive delays. The default value is 30 seconds. This property may be overridden at the Command object level for particular commands.

The ConnectionString property stores the string used to connect to the data source. The *Open* method (described earlier) allows an optional ConnectionString parameter. If none is passed in the *Open* method, the string is retrieved from the ConnectionString property. When a parameter is passed through the *Open* method, the new string overwrites the string stored in the property.

The DefaultDatabase property holds the name of the default database to be used when the connection is opened. This may be set in the data source values so that you may not be able to change this property once the connection is made.

The IsolationLevel property governs the isolation level of transactions within a BeginTrans...CommitTrans structure. This property may be set to the values: adXactUnspecified (-1), adXactChaos (16), adXactBrowse (256), adX-actReadUncommitted (256), adXactCursorStability (4096), adXactReadCommitted (65536), and adXactIsolated or adXactSerializable (1048576). If the data source cannot comply with your isolation level, the next greater isolation level may be returned.

The Provider name holds the name of the provider for the particular data source. If the Provider will be an ODBC driver or if there is no Provider set, the MSDASQL provider will be used as the default. As more products acquire OLE DB native interfaces, more Providers will become available.

The Version property will return the version of ADO being used. This property is stored as a string value. The version of the Provider is stored in the Properties collection.

The Mode property selects the type of connection that will be created. It accepts integer values to make the connection ReadOnly (1), WriteOnly (2), Read/Write (3), Prevent others from opening with read permissions (4), Prevent others from opening with write permissions (8), Exclusive read/write (12), and Completely exclusive (16).

The ConnectionTimeout property contains the amount of time to wait before aborting a connection attempt. Setting this for an appropriate time prevents the user from endlessly waiting for a response and saves the processor overwhelmed with requests from trying to handle them all.

Command Object The Command object executes an operation against the data source. That operation may be the creation of a Recordset object, execution of a bulk operation, or changing the structure of the data source itself.

The CreateParameter method is used to create a new Parameter object. A new parameter needs a specified Name, Type, Direction, and Value. Although this method creates a Parameter object, it is not automatically appended to the Parameters collection in the Command object. Use the *Append* method for this.

The *Append* method is used to change the structure of the data source. It will add an object to the Parameters collection within the Command object. Before you execute the *Append* method, you must first set the Type property of the Parameter object to be appended.

The ActiveConnection property must hold the reference to a currently active connection. This parameter must be valid before the *Execute* method is called, or an error will be generated. The Command object may switch its base connection by having this parameter first set to Nothing and then set to a new Connection object.

The CommandText property contains the text of the command to be sent when the *Execute* method is activated. This property is usually set to equal an SQL command.

The CommandTimeout property can be set to allow a specified command to override the value of this property at the Connection object level. This allows a designer who knows a particular operation will take longer than the default timeout will allow to set this value specifically for this command.

The CommandType property indicates the type of Command object. It can contain the values: adCmdText (1), adCmdTable (2), adCmdStoredProc (4), and adCmdUnknown (8).

The Prepared property is a Boolean property that notifies the provider whether the command stored in the CommandText should be compiled. This option will take longer for the first execution, but if this command needs to be activated repeatedly, it will save time in the long run.

Execute Method The *Execute* method is used to send SQL to the data source. It can be used on either a Command object or a Connection object.

If the source is an ODBC data source, the SQL command will be interpreted through ODBC to access the data. If the source is a direct OLE DB driver and the source can accept SQL commands, the driver merely passes the execution statement through to the source for processing.

When the Execute statement has completed its operation, it will return the number of records that were affected. If the operation directly affects no records, the number 0 is returned. This would be the case if the operation were the creation of a stored procedure.

The *AddNew* method is used to create a new record in the current data source. Once the *AddNew* method has been used, the current record points to this new record. Therefore, any modification to the fields will be saved in this new record.

Errors Object The Errors object is used to return error code information about attempted operations, including updates, queries, and inserts.

The Description property describes in text what error occurred, the Number property stores the error number, the Source property contains the name of the property that caused the error, and the HelpContext and HelpFile properties indicate the Windows help files that are relevant to the error, if any.

The Errors object also contains information provided by the driver if the error occurred through the data source. The NativeError and SQLState properties contain error information returned by the driver.

All the Errors objects are contained within an Errors collection, and they can be referenced by individual item number or by error type.

Parameter Object The *AppendChunk* method is used to append binary data to a current field. Use the *AppendChuck* method to store OLE objects, pictures (BMP, GIF, JPG, etc.), or other binary data into a database. The AppendChunk command should only be used with the General type field.

The *Refresh* method can be used to update all objects contained within a collection, including connections to and from individual Properties objects. This method will repopulate any dynamic properties that are exposed by the provider.

The Count property may be used to determine how many Parameter objects are contained within a Parameters collection. This property may be used only against the collection itself.

The Item property can be used with an index value to return a specific item within a collection. The name of the item may also be used to retrieve the object. The Item property returns the reference to an object.

Property Object Property objects may be created in the collections of many different objects, including the Recordset object, Command object, Collection object, and others. The Property object is a dynamic object usually created by a vendor of a specific database. If a vendor such as Oracle wanted to provide capabilities or information not supported by the generalADO object, these could be added through Property objects added to other objects.

The *Refresh* method can be used to update all objects contained within a collection, including connections to and from individual, Properties objects. This method will repopulate any dynamic properties that are exposed by the provider.

The Count property may be used to determine how many Property objects are contained within a Properties collection. This property may be used only against the collection itself.

The Item property can be used with an index value to return a specific item within a collection. The name of the item may also be used to retrieve the object. This property returns the reference to an object.

Recordset Object The Recordset object actually holds the records retrieved from the query. It is the key object when accessing data sources. Using the methods included in the Recordset object, you may move within the available records, update data, insert new records, and set a filter to view only specific records within a data set. The Recordset object is very flexible, and multiple recordsets may be created from a single session.

The simplest example of accessing a recordset is to create a new Recordset object and execute the *Open* method. A Connection object will automatically be created for the recordset, and the connection will be made.

```
set rstMain = CreateObject("ADODB.Recordset")

rstMain.Open "SELECT * FROM authors",

"DATABASE=pubs;UID=sa;PWD=;DSN=Publishers"
```

The password sent to the data source in the ASP file is hard-coded into the connection string above. Be careful if you decide to implement password verification through a standard HTML form because sending the data over the insecure Internet could result in a captured user name and password. It is best to register for a verified certificate for your server from a trusted company like Verisign. When a connection is then made between a user's browser and your server, an encrypted SSL channel is created, making interception and decoding of the password nearly impossible.

The Recordset object supports transaction processing: Of a series of database changes, either all will occur or none, thereby preventing data corruption.

The classic example of a database system handling the transfer of money from account A to account B illustrates the need for the Recordset object: Money must first be removed from account A and then credited to account B.

These actions together form a transaction, which must be completed before any other process is allowed to access account A or account B. If a second process read the balance of account A prior to the debit and then performed a credit afterward, the debit would disappear. If account A is mine, I like this. If I'm the bank or its programmer, I'm not so happy.

Transactions encapsulate multiple operations within a single event. The *BeginTrans* method is used to open a transaction. When all the operations have been entered, the *CommitTrans* method can be called to commit the changes to the data source. If an error were to occur, the *RollbackTrans* method might be invoked to roll back and eliminate all the transactions at once.

To update any changes made to the current record, you can use the *Update* method. To cancel these changes, you can use the *CancelUpdate* method. The *Update* method will send the OLE DB driver the signal to attempt an update, which might include a SQL *Update* command.

In many cases, updating a number of records in a given data source is necessary. Loading each record and subsequently submitting an update to the data source can be time-consuming. If all updates could be cached at the recordset until an update was requested, then all record modifications could be sent to the data source at once. Batch updates should be performed only with keyset or static cursors.

To start a batch update, the Recordset object LockType must be set to adLockBatchOptimistic (4) before the recordset is opened. When the recordset is opened in this mode, updates do not occur until the *UpdateBatch* method is called. The *UpdateBatch* method writes all the record changes to the data source.

If the updates need to be aborted, you can use the *CancelBatch* method; the CancelBatch method will cancel all the operations buffered in a batch update function.

To navigate the recordset, methods such as *Move*, *MoveFirst*, *MoveLast*, *MoveNext*, and *MovePrevious* are available.

Once all the necessary properties for the Recordset object have been set, the *Open* method may be executed to establish the connection between the data source and the Recordset object. If no Connection object is specified but all parameters are in place, the Recordset object will establish a connection. The optional Source argument may be used to specify the necessary connection.

Once the Recordset is no longer needed, the *Close* method will flush all records contained in the recordset. The method closes any dependent objects and frees the system resources associated with them. Using the Close command does not eliminate the Recordset object, so properties for the object itself may still be changed and an Open command executed to re-create the structures it represents.

The *Requery* method is used to requery the data source and retrieve any changes that may have occurred or any new records that meet the criteria in the original query. Requery is often necessary if a great deal of time has passed since the data's original acquisition. It may also be necessary if changes were made to the database using direct SQL commands rather than interfacing through the ADO methods such as *Update*.

The *GetRows* method is used to copy rows from the recordset into an array. This method can be used effectively if you need to display a certain number of records on the screen at a particular time.

The *Clone* method is used to duplicate a recordset from the current recordset; for example:

```
<% Set newRS = oldRS.Clone %>
```

The *Delete* method can be used to eliminate the selected record. Delete commands, like Update commands, are encapsulated within the batch process.

If the recordset is based on a compound command set, the *NextRecordset* method will clear the current recordset and execute the next command. A compound recordset is one created with a command string that contains multiple queries. For example, the command string might be equal to "Select * from MyTable1; Select * from MyTable2." If there are no more recordsets to use, the recordset returned will be empty. If both the BOF and the EOF properties are set to TRUE, the recordset is empty.

The *Resync* method synchronizes the data with the underlying database by refreshing the data. The *Supports* method allows the driver to be queried to determine whether it supports a particular type of cursor usage. Cursor options such as move forward and backward may be determined through this method.

The BOF and EOF functions are set to TRUE if the current record is either the beginning of the file or the end of the file, respectively.

ActiveConnection provides a pointer to the current connection. This property cannot be changed while the recordset is open.

The Filter property allows you to set a particular type of filter on the recordset. When the Filter property is set, it automatically requeries the data for those that comply with the new specifications. The first record to comply with the new filter parameters becomes the current record.

The LockType property is used to determine how multiuser access of the data source occurs. The LockType property has four settings: Access recordset in read-only mode, pessimistic locking, optimistic locking, and batch update optimistic locking. Pessimistic record locking locks each record as the record is edited. Optimistic locking locks the record only when the Update method is issued.

The *RecordCount* method will return the number of records available in the current recordset. Use the *Requery* method to make sure this number is current.

The Source property contains the name of the data source where the Recordset object retrieves its data. This property string might contain the name of a table, a query, a Command object, or a stored procedure. If the Source indicates a Command object, the ActiveConnection of the Recordset object will be set to match the equivalent property stored in the Command object.

The PageSize property is used to define the number of records present on a "page." Pages are used to navigate or browse effectively through large data sets.

The AbsolutePage property indicates the page of the currently selected record within the Recordset object based on the number of records per page, as defined in the PageSize property.

The PageCount property describes the total number of pages contained within the recordset given the setting of the PageSize property. The end of the recordset can be determined by comparing the AbsolutePage property value with the PageCount property value.

The position of the current record is stored in the AbsolutePosition property. This position is located as the RecordCount property identifies the total number of records and the first available record is numbered 1.

The Recordset object allows the creation of a bookmark to store a position at a current record. Using bookmarks, the user can page within the recordset and still return to a particular record. If the recordset is closed, the bookmark values are flushed from memory. Only one bookmark may be created per record, and not all data sources support bookmarks.

The CacheSize property determines how many records will be read into a recordset object at a time. By determining the ideal CacheSize for each application, you can optimize the user's experience. If the cache is set too high, too much memory and time are used before the user ever sees the data stored in the recordset. If the cache is too small, the system constantly requeries the data source and consequently hinders performance. You can determine the correct cache size only by judgment and trial and error. The default number of CacheSize is set to 10.

The cursor supported by a particular data source is stored within the CursorType property. The available types include forward-only, keyset, dynamic, or static. Visual InterDev features an effective interface that can determine the cursor types that the intended data source supports.

The EditMode property indicates the status of the current record. If the record has been edited but not saved, the value is set to 1. If a new record has been added using the *AddNew* method, the value is set to 2. If no editing is in progress, the property is set to 0.

The MaxRecords property can be used to limit how many records are loaded into a recordset. By default, this value is set to 0 and so disables a maximum number. If memory overloads are a problem, you could use the MaxRecords property. When most recordsets lived on the client machines in applications such as Visual Basic, this property was rarely used. As more and more ASP files are created on servers, this property will probably be used heavily to control resource usage.

The Status property reports on the status of the current record regarding batch updates and other bulk transactions. Values in this property indicate whether the record is new, updated, modified, deleted, or bookmarked.

Connection Pooling

The newest ODBC driver, ODBC 3.0, features a new capability, *connection pooling*. Many information systems need periodic access to a database. In traditional data-access models, each database user opens a connection and begins a session with the database. The session keeps track of all security privileges and other information concerning the user. Sessions are expensive in terms of server resources. Maintaining a connection and all the information and processing that this implies can become prohibitive to system performance if the number of users becomes too great, as it often does in Internet applications.

Consumption of server resources is a significant problem with Web database access, where connections must be routinely created and destroyed. Because no login or other process occurs to create a true database session, the user may move through a Web site and, by the nature of the pages he or she selects, create several connections.

To resolve this problem, ODBC 3.0 features connection pooling, in which many open connections are kept idle until they are needed. When a connection is requested, it is removed from the pool and activated for the duration of the task. The connection then remains live for generally 60 seconds of inactivity. After this time, the connection is once again put in suspended mode and returned to the connection pool.

Use of the connection pool occurs completely in the background to ASP users. Certain programming methods should be followed to best enable the system to work effectively. Although the ADO connection should be created and destroyed with each page access, the following is recommended:

```
Session("ConnectionString") = "dsn=AdvWorks;uid=advworks;pwd=advworks"
```

On each page:

```
<OBJECT RUNAT=Server ID=Conn PROGID="ADODB.Connection"></OBJECT>
```

To open the session:

```
Conn.Open Session("ConnectionString")
```

When the session is complete, use the *Close* method as you normally would.

```
Conn.Close
```

You can alter various aspects of the connection pool in the registry. For more information on the specific entries, see the Active Server Pages or the ODBC 3.0 documentation.

ADO Security Issues

You may be tempted to use a single data source for all the solutions you develop with ADO. A problem arises when a single-source database access skirts traditional security settings and password validation. If all your users access data through an ASP that uses a single ADO data source, then all those users have the same level of security access.

The unification of DAO and RDO under the ADO specification may centralize some of the available security. If OLE DB evolves to become a unified security model, security that was an afterthought may be used as a matter of course.

The Future of ADO

Because ADO provides the simplified user interface for OLE DB, it will become a centerpiece of Microsoft's database access strategy. OLE DB will be implemented enterprise-wide and across every platform on which ActiveX is available. Through Component Object Model (COM) and Distributed COM (DCOM), the foundation technologies for ActiveX, OLE DB can be accessed by any program and even across any network.

The OLE DB specification is an open standard, much like ODBC. Microsoft plans to adopt OLE DB as its standard way of addressing heterogeneous data sources. If Microsoft is as effective at promoting OLE DB as a standard as it was with ODBC, OLE DB may become the premier object data store access method.

Instead of having ODBC data sources, OLE DB introduces the new concept of data providers. A *data provider* essentially is an object that supplies all drivers needed to access a database. All data handling occurs through the data provider object. In this way, queries can reach into data not accessible by traditional SQL engines and heterogeneous data such as mapping information, image and document databases, and even real-time data suppliers.

ODBC 3.0 is an upgrade from the 2.5 specification that adds to the ODBC data model in several ways; the most significant is its ability to add connection pooling, described earlier. ODBC 3.0 also complies more closely with the transparency between data sources by providing complete access to stored procedures.

ADO will also lead the way to conditional optimization scripts for different data sources. If the query can be most effective when executed on a particular server using a different type of script, the DAO can be created to automatically make this selection and optimize itself. All of this activity would be transparent to the user, who sees only better data performance.

Content Linking Component

The Content Linking Component will be used mostly for online magazines, journals, and newsletters. It allows the creation of an electronic table of contents. The objects contained in the Content Linking Component can be used to navigate the links of a Web page.

To get the total number of pages contained in the content linking file, use the *GetListCount* method. It returns an integer of the number of pages when it is passed a URL.

You can retrieve the index number of the currently accessed page by using the *GetListIndex* method. The first item in a list is given the number 1, and each page after that is numbered sequentially. If the current page is not part of the content list, the value 0 is returned. The *GetListIndex* method requires that the list's URL be passed to it.

You can use the *GetPreviousDescription* and *GetNextDescription* methods to retrieve the pages before and after the current page. If *GetNextDescription* is used and the current page is not in the link list, the last link in the file is returned. If *GetPreviousDescription* is used and the current page isn't in the list, the first link is returned.

The *GetNextURL* and *GetPreviousURL* methods serve the identical functions except they retrieve the URL of the desired page. If the page is not on the list, the first page is returned in the case of *GetPreviousURL*; the last page is returned when a *GetNextURL* is used.

The *GetNthDescription* and *GetNthURL* methods allow you to retrieve specific items from the Content Link list. You may find these methods most useful for creating a Goto page for explicit navigation. They may also prove effective when you create a table of contents or index for the site.

Link File Format

The catalogue of links is contained in a file used by the CL control. The link file is stored in a standard ASCII text file created using a program such as Notepad. If you're using Visual InterDev, remember to add the file to your project so that it may be updated and you may update and change the placement of your Web page content.

The link file is made up of line references to each of the necessary files. The actual line is structured with the Web page URL, followed by the description of the file and an optional comment related to the entry. Each of these three fields should be separated by a TAB character. The following is an example of a link field with seven entries, each pertaining to the subject of Active Platform.

```
story1.htm Highlights From the Hockey Playoffs

story2.htm Congress Passes New Welfare Initiative

story3.htm Cider Recipes to Warm Long Winter Nights

story4.htm Winter Storm to bring more snow to East

story5.htm Reducing Stress on the Job

main.htm Return to the table of contents
```

FileSystem Component

The FileSystem component is very useful, but it may be the most dangerous component for ASP to use. Through the FileSystem control, code can completely manipulate the file system on the server, including modifying, moving, and deleting files and folders.

The *CreateTextFile* creates a new file at the specified path. This method takes three parameters: the file name, the overwrite, and the unicode parameters. The overwrite parameters tell the method how it should function if the file to be created matches the name of a file that already exists in the given path. If set to TRUE, the file is written over. If FALSE, the file is left alone and the new file is not created. Also, an error is generated in the runtime object, so the user may be alerted why the operation did not take place.

The Unicode flag allows the file to be created in Unicode format. This is useful most for the international version of the server.

The *OpenTextFile* method is used to open a file, but not only for reading. *OpenTextFile* is also used for appending to the file and reading from it. The syntax of this method can be seen here:

```
Set Instream = FileObject.OpenTextFile (Server.MapPath ("/AdvWorks") &
"\tips.txt", 1, FALSE, FALSE)
```

The file name must be given, followed by the access method. The access method can be one of three types, 1=Read the text file, 2=Write to the file, and 8=Append to the file.

VB Script does not implement any file access commands that are traditionally available in Visual Basic. Instead, all file access on the server occurs through the FileSystem component. The following sample code picks a tip from a file of single-line Active Platform tips:

```
<HTML>

<BODY>

<%


' Open the file with Active Platform tips

Set FileObject = Server.CreateObject("Scripting.FileSystemObject")


Set Instream = FileObject.OpenTextFile (Server.MapPath ("/APSourceBook") &

"/tips.txt", 1, FALSE, FALSE)




' Find how many tips there are

NumTips = CInt(Instream.ReadLine)

Randomize

' Select a random tip

TipNum = Int(Rnd*NumTips)
```

```
' Move to the tip chosen in the random routine

For i = 1 to TipNum -1

      InStream.SkipLine()

Next


Response.Write Instream.ReadLine

%>

</BODY>

</HTML>
```

When the file access occurs, you'll notice that the file type is set to the value of 1. VB Script does not automatically understand constant values. Therefore, if you see sample code that includes a constant, make sure that the constant's definition is contained within the source code or it will be treated as a variant variable when placed in the code. By default, this variant will be set to a value of 0.

TextStream Component

Once a file has been created or opened using the FileSystem component, that file can be read and written into using the TextStream component.

A text stream most often is a standard text file that needs parsing. With all characters that are read or skipped, the *column* property advances. When a newline character occurs, the column property is reset to 1 and the Line property is incremented by 1. When a file is first opened, both the Line and the Column properties are set to 1.

The AtEndofLine property can be used to read through a file, character by character, until the line is processed. The property is set to TRUE if the end of the line is reached or to FALSE otherwise. For example, the following code will check a line to see if it is the beginning of a <BODY> tag:

```
<%
'Create an object reference to the file system
Set fs = CreateObject("Scripting.FileSystemObject")
' Open the file to check if the first line contains a <BODY> tag
Set myFile = fs.OpenTextFile("c:\checkhtml.txt", 1, False)
Do While myFile.AtEndOfLine <> True
    CurLine = CurLine + myFile.Read(1)
    if CurLine = "<BODY" then
            Response.Write "Found a <BODY> tag"
      end if
Loop
myFile.Close
%>
```

If the text stream has been opened not for reading but for writing or appending, this method will generate a runtime error.

The AtEndofStream property can be used to detect the end of the file. A Do While...Loop can be used to scan the entire file until the AtEndofStream property is TRUE. A routine could be written that would scan a file and report all the individual lines that contained <BR> tags. Such a routine would look like this:

```
<%
'Create an object reference to the file system
Set fs = CreateObject("Scripting.FileSystemObject")
' Open the file to count the number of <BR> tags
Set myFile = fs.OpenTextFile("c:\checkhtml.txt", 1, False)
numlines = 0
```

```
Do While myFile.AtEndOfStream <> True
    CurLine = myFile.ReadLine
    if CurLine = "<BR>" then
            numlines = numlines + 1
      end if
Loop
Response.Write "Number of individual <BR> tags:" + numlines
myFile.Close
%>
```

The *Close* method will actually close the text stream that was opened using the FileSystemObject. Any methods that reference the TextStream object after the file has been closed will generate a runtime error.

The *Read* method reads a specified number of characters from the current text stream object. The characters are returned as a string. The *ReadLine* method will read characters until it reaches a newline character. The method will read up to the newline character, but the newline will not be included in the string.

The *ReadAll* method will read the entire file into memory. The ReadAll command should not be used for large files. It is more effective to use the Read or ReadLine files to load the file as it is needed or processed.

The *Skip* method acts in the same way as the *Read* method in moving the pointer forward in the file, but it instead discards the characters. The *SkipLine* method will skip all the characters including the newline character that defines the line. Both the *Skip* and *SkipLine* methods can be used to move over defined file headers in order to read the primary body of the file.

The *Write* and *WriteLine* methods write a specified string of characters to the current text stream file. Although they accomplish nearly the same function, the *WriteLine* method adds a newline character after the included string.

The *WriteBlankLines* method adds a specified number of newline characters to the current text stream file. This method can be especially effective when you are formatting a particular HTML file for display. The number of blank lines is passed as a parameter to this method.

Browser Capabilities Component

Using the Browser Capabilities Component, an Active Server Page can determine the browser's abilities as it accesses the page. The page can then be instantly modified to suit the particular client. For example, if the browser that is accessing the page cannot execute Java applets, the ASP file can use If...Then statements to eliminate the Java applet from the HTML page fed to the client.

```
<HTML>

<HEAD><TITLE>Browser Properties</TITLE></HEAD>

<BODY>


<%  Set bc = Server.CreateObject("MSWC.BrowserType") %>


<H1>Browser properties:</H1>

Browser Type: <%= bc.Browser %><P>

What Version: <%= bc.Version %><P>

Major Version: <%= bc.Majorver %><P>

Minor Version: <%= bc.Minorver %><P>

Frames: <%= CStr(CBool(bc.Frames)) %><P>

Tables: <%= CStr(CBool(bc.Tables)) %><P>

Cookies: <%= CStr(CBool(bc.cookies)) %><P>

Background Sounds: <%= CStr(CBool(bc.BackgroundSounds)) %><P>

VBScript: <%= CStr(CBool(bc.VBScript)) %><P>
```

```
JavaScript: <%= CStr(CBool(bc.Javascript)) %><P>

<P>

</BODY>

</HTML>
```

If you load this code into your browser, you will be able to display all your browser's characteristics. The browser itself does not provide all the information. Rather, the information is stored in a file called browscap.ini. This file is a lookup file with one entry for each browser that it recognizes. The characteristics for that browser are contained in the entry of the INI file. If no entry is found for the browser type, the returned characteristics are all set to UNKNOWN.

Advertisement Rotator Component

Most professional sites on the Internet feature a banner advertisement at the top of the main page. Users can click on the banner to jump to a site related to the ad itself. Many popular sites charge about $20 for each 1000 times a user sees a particular ad. Included with Active Server is the Advertisement Rotator Component. This component eliminates the drudgery of implementing the routines that rotate through a list of advertisements by supplying most of the necessary logic. Every time that a user browses your page, an ad from the ad file is displayed.

The interface to the Ad Rotator is quite simple. It relies on a file held on the server to list all the necessary ad pictures (in GIF or JPG format), the frequency with which each ad will be displayed, the link that takes the user to the site the ad represents, and other information. When the user clicks on a particular banner, this information can be recorded in the Web server logs. The log data allows you to track how often users click on a particular banner.

The Ad Rotator component has several important properties:

Border property. The Border property contains the width of the border that will surround the ad.

Clickable property. The Clickable property determines whether the user can click on the banner.

TargetFrame property. This property indicates the URL of the target when clicked.

The component features only a single method, the *GetAdvertisement* method, which you embed in your ASP code to automatically insert the banner advertisement into the final HTML code.

Using the Rotator Schedule File

All the information for the banner ads is stored in a specially formatted file. This file contains information about the ad, including these items:

Name

Location

Frequency of display

The Rotator Schedule file is divided into two parts: the header and the body. The header describes conditions that will be applied to all the banners contained within the file. The body contains all the individual banners and their associated properties. The header is separated from the body by a line containing a single asterisk (*).

The header contains four parameters: redirect URL, width, height, and border. The width, height, and border all define the appearance of the banner ad. The redirect URL specifies the address of the ASP that redirects the click after the user has clicked on a banner ad. This redirection page is optional, but it is necessary to recorder the number of times users selected a particular advertisement.

The body portion of the Rotator Schedule contains one entry for each banner that will be displayed by the component.

Now it is time for you to create your own Rotator Schedule file.

1. Create the Rotator Schedule file so that it looks like the listing below. Save the file as adSchedule.txt.

```
redirect adRedirect.asp

width 460

height 60

border 1
```

```
*

ad_1.gif

http://www.coherentdata.com

Coherent Data

20


ad_2.gif

http://www.coherentdata.com/cscentral

Client/Server Central

20


ad_3.gif

http://www.dbmsmag.com

DBMS Magazine

30
```

2. Now you need to create a sample page that will show the banners. Each banner will automatically be placed in the Web page according to the frequency indicated in the rotator file. You can create the main page for the rotator in Notepad or Visual InterDev and save it as adRotate.ASP. Here is an example of the HTML source code you should write:

```
<HTML>

<HEAD><TITLE>The Advertisement Rotator component</TITLE></HEAD>

<BODY BGCOLOR=#FFFFFF>

<H3>The Advertisement Rotator component</H3>


<%  Set Ad = Server.CreateObject("MSWC.Adrotator") %>
```

```
<%= Ad.GetAdvertisement("adSchedule.txt") %>


<P>Click on the banner ad shown above.

</BODY>

</HTML>
```

> **TIP** The redirector file will record which banner ad was selected before the transfer occurs. Be sure to include in your redirect file a manual redirection link. If a server becomes too busy, the user will have to wait until extra processor time is available for the transfer to occur. On Microsoft's own site, this wait can sometimes stretch to more than 30 seconds. Therefore, as a courtesy, it is wise to provide a manual link as well.

3. Enter the following code into Notepad or Visual InterDev. Note that there are no HTML tags or Body tags in this code. Because it is a redirector page, HTML code will not allow it to function correctly. Create the file and save it as adRedirect.ASP:

```
<%

      On Error Resume Next


      ' Setup FileSystemObject to access our text files

      Set FileObject = Server.CreateObject("Scripting.FileSystemObject")

      ' Create a variable that contains the path to the file

      CountFile = (Server.MapPath ("/APSourceBook") & "\adLog.txt")


      ' Open the file for appending

      ' Parameters: 8=Open for appending, False=Don't create if none
exists

      Set outStream = FileObject.OpenTextFile (countFile, 8, FALSE)
```

```
    ' Write the current time, date, and the requested URL

    outStream.WriteLine (Now & chr(9) & Request.QueryString("url"))

    ' Clear the outStream object

    Set OutStream = Nothing


    ' Redirect to selected banner URL

    Response.Redirect(Request.QueryString("url"))

%>
```

4. Create a blank text file with the name adLog.txt. This is the file where user selections will be stored. You will also need three GIF files for the banner ads themselves. In the Schedule file, you have named our three banners ad_1.gif, ad_2.gif, and ad_3.gif. If you don't use these file names, make sure you change the schedule file to match the new names.

Adding a Counter

Some of the most popular CGI programs are the ones that add a counter to a Web page so users can see how may people have visited a particular site. The built-in component makes adding a counter extremely easy.

The sample counter you will create uses a text file located in the APSourcebook directory called *count.txt.* This file contains only one line, which contains the numeric counter. Each time a user accesses the page, the counter is incremented by 1 and the file is written over.

Using either Notepad or Visual InterDev, enter the source code for the following file and save it as Count.ASP:

```
<HTML>

<BODY>

<H1>Counter Example ASP file</H1>


<%
```

```
' In case two instances access the file at exactly the same time,
' ignore the error and therefore the update
On Error Resume Next

' Setup FileSystemObject to access our text files
Set FileObject = Server.CreateObject("Scripting.FileSystemObject")
' Create a variable that contains the path to the file
CountFile = (Server.MapPath ("/APSourceBook") & "\count.txt")

' Open the file
' Parameters: 1=Open for reading, False=Don't create if none exists
Set inStream = FileObject.OpenTextFile (countFile, 1, FALSE)
' Read the first line which should contain the current value
counterStr = Instream.ReadLine
' Clear the inStream object
Set inStream = Nothing

' Convert the string to a number
tempnum = CInt(counterStr)
' Increment the number
tempnum = tempnum + 1

' Recreate the file for new output
' Parameters: True = Overwrite existing file, False = No Unicode
```

```
        Set outStream= FileObject.CreateTextFile (countFile, True, False)

        ' Write the incremented counter number

        outStream.WriteLine (tempnum)

        ' Clear the outStream object

        Set OutStream = Nothing

%>


<P>

Current Visitor: <%= tempNum %><BR>

</BODY>

</HTML>
```

Creating Components

You can create a component in any number of languages that support COM objects, but you will primarily use C++, Java, and Visual Basic. Each has its strengths and weaknesses; their primary strengths can be summarized as follows:

- C++ executes most quickly, gives the most access to system calls, and allows encapsulation of existing C++ code
- Java programming is portable across platforms, and it is very similar to C++ but simplified
- Visual Basic leverages knowledge of VB/VBA/VB Script for more than 3 million programmers

When components are created, they are also easier to maintain because all the source code for all the routines they contain can be stored in a single project file. This approach yields a system that is easier to maintain than the numerous ASP files that have no direct connections.

The Active Server Pages system makes no distinction between server-side and client-side components (see Figure 9.6). Therefore, beware of how you use the components because the user interface portions of particular controls can affect the functioning of the server operation. For example, if you used Excel as a server-side control and requested it to write to a file name that already exists, it would activate a Yes/No save dialog box on the server. This dialog box would never appear in the the browser client; users would think that the system has "hung."

If you want to create a server-side solution that, on request from the client, e-mails a message, you could do so using the MAPI messaging controls included with Visual Basic 5.

In Figure 9.7, you can see how the control object appears once it has been inserted into the ASP.

Figure 9.6 The ActiveX control menu shows not only server-side components but client-side components as well.

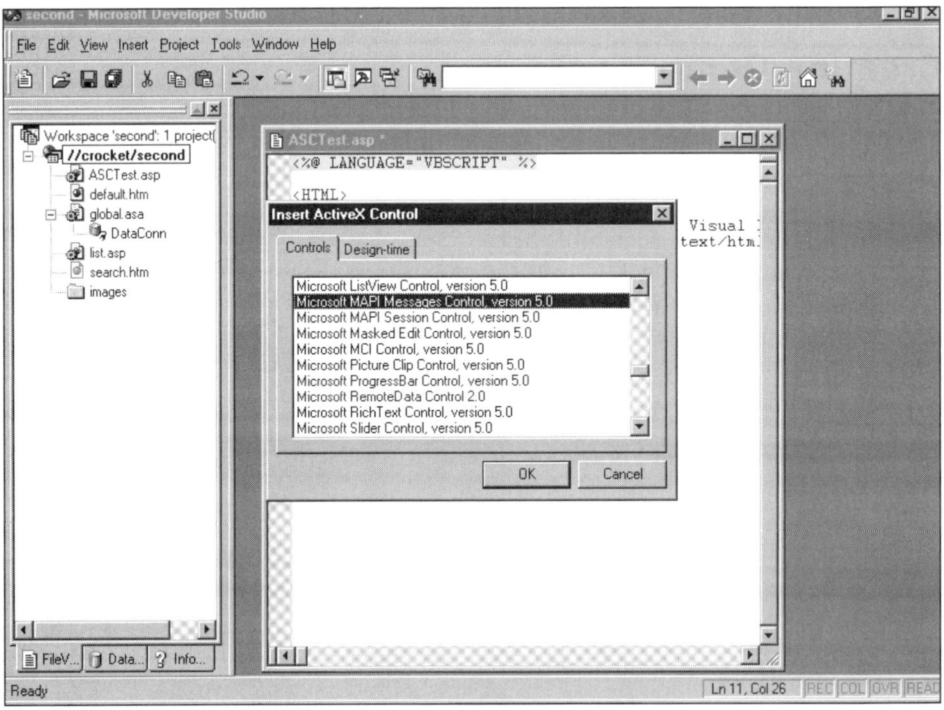

The number of server-side components being created for real-world deployment is growing. Some of these new components include the following:

- Online shopping software
- SMTP mail
- POP3 component
- DNS lookup component
- Calendar generation component
- FTP get and put component
- Credit card checker component

Figure 9.7 The meta-data heads that supply information to the controls when they are re-activated are nearly identical to the ActiveX control header.

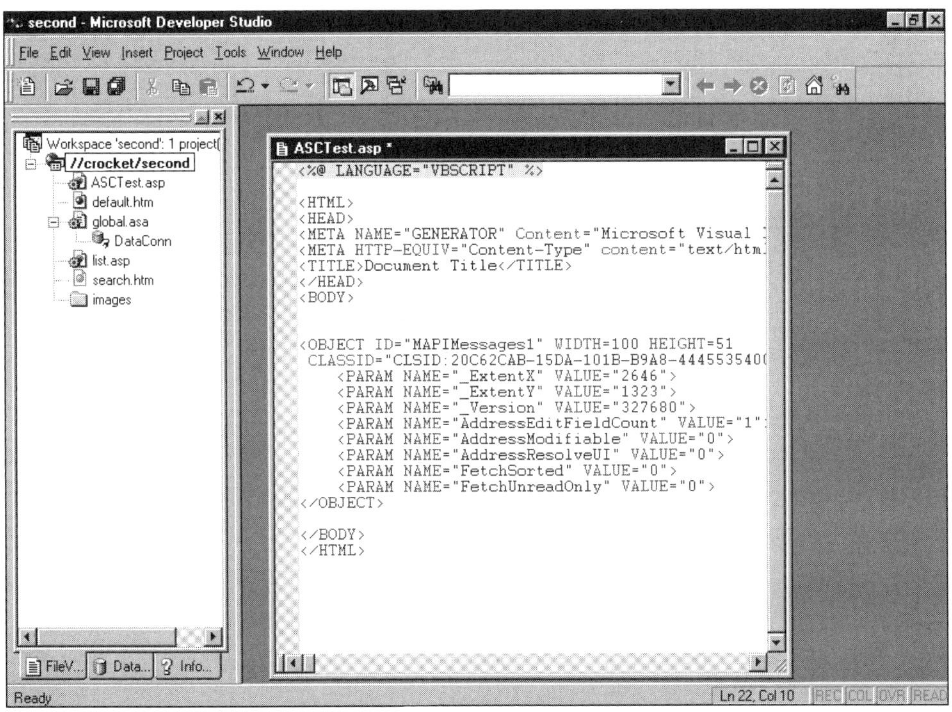

The Microsoft Web site has other server components with source code that you can download for free. Here is a list of just some of those server components:

- Content Rotator component
- HTML Table component
- Page Counter component
- Registry Access component
- Text Formatter component
- Threading models

How effectively an ASC executes largely depends on the threading model used for the component. Threading essentially defines memory usage and the creation of instances of the object.

Single-threaded components are essentially the most ineffective type of ASC. As in a CGI application, a separate process must be developed every time an instance is created. All information exchange must take place through a single thread. When a new instance is needed, the amount of memory and resources must match an entirely new copy of the component.

Visual Basic 4 could create only single-threaded components. This meant that each instance of the application consumed a minimum of 500K of memory. If 10 users accessed the page using the component simultaneously, the server would use more than 5 MB of memory to execute that single component!

Apartment threading allows multiple threads to access the same object, while free-threading opens up even more flexibility.

C++ Components

Components written in C++ will most likely execute faster than components created using Visual Basic or Java. They are significantly more difficult to write, however, unless you are intimately familiar with the C++ environment.

The easiest way to create a component in C++ is to use the Active Template Library (ATL). ATL creates smaller and faster components than the OLE component libraries. Applications created with ATL can support all three threading models: single, apartment, and free-threaded. ATL will aid you in creating controls of varying levels of complexity including minimal COM object, Internet Explorer ActiveX controls, and full OLE controls.

To use the ATL, the COM AppWizard and the ATL Object Wizard will automate the setup and core routines. The C++ IDispatch interfaces are used to access all the key ActiveX or OLE routines within the object being created.

Java Components

One of the technologies generating the most press coverage in recent years is the programming language Java. Java's machine-independent nature makes the possibility of cross-platform application generation an enticing promise. Microsoft has provided one of the best Java development tools in the industry in the form of the Visual J++ development environment. Through Active Platform, Microsoft has also made Java deployment more effective.

Active Server Pages allow Java components to be run on the server. By creating a single application in Java, perhaps using JavaBeans components, core business functions can be encapsulated, allowing an application to be used on diverse server platforms.

Creation of Java components for use with ASP relies heavily on Microsoft's own Active Server Pages Object Library. This library that may be generated by the Java Type Library Wizard included with Visual J++.

Market availability of JavaBeans may create many usable server components for cross-platform implementation. Currently, a Java application must be compiled with the object extensions included with Visual J++, which are known as the ASP Classes. They provide the gateway to the Request, Response, Application, Server, and Session intrinsic objects.

Installation of Components

Any components that are installed on the server must be registered so that the ActiveX system can find them. There are three primary ways to register a component on the server:

- Download via a CAB file, which automatically registers the control
- Manually register it using the regsrv32.exe program
- Use the Browse command to access the TLB or SBL file

The best way to check the objects registered on the current system and the methods and properties they support is to look in the Object browser. The Object browser is available in all the Office applications, Visual Basic 5, Visual C++ and J++, and Visual InterDev.

Make sure that you have checked the References dialog to see whether it is available to the current application (see Figure 9.8). A program must specify the components from which it needs access to create instances. If every application automatically loaded the headers of every register component, execution would be very slow. Therefore, if the control doesn't appear in the Object browser, check the References dialog.

Figure 9.8 Object browser displaying the Excel object that is registered on a system.

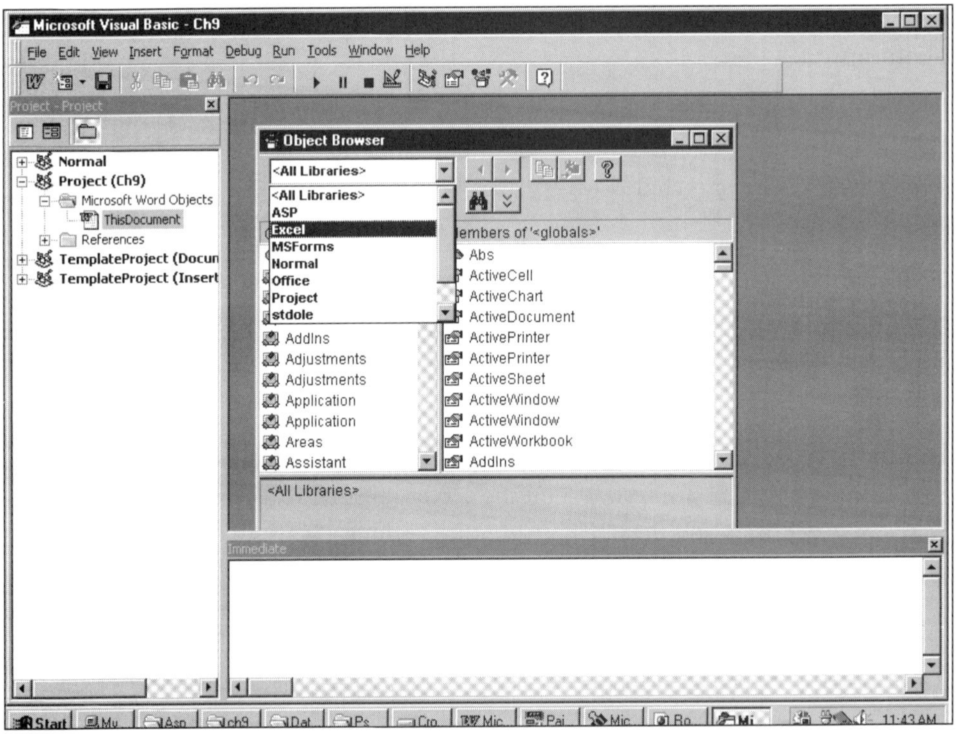

In Visual Basic for Applications (such as Word, Excel, Access, and PowerPoint), you can show the Visual Basic Editor window by pressing the Alt-F11 keys. The F2 key will show the ObjectBrowser. Check for the ASP controls we've just created. If they are missing, under the Tools menu select the References option. You should find the ASP class in the list. Put a check in the box to the left of the entry. Now when you open the Object browser, the ASP classes appear.

When you move the component to another machine, it will not be registered there. If you look in the folder that contains the ASP.DLL file, you will also see a file labeled ASP.LIB. This library file contains the information necessary for the control to be registered.

When a component written in Visual Basic is moved to a new server, you must make sure the VBRUN500.DLL is present on the new machine as well as any other ActiveX controls that the component may use. The best way to accomplish this process is to use the Setup Wizard. It will create a cabinet (CAB) file that contains all the necessary elements (controls, DLLs, and more) that your component needs to function.

Registration

The RegSvr32.EXE can be executed to register a component on a particular system. Use the Command Prompt window, and locate your file with either a TLB or LIB extended file. If you need to register the ASP control, for example, you could type:

```
regsvr32 asp.dll
```

This command needs to be executed within the directory where the control and the TLB or LIB file are stored. You can then use the Object Browser to make sure the component is active and available.

Registration in the OLE Registry is an important part of object creation. ActiveX controls can be registered to be located either on the local server or on a distributed machine.

Using Excel as an Active Server Component

Any OLE Automation Server can be used as an Active Server Component. Although using Excel as an Active Server Component in most cases would be inefficient, we

> **WARNING** This example is meant to show you that out-of-process servers may be accessed using the Active Server Component framework. Microsoft recommends against using out-of-process servers for two reasons: security and server efficiency. When a new user accesses a currently out-of-process server, he or she automatically inherits the security privileges of the last user. Also, out-of-process servers use an excessive amount of server resources (processor time, system speed, and memory). Therefore, examine the issues closely before you consider putting a solution like the example presented here into a production environment.

will demonstrate this arrangement to illustrate the power of using ASP files effectively.

In this example, you will have a user input information on a Web page. The Web server will then take this user information, create a custom spreadsheet using Excel as a component, and save the custom sheet in the FTP folder for user download.

1. First you'll need to use the RegEdit32.EXE application to modify the Web server information so that it allows the out-of-process Excel component to function. Make sure you back up the registry before you make any modifications. Execute RegEdit and drill down through the hierarchy until you find the AllowOutOfProcCmpnts entry. Locate the parameter by following this path:

```
HKEY_LOCAL_MACHINE\SYSTEM

        \CurrentControlSet

                \Services

                        \W3SVC

                                \ASP

                                        \Parameters
```

2. Change the value of the AllowOutOfProcCmpnts parameter from 0 to 1. Now reboot the machine to enabled the change to take effect. After you test this sample, restore the parameter to its original value of 0.

3. The first ASP file will input the file name to use for the Excel file and the number of random numbers to insert in the spreadsheet. Use a standard HTML form that accepts two parameters: name and loopnum. These variables will automatically be stored in the Request object when the user clicks on the button labeled Create Excel file. Using Notepad or Visual InterDev, create the following file and save as excelAdd.ASP:

```
<HTML>
<HEAD><TITLE>Dynamic Excel Creation</TITLE></HEAD>
<BODY>
<H1>Server-side Excel document creation</H1>

<%
On Error Resume Next
%>
<P>Make sure you have Excel properly installed on your server.
<P>
<HR>
<H2>Please enter the parameters to dynamically create an Excel document on
the server.</H2>
<FORM METHOD=POST ACTION="excelProcess.asp">
      <P>File name for created spreadsheet (i.e. mysheet.xls) :
      <INPUT TYPE=TEXT SIZE=50 MAXLENGTH=50 NAME="name"><BR>

      <P>Number of random numbers for placement in sheet :
      <INPUT TYPE=TEXT SIZE=4 MAXLENGTH=4 NAME="loopnum"><BR>
<HR>
```

```
        <P><B>Please be patient, creation may take up to a minute.</B>

        <P><INPUT TYPE=SUBMIT VALUE="Create Excel file"><INPUT TYPE=RESET
VALUE="Reset Form">

        </FORM>

<P> <A HREF="default.htm">Return to home page</A>


</BODY>

</HTML>
```

4. Now create an ASP file that takes the file name information supplied by the user and creates the necessary file. The ASP must instantiate the Excel application as an Active Server Component. Once this has occurred, commands can be sent to the object through VB Script. In the code, you create a new worksheet, insert values into various cells, and save the file by the file name provided on the excelAdd.ASP page. Using either Notepad or Visual InterDev, create the following file and save it as excelProcess.ASP:

```
<HTML>

<BODY>

<% If Request.Form("loopnum") = "" or Request.Form("name") = "" Then %>

   <P>You did not provide a current loop number or file name.

<%  Else %>

        <%

        'On Error Resume Next


        ' Create a variable that contains the path to the file

        excelFile = (Server.MapPath ("/APSourceBook") & "/" &
Request.Form("name"))
```

```
' Create an instance of the Excel application
Set AppXL = Server.CreateObject("Excel.Application")
' Create a reference to the application object
 Set xl = APPXL.Application
' Add a new Workbook to the collection
 xl.Workbooks.Add
' Create reference to the current active worksheet
 Set ws = xl.ActiveSheet
' Set the name of the sheet
  ws.Name = "MySheet"
' Set the value of the first cell to match the filename
  ws.Cells(1, 1).Value = Request.Form("name")
' Set the loopnum variable equal to the user input for # of random
#s
loopnum = CInt(Request.Form("loopnum"))
' Set the values of the first column of cells
for i = 1 to loopnum
      ws.Cells(i+2, 1).Value = Rnd
next
' Save the workbook file
  xl.ActiveWorkbook.SaveAs excelFile
' Close the workbook
  xl.ActiveWorkbook.Close
' Set all about references to Nothing
```

```
        Set ws = Nothing
        Set xl = Nothing
        Set AppXL = Nothing
        %>
        <H1>Excel file created.</H1><P>
        Your file: <A HREF="<% =Request.Form("name") %>"><%
=Request.Form("name") %></A>
<%  End If %>
</BODY>
</HTML>
```

5. Access the excelAdd.ASP file on your Web server and input a file name. The Excel file will be created and, with this technology, can be instantly downloaded. No code was put into place, however, to delete the created file nor is there any code to prevent an error if the file already exists. The potential of using a commercial component containing the functions that your need can decrease development and deployment time tremendously.

Building custom components, however, is necessary for many special solutions. Using Visual Basic makes this process not only possible but economical.

Create a Simple Control

By creating ActiveX Server controls, a company can also encapsulate any necessary core logic within a self-contained ActiveX DLL. This logic might include line-of-business objects for typical business rules. To demonstrate the usefulness of using controls on the server side, begin by creating a simple control that provides a feature not currently available in VB Script.

The simple control that you will build places the time as a string that can be inserted into the HTML presented to the user. As you know, VB Script does not include a Time keyword as Visual Basic does.

1. Execute Visual Basic 5; when you are prompted for the time of project to create, select the ActiveX DLL option and let VB create a new project. You could create an ActiveX control, but an ActiveX control does not allow apartment threading. If you prefer to create the component as a control the procedure is essentially identical, although the final result will have the file extension OCX rather than DLL.

> **TIP** Microsoft has produced a free version of Visual Basic called the Control Creation Edition that is available for download on the Microsoft Web site. This version of VB allows you to create complete ActiveX controls. The screenshots in this book will come from the full version of Visual Basic 5, so don't be confused if your screens do not match the ones shown here.

2. An ActiveX DLL has no visible component, so you will be creating a Class file to execute the function. Set the (Name) property of the control to ctlTime, and set the (Name) property of the project to ASP. These names will be used to define the ASC within the Active Server Page code that we will create using VB Script. The names used in the (Name) properties are the ones you include in the Server.CreateObject() method call.

3. To the general declarations section, add the following variable:

```
Public CurrentTime
```

4. Under the Tools menu, select the Add Procedure option. Name the procedure GetTime and make sure that it is selected to be a Public procedure, so it may be accessed from outside the control. The left combo box should remain in the (General) category.

5. Using the right combo box, select the GetTime procedure, and enter the single line of code so that the procedure matches the listing below:

```
Public Sub GetTime()
```

```
    CurrentTime = Time

End Sub
```

This code creates a method called GetTime that, when called from our ASP file, will place the current value of time into the CurrentTime variable. Because the variable is a public property, this value can be retrieved by our VB Script code.

6. Then save the project and compile the ActiveX DLL. Save the control as ctlTime.ctl and the project as ASP.vbp, then select the Make the ASP.DLL option under the File menu. The ActiveX DLL will compile and automatically register itself. To check that everything worked correctly, look at the Object Browser window.

   You can show the Object Browser by either selecting it under the View menu or pressing the F2 key. The combo box that selects the object library you wish to view is set by default to <All Libraries>. Click on the combo box to see the ASP option in the list. Select this option to see the class ctlTime appear in the box to the left. Scroll in the box to the right to see the GetTime method (see Figure 9.9).

7. Now that your control is compiled and verified on the system, exit Visual Basic. Next you need to create the ASP file that uses the component. You will use VB Script code to instantiate a ctlTime component and execute the *GetTime* method. The value of the CurrentTime variable can then be added to the resultant HTML. Execute Notepad or Visual InterDev, enter the code below, and save the file as ctlTime.ASP:

```
<HTML>

<BODY>

<H1> Using the ctlTime component </H1>

<P>

<%

' Create instance of ctlTime object

Set MyTime1 = Server.CreateObject("ASP.ctlTime")
```

Figure 9.9 Showing the *GetTime* method of the ctlTime class.

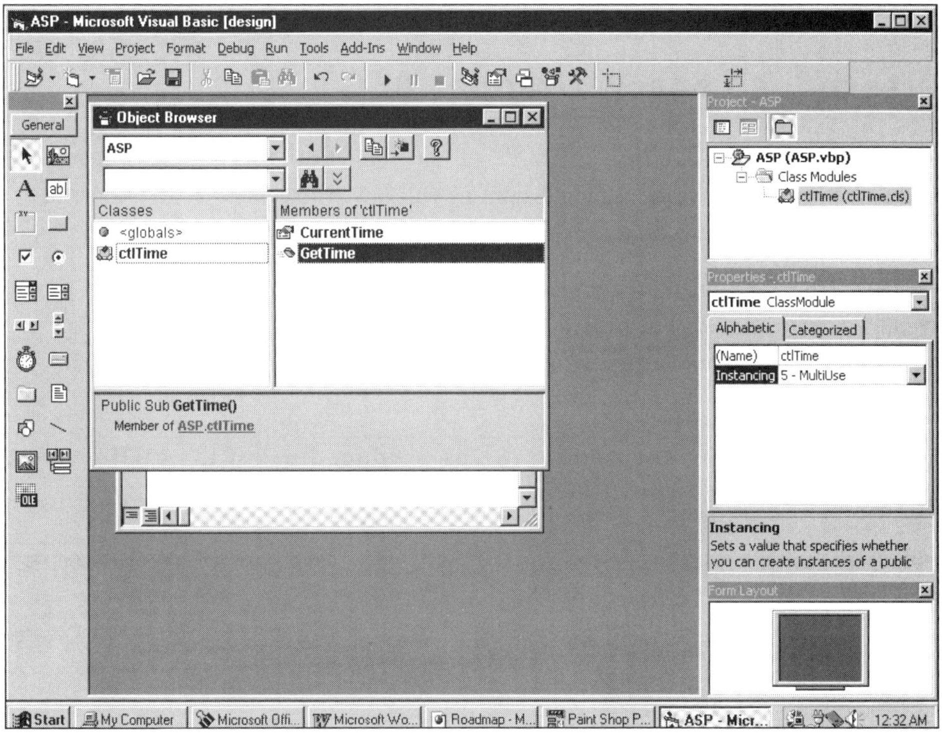


```
' Execute GetTime method which will load the CurrentTime variable

MyTime1.GetTime



Response.Write "The current time is: "

Response.Write MyTime1.CurrentTime

%>

<P>

</BODY>

</HTML>
```

8. Now execute this ASP file in your browser. The display should look like the one shown in Figure 9.10. See how easy creating components can be? Now that you have created an extremely rudimentary control, it's time to create

one that might have a future application. The next ASC will access some legacy data stored in a text file and display it in the Web page.

Creating a Legacy Wrapper ASC

Many organizations have legacy data that is available from older systems in some odd data format. Often the legacy programs will have the capability to export the data into a text file or another file format that Visual Basic can read.

Many large and midsized companies closely monitor the maturity of the current Web tools with the hope of providing wide access to legacy information through a standard Web browser. Legacy information is older data, usually residing on an

Figure 9.10 The current time that was produced using the ctlTime component.

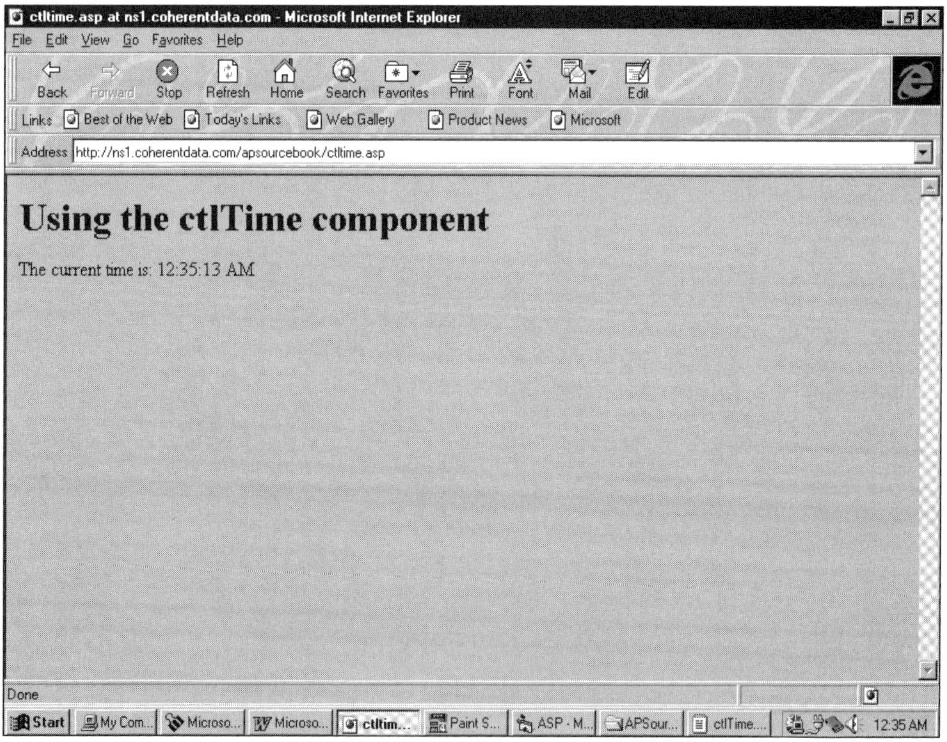

aging system such as a Unix platform, minicomputer, or mainframe. Providing Web access allows any browser-equipped computer to access the information without using a specific terminal or a command-line-driven program.

Active Server Components make this kind of access not only possible, but affordable. As an example, we will create an ActiveX DLL using VB5 (or VB 5 Control Creation edition) to read and parse a text file for live information retrieval. In our example, the central data file will be stored on the Web server. The ActiveX DLL, when activated by an ASP file, will read the file, compile the information, and output it in an HTML table.

As a real-world example, the Portland, Oregon, Police Bureau has exactly this type of data problem. The computer-aided dispatch system that tracks all patrol unit dispatch information keeps the data in its own proprietary format, but it enables output of the information as formatted text files. If the PPB needs to provide access to this information over its intranet, it could create a control that actively reads the data off a network shared dump file containing the latest data.

You've already created a project for the last control. Now you will add a second control to this project.

1. Select the Add Class Module option from the Project menu. Set the (Name) property of the class to ctlWrapper.
2. You will also need to use the Active Server Pages Object Library in this control because we will write into the server page. Therefore, select the References option under the Project menu. Place a check in the box labeled Microsoft Active Server Pages 1.0 Object Library. The file associated with this object library is the ASP.DLL file.

> **WARNING** Testing a server component after it has been loaded by a Web page requires restarting the Web server. Both Personal Web Server and IIS keep an attachment to the control open after a page containing the control is opened. Therefore, if you make a change and try to recompile the DLL, a Permission Denied error will occur, saying that the control is in use. To recompile the component, stop the Web server, compile it, and restart the service.

3. Next, create some object variables to hold the references to the Intrinsic objects. You also need to create a public property that we can demonstrate for setting and reading from our server-side VB Script. Add these values to the General Declarations:

```
Option Explicit


' Create property accessable from ASP file

Public myProperty As String


' Create object references for intrinsic ASC objects

Dim myRequest As Request

Dim myResponse As Response

Dim myServer As Server

Dim mySession As Session

Dim myApplication As Application
```

4. The variables in the general declarations section are meant to contain references to all intrinsic controls. They must be set to point at the correct objects when the object is initialized. Two event routines, OnStartPage and OnEndPage, are automatically executed on page events. If you place code in routines that match these names, the code will be executed when these events occur.

   The OnStartPage routine accepts the ScriptingContext property. This property contains all necessary object references. Use the Set command to point local variables at these objects. When you have finished with the Web page, the OnEndPage function will activate to destroy the variable references. Create two functions with the appropriate names and make them match the following:

```
Public Function OnStartPage(myScriptingContext As ScriptingContext)
```

```
    Set myRequest = myScriptingContext.Request

    Set myResponse = myScriptingContext.Response

    Set myServer = myScriptingContext.Server

    Set mySession = myScriptingContext.Session

    Set myApplication = myScriptingContext.Application


End Function


Public Function OnEndPage()


    Set myRequest = Nothing

    Set myResponse = Nothing

    Set myServer = Nothing

    Set mySession = Nothing

    Set myApplication = Nothing


End Function
```

5. You also need the central method that will be used to read the data file and create a table from the file. This routine will parse a comma-delimited file into separate fields, and each field will become a column in the HTML table. The method will be called *GetData* and will require that the name of the file to be parsed will be passed to it.

   GetData will open the file and add rows to a table until all lines of the record have been read. When the end-of-file has been reached (EOF=True), the final row and the table are closed with the proper HTML tags. Create a new procedure called GetData and enter the following:

```
Public Sub GetData(tempFName As String)
    Dim inp, firstLoop, OKFlag As Integer

    ' Open the file as #1 for table creation
    Open tempFName For Input As #1
    ' Write the table header
    myResponse.Write "<TABLE BORDER=1>"

    ' Set flag for special processing first time through the loop
    firstLoop = True
    Do While Not EOF(1)
        ' Input first parameter
        Input #1, inp
        OKFlag = True
        ' Check if end of line has been reached
        If IsEmpty(inp) Then
            OKFlag = False
        End If
        ' Normal column input
        If OKFlag Then
            ' If first loop, add a new row
            If firstLoop Then
                myResponse.Write "<TR>"
                firstLoop = False
```

```
            End If
            ' Write a column into the table
            myResponse.Write "<TD>" & inp & "</TD>"
        Else
            ' If input was empty, but end of file was not reached,
process
            If Not EOF(1) Then
                myResponse.Write "</TR>"
                myResponse.Write "<TR>"
            End If
        End If
    Loop
    Close #1
    ' End last row
    myResponse.Write "</TR>"
    ' End the table
    myResponse.Write "</TABLE>"

End Sub
```

Now that you've created the necessary code for the component, compile it using the Make ASP.DLL option under the File menu. Now both controls are contained within the ASP control. We need an ASP file to instantiate our control and pass it a file name.

Using Notepad or Visual InterDev, create a file that contains the following ASP code and save it as ctlWrapper.ASP:

```
<HTML>
<HEAD>
<TITLE>Using the ctlWrapper</TITLE>
</HEAD>
<BODY>
<H1>The table created below was made entirely using HTML from the
ctlWrapper component.</H1>

<% Set myobj = Server.CreateObject("ASP.ctlWrapper") %>

The current Value of myProperty = <%= myobj.myProperty %><BR>
<% newvalue = "AP SourceBook" %>
Set myProperty to <%= newvalue %>
<% myobj.myProperty = newvalue %><BR>
The myProperty Value is now: <B><I><%= myobj.myProperty %></I></B>

<P><H2>Executing the GetData method: </H2>
<P>
<% myobj.GetData "C:\test.DAT" %><BR>

</BODY>
</HTML>
```

This ASP file first creates an instance of the ctlWrapper object, and it then displays the myProperty value (which will be empty). The ASP then demonstrates setting the property and displaying the new value. The core of the file is the execution of the *GetData* method. Notice the simplicity of code for the amount of HTML that it will generate.

For the demo to work, you will need a sample data file. The sample can be any comma-delimited data. Use notepad to create the following sample data file and save it as TEST.DAT at the root directory:

```
Line 1,1,1,"shapeColor","0 1 0",

Line 2,2,1,"position","1 2 3",

Line 3,0,2,"position","3 1 0","shapeColor","0 0 .5",

Line 4,3,1,"position","3 2 5",

Line 5,2,1,"position","-3 1 4",
```

Figure 9.11 The ctlWrapper results in a Web browser.

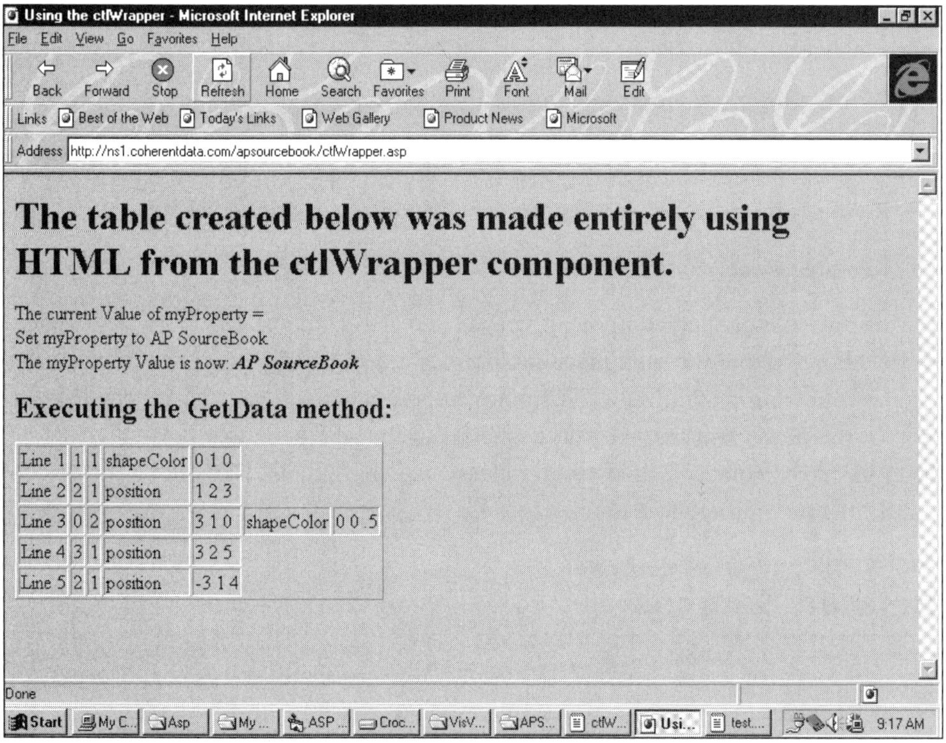

Access the ctlWrapper.ASP file from your Web browser. When you access this ASP file, it displays a screen like the one shown in Figure 9.11. The data file is read into memory and parsed for dynamic creation of an HTML page.

You have developed a component that actually accesses a custom data file format and places the data into an HTML table. By creating more components such as this one, your server can become the central place to store business objects.

Using Remote Components

You now understand how components located on the server are used, but did you realize you could also use controls located on other servers? Chapter 10 will introduce you to distributed computing. Distributed computing allows objects or components on different computers that are dispersed on a network to communicate with each other.

There are a great number of advantages to using remote objects:

- The load for processing can be distributed.
- Business logic particular to a division can be kept on that division's servers.
- Specialized servers can be optimized for execution of particular object types.
- Remote objects can give end users the illusion of a single server.
- Remote objects can tighten integration with OS services.

The data file parsing component you just created could be used as a distributed object. It could execute on a machine that has a dedicated process to retrieve legacy data from a mainframe. The remote component software makes the location of the object transparent to the system, so the ASP code that created an instance of the control would remain identical. The ActiveX DLL, however, would be located on a different computer.

Related Sources

The resources for Active Server Pages on the Web are significant. The following is a list of resources that supplement the information presented in this chapter.

If you are going to develop your own ASCs, we recommend that you download the free ActiveX SDK (http://www.microsoft.com/intdev/sdk/docs/olescrpt). It provides information on ActiveX controls, the interaction between controls and the scripting environment, and sample code.

The Microsoft IIS page (www.microsoft.com/iis) has a number of sample Active Server Components with source code for free download. These components are written in Visual Basic, Java, and C++, providing a wide variety of possible foundation code.

Because ADO relies on OLE DB for database access, the Microsoft OLE DB page (www.microsoft.com/oledb) contains a good amount of information for people planning to access databases through this component.

Conclusion

You have become a full-fledged Active Server Component developer! If you created the sample component using Visual Basic 5, you should be able to design and build a server-side ActiveX DLL or control. Server controls are far easier to test than client-side controls because all testing can occur on a single machine without worrying about compatibility across several machines.

Advantages of server components. These include performance, source control, and object reuse.

Intrinsic controls. These controls are built into the server for immediate access.

ActiveX Data Objects. The ADO can be used to access an ODBC or OLE DB data source to retrieve, add, edit, or delete records.

Content Linking component. For sites that present a newspaper, magazine, or similar format type, this component will create an electronic table of contents for easy navigation by users.

FileSystem component. Even though VB Script does not contain file commands for security reasons, access to the file system on the server is essential. The FileSystem component allows files to be read, written, or appended.

Browser Capabilities component. Modifying the actual content sent to the user based on the capabilities of the browser in use could be easily accomplished by checking the properties contained in this component.

Advertisement Rotator component. Many Web sites attempt to use the advertisement business model to pay for upkeep. This component, included with ASP, can help you set up banner ad rotation almost instantly and allow you to track the users who click on various banners.

Server-side Java components. Java applications of JavaBeans components can be executed on the ASP server in the same manner that other components can be used. This type of component allows a heterogeneous server environment (such as a Netscape Unix server) to share core business logic without extreme difficulty.

Creating a legacy wrapper. Older data can be wrapped in an Active Server Component so that the user transparently accesses the legacy data using a standard Web browser.

Control registration. There are three ways of registering an ActiveX control: automatic registration through the programming environment (such as VB 5), manual registration using the regsvr32.EXE utility, and browse registration using the TLB files.

Remote components. Distributed computing is quickly becoming the technology of tomorrow. ActiveX components can be easily registered for use over a network as DCOM objects. Active Server Pages can treat a remote component as if it were a local Active Server Component.

Chapter

10

Distributed Component Object Model

History has clearly illustrated that communication is the key to development. Until now, this illustration has been limited to one human making audible noises, and beating on his chest, signals that other humans have successfully interpreted. In today's new Information Age, software objects will be doing most of the communication; this chapter will describe one language that may be used extensively.

One of the first steps in the direction of software object communication is Microsoft's Distributed Component Object Model (DCOM), which lets components communicate over a network. As the programming world shifts to object-oriented and component-based design, network object services will become increasingly important. In this chapter, we will examine both DCOM and Microsoft's new Transaction Server, which can manage objects from a central server.

So far in this book you have been using the Active Desktop and the Active Server for all solutions on both the client and the server sides. In Figure 10.1, you can see the technology used for these two platforms. The Active Desktop consists primarily of the browser, which can read and display HTML files, execute scripts (VB Script and JavaScript), manipulate client-side controls

(ActiveX controls or JavaBeans), and run Java applets. On the Active Server, the Web server can send HTML, construct HTML from ASP files consisting of VB Script or JavaScript, and use Active Server Components, in the form of ActiveX Controls, ActiveX DLLs, or Java programs. All communication between the Active Desktop and the Active Server has been based on the HTTP protocol, the Internet protocol used to send and receive information between World Wide Web programs.

Of course, the HTTP protocol is not the only one that can be used over the network. The base protocol of the Internet is called TCP/IP, on which all Internet protocols rest. Think of a protocol like a language: If both computers can speak the same language, they can communicate.

Protocols are also stackable. You can stack one protocol on top of another, so the lower-level protocol handles the data transfer, while the higher protocol communicates other information. In Figure 10.2, you see that the Web protocol (HTTP) sits on top of the TCP/IP protocol. Any HTTP request is carried or "wrapped" within TCP/IP packets. When it reaches its destination computer, the HTTP information is unwrapped and read by the HTTP receiver. The Web browser and the Web server, therefore, use HTTP as their standard language to communicate.

Of course, protocols are not limited to communication over networks. Various protocols are used to allow software and hardware within a single computer to communicate. On the Active Platform, for object communication, components use a protocol called the *Component Object Model* (COM). In the last two chapters, VB Script was used to call Active Server Components, while the Active Server used the COM protocol to provide exchanges between VB Script and the objects. For objects

Figure 10.1 Active Platform communication as covered.

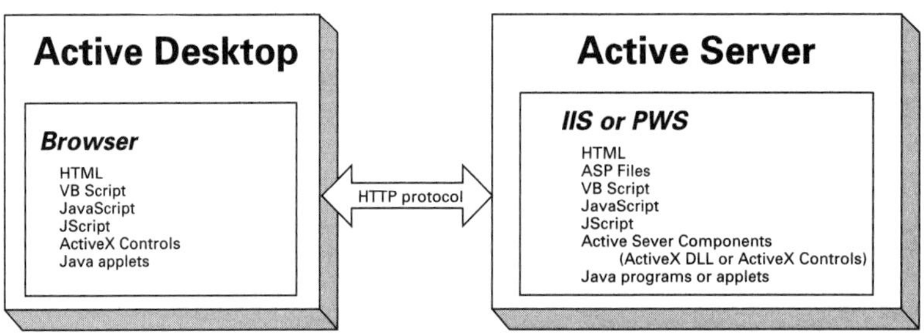

Figure 10.2 TCP/IP with HTTP on top for communication.

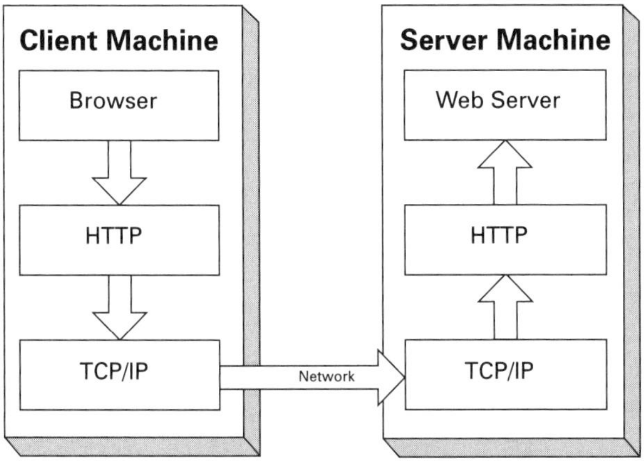

to talk over a network, a slightly different protocol called *Distributed Component Object Model* (DCOM) is used.

What if you want the control or DLL to execute not on the particular machine that is using it, but on another machine altogether? In this case you need *distributed objects*. Distributed objects can be located on any machine, including traditionally incompatible platforms such as Unix and Macintosh, on the network. An object could be located in another country and instantiated and used by a local computer.

Introducing DCOM

DCOM allows two or more objects to communicate with each other over a network. This communication can include passing data, calling methods, or creating instances of objects. Instead of using the HTTP protocol that is customized for best use with Web pages, DCOM uses its own protocol to communicate between a DCOM client stub (the access piece executing on the client machine) and the DCOM server. In Figure 10.3 you can see that the DCOM client stub makes a call to a remote DCOM object through the DCOM protocol to the DCOM Server running on a remote machine.

Figure 10.3 TCP/IP with DCOM protocol on top for communication.

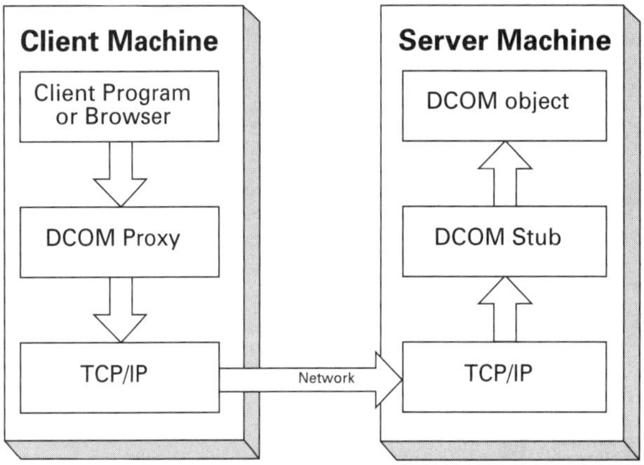

You might be wondering what this DCOM client stub looks like. Actually, to the client machine, it looks just like any other ActiveX control or OLE Automation Server. DCOM does not replace COM; instead, it integrates transparently with it. When a program calls an object on a machine (an ActiveX control, for example), a request is passed to the COM driver. COM checks if the object is located on the current machine. If not, it passes the request to the DCOM driver for complete network processing. A DCOM object might appear in a program or a Web page just like a traditional object. The CreateObject() method and the Set methods in VB Script can be used with a DCOM object.

DCOM is much more than a simple protocol. DCOM allows remote execution of objects on a remote machine. For example, a scientist might need to run particular wind tunnel tests that require far more computing power than that available on a typical desktop machine. A wind tunnel DCOM object could be created to run on a supercomputer. From a desktop machine, the scientist could instantiate the wind tunnel object (his or her machine would send a signal to the remote DCOM object to create an instance) and send it commands. The resultant data could be stored in some of the object's properties. Although all the processing took place on the remote DCOM object on the supercomputer, to the scientist, it would appear the object was located on the local machine.

Using a supercomputer is an extreme example, but it does show some of the fundamental benefits of distributed component systems. All the logic or programming for a remote object can be stored on a remote machine. The object server can be optimized for particular object execution. From the perspective of the user and the programmer, this distributed object access can appear nearly transparent.

Microsoft has created DCOM for Windows 95, Windows NT 4.0, and future operating systems. Microsoft is also actively developing DCOM for the Macintosh as well as aiding partners such as Software AG in developing DCOM for the Unix platform. Because the objects execute remotely, this cross-platform strategy promises to allow DCOM clients to use objects on any operating system running a DCOM server.

DCOM emerged from the C++ world, so for many Web developers, some of these concepts may seem difficult. Not to worry, because almost all of these processes occur in the background if you develop your objects in Visual Basic. Understanding what is happening behind the scenes, though, will allow you to understand some of DCOM's limitations as well as optimize your system for the best use of DCOM.

The DCOM technology is automatically incorporated into the Windows NT 4.0 system. For Windows 95, it must be separately installed. The next version of Windows should include the DCOM services natively. For real enterprise deployment of DCOM, however, you will want to use the Microsoft Transaction Server, which will be briefly described later in this chapter.

Top Five Reasons for Distributed Computing

Distributed computing is the term used to describe a system where objects and processing for an organization are spread across the network. DCOM will bring distributed computing to a majority of enterprises. The advantages of distributed computing might not be immediately apparent, so we've noted the top five reasons to implement a distributed system:

1. Encapsulating business logic
2. Intense or specialized calculations
3. Custom processes—credit validation
4. Encapsulating department logic
5. Shielding data access

Using objects to encapsulate business logic will most likely be the primary early use of distributed computing. By creating business rules within objects, updates to the rules can be made by changing a single object rather than each client application that needs the logic it provides.

A simple example of this would be the size of a transaction before a credit check process was enabled. If the level for the required credit check was raised from $1000 to $2000, the credit level could be updated instantly. For more information about business objects, see the section "Three-Tier Architecture," later in this chapter.

Particular machines are often optimized in either their processor capabilities or their resources (memory, hard disk space, and so on) so that they can process particular types of calculations. There are many examples in which distributing complex or specialized calculations can be an effective solution. Some of these include:

- Graphic display imaging, such as visualization or high-quality rendering
- Scientific calculations requiring great accuracy, such as those requiring solutions built with processor-optimized FORTRAN implementations
- Modeling problems that require massively parallel processing
- Risk analysis of loans
- Stellar cartography

Custom processes that require specialized software or hardware can also benefit from distributed object deployment. For example, when a credit card check is required, the check must take place through a special piece of software (in small companies the software is actually stored in the credit terminal). The software might even need to access a phone line to interface with the credit authorization service. For an organization, it would be far easier to create an object that handled all credit card checks. Any program that required this feature could feed the correct information into the object and await the return of the approved or declined message from the credit object. For the security of particular custom processes, it makes a great deal of sense to centralize the logic within objects that may be placed on a particular secure server.

Within large organizations, distributed computing can be used to centralize departmental logic. For example, now the accounting department would be responsible for the objects that directly affect their information systems, and the most appropriate decisions for modifications could take place within the department they affect. This approach also separates business logic into functional areas, so problem tracking is simplified.

In current client/server systems, the structure of the core system databases must be exposed to each client application. Updates, reads, or modifications to the database occur through SQL calls that directly access the core database or, at best, access a view to the main database. Creating objects that provide a front-end for most database access shields the data from the applications. A simple example of the efficacy of this solution occurs when the structure or field names of the main database need to be changed. If access occurs through a set of objects, the client applications will be unaware that any change occurred.

These are just the most common types of problems that can be solved using a distributed system. DCOM brings the distributed object model to all Windows machines and, soon, to most Unix and Macintosh platforms. Now that you understand the usefulness of deploying a DCOM system for these different applications, let's learn how the DCOM system itself functions.

DCOM Overview

Before you can utilize DCOM in your applications you need to first understand how it works. The entire object model is shown in Figure 10.4. You can see that when a program requests an object, COM first checks if the object is in-process or out-of-process (for more information on these types, see Chapter 9). If the object is in-process, all communication can occur quickly by passing a pointer to the object to exchange data and commands. If the object is out-of-process, COM must determine whether the object is located locally on the machine or across the network. If local, COM instantiates a new object and begins communication across the operating system; if the object is remote, DCOM is activated to handle the remote transactions.

To retrieve the information on the object's location, DCOM first accesses the necessary dictionary to determine the specifics about the object. In Figure 10.5,

Figure 10.4 COM and DCOM functional diagram.

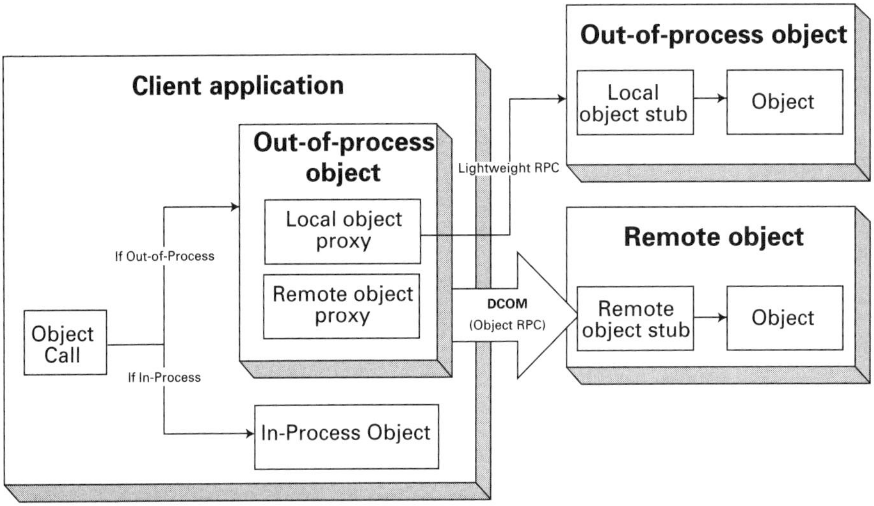

you'll see the Remote Automation Connection Manager. This is a program included with Visual Basic (both versions 4 and 5) that allows individual objects to be configured for remote access. To access a remote object, it must be registered on the local machine. The reference is then redirected to point to the new location across the network.

In addition to the Remote Automation Connection Manager on the remote machine, either an object server (such as Microsoft Transaction Server) or the Automation Manager must be executing. These pieces of software act much the way a Web server does for Web pages. When an object is requested from a remote client, these object servers accept and process the various requests.

Each DCOM object is registered on one or more client machines but is actually located on another machine on the network. Any machine may be a DCOM server, but most implementations will centralize objects on particular machines using the Microsoft Transaction Server. The client requests an instance of the object, and the DCOM technology creates the connection across the network. You should realize that a DCOM object works much the same way as a COM object; therefore, understanding DCOM objects begins with the basic COM interface, which provides the programming interface that an application accesses whether the object is located on the local machine or across the network.

Figure 10.5 Remote Automation Connection Manager.

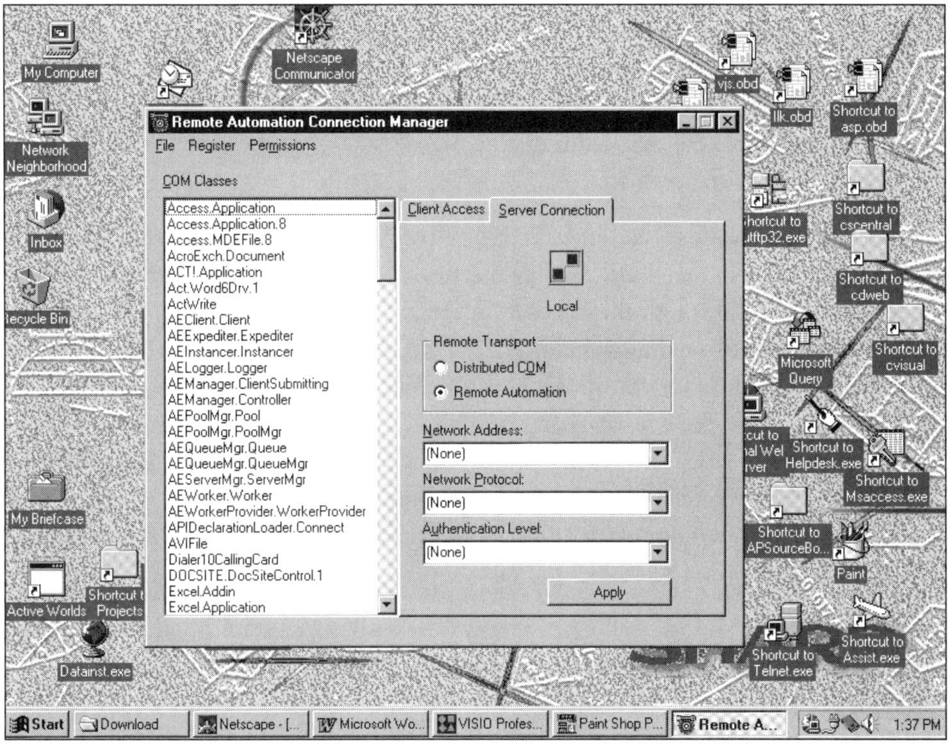

COM Interfaces

The structure of a COM object is fundamental to the network extensions of COM, referred to as DCOM. Visual Basic, included in the ability to create an ActiveX DLL, does most of the COM interface creation work for you. The ActiveX DLL automatically creates all interfaces needed for accessing the object. (If you create ActiveX DLLs in Visual Basic for deployment by someone else, you may consider skipping this section completely because you will probably never encounter these specifics.) If you are deploying a distributed system, however, understanding the fundamentals of the entire COM interface system is important. Just keep in mind that most of this process will occur behind the scenes if your primary development environment is Visual Basic.

When communication with an out-of-process COM object occurs, the exchange actually takes place through an interface called Lightweight Remote Procedure Call

(Lightweight RPC). RPCs provide a standardized, language-independent way for processes to communicate. You can think of RPCs much like the Universal Translator in Star Trek, which allowed everyone from Vulcans to Klingons to communicate easily. Typically, a program in C++ cannot invoke a call in memory to a function written in Visual Basic. Using a standard such as RPC, functions can be invoked regardless of the original implementation as long as both the sender and receiver understand the protocol.

Programs make calls to an object interface through the Lightweight RPC. A COM object is a set of methods and properties bundled in a self-contained object and accessible only through the exposed interfaces. You can think of a COM object like an automobile. To get anywhere you don't have to tell the automobile engine when to fire a spark plug; you simple press the gas pedal, which causes a series of actions that result in the car's moving. Much like the gas pedal of an automobile, COM objects have interfaces, which are sets of methods categorically related to each other; when selected, the interfaces will result in the COM object's performing a series of activities. Of course, a COM object may have any number of interfaces.

The interfaces exposed by a COM object are the only means of connection between the object and the calling program. The calling program never actually has access to any part of the object, but instead must pass all requests or invoke any functions through a particular interface. The most common interfaces include the IUnknown and the IDispatch interfaces.

IUnknown Interface

The single interface required by all COM objects is the *IUnknown* interface (see Figure 10.6). All access to the COM object proceeds from the IUnknown interface, which has three basic methods:

QueryInterface

AddRef

Release

The *AddRef* and *Release* methods are used to handle the object instance of the counter that tracks how many processes are using the object. The *QueryInterface* method is used to determine which methods the particular interface supports.

Figure 10.6 The IUnknown interface and its three exposed methods.

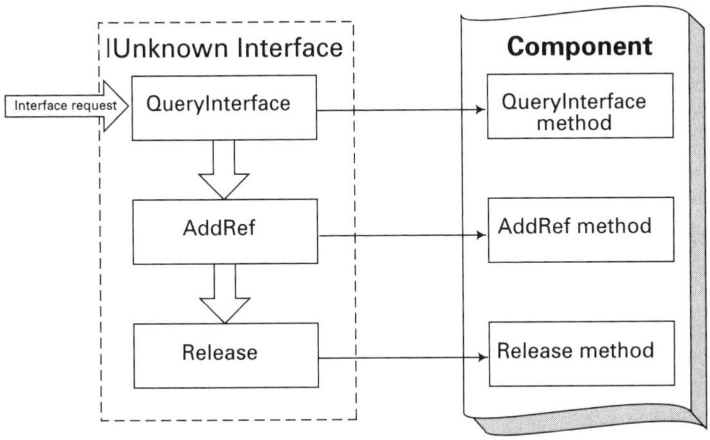

When the *CreateObject()* method is called (or the C++ *CoCreateInstance* method), the *AddRef* method automatically executes and increments the Reference Counter. The Reference Counter then holds the number of instances in use and begins at 1 when the first instance is created.

The *Release* method tells the object that it is no longer needed. Calling this method decreases the Reference Count by 1; when the Reference Count reaches 0, the object is set to be purged from memory.

Often before your program makes a call to an interface on a particular COM object it must first determine if that interface is even available; at which point it uses the *QueryInterface* method. This method returns a pointer to the requested interface if it is located. By doing so, the *QueryInterface* method can be used to judge the version of the object accessed. If a particular interface known to be in a version returns an interface error, the object being accessed is most likely an older version of the component.

A program can use a certain property to determine if a particular object supports automation features and hence can be used with the DCOM system. If either the IDispatch interface or the IUnknown interface contains the attribute name *oleautomation*, it can be used as an OLE Automation Server.

IDispatch Interface

Like a car, before you can effectively use a COM object, you need to determine its capabilities—Do you have a Corvette or a Yugo? The IDispatch interface provides a primary access interface to determine the methods available for the COM object at runtime. IDispatch allows querying of an object's methods and properties as well as invoking of methods. Access to methods through the IDispatch interface are primarily for runtime execution, so they are labeled late-bound or name-bound.

Class Factory Interfaces

In addition to these basic interfaces, there are several other important interfaces known as Class Factory interfaces. When an object needs to be created, an instance is requested from the Class Factory interface that must create the instance. Every DCOM object must have a Class Factory method to create an instance of the object.

We will cover the role of the Class Factory interface later in the "DCOM Process" section, but it is important to know about the alternate to the IClassFactory interface. Instead of the standard IClassFactory interface used by most general objects, the IClassFactory2 interface can be used when the component is a commercial or proprietary object.

In addition to the *CreateInstance* and *LockServer* methods included with the standard IClassFactory interface, IClassFactory2 supplements these methods with three additional methods:

GetLicInfo

RequestLicKey

CreateInstanceLic

Considering that most software developers do not enjoy working for free, the methods supported by Class Factory 2 are made so commercial component vendors can require license files to be checked before the instance may be created. The license may be contained on the hosting machine, or the object may direct the method to search on a different machine for the license file. Unfortunately, the licensing interface is fairly primitive, and it will not track the number of instances that may be created with the license.

Identification of Object

For any COM objects, you also need a way to identify and access them. Because objects will be frequently exchanged, Microsoft has adopted an algorithm for creating unique identification numbers for both the objects themselves and each interface within an object.

In the last chapter, we briefly examined the ProgID and the ClassID used to identify a particular object. Either identification can be used to create a new instance of an object using the *CreateObject()* method. A ProgID uses the form of company.class.version (that is, mycompany.myobject.1) to specify the necessary object. The ClassID uses a series of numbers (that is, "{10722D20-FD67-11CE-A6C7-4445535400FF}") that uniquely identifies the object.

In the previous examples, the client-side script required use of the ClassID to avoid confusion among multiple controls that could exist on the client. On the server side, you can use either the ProgID or the ClassID for object creation.

The ClassID is stored in the hexadecimal format approved by the DCE standard; that is, a 128-bit identifier in the following format: {01234567-1234-1234-1234-012345678AB}. This number is generated based on the time and date of the ID creation, the network card's ID number, and several other factors. The main objective in the creation of the ClassID number is to create a unique number, one that will not match the numbers created for any other COM objects.

Part of the process of loading an object onto a computer system is registering it. The ClassID itself is contained within the object. The system, however, does not know how to find the object until its entry has been added to the registry. Registration of components occurs in two subkeys in the registry:

Classes. The Classes subkey occurs in the registry path of HKEY_LOCAL_MACHINE/SOFTWARE/Classes and holds all the components currently registered on a machine.

Microsoft/OLE. The Microsoft/OLE subkey uses the HKEY_LOCAL_MACHINE/SOFTWARE/Microsoft/OLE path for the call-level security of the DCOM interface.

ActiveX or OLE controls are really COM objects, so the ClassIDs that you have already used are actually COM ClassIDs. You have never had to use an ID to call an interface because VB Script resolves the identification for you. When an interface is created, you must assign it a *universally unique identifier* (UUID), often referred to as an *interface identifier* (IID). The IID is also used to prevent two interfaces of an object from being mistaken for each other and thereby causing conflicts. The IID also allows a single object to have multiple versions of an interface active simultaneously. Rather than putting versions on the interface, each UUID is unique for the object at its creation.

In a C++ program, the required IID is coded in the same way a ClassID may be included in VB Script code. At runtime, the C++ program requests, through the IUnknown interface, a pointer to the requested interface. If the object has an interface that matches the IID, a pointer to the interface is returned.

For interfaces, the unique IID numbers are used not only to differentiate between different interfaces, but also to allow a single object to contain multiple versions of the same interface. As many people may know, one of the most difficult issues that an enterprise must address is upgrading and testing new applications. With objects, the process becomes even more difficult because numerous applications may use the same object. A problem with the new object could cause system-wide calamity. Because each interface within an object has a unique identifier, a new version is given a new IID. This prevents requiring complicated version control on individual interfaces, and it also prevents your IS department from coming up with excuses for why the server is down.

Each object has interfaces with IIDs that are used to provide communication between objects and programs (or other objects). As stated earlier, a program never actually accesses an object directly; instead, it limits all interaction through the interfaces. It is the use of marshaling that puts the communication layer in place.

Marshaling

When information is sent between a program and an object, the process known as marshaling provides the communication. Marshaling essentially maps a local memory location to a structure that can be accessed by a remote machine. Marshaling creates a *proxy* object and a *stub* object that handle communication between the pieces. Any exchanges between the program and the object occur through the proxy and the stub.

An advantage of this system is that it provides a safeguard against failure of the entire system if the remote object were to fail. If the object were to become disconnected, only the stub connecting the object would disappear. The proxy that the client communicates with would remain in place. Therefore, any calls to the proxy still execute, but they return an error indicating that the stub cannot be reached. If the client program makes direct calls to the remote object, the object's disappearance would make the call attempt to execute something no longer functioning, which could have disastrous consequences for the system.

Persistent Storage

In most object models, there is no way for the current state of an object to be stored for later retrieval. A process that is partially completed, if aborted, loses all the progress that has occurred. Persistent storage allows an object's properties and state to be written to a nonvolatile medium (such as a hard disk) for later activation.

The COM specification contains a complete implementation of persistent storage and even allows the storage in a special type of document called an OLE Structured Storage document. These documents are stored in a hierarchical fashion, and particular objects can be read, added, or updated within the hierarchy without accessing the entire file. The Microsoft Office applications (including Word and Excel) use this structured file to store their documents.

Microsoft recently announced the addition of persistent storage to the Java COM model. Therefore, Java programs can now store files using the structured file format. At the time of this writing, Microsoft offers no way to use structured storage from Visual Basic.

Creating persistent storage for a remote object is far more difficult because the proxy and the stub are split across separate machines. Microsoft has not announced any plans to add persistent storage to DCOM; however, persistent storage is included in the JavaBeans specification. Because the Java-CORBA technologies compete with DCOM, we may see this feature in DCOM in the near future.

Inheritance and Aggregation

Many object systems, including the Common Object Request Broker Architecture (CORBA), allow objects to inherit properties and methods from each other. This *inheritance* feature can allow software to be easily extended by creating an object based on another object, inheriting all of its behavior.

For example, a bank might need to create an object that makes several deposits. If an object already exists that makes a deposit, another object could be written to activate this object several times and make several different deposits. Like any out-of-process instance, the speed of the objects would slow as communication occurred between the primary and the subobjects. What if the bank needed to use the multiple deposits more than just this once? Another user would now need access to the new multiple-deposit object as well as the other single-deposit object. What if the primary object could be extended to include the new operations?

This extension capability is exactly the point of inheritance. It would be a simple process to extend the object to include a new multiple-deposit object. By inheriting the behaviors of the primary objects, any changes in the primary object are automatically reflected in the objects that inherit from it. If the procedure for recording deposits changed, a single change to the primary object would automatically be used by any objects that inherited from it.

Of course, DCOM does not support inheritance. If inheritance is so great and useful, why isn't it included in DCOM? The answer to this question is called the fragile base class problem. Microsoft realized that the future object systems would be used in mission-critical systems for everything from emergency room tracking systems to financial markets. Imagine a large system where hundreds of objects inherit behavior from a primary foundation class. Any change made to this primary object would immediately be felt throughout the inheriting objects. This is a great and powerful function if all changes are effective, but what if a bug is introduced? All dependent objects would fault, and the whole system might collapse. In systems where the lives or financial well-being of numerous people are at stake, inheritance could be a potentially dangerous design flaw.

To create an alternative, DCOM supports a methodology called aggregation. Aggregation allows an object to encapsulate and override the behavior of an object. Therefore, if we have deposit object A (version 1) and we need to make a multiple-deposit object, we can encapsulate the deposit object within our new object. We could then encapsulate our multiple-deposit object within another object, and so on, to aggregate the features.

When you create an upgrade of the original deposit object A to version 2, nothing changes automatically. All objects that use the deposit object must be recompiled to use the new object. This process is more time-intensive than the inherited model, but it has the advantage of safety. Objects can be upgraded and tested individually. If an error occurs, it would occur in a single area, rather than throughout the entire system.

Aggregation is possible because multiple interfaces may be defined for each object. Therefore, an object that is encapsulated within another DCOM object may still expose its interface. Alternately, the DCOM object might practice *delegation* where the interface of the encapsulated object would be duplicated in the primary object's interface. When calls are made to the functions of the primary object, it would, in turn, pass parameters and make calls to the contained object.

The DCOM Process

Now that you understand how COM functions, you can see that the differences between COM and DCOM are slight from an administrator's point of view. Instead of using the Lightweight RPC for object communication, DCOM uses a complete Object RPC. This difference is transparent to the programmer. The process with which a DCOM object is created is nearly identical to that of a COM object.

Any program may request a DCOM object. When a client requests the creation of a DCOM object, a series of operations are set into motion. These operations occur in the following steps:

1. Determine that the requested object is a remote object.
2. Make a connection with the server that contains the object.
3. Create a connection to the Class Factory of the object.
4. Request the creation of an object instance.
5. Server returns a reference to the new instance to the client stub.

When the original COM call occurs, the system itself must determine the location of the object. The object may be located on the local machine or on a remote server. This determination is made with the COM Service Control Manager (SCM), which automatically attempts to locate the object entry in the registry. If it is a remote object, the DCOM system is activated.

The information contained in the registry provides security and location information for the machine hosting the remote object. The remote procedure call routines are activated to establish a connection with the server that contains the object. A proxy is created on the client, and a stub is generated on the server to allow communication.

Once the connection has been made, a pointer to the Class Factory interface must be created. The Class Factory contains the methods used to create an instance of the object and initialize all primary variables. The object is located using the ClassID that the client passes to it.

The DCOM routines then request the Class Factory to create an instance of the object. If a Class Factory 2 (for licensed objects) is used, the license is checked on the host machine. If there is a problem with creating the instance, the original calling routine will receive an error.

Finally, the remote DCOM returns a reference to the newly created instance. The client application can use this reference pointer to access this instance until it is no longer needed. In VB Script, setting the reference to Nothing, as we did in much of the source code in the last chapter, decreases that object's Reference Count. When no more processes access the object, the instance is destroyed.

All actual data connection and exchange occurs through the DCOM Object Remote Procedure Call. Instead of the Lightweight RPC that is used to communicate between out-of-process COM objects, DCOM uses a complete RPC interface to invoke methods and pass variables across the network.

Object Life Cycle

Because objects execute on the server itself, tracking the life cycle of an object is very important. If clients routinely created objects but didn't dispose of them, the server would consume an increasing amount of resources to maintain dead objects. On the other hand, if an object was being accessed by several users and each user could dispose of the object, the object might be eliminated while a user still needed access.

To prevent either of these situations, DCOM keeps an instance tracking number. Each time a user creates an instance of an object, the number is incremented. When the user finishes using the object, the sequence is decremented. When the number of users accessing the object equals 0, the server marks the object for elimination. This step doesn't eliminate the object from the server; it simply frees all the memory from the instances of the object. The object is not instantly removed in case another process should activate it shortly after all current connections are lost. Instead, it is marked for removal, and the DCOM server will occasionally (at various time intervals or when server resources are low) execute a process known as *garbage collection,* which removes all unused objects from memory.

A client machine may often shut down for a number of reasons, including a severed connection, a system crash, or a power loss, without having released the instances of the objects it was using. To prevent numerous instances of these objects remaining on the server long after the client does not need them, Microsoft implemented automatic *pinging* in the DCOM system.

While the systems are communicating, they routinely activate a ping that keeps alive a process. The absence of a ping after a specified period of time indicates to DCOM that the object has died and that the instance is shut down. To decrease network traffic, DCOM will send a single ping only between machines that may have multiple open connections. This approach prevents the additional network traffic that would be caused if a ping was used for each process.

Additionally, the Class Factory interface contains a method known as *LockServer*. This method locks the object that is running on the server so that even if the reference count is reduced to 0, the object is not destroyed.

Binary Interoperability

To access DCOM objects, the language must be able to find the properties and methods of the object. C++, for example, normally uses different object headers than Visual Basic. The COM/DCOM model, however, creates a binary compatible header so that any language may use these objects.

As described earlier, the ActiveX/OLE framework sits on top of the COM/DCOM object model. It is the foundational COM *binary interoperability* that lets the same ActiveX control be used in numerous programming environments, including C++, Visual Basic, Delphi, Internet Explorer, and Active Server.

Binary interoperability is aided by the IDispatch interface, which allows for runtime resolution of the interfaces available for the objects. IDispatch can be used to invoke available methods so that the interface does not even require coding into the program.

Threading Model

Distributed COM promotes the use of either the single-thread model or the apartment threading model. Single threading creates an entire process for each instance of the object that is required. This model is typically invoked when the object is an EXE component, such as Excel. This threading model takes a tremendous amount of system resources for every instance and is, therefore, not recommended for use in a distributed object system.

The only threading model actually supported by Microsoft's Transaction Server is the apartment threading model. Apartment threading creates a process the first time an object is instantiated. All subsequent instances of the object are created within the original process, saving a tremendous amount of processor time and resources.

Free threading, the ability of a single program to create multiple threads within itself, is not recommended for a distributed object system. For a normal program, free threading is ideal because a thread can be created for each process that needs to be completed.

For instance, a spreadsheet might create a recalculation thread and a printing thread that can be processed simultaneously. The operating system can optimize these threads separately for best performance. In a distributed object system, however, the server can optimize performance much better by handling an object as a single point of execution. With multiple threads in multiple instances, a great deal of overhead is consumed managing all the subprocesses.

If you build the components for distributed computing, use the apartment threading model. If free-threading is used, the individual components must handle threading coordinates and optimization. With apartment threading, COM automatically handles the necessary thread synchronization. This will establish a strong baseline of compatibility with future Microsoft object solutions.

Security

Like every other aspect of software communication, security is an important issue. The security available through the DCOM model is fairly significant. Because objects can begin processes that may be intensive in server resources or can access and modify secure data, a complete security and authentication system is built in to the core of the DCOM model.

The control of the security is set during the deployment stage rather than at compile-time. Therefore, a single component can be configured for various levels of security, from none to a strict security environment, without requiring a recompile of the component itself.

Component security is stored in Access Control Lists (ACLs) that are present on the system hosting the object. ACLs are configured with the DCOMCFG utility described earlier. This utility specifies the users and groups that will have access to the object and the level of access available to them. The restrictions allow an administrator to specify whether the user or group can instantiate the object at all and which methods may be executed.

DCOM also supports a machine-wide default so that security can be configured for all users. The DCOMCNFG utility can be used to set the various defaults for a machine, and it can also be used to set security options for individual objects.

Unfortunately, this security is not integrated with the rest of the security structures available on Windows NT. Microsoft obviously will have to consolidate some of its security models available on various servers, although DCOM security adds to the already separate security administration required for NT, SQL Server (there is some integration here), Exchange Server, Access security, and Internet Information Server security.

Microsoft Interface Definition Language (MIDL)

Every object to be used on a machine must be registered in the registry. Registration occurs through the use of a TLB file. In the last chapter, we explained how to use the REGSVR32.EXE program to register an object on a particular machine. Visual Basic automatically generates the Type Library (TLB) file needed to register the component. In C++ and other languages, the TLB file often needs to be created by hand to specify exactly which interfaces will be included in the object.

Creating the interface is done using the Microsoft Interface Definition Language (MIDL), based on the Distributed Computing Environment (DCE) IDL specification. The IDL file must be run through an interface compiler that generates the necessary TLB file. For Visual Basic, the TLB file is automatically generated so that no MIDL file is required. For C++ and other environments, a certain compiler must be used to convert the MIDL file into the type library file.

The MIDL file is used to specify both the proxy and the stub that will be used to communicate with the object. The MIDL format uses C++ type definitions to create the proper COM headers. Not all data types are supported, so be sure to check the types you need to send across the COM interface before you begin implementation.

If you use the MIDL or another utility to create the TLB file and if the object is registered on your system, you still need to configure it for remote access. The DCOM configuration utility, known as DCOMCNFG, can be used to specify not only security for registered objects, but also where execution will take place.

DCOMCNFG

The DCOMCNFG.EXE program allows individual objects to be set to execute in a particular place and sets the security of objects, the default security settings for the computer, and the default communications properties. When the DCOMCNFG application is executed, it will show all the objects currently registered on your machine (see Figure 10.7).

The Default Properties and the Default Security tabs allow you to set up the security for the machine on which the program is running. If you select one of the applications and click the Properties button, you can edit individual options for a particular object. The General tab describes the object's name, type, and location. The Location tab allows you to specify where the component will be run; in Figure 10.8 you can see that this component is configured to run on a remote machine.

The Security tab allows you to set custom permission for this particular object. These permissions are best set using the Transaction Server for objects that will be executed off it. Any DCOM-capable machine, however, may serve remote DCOM

Figure 10.7 DCOMCNFG opening screen showing all currently registered components.

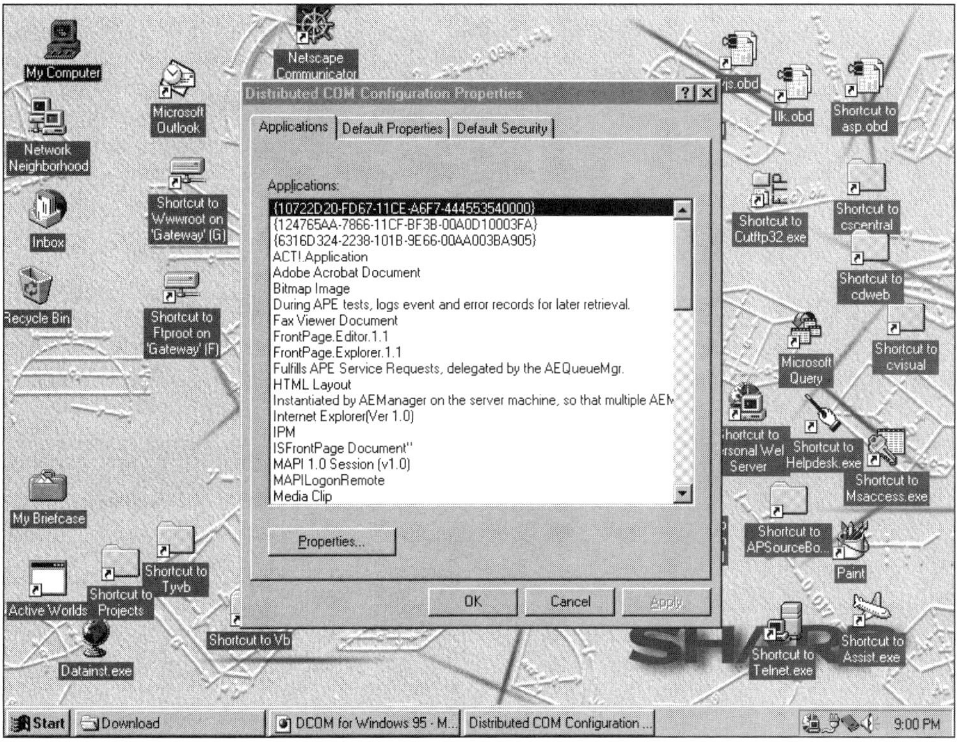

objects. This configuration allows you to set the users or groups that can access the object.

The DCOMCNFG application is included with Windows NT, but it is not natively included with Windows 95. Note that it is not installed generically with Windows 95 DCOM because it is an administration utility. Therefore, it requires a separate installation (and download) to use.

Administration Issues

Of course, administration on a DCOM system is not an easy task. Even if Transaction Server is used to maintain the server-side objects, each object must still be registered on every client machine that needs to use it.

Figure 10.8 The DCOMCNFG utility when accessing the Location tab of a component.

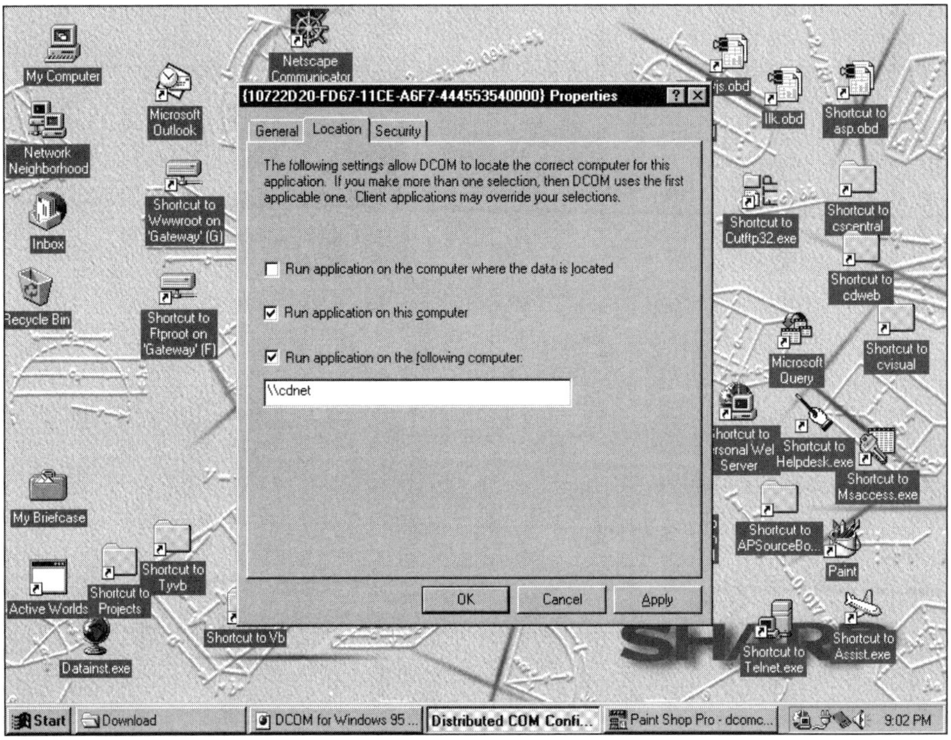

Not only does each object on a client need to be separately registered and configured, but the individual objects must also be pointed at the proper server to work correctly. If the object is moved to a different server, each client machine and all its registry pointers must be reconfigured.

Microsoft will most likely need to address these issues in the coming year. The simplest solutions will come through the Active Directory technology, which provides a wide variety of directory service, allowing objects to be directed to the Active Directory, which could locate the necessary object server.

DCOM and CORBA

In emerging field of object communications, DCOM has yet to be established as the Ma Bell standard. An often mentioned competitor for DCOM is the Common Object Request Broker Architecture (CORBA). CORBA seeks to be a vendor-neutral specification, unlike DCOM, a product of Microsoft that is designed to work on the Windows platform. CORBA's main goal is to be an open standard that can execute on any platform. The advantages and disadvantages of using one technology over another have escalated to the point of nearly becoming a religious argument.

Many companies are betting on DCOM for one simple reason: It is backed by Microsoft. CORBA is a standard that was created and continues to be modified by a committee, one that often appears to be plagued with the hundred chiefs and one brave syndrome, resulting in a standardization and evolution process that is slow and consensus-oriented. CORBA's leading problem to date has been difficulty with interoperability among vendor implementations of pieces of the CORBA specification. Many vendors are pushing forward with the CORBA standard, and Netscape is even incorporating the ability to use CORBA objects in its next-generation browser.

Over the next few years, a battle will be fought for dominance of the distributed computing world. Microsoft's demonstrated ability to turn ODBC into an industry standard has many industry veterans betting on Microsoft.

There are signs that the problem of one object model versus another may be solved with the use of bridges. For example, if you need to incorporate a CORBA object system within a DCOM-based Windows solution, Digital Equipment Corporation has created a DCOM-CORBA object bridge. How well this interoperability will work is anyone's guess at this point because poor interoperability—even between standard CORBA systems—has been the major barrier.

Using DCOM with the Active Desktop

Right now, configuring all your objects and locating the proper server are fairly difficult. One of the simplest ways that would allow you to create a connection to your object is to put the connector on a Web page. When you need to access your

Figure 10.9 DCOM and browser synergy.

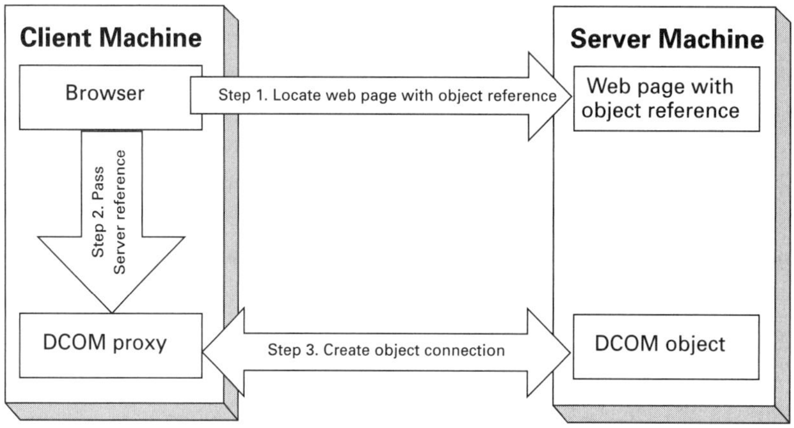

object, you activate the proper Web page in your browser or on your Active Desktop.

As you can see, the Web page can act as a facilitator by instantiating the DCOM object proxy on your machine and then allowing the remote object instance to communicate on a remote server. Once the connection between the DCOM object and its proxy is created, the browser is no longer needed. The browser can then be exited because its only role was to locate the object directory.

Using the browser as a facilitator is shown in the three steps of Figure 10.9. The browser is used as the basic human communication layer.

This type of strategy is especially effective when a constant feed is required after the connection is made. If the connection is always needed, the DCOM link could be opened on boot; however, if the connection is necessary only under particular circumstances, using a browser provides the perfect solution.

For example, imagine you had an agent object that ran on your bank's server. It constantly watched your transactions, fluctuations in the currency market, and the value of your stocks. Although you want this process to be occurring constantly and the updates to the object itself to be continual, you do not want a constant connection to be made between the object and your client machine every time your machine is booted. By using the browser, you can initialize the connection as needed.

As DCOM becomes more easily deployable and Active Desktop becomes standardized on the enterprise, Microsoft will use this type of object browsing to bring easy object access to the desktop.

Transaction Server

Microsoft plans to make DCOM the next major technology for enterprise deployment. Organizations first used networks to exchange files using file servers, then they exchanged data over networks with database servers. With the development of the Internet and intranets, Web servers now retrieve HTML information. For many experts, the next major technology will be the use of *object servers* to provide wide network access to programs and components.

The Transaction Server is different from most other types of servers in that it *does not do any of the actual processing*. It essentially acts as a type of "middleman" to allow requests from clients to instantiate objects and provide security, administration, and garbage collection facilities. All actual execution, however, occurs in the individual component objects. The Transaction Server primarily acts to introduce the requests to the objects. Even initialization and destruction are handled by the objects themselves.

The Microsoft Transaction Server allows objects placed in a server to be accessed by various DCOM client machines. Most Transaction Server management takes place within the Transaction Server Explorer. As you can see in Figure 10.10, the interface is similar to that used for file management or SQL Server administration. In the left pane of the Explorer you can see that all the computers to be administered appear there. As with the SQL Server administration tools, you can control more than the local machine from the Explorer.

Selecting a computer will show all the packages installed on the machine, the remote component registered for access, the current transaction list, the transaction statistics, and the trace messages.

All components stored on the Transaction Server are contained within *packages*. Opening a package allows you to examine the current status of components stored there. Included with the Transaction Server are two sample applications: Hockey and Sample Bank. In Figure 10.11, you can see all the components of the Sample Bank application.

Figure 10.10 The Transaction Server Explorer.

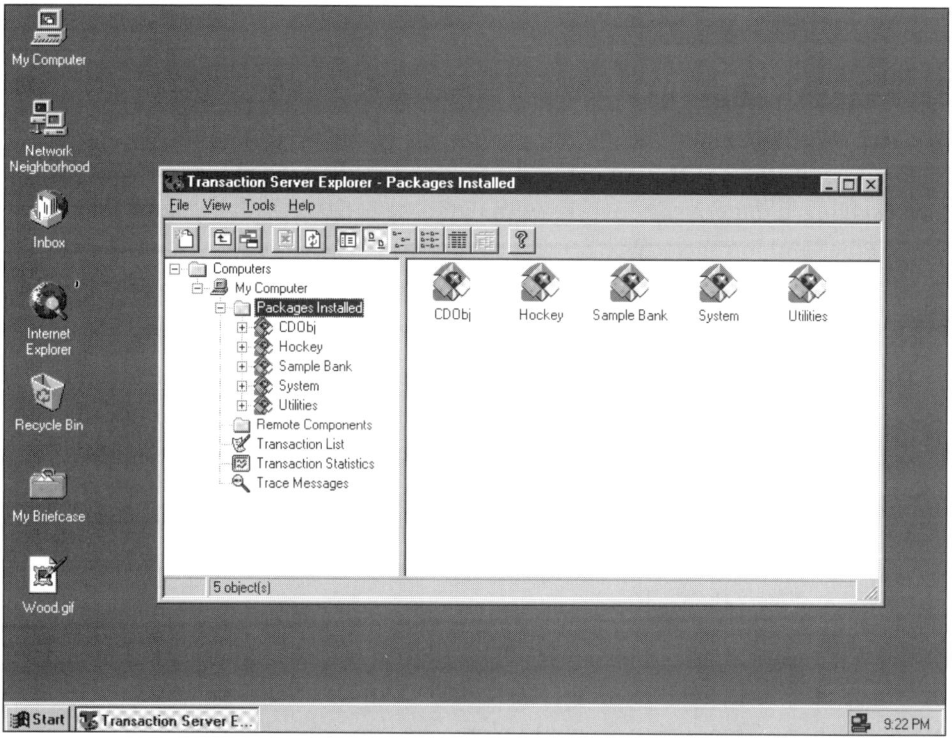

Each Sample Bank component is registered with this server. The properties of the component (accessible by clicking the right mouse button) allow you to set various options including the transaction abilities of the component, the activation level, and the security. The transaction settings allow four different levels with these characteristics:

- Requires a transaction
- Requires a new transaction
- Supports transactions
- Does not support transactions

The activation level allows the administrator to specify how the component will be created in the server process, in the creator's processor, or even in a remote server process.

The Explorer allows you to examine registered components all the way down to their methods. In Figure 10.12, you can see that we have exposed all the methods contained in the IAccount interface of the BankAccount.VC object.

The Transaction Server supports automatic thread and process management including thread pooling. The object must support the IobjectControl interface for it to participate in object pooling. Pooling allows an instance of an object to be created and to wait until the object is requested. When the request occurs, the instance is taken from the pool and passed to the user. When the instance is no longer needed, it returns to the object pool. This saves time for frequently used objects because they don't have to be instantiated from scratch every time they are needed.

Figure 10.11 The components of the Sample Bank package.

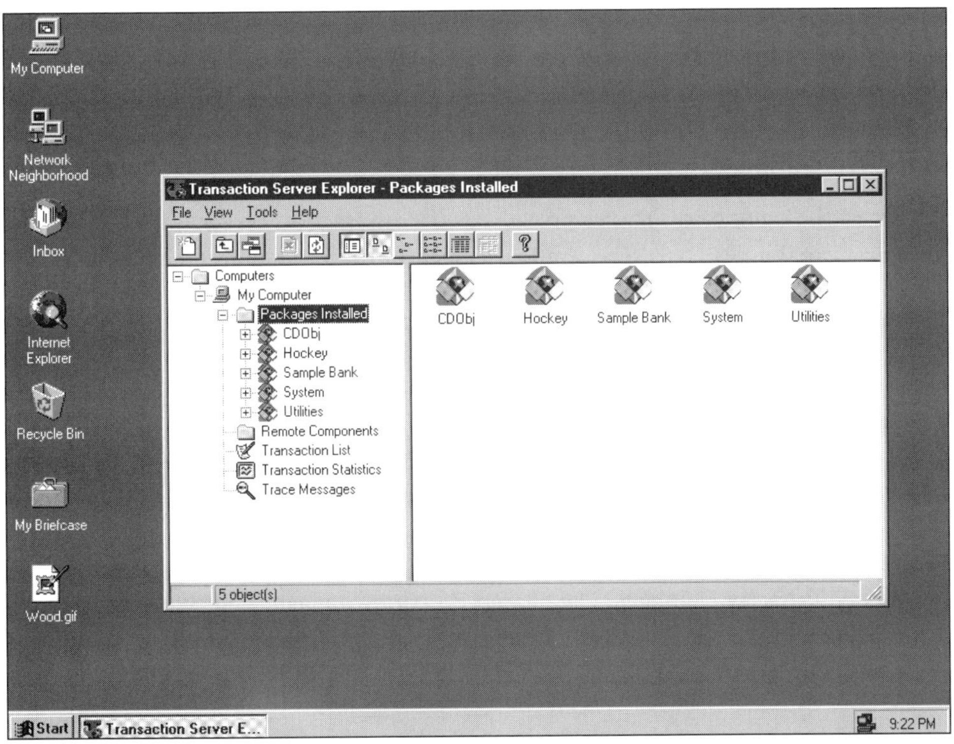

Figure 10.12 The methods of the IAccount interface.

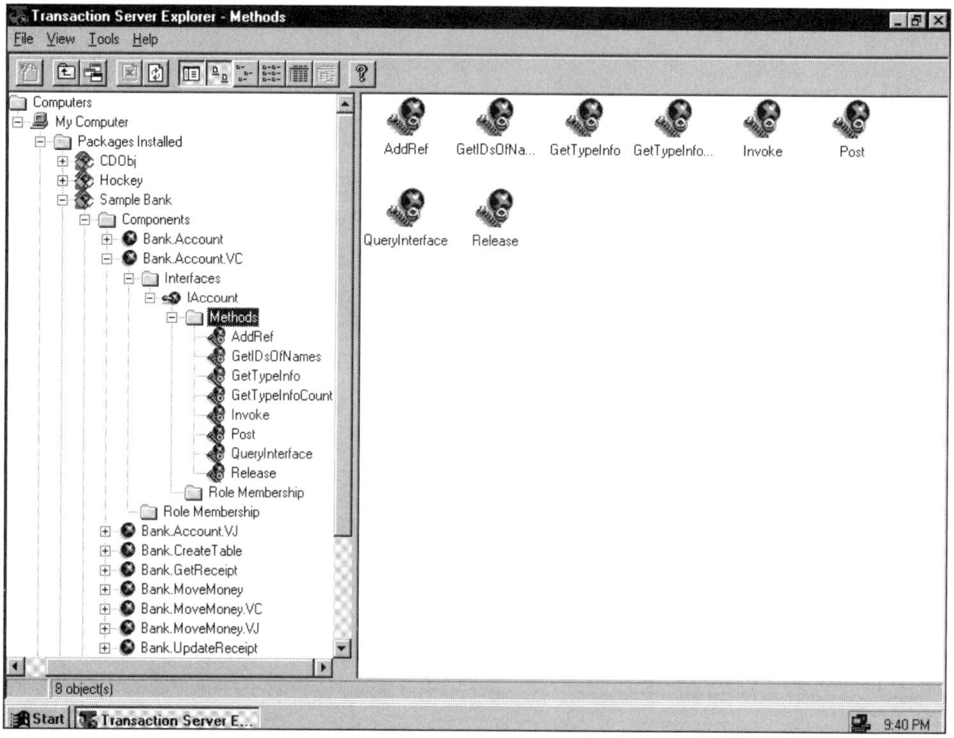

One of the significant services provided with Transaction Server is its *resource dispenser* capabilities. This service allows synchronization and administration of resources within a process. Resource dispensing occurs within a component and must be coded there. Two resource dispensers are included with the Transaction Server.

ODBC Resource Dispenser. The ODBC resource dispenser allows pooling of database connections. The ODBC 3.0 driver supports database connection pooling through the Transaction Server API. By pooling data connection resources, sessions to a remote data source are maximized.

Shared Property Manager. The Shared Property Manager will share the global state within the server process. Interfaces such as CreatePropertyGroup and CreateProperty are exposed.

Distributed Transaction Coordinator

The Distributed Transaction Coordinator (DTC) is a system service that can be used to coordinate remote transactions. First released with SQL Server 6.5, the Microsoft DTC is a system service that can coordinate multiple operations across system resource services. The Transaction Server integrates with the DTC to extend its transaction capabilities to include objects administered by the server.

DTC is available on both Windows 95 and Windows NT platforms. It is listed as the MS DTC item in the Control Panels folder, and you can configure it to have the transactions managed by one particular server (see Figure 10.13). Configuration of the protocol settings is located in the Settings directory.

A common framework for judging transaction capabilities in the database industry has been the use of the ACID system, which describes four different areas of

Figure 10.13 Configuring the Microsoft Distributed Transaction Coordinator.

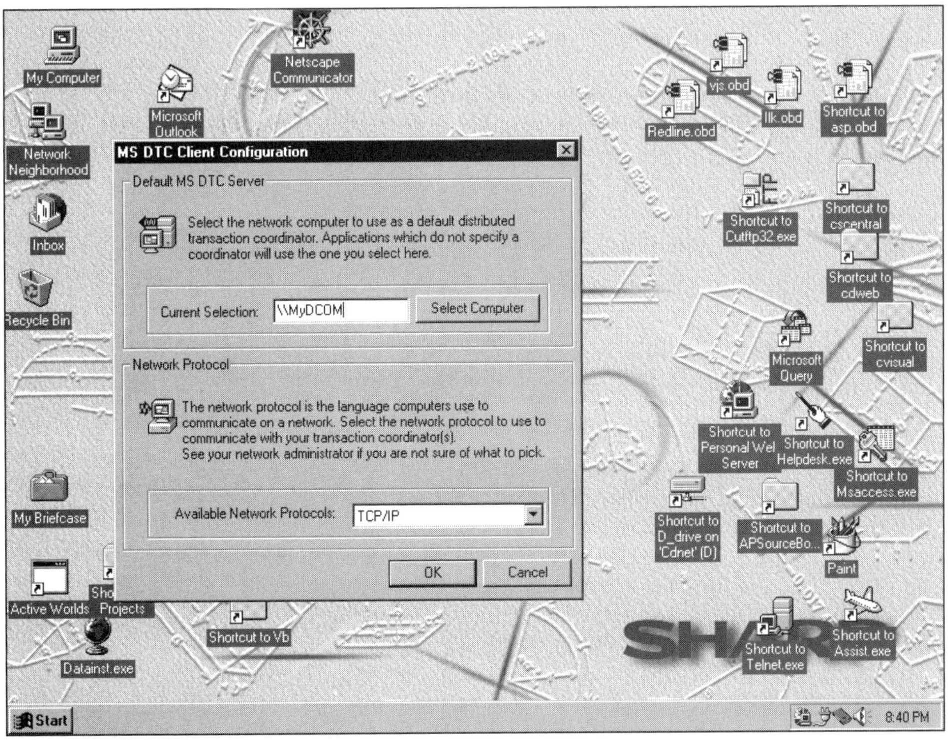

transaction security. If a system complies with all four areas, the system is said to support true transactions.

Atomicity. A transaction is an indivisible unit.

Consistency. Either all the operations are executed or the transaction must abort.

Isolation. The transaction is independent of other transactions and not affected by them.

Durability. The transaction, after it is committed, is permanent and will survive a system failure.

The MS DTC supports the ACID framework. The DTC guarantees atomicity of the transactions. Atomicity can be ensured even if the span of the transactions crosses multiple Resource Managers. The Resource Managers used by the Transaction Server cooperate with other system services to guarantee the ACID model.

The MS DTC has been included in both Windows 95 and Windows NT for quite some time. It currently supports both OLE Transactions and X/Open XA protocols; future releases are expected to implement SNA LU6.2 and Transaction Internet Protocol (TIP).

Microsoft and Tandem both support the Transaction Internet Protocol (TIP) protocol. To advance the adoption of this standard, Microsoft and Tandem created a free reference implementation written in Java that is available on the Microsoft Web site.

The DTC also offers a Statistics window that shows a variety of transaction statistics:

- Number of active transactions
- Peak number of transactions
- Number of committed or aborted transactions
- Total number of transactions processed
- Response times

The Transaction Server includes the DTC because it is used as a basis for transaction support. An object or a number of objects can be set on the server to perform a transaction. By coordinating through the DTC, transactions from all Windows databases or objects can be handled by a single central service.

Transaction Objects

When using a database, the ability to encapsulate several operations in a transaction provides a safeguard against several types of operational failures. Having transaction abilities ensures the data integrity of the information stored in the database. Transaction Server allows the identical type of Commit/Rollback features within a series of object operations.

It can interface with the MS DTC system to provide complete ACID transaction support. Through the MS DTC, it also can interface to other protocols. Because the DTC is fundamental to SQL Server, be sure that the database server you run on Windows NT supports transactions through the DTC in order to make the transaction objects usable with the data source.

Transaction objects, because of their ability to rollback changes, require extra overhead and processing power. The transaction is handled on the Transaction Server, which allows for much more administrative control than a typical system where the client must open and then commit the transactions.

Nontransaction Objects

If you are not doing database work, most of your objects will not need many of these basic safeguards. Without the need to commit or rollback a series of operations, performance can be increased for objects that perform particular tasks.

Nontransactional objects are typically made up of calculation objects, process objects, and other objects that don't make actual changes to the system or database; instead, they carry out a series of operations. You may specify a complete database system to be a nontransaction object. The object type is not limited within the construction of the object itself because the only difference between the two types of objects is the configuration settings.

Monitoring Components

The Microsoft Transaction Server provides significant features for monitoring the actual object transactions taking place. Widespread use of distributed object systems is relatively new to the computing world. The system resources and the loads created by these systems are just beginning to be understood. If you are deploying a distributed system for he first time, you must closely track the usage that takes place on your server to understand and optimize for the most often used operations and best server performance.

To this end, the Transaction Server allows usage monitoring in several practical ways. The Component Usage and the Transaction Statistics windows provide the primary way that current processes occur. To examine the status of a particular component, select the Components folder that you want to examine. Then select the Status option under the File menu.

The Transaction Server even allows you to shut down the server processes. This can only be done to the entire computer's Transaction Server processes, but it is available as the Shutdown Server Processes option under the Tools menu.

Packaging Objects

A set of objects may be encapsulated in a single package that can then be deployed on a particular server. This helps administration when many objects must be used in conjunction to provide an application. Security may also be assigned to a particular package.

Although similar functionality does not exist for the clients, packaging allows a set of objects to be moved to another Transaction Server and activated instantly. They would retain not only their identities, but also the configured security settings.

System Package Components

None of the System Package components can be modified. All of the internal states of the Transaction Server are stored in this package and can be viewed as read-only because the System Package is really a reflection of the local machine's state.

Transaction Server uses the *declarative security* model to limit access to all items available through the Explorer. Roles are assigned to individual users and components. A role determines which packages, components, and interfaces are available to the user. Everything in the Explorer is stored in the main server *catalog*. The system process represented by the System Package must execute in the local Administrators group to get the necessary access. The System Package can then access the registry of the local system.

Active Directory

When accessing the Web, a user needs to type a domain name (for example, www.coherentdata.com) to locate a Web server. The domain name is converted into an IP number, the address where the computer is actually located. For the person running the Web server to change the machine accessed by a particular domain name, he or she changes the name at the central directory services; users that enter the domain name will now be pointed to the new computer.

The objects demonstrated so far have been configured to run on a particular computer. If you want the DCOM object to be located on a different computer, all client machines that point at the object would have to be reconfigured. Microsoft's new Active Directory is meant to solve this problem.

The Active Directory contains the references for the various objects so that when an object is moved, the entry in the Active Directory must be changed, and all requesters will now look at the object on the different computer.

Future Integration with OLE DB

Microsoft intends to make OLE DB the standard way to access all corporate data. Components that access OLE DB will be easily integrated and most likely will become DCOM components themselves.

Microsoft is positioning nearly all data access that occurs on the enterprise to take place through objects. Linking OLE DB and Transaction Server not only will allow transaction-based access to most databases, but will also provide nonrelational stored data to be protected under the transaction model.

Java-DCOM Interface

Microsoft is now committed to providing an interface for Java to DCOM objects as well as the creation of DCOM objects within the Java environment. Accessing a DCOM object is as simple as calling the proper API functions through the COM class. Programming with DCOM objects within Java is even simpler than doing the same with C++!

Currently, building a DCOM object using Java is a tedious process. You can create a DCOM component with DCOM in two ways: using a DCOM wrapper or creating the compiled Java component using the DCOM classes available with Java.

If you have already made your Java code in the standard Java component format (JavaBeans), you can use an ActiveX wrapper to make the JavaBean appear as if it were a standard DCOM component. This way is certainly the easiest, but it limits the capabilities of your component and creates a substantial performance penalty.

The Java development system from Microsoft, Visual J++, comes with several features and utilities to make DCOM creation possible. To create a component, you must define the interfaces to all of your functions within an MIDL file for later compilation into the necessary type library file.

You can then use the utility included with Visual J++ called the GUID-generation utility to generate all GUID and UUID numbers for your classes and interfaces. Then you will be ready to compile the MIDL file into a usable TLB file.

The JavaTLB tool can be used to create a .class file from the TLB file just created. This tool also generates a template for the Java interface definition of the class.

Now you need to write the actual object that conforms with the interfaces stored in the TLB file. The template that the JavaTLB utility provided gives you a starting point. When you're finished, compile the object.

Open the Windows command-line interface and run the JavaReg utility that will register the component as a DCOM object. This utility is the parallel of the REGSVR32 program created specifically for Java components. The JavaReg adds the component to the registry. You will need to execute this program on any client machine where you use your component. The ClassPath variable that Java uses to execute code must also be set so that the Java Virtual Machine can find your component.

To access your new component through Java, you will need to use the COM class. All interfaces for a DCOM object are added to the *com.ms.com.IUnknown* class. Of course, using this class violates the "100% Pure Java" specification, but the extra power gained is significant. You will need to use an include to import the type library, which lets the Java VM know that the DCOM object will be used.

Recently, Microsoft has taken several additional steps toward extending the COM interface into Java by including disconnected operation, garbage collection, persistence, and distributed debugging. Microsoft's apparent commitment to Java will make the interface between the two more seamless in the future. The machine-independent nature of Java will also be sacrificed.

Three-Tier Architecture

You may have heard of three-tier architecture for business systems, but you may be unaware of just what it represents. Traditional client/server is considered a two-tier architecture in which a client program talks to a server, such as a file server or a database server. Adding a third tier seeks to separate the business logic from the actual database access, as we have shown using DCOM in this chapter.

A three-tier logical layering system (see Figure 10.14) makes access to the data occur through a tier of business objects. This separates the logic from both the client applications and the actual data source. By isolating particular program logic in this fashion, changes to either the client tier or the database tier can be made transparently to the other layer by modifying the objects.

DCOM integration with MSMQ

If DCOM is like making a direct phone call to an object, messaging is more like sending a letter. A growing sector of the client/server industry is known as message-oriented middleware or MOM. By sending messages containing various requests that may be queued, MOM can be used to create an asynchronous system. Microsoft has created a new messaging server tentatively called MSMQ (code name Falcon).

DCOM cannot handle asynchronous requests. For example, if a program needed a query processed but wanted control returned, using DCOM objects does not present a simple solution. However, if linked with a MOM system, a message could be sent requesting the query, and the client application could allow the user to continue with any other tasks at hand. When the queued message could finally be executed, it would return the resultant information in another message to the original calling application. The user could then be alerted that the query was completed and the results available.

An additional advantage of a MOM system is the ability of either the client or the server to be unavailable without any loss of data. If the request is sent to a

Figure 10.14 Three-tier architecture.

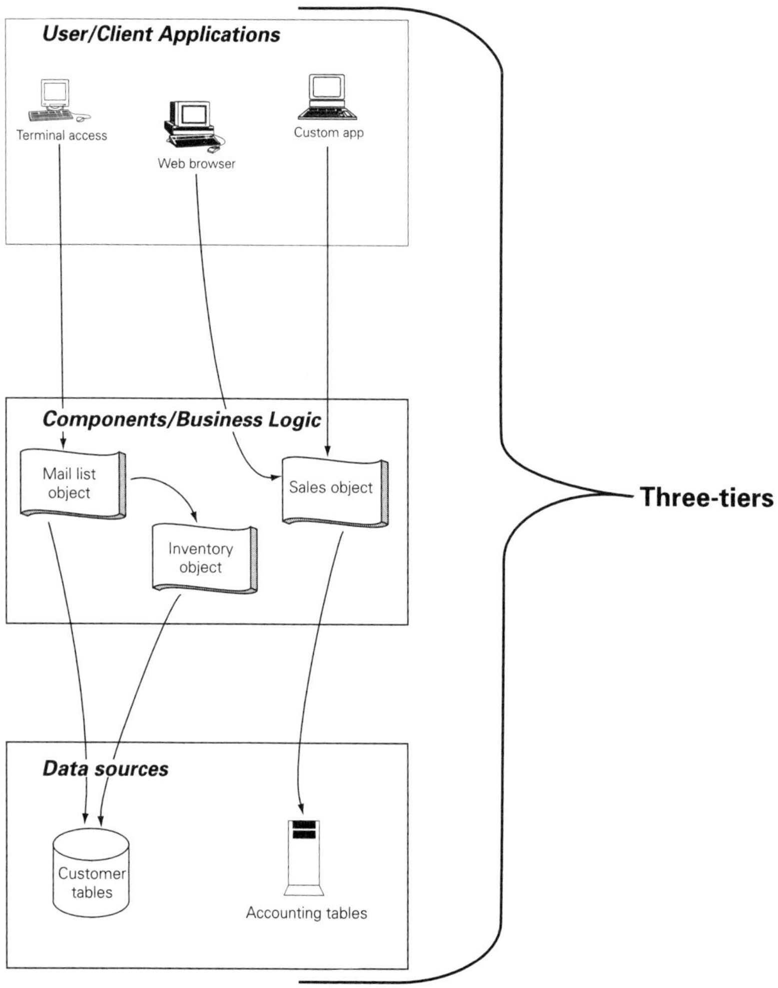

server that is unavailable, the request is queued. When the server becomes available, it will process the request. In the same way, a client machine could send a request or activate a process and then shut down for the night. The return answer would remain queued in the server until the client becomes active again the following day.

This type of system is also ideal for a system that relies on laptops. A sales processing system, for example, could record all on-the-road sales to the necessary objects and post them in a message queue. When the laptop is hooked up to the local area network or dial-in support is available, all the object messages could be sent to the system for processing.

The content of particular requests can also be filtered. In an object-based system, this might include sorting and grouping object requests of the same type. The server could then instantiate the proper objects of a particular type, and all of those requests can be processed in order. This approach would maximize the performance of the server system and use of its resources.

Related Sources

The resources for Active Server Pages on the Web itself are significant. The following is a list of resources that supplement the information found in this chapter.

Microsoft has a page dedicated to OLE/COM/DCOM at http://www.microsoft.com/oledev that contains technical information, news, and the downloads for Windows 95 DCOM. From this page, you can also subscribe to a DCOM-related e-mail mailing list.

For database related information about DCOM, check out *DBMS Magazine* (www.dbmsmag.com). Past articles have covered distributed component deployment and DCOM's role in transaction systems.

Informix's Universal Server provides relational database capabilities with object storage integrated with Microsoft Transaction Server and DCOM. In fact, no server changes are required to use Transaction Server with the Universal Server.

The Transaction Server made by Microsoft is not the only DCOM server available for the Windows platform. Consistently getting excellent reviews is the Borland (www.borland.com) technologies, Multi-Tier Distributed Application Services (MIDAS), that have been gathered under the MIDAS banner. The Borland suite of products includes features such as load balancing, object brokering, and failover capabilities that were not included in Transaction Server at the time of this writing. The MIDAS technologies also come bundled with Borland's Delphi programming package in the Delphi Client/Server suite.

Although the entire focus of the book is primarily on the CORBA object specification, the book *Client/Server Programming with Java and CORBA* by Robert

Orfali, Dan Harkey, and Jeri Edwards (also published by Wiley) has a good chapter on DCOM when compared with CORBA. Although extremely biased toward the CORBA system, the writing and clear explanation of this technical subject are excellent.

Conclusion

The DCOM technology is evolving rapidly because of many organizations' need to implement it. The material covered in this chapter should provide a good foundation for you to use when attempting to examine future developments. The following is a brief summary of some of the key topics that you might need to refer to in the future.

DCOM System. DCOM must be installed on both the client and the hosting machine. DCOM is available currently for Windows 95 and NT, and soon for Unix and Macintosh. DCOM objects function as OLE Automation Servers, and objects must be registered in the OLE Registry on every machine that uses them. Third-party vendors are creating tools that allow DCOM to interface with other object technologies including JavaBeans and CORBA.

COM/DCOM. The Component Object Model (COM) that provides the foundation for OLE and ActiveX technology has been extended to work over a network using Distributed Component Object Model (DCOM). When an instance of a DCOM object is created, a DCOM proxy is created on the client machine that connects to a DCOM stub on the hosting machine. The proxy is connected to the client application and the stub is connected to the remotely executing object. To the client application, the connection is transparent; to the application, the object appears to be executing on the client machine.

DCOM and CORBA. These two competing object standards have a great deal in common but proceed from entirely different beginning points. DCOM, from Microsoft, uses the Windows OS as its primary launching point and seeks to extend to other platforms. CORBA is the object standard by committee, so it has begun on many platform and now seeks widespread acceptance. It remains to be seen what level of interoperability will occur between the two.

Microsoft Transaction Server. The Transaction Server acts as a general manager to distributed objects by providing security, administration, and garbage collection. The Transaction Server can accept only ActiveX DLLs for components.

Java support. Accessing DCOM objects from within Java is done through the COM object class. All DCOM interfaces are well supported, but the COM interface is only partially implemented. Creating DCOM objects using Java requires numerous pieces to be brought together and, as such, is not a simple process.

MSMQ Messaging. The new MSMQ Server is used to provide DCOM with asynchronous object interaction. Messages for the objects may be queued and sorted by the server.

Index

B

C

D

E

F

G

H

I

J

S